Contemporary Anthropology of Religion

A series published with the Society for the Anthropology of Religion

Laurel Kendall, Series Editor
Curator, Division of Anthropology, America Museum of Natural History

Published by Palgrave Macmillan:

Body / Meaning / Healing
By Thomas J. Csordas

The Weight of the Past: Living with History in Mahajanga, Madagascar
By Michael Lambek

After the Rescue: Jewish Identity and Community in Contemporary Denmark
By Andrew Buckser

Empowering the Past, Confronting the Future
By Andrew Strathern and Pamela J. Stewart

Islam Obscured: The Rhetoric of Anthropological Representation
By Daniel Martin Varisco

Islam, Memory, and Morality in Yemen: Ruling Families in Transition
By Gabrielle Vom Bruck

A Peaceful Jihad: Negotiating Identity and Modernity in Muslim Java
By Ronald Lukens-Bull

The Road to Clarity: Seventh-Day Adventism in Madagascar
By Eva Keller

Yoruba in Diaspora: An African Church in London
By Hermione Harris

Islamic Narrative and Authority in Southeast Asia: From the 16th to the 21st Century
By Thomas Gibson

Evangelicalism and Conflict in Northern Ireland
By Gladys Ganiel

Christianity in the Local Context: Southern Baptists in the Philippines
By Brian M. Howell

Missions and Conversions: Creating the Montagnard-Dega Refugee Community
By Thomas Pearson

Gender, Catholicism, and Morality in Brazil: Virtuous Husbands, Powerful Wives
By Maya Mayblin

Direct Sales and Direct Faith in Latin America
By Peter S. Cahn

Shamans, Spirituality, and Cultural Revitalization: Explorations in Siberia and Beyond
By Marjorie Mandelstam Balzer

Spirits without Borders: Vietnamese Spirit Mediums in a Transnational Age
By Karen Fjelstad and Nguyễn Thị Hiền

The Halal Frontier: Muslim Consumers in a Globalized Market
By Johan Fischer

Faith in Objects: American Missionary Expositions in the Early Twentieth Century
By Erin L. Hasinoff

The Christianity of Culture: Conversion, Ethnic Citizenship, and the Matter of Religion in Malaysian Borneo
By Liana Chua

Communitas: The Anthropology of Collective Joy
By Edith Turner

Questioning French Secularism: Gender Politics and Islam in a Parisian Suburb
By Jennifer A. Selby

Language, Charisma, and Creativity: Ritual Life in the Catholic Charismatic Renewal
By Thomas J. Csordas

Shamans, Spirituality, and Cultural Revitalization

Explorations in Siberia and Beyond

Marjorie Mandelstam Balzer

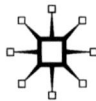

SHAMANS, SPIRITUALITY, AND CULTURAL REVITALIZATION
Copyright © Marjorie Mandelstam Balzer, 2011.

All rights reserved.

First published in hardcover in 2011 by PALGRAVE MACMILLAN® in the United States—a division of St. Martin's Press LLC, 175 Fifth Avenue, New York, NY 10010.

Where this book is distributed in the UK, Europe and the rest of the world, this is by Palgrave Macmillan, a division of Macmillan Publishers Limited, registered in England, company number 785998, of Houndmills, Basingstoke, Hampshire RG21 6XS.

Palgrave Macmillan is the global academic imprint of the above companies and has companies and representatives throughout the world.

Palgrave® and Macmillan® are registered trademarks in the United States, the United Kingdom, Europe and other countries.

ISBN: 978–1–137–00556–4

The Library of Congress has cataloged the hardcover edition as follows:

Balzer, Marjorie Mandelstam, 1950– author.
    Shamans, Spirituality, and Cultural Revitalization : Explorations in Siberia and Beyond / Marjorie Mandelstam Balzer.
        p. cm.—(Contemporary Anthropology of Religion)
    ISBN 978–0–230–11091–5 (hardback)
    1. Shamanism—Siberia. 2. Shamanism. I. Title.
BL2370.S5B28 2011
201'.44—dc22   2010049474

A catalogue record of the book is available from the British Library.

Design by Newgen Imaging Systems (P) Ltd., Chennai, India.

First PALGRAVE MACMILLAN paperback edition: June 2012

10 9 8 7 6 5 4 3 2 1

Printed in the United States of America.

Transferred to Digital Printing in 2012

To all my friends and colleagues with shamanic ancestry and/or sensibility:

May your empathy serve you well.

Previous Publications

Culture Incarnate: Native Anthropology from Russia, ed. (1990)
Russian Traditional Culture, ed. (1992)
Shamanic Worlds: Rituals and Lore of Siberia and Central Asia, ed. (1997)
The Tenacity of Ethnicity: A Siberian Saga in Global Perspective (1999)
Religion and Politics in Russia, ed. (2009)

Contents

Photographs ix

Credits and Confessions xi

Introduction: Shamans, Spirituality, and Cultural Revitalization 1

Chapter 1
Sacred Trust: Ethnography as Renewed Relationships 15

Chapter 2
Spirits Under Siege: Shamanic Communities of the North 35

Chapter 3
Doctors or Deceivers? 57

Chapter 4
Poetics of Sacred Language Through Time and Space 79

Chapter 5
Flights of the Sacred: Birds, Trees, and
Open-Body-Mindedness 107

Chapter 6
Urban Shamans? Unmasking Leadership and Creativity 131

Chapter 7
Sustainable Faith? Multiple Generations of
Healing and Spirituality 163

Chapter 8
Social Medicine? Religious Movements in
the Siberian Far East 183

Reflections 211

Notes	229
References	251
Index	277

Photographs

Cover: The late Iakim Izbekov, retired shaman's assistant and choreographer, with wooden *émégét* birds perched in a row on a pole slanted skyward at his homestead. Part-Sakha ethnographer Alexander A. Popov was told, "the first shaman cut, from pieces of willow, *ämägkät*, birds and animals, and made them whole, breathed life into them with his breath, after which they hid themselves. Since then have shamanic helper spirits existed" (1947:290).

1 Sakha (Yakut) musicians Maria Osipova, German and Klavdia Khatylaev, with the author after Glen Echo Town Hall concert. Photo by Harley Balzer, 2008 — 14

2 Historical anti-shaman election poster - "Vote Workers for the Native Council. Do not Allow Shamans and Kulaks." Artist G. Khoroshevskii, 1931 — 34

3 Maria Vagatova, Khanty (Ostiak) poet, daughter of a shaman. Photo by Marjorie Mandelstam Balzer, 2010 — 56

4 Line dance and chant "okhuokhai," Suntar 1986 *yhyakh* summer solstice ceremony. Photo by Marjorie Mandelstam Balzer, 1986 — 78

5 The late Vladimir Kondakov, founder of the Association of Folk Medicine, holding a photo of legendary shaman Niikon, Photo by Marjorie Mandelstam Balzer, 1993 — 106

6 Laughter therapy after a *khomus* séance, led by Klavdia Maksimova. Photo by Marjorie Mandelstam Balzer, 1995 — 130

7	Andrei S. Borisov, Minister of Culture, at epic poetry performance, Gornyi *ulus*. Photo by Marjorie Mandelstam Balzer, 2010	130
8	Aleksandra Chirkova, wearing the cloak of her deceased father Konstantin *oiuun*, Abyi *ulus*. Photo by Marjorie Mandelstam Balzer, 1993	162
9	Tuvan-Russian shaman Natasha at a sacred spring, Republic of Tuva (Tyva). Photo by Marjorie Mandelstam Balzer, 2005	182
10	Buriat shaman with supplicant, *tailgan* ceremony Tunka Valley. Photo by Marjorie Mandelstam Balzer, 2010	210
11	Olkhon Island, Lake Baikal, near sacred rock, with sun-kissed offerings tree. Photo by Marjorie Mandelstam Balzer, 2005	228

Credits and Confessions

Mysticism runs like a beautiful blue vein through the discourse of many, not all, of my Sakha (Yakut) friends. I begin with them, for opening my heart-soul-mind-body to their stories and for giving me the chance to study an unlikely place I have come to love: Siberia. To my plaintive query in 1992, "Where have all the shamans gone?" the recently appointed Minister of Culture of the Sakha Republic Andrei Savich Borisov wryly answered: "I am sitting here." My appreciation for his moral and occasionally institutional support from 1986–2010 is enormous. To friends and their families who have hosted me, sometimes for long stretches, I have a special debt of deep gratitude: Zinaida Ivanova-Unarova and Vladimir Ivanov-Unarov, Uliana Vinokurova and Petr Vinokurov, Ivan Alekseev and Lisa Alekseeva, Albina Diachkova and Anatoly Gogolev, Irina Maksimova and her daughter Aiza Reshetnikova, founder of the Museum of Music and Folklore. The beauty of Vladimir, Petr, Lisa, and Irina lives on in our memories. The flourishing families of Vera and Zhargal Solovyev, founders of the Sakha diaspora group Sakha Open World (www.sakhaopenworld.com), and ethnomusicologist Eduard Alekseev with Zoya Alekseeva have been enormously significant in helping me bridge worlds of "East" and "West."

My first sense of the extensive beauty of the Sakha epic poetry *olonkho* came from my Sakha language teacher Klara Belkin, during sessions in the Bronx, and continued with awe for my friend Stepanida Borisova's epic depictions on stage. My first guide in Sakha villages in 1986 was ethnographer and university professor Anatoly Gogolev, who helped organize the ground breaking 1992 international conference "Shamanism as Religion." My first taste of the power of Sakha healing came from the warm hands and passion of Aleksandra Chrikova, daughter of the great shaman Konstantin; it continued with Vladimir Kondakov, founder of the Association of Folk Medicine. My introduction to the power of Sakha music came from Anastassiia Varlaamova, the wonder of Ivan Alekseev's and Spiridon and Nikolai Shishigin's *khomus* (jaw harp) playing, and the astonishing talent of Klavdia and German Khatylaev. I am indebted to the founders of the group *Kut-Siur*, filmmaker Aleksei Romanov, his wife ethnographer Ekaterina Romanova, and the linguist Lazar Afanas'ev (Téris), as well as to Ksenofont Utkin and Uhhan (Ivan Nikolaev) for conversations about the repression of shamans and the principles of *kut-siur* (glossed as heart-soul-mind-body). Doors of the House of Purification and of perception have been opened by director Nadezhda Tolbonova and master prayer singer Afanasy Fedorov.

I am grateful to my ethnography, folklore, and sociology colleagues (the late) Nikolai Alekseev; Anatoly Alekseev; Roza Bravina; Liudmilla Egoreva; Luisa Gabysheva; Villiam Iakovlev; Wanda Ignateva; Svetlana Mukhopleva; Platon Sleptsov and Valery Vasilev for numerous insights over the years. Egor Shishigin, historian and director of the Yaroslavski Museum, has provided perspective on Christianization. Welcoming heroes of the Sakha art world include museum founder Asa Gabisheva; Fedor Markov; Afanasy Osipov; (the late) Vasily Parnikov; and craftswoman Annya Zvereva.

In villages and *ulus* (district) centers over the years, many have aided my far-flung work in a republic nearly the size of India with atrocious roads and scary prop planes. From the Viliuisk region, I am enormously grateful to the young shaman Fedot Ivanov; the elder Nikolai Ignat'ev; the healer Galina Safronova; and the blacksmith Ivan Zakharov. Consultants of Kachagatsa village were the memorable shaman's daughter Anna Spiridonovna Semenova, and my guide there, the stimulating schoolteacher Gavril Gerasimov. From Megino-Kangalas, special hosts and interlocutors included Nikolai Shishigin, Matriona Ilina, and Marfa Zamorshikova of Tiuktiur, the curer Evdokiia Semenova of Nemegiuntse, plus the sisters Ekaterina Pavlova and Fatima Danilova of the recently flooded village of Oktemsk. In Tatta, the healer Mikhail Chashkin was generous and sobering. In Srednaia Kolyma region, Arsan Laptev (grandson of the shaman Kursan), Igor Laptev, and Innokenti Volkhov provided astonishing tales and charm. From Belaia Gora, major sources were Aleksandra Chirkova and her sister Matriona, plus Matriona Yakovleva, and Petr Iliakhov, son of one of Konstantin's helpers and himself an historian of Sakha shamans. In Verkhoyansk, Victor Struchkov and Mir Umchanov literally went the extra kilometers for me, and Liubov Starostina was an eager helper. My shamanic sources and friendships in Kangalas, where I have lived and travelled repeatedly, must remain anonymous, in part because of their competition with each other.

My fieldwork in the Khanty-Mansi Okrug, beginning in 1976 while on the official US-USSR cultural exchange, has been much less extensive, despite a follow-up field trip in 1991, and periodic contacts since then. Major Kazym consultants were members of the talented Moldanov family; I have cherished my friendship with Tatiana Moldanova, Khanty ethnographer and activist, and her reindeer-breeder turned folklorist husband Timofei, now living in Khanty-Mansisk. I am grateful to the writers Eremei Aipin, Maria Vagatova, and Yuri Vella. Anastasiia Vagatova reinforced the power and tragedy of the Kazym "rebellion" with her family stories in 1991, after years of keeping them secret. The artist Galina Obatyna opened my eyes to the significance of reincarnation. The folklorist Maina Lapina is a more recent kindred spirit from conversations in 2010.

In the Republic of Buriatia and its adjoining regions, where I travelled in 2005 and 2010, I found fascinating resonance with trends in Sakha Republic. But I leave deeper insights to those with Mongolian language skills. The experienced and impressive Buriat shamans Svetlana Daribazarova, Bair Rinchinov, and Bair Zyrendorzhiev (head of the shamanic Tengeri Association) have jolted me with their fervor, while the shaman-blacksmith Budazhap Shiretorov kindly took me to a sacred mountain peak to absorb and honor magnificent waterfalls of the Tunka Valley. I am grateful to Buriat ethnographers and historians Lubov Abaeva, Chimita Garmayeva, Darima Nikolaeva, Olga Shoglanova, and Irina Urbanaeva. Zoia Morokhoieva, my Fulbright Fellow at Georgetown University, and fellow traveller in a Michael Harner shamanic workshop, has a special place in my spiritual and intellectual journeys. By 2007, my houseguest, the Buriat journalist and student of comparative politics Marina Saydukova-Romanova crucially confirmed that shamans were increasing in the younger generations.

In Tuva (Tyva) Republic, where I travelled in 2005 as an American Museum of Natural History "study leader," sources of inspiration include my guide and friend Aldynai Seden-Khuurak (first met at the University of Virginia); the great recoverer of shamanic traditions Mongush Kenin-Lopsan (first met in Garmisch, Germany); the folklorist Valentina Suzukei; the shaman Aichurek; and the Russian-Tuvan shaman Natasha. For friendship and hospitality over many years, I am especially grateful to my Fulbright Fellow, Tuvan sociologist Zoia Anaiban.

A few distinguished Russian colleagues have shared my enthusiasm for Siberia. The late sociologist Alexander Pika was generous in emotional support during Soviet bureaucratic frustrations, and in sharing archive notes on the Kazym "rebellion." I am grateful to path-breaking ethnographers Dmitrij Funk and Valentina Kharitonova, sensitive to issues of "reflexive anthropology," who encouraged me to write about my field relationships. Folklorists Olga Balalaeva and Elena Novik have been long-term friends. Famous anthropologists Sergei Arutiunov and Natalia Zhukovskaia have been models of field diligence and personal integrity, as well as sources for some of my best leads. Activist Olga Murashko, author of important laws defending indigenous peoples, has been a guide and inspiration against cynicism. Director of the Institute of Ethnology and Anthropology Valery Tishkov has been a major sparring interlocutor and friend for many years.

I have been pleased to find that European colleagues who study shamans are just as idiosyncratic as the rest of us. I especially mourn my brilliant co-conspirator, pioneer in "neo-shaman" research, anthropologist Galina Lindquist. Hungarian founder of the International Society for Shamanistic Research and its deservedly long-lasting president Dr. Mihály Hoppál was an unseen rival in shamanic studies before 1992 and has been a collaborator and friend ever since. I honor that epitome of academic rigor combined with warmth and wisdom, Professor Ulla Johansen, whose extraordinary doctoral student Dilmurat Omar became head of the anthropology department of Xinjiang Normal University and was our wonderful guide in villages on the Chinese-Kyrgyz border in 2003. German giants Michael Oppitz and Erich Kasten, each combining museum and field savvy, have given me unexpected morale boosts. Ugrian specialist Ildiko Lehtinen, curator, Helsinki National Museum of Finland, was generous with time and access to collections when I most needed it. Professors Juha Pentikainen and Anna-Leena Siikala have been kindred spirits. Dean of Siberian studies, St. Petersburger turned Parisian Boris Chichlo has been a friend and inspiration since 1975. Renowned French anthropologist of Buriatia Roberte Hamayon was a welcoming host in 1997, despite her insistence she was "post, post, post-modern." Cambridge anthropologists Caroline Humphrey and Piers Vitebsky have set high standards for me and for colleagues and students all over the world, including the dynamic Bumochir Dulam, now head of the anthropology department at Mongolia's state university. I treasure Greek anthropologist Diana Riboli's friendship and shamanic insight. Polish ethnographer Maria Kosko, who shares my interest in the interconnections of Sakha and Éven summer solstice ceremonies, was a great host in 2002. Estonian anthropologist Art Leete, sharing my interest in the Kazym war, was an excellent sponsor of an International Society for Shamanistic Research conference in 2000 and another of my Fulbright Fellows.

U.S. and Canadian colleagues, friends and spiritual guides are hard to separate into distinct categories and impossible to rank. I am indebted to Frederica de Laguna for launching me in Northern studies; and to Demitri Shimkin, one of the founders of Siberian studies in the U.S., for rescuing me in 1979 when as a young scholar on a very overgrown path I most needed help. I am grateful to Peter Furst for planting the idea of collecting my work on shamans in one book, and to Laurel Kendall for helping me see it through. I thank Bruce Grant and Julie Criukshank for reading the ms. and becoming colleagues of many dimensions. Fellow Northernists Gail Fondahl and Antonia Mills have shared amazing stories and made my trip to Northern Canada in 1996 memorable. The ethnomusicologist Theodore Levin has provided inspiration, support and been a writing style model, as have anthropologists Barbara and Denis Tedlock and Michael M. J. Fischer. I honor Edith Turner for her warmth- infused intelligence and Joan Koss-Chioino for opening my eyes to the dynamics of "radical empathy." I am grateful to Doctors Ronald Dubner and Candace Pert of the National Institutes of Health for cluing me in 1982 to possible biochemical responses of patients during shamanic séances. NIH doctor Lev Goldfarb provided a video he made of famed E'dii Dora's healing techniques. Mira Amiras and Alexandra Maloney Kim were excellent orchestrators of people and collaborative research. John Baker, president of the Association for the Anthropology of Consciousness, and Stanley Krippner have helped me understand the wide range of shamanic interest in Europe and the Americas. Contrasting conversations with Alice Kehoe, Larry Peters and Marina Roseman were augmented by stimulation from Ana Mariella Bacigalupo, Beth Conklin and Harald Prins. Scholars of Buriatia and Mongolia Anya Bernstein, Joseph Long, Katherine Metzo, Justine Buck Quijada, and Manduhai Buyandelgeriyn have filled considerable gaps in my knowledge of changing shamanic practices in this crucial region. Anthropologist Brian Donohoe has done the same for Tuva, and Alexander King for Kamchatka. The support of Paul Goble, Lenore Grenoble, Alfred J. Rieber, and Blair Ruble is hugely appreciated. Friendship with the Cherokee healer C. W. Duncan Sings Alone and his wife Priscilla Cogan since 1991 is valuable beyond words, as has been my rapport with Michael and Sandra Harner. The intuitive mainstays of my drum circle Marilyn and Knox Hayes, Steven Vogel and Deborah Harrigan have been wise, kind and patient.

I am indebted to Georgetown University, the International Research and Exchanges Board (IREX), the Social Science Research Council (SSRC), the National Endowment for Humanities (NEH), the American Museum of Natural History, the Kennan Institute of the Smithsonian's Woodrow Wilson Center, the Ammosov Northeast Federal University (formerly Yakutsk State University), the Academy of Sciences Humanities Institute (formerly Institute of Languages, Literature and History), and the Arctic Institute of Culture and Art for fieldwork and/or research support. Many thanks are also due to Joel Breuklander, Rohini Krishnan, and Brigitte Shull of Palgrave Macmillan, and to Patricia Carley.

Beyond the scope of any institutional or personal support, I most appreciate the love, intellectual stimulation, humor, editorial skill, and encouragement of my life partner Harley David Balzer.

I follow Library of Congress transliteration style, unless a name has become entrenched in the literature in another form (Yakutia rather than Iakutia). For Sakha words, I use the é instead of a backward e since they are nearly the same sound. Terms provided here are mostly from the Turkic Sakha language. Where other language terms are relevant, for example from Russian, I indicate their provenance.

Partial use of the following articles that have been updated here is gratefully acknowledged

1991 "Doctors or Deceivers? The Siberian Khanty Shaman and Soviet Medicine," *Anthropology and Medicine*, ed. L. Romanucci-Ross, D. Moerman, L. Tancredi, 56–80. 2nd ed. New York: Bergin and Garvey. [Praeger—Greenwood Group pages 56–72 without charts.]

1996 Flights of the Sacred: Symbolism and Theory in Siberian Shamanism. *American Anthropologist* 98(2):305–318. [permission for pages 305–310, and 313–315.]

1997 "The Poetry of Shamanism" *Poetry and Prophecy: Cross-Cultural Perspectives on Inspiration and Verbal Art*, John Leavitt, ed. Ann Arbor: University of Michigan, 93–127. [permission for 93–119.]

2001 Healing Failed Faith? Contemporary Siberian Shamanism. *Anthropology and Humanism* 26 (2): 134–149. [permission for 134–144.]

2001 "Shamanic Communities in the Soviet North" *Politik und Religion in der Sowjetunion 1917–1941*, C. Gassenschmidt and R. Tuchtenhagen, eds., pp. 237–255. Wiesbaden: Harrassowitz Verlag. [permission for 238–250.]

2006 "Sustainable Faith? Reconfiguring Shamanic Healing in Siberia" *Spiritual Transformation and Healing*. Joan Koss-Chioino, Philip Hefner, eds. Lanham: Rowman and Littlefield, 78–100. [permission for 78–96.]

Introduction: Shamans, Spirituality, and Cultural Revitalization

Shamans of the twenty-first century, like those of centuries before them, attract controversy and fascination well beyond their numbers. As healers of wounded souls and body politics, they can and have become the locus of cultural debates and medical discoveries. This book represents my personal and analytical forays into shamanic studies, based on extensive, periodic fieldwork in several areas of Siberia and Inner Asia, beginning in 1976 in the Ob River (Khanty-Mansi) Region, sustained by long-term research in the Sakha Republic (Yakutia), and including trips to Tuva (Tyva) and Buriatia of the Russian Federation as well as the Xinjiang (Uighur national) region of China. It is at once historical and current, ethnographic and reflexive, geographically specific and oriented toward cautious comparisons. My goal is to provide new angles on our understanding of the intersections of spirituality, religion, and politics. Along the way, I interpret a vast literature representing appropriately eclectic claims to expertise. I also use seemingly esoteric or "exotic" narratives about shamanism to probe social and political issues of postsocialism, modernity, authenticity, and indigenous rights.

One dramatic cure has haunted me for many years, and may serve to intrigue. I first heard of Fedot Ivanov, one of the younger shamans of the Sakha Republic (Yakutia), where I have done fieldwork since 1986, because Sakha friends claimed he had inherited the skills and talents of one of the greatest shamans of the twentieth century, Niikon. A sensational story buzzed in the capital, Yakutsk, about a Russian woman doctor whose cancer he had cured. This woman, knowing well the pitfalls of Soviet surgery, secretly had gone to Fedot around 1990, after Japanese scanning technology revealed she had a tumor. Fedot worked with her during numerous séances in the forest near his home over the course of a month. When she returned to her hospital, her doctor-colleagues were furious that she had delayed her operation. But they were completely confounded when they found no tumor and learned where she had been.

Cases such as that of the Russian woman doctor cured of cancer by a remote rural Sakha shaman are just what a social doctor of an injured post-Soviet society might have ordered. I have never been able to track the Russian doctor to confirm her recovery. But the account is at minimum a widespread affirmation of faith in traditional healing, in the revitalization of shamanic traditions, and in the spiritual transference of shamanic power to a new generation. Fedot in the post-Soviet period represents this and more, for his satisfied patient list has been growing. For them, he is more than a Western-style medical doctor taking individual "cases," and they are more than "patients" or "clients" on a list of successes to be advertised.

Fedot is one of several shamans and shamanic musicians featured in this book. Their astonishing lives merit probing and profiling. I weave them into my narratives while honoring requests for discretion. One of the many paradoxes of shamanic studies is that those shamans who promote their own high profiles are likely to be the very ones less worthy of profiling. The most modest are often the most secure, effective, and elusive.

Multiple Interpretations, Many Levels of Analysis

What are we to make of shamanic curing histories and dramatic séances for diverse purposes? Why have shamanic musical traditions and prayer chants been rekindled across the generations in diverse indigenous contexts in Siberia and elsewhere? Siberian studies and accounts from my fieldwork are rich, suggestive and sometimes poetic to the point of unknowability without direct experience. Various modes of interpretation are possible, each potentially rewarding but none culminating. They can build on each other, with an interpenetrating layering. Classic studies of shamanism in Siberia, Inner Asia and North America, including some by indigenous scholars, often focus on historical diffusion and the importance of using histories of shamanic activities as leaders, doctors, psychics, and pioneers to trace cultural roots. I adapt functional and historical interpretations here, joining them with exploration of more recent approaches that feature the intersections of medicine, music, theater, politics, and anthropology.

Some shamanic healers understandably resent the implication that their séances work only because they provide "placebos," or cathartic theater. My colleague and friend Aleksandra Chirkova (2002), daughter of renowned Sakha shaman Konstantin, became a European-trained surgeon on the advice of her father, and later selectively integrated shamanic healing into her practice. One of the stars of this book, she has taught me much of what I know about Sakha healing and spirituality. From her vast knowledge of multiple philosophies behind curing regimes, she explains that what she does to help patients cure themselves is far more than theater, and more than psychological therapy or mind manipulation.

Aleksandra also stresses the importance of shamans for solving community emergencies. A narrative she tells about her father is that two panicked men once arrived on his doorstep during the Soviet period saying a fire had started in their nearby village and was spreading house to house. Konstantin ushered the men into his cabin, offering tea. He excused himself and was seen exiting with a pail of water. When he returned a few minutes later, they reiterated that their problem was urgent. "Ah," he said. "Don't worry. I've already doused the fire: they've had rain, a cloudburst has taken care of it." Sakha today retell this story, wondering what it means, whether "scientific explanations" can be found, or whether the tale is apocryphal.

I prefer interpretations of such narratives, and of the diverse shamanic practices that this book describes, to be grounded, meaning situationally sensitive and down to earth. This requires forgoing the luxury of abstraction and over-generalization while nonetheless communicating comparatively across cultural and disciplinary boundaries (compare Grim 1983; Atkinson 1992; Hultkranz 1992). The anthropologist's dilemma is balancing personal accounts with broader meaning so that readers can relate new material to their own experiences without astonishing distortions in translation and perception. For me, three defining keys to shamanic power surviving over time in Siberia are that the shaman is spiritually selected, often against his or her will; mediates among complex cosmological worlds for a purpose; and suffers throughout a lifetime of pain in order to become more attuned and empathetic in solving problems that are often, but not only, about healing.

What does it mean to be "chosen by the spirits," as the late Vladimir Basilov (1997) so eloquently emphasized? And which spirits? A range of criteria may guide the relevant powers that enable spirits to become effective helpers, whether it is an owl's dark-penetrating eyesight, the eagle's all-seeing pivot eyes, the bear's acute senses, wisdom, targeted violence, size, and nurturing ability, or the horse's strong reliability. Animal helpers can be understood in the context of multiple, interpenetrating natural systems and their depiction. In the Sakha language, the very word for "nature," *aiyylgha*, contains the word for "spirit." The helpers of Siberia often are replete with contradictions, ferocious yet kind, indirect and effective, literal and creative. Similarly, but not the same, all-too-human spirit helpers in Korean and South Asian contexts can be greedy and playful on their way to helping near-desperate supplicants solve economic as well as health problems (Kendall 1996; 2009). Since economic uncertainty, local politics, and dis-ease are often intertwined, divisions of medical and social labor can be unproductive. They may be moot in more holistic, socially grounded shamanic approaches to health. This need not contradict specialization through honed talent for specific tasks, for example the Siberian Khanty dream-interpreter or the Sakha diviner who finds dead bodies for the police.

My study of healing and creative processes sparked through spiritual transformation encompasses many gradations of private and public shamanic practices. I have confirmed in numerous conversations and observations the "classic" model of spirit initiation. This occurs when future shamanic healers begin their practices by healing themselves through personal revelation, often but not only through altered consciousness states. It involves the frequently traumatic shamanic experience of spirit negotiation through suffering, dismemberment, and its transcendence. Well known in the ethnographic literature, it can stimulate a "radical empathy" that brings results (Koss-Chioino and Hefner 2006). A healer lives through the pains of specific illnesses, in order to bring the gift of empathy to patients experiencing analogous illnesses. Such initiations are not meant to be for the benefit of shamans or their immediate families alone. Indeed, many shamans mourn that they are often too emotionally distraught about their own families to cure them, and that misuse of their newfound powers can redound against loved ones, a point returned to in my conclusions.

Exuberant shamanic séances are the heart and soul of much analysis of shamanic success (Siikala and Hoppál 1992). More than tidy liminal ritual and symbolic systems that return participants to some status quo, séances are often open-ended and adaptive. They address familial and community misunderstandings as well as specific illnesses. They may stimulate endorphins (with drumming and other means) at the same time they entertain and resonate with emotional power. They may constitute the beginnings rather than the ends of healing processes. The late, famed Évenk shaman Maria Kul'betinova was known to give patients, as follow-ups to their séances, small bells to ring in emergencies. A grateful patient explained to me in 1995 that this enabled Maria to fly through the tundra to that patient's aid. The patient, touching the bell with awe in her high-rise Yakutsk apartment, confided that she has used this boon with success, but sparingly. The Tuvan shaman Nadia told me in 2005 that she continually renews her relations with water spirits on behalf of her human supplicants through monthly rituals at a sacred spring. Repeat visits and continuity of care are built into such systematic and creative practices. But the language and thought in which they are embedded often seem alien or irrational to Western skeptics used to deriding "beliefs" as "superstitions" (Lindquist and Coleman 2008).

Analyses that require us to differentiate beliefs in multiple spirits from faith in a single higher God or determine whether shamanic cures work best in personal, familial, or community-based contexts may be unnecessary, given the interpenetrating social and symbolic dynamics of séances. However, a 2004 trip to China provoked me into privileging the significance of community orientation. Despite aspects of "ethnographic tourism" characterizing the trip, our small research group, led by the German-educated Urumqi anthropologist Dilmurat Omar (2003), witnessed an intense Kyrgyz séance done for a community of believers in the remote Tien Shan mountains of Xinjiang province (compare Kara, Hoppál, Sipos 2007). Over 50 people were crammed into a yurt at night for a séance that began and ended with Moslem prayers. At its peak, 12 villagers were herded (made to race) around a fire by an elderly Kyrgyz shaman (*baqshi*) waving a whip. The *baqshi* seemed to be everywhere as he tried to drive "evil spirits" away from alcoholics, women haunted by nightmares, and villagers with other complaints. Some were pulled up from the seated crowd, pushed down, and stepped on by the shaman or his female assistant. Far more participants than the shaman and his assistant appeared to be experiencing altered consciousness. The Kyrgyz group orientation and dynamic of communal solidarity to heal through a spirit-calling ritual was "traditional," with an archaic feel. It had been maintained in flexible yet similar ways for many generations. Or was its seeming agelessness a reflection that I know less about this field context?

My task here is to communicate the unevenness of cultural change, and differences in shamanic practice over generations, usually after considerable suffering and repression, whether due to Soviet rule in Siberia, Central and Inner Asia, or Christianity, Islam, and Buddhism in much of the world (compare Walter and Fridman 2004). Many chapters highlight ripple effects of social stress, using shamanic wisdom and practice as a way to probe the multigenerational flexibility of community self-definitions and concerns for survival. As anthropological approaches are tested against various degrees of insider, esoteric knowledge, one of the greatest challenges is to understand how crucial, culturally salient meaning, belief, and practice may have been lost, changed, or (re)invented in successive interactions and generations (Fernandez 1986; 1991). Analysts need to gaze backward to gain understanding of ambiguous nostalgia and forward to reveal the ways rituals can help (re)construct social realities. Debates within communities can be featured, not masked.

Concerns have emerged within post-Soviet Siberian intelligentsias over the effectiveness of shamanic curing and the usefulness of huge shamanic festivals for seasonal rituals of fertility and renewal. Spiritual cacophony and pain have produced some creative and usually healthy experiments in group and individual therapy, including powerful group music therapy with jaw harps (*khomus*, also called Jew's harp) as well as drums, plus "laughter therapy" and lessons in opening creative energies for full human potential. Such experiments can be correlated with "new age" shamanism in America and Europe (Harner 1990; Lindquist 1997; Jacobsen 1999). But in indigenous contexts, they become therapeutic at the level of rebuilding community confidence, sometimes enabling positive aspects of nonchauvinist nationalism to stimulate an ethos and morale that was sorely lacking in Soviet times (compare Tamir 1993; Fortun et al. 2010).

Once associated with discredited "deceiver-shamans" in the Soviet period, spirituality has become more openly revered in the post-Soviet period by many Siberians and some Russians. However, zigzags of community support for shamanic cures have resulted in both openings and closings of "traditional healing centers." The Center of Folk Medicine, founded by the late shaman-historian Vladimir Kondakov, using Sakha therapies as well as Chinese medicine such as acupuncture, has had considerable success attracting healers and patients. Yet neither urban nor rural Sakha deem the majority of their healers to be full-fledged *oiuun* or *udagan*, the Sakha terms for male and female shamans, respectively. For this, consultants say, one needs a shamanic lineage, spirit torment-inspiration called *ettéénei* [or *ettéétén yald'ar*, shamanic illness], and a many-staged apprenticeship to a knowledgeable elder. While the proportions of these elements may vary individually, all are desirable to create the personal synergism needed for curing through experience-rooted empathy [*ahynyy*]. A effective healer like the late Sakha elder Niikon literally and symbolically stripped his patients naked to cleanse them of their fears and their community-defined "sins," to make them feel whole again, welcome, humble, and respectful in an imperfect world. Various kinds of empathy, intuition, and their resonance were activated in the shamanic powers exemplified by Kondakov and Niikon, whose voices and stories are featured here.

Sakha terms for spiritual healing are particularly revealing. A shaman, and a few others, is said to be "a person with an open body" [*ahaghas éttéékh kihi*], bravely open heart-soul-minded to all experience. Perceptive healers have "eyes on the spine" [*køkhauger kharakhiakh*], akin to the concept of a "third eye." They also may have genetically passed on creativity, similar to musical talent that includes synesthesia. All are adept at intuition-based diagnosis, and at stimulating the life forces of *kut-siur* [soul-mind-life force; or heart-soul-mind-spirit] through mutually reinforcing prayers-and-blessings [*algys*]. But to reduce the healing process, and its transforming effects, to the power of prayer and purification misses the integration of many kinds of spirituality and information reception in shamanic practice.[1]

Tensions between individual and community-oriented curing play out differently in diverse cases, especially given that many Siberian communities, as elsewhere, are highly multiethnic. The more cultural boundaries are blurred, the harder it becomes to identify fixed etiologies and philosophies of curing that can be linked to particular ethnic groups or specific language-based chants and mantras (Langford 2003; compare Dulam 2010). The work of the Native American M.D. Lewis Mehl-Madrona (1997) in bridging cultural gaps in healing regimes is particularly relevant for open-minded supplicants, including cancer patients.

Gender issues are interwoven through the book, especially since recognition of the importance of sexuality in shamanic practice has led interpreters in interesting, post-Freudian directions. Those who imply or claim the most significant shamans were usually male (Seroshevsky [Sieroshewskii] 1896; Schenk and Ratch 1999) can be balanced by understanding "the woman in the shaman's body" (Tedlock 2005). Some have productively stressed the principle that the strongest shamans often utilize both male and female potentialities or transcend gender stereotypes entirely (Saladin d'Anglure 1992a,b,1993; Lang 1996; Roscoe 1998). Certain shamans have revealed that their spirit interlocutors are "brides" and "grooms" of the opposite sex, rendering a few fieldwork-oriented ethnographers into intrigued would-be voyeurs. The relevant literature does far more than reflect the "trendiness" of gender studies: some of our best data derive from early ethnographic sensitivity.[2]

Analysts in Russia and elsewhere have too often seen "folk healing" in terms of extremes: either disastrous or miraculous, "black" or "white," and some have projected these images onto shamans. However, shamanic intension and effectiveness is now and probably was in the past far more mixed. As a new generation of healers and their supplicants become comfortable with the creativity and energy of cultural (re)vitalization, they are also (re)kindling a vibrant and pliant understanding of healing itself. To adapt Lewis Hyde's (1998: 293–300) perspectives on cultural creativity, some gifted shamans can cross boundaries and become the creative tricksters of cultural revitalization. Thomas Csordas (2002: 5) warns that "healing is much more like planting a seed or nudging a rolling ball to slightly change its trajectory so that it ends up in a different place, than it is like lightening striking or mountains moving." Combining these insights, we can see that the "nudge" of renewed faith in benevolent and active healers and ancestral spirits may be making possible the effectiveness of newly revitalized shamanic therapies. Occasionally, when a few living shamans themselves evoke the sacred mountains, rivers, nine heavens, and lightning of a culturally constructed Sakha cosmos in their prayer-chants, an incremental cure may occur so speedily as to seem miraculous.

The American poet Emily Dickinson once said, "tell all the truth but tell it slant." Her refreshing honesty may seem charming in a poet, but not in an anthropologist presumed to be a social scientist. I am neither poet nor "scientist" here, but a sharer of selected narratives that push us to take more seriously, without romanticism, traditional indigenous wisdom concerning ecology and animal-human relations as potentially reciprocal.[3] Aware of debates over "indigeneity" and "tradition" in contexts of continual cultural change, I am inspired by the deceptively simple folklorist mantra (used on satellite radio) "tradition pushing forward," as played out in tension with contemporary political searches for "useable pasts." Similarly, I apply or adapt theories with the hope that I can transcend national boundaries identifying some analytical lenses as "American" and others as "European" or "Russian." In our globally connected world, we need no longer peg "Americans" as more likely analysts of social- psychological dynamics, French as more likely structuralists, Eastern Europeans as especially sensitive to language and symbolism, Russians as residual materialists.

While discrepancies exist among many theoretical positions and their predominant advocates, much can be resolved by acknowledging that their observations often stem from contrasting and varied field experiences. If powerful enough, these can override a researcher's previous assumptions.[4] Most significant, research over many years of revisiting the same or similar field sites shifts and deepens one's perspectives. Laurel Kendall (2009: 49) perceptively terms this "memory horizons," noting "Like any lens, structuralism gave only partial vision, but it brought some things into focus that might otherwise not have been seen." She went on to "follow the money," the political economies of the Korean popular religious rituals called *kut*. I have more diffusely followed people and tried to chase their narratives.

Presenting Shamans and Shamanic Cosmologies Through Essays

The first chapter summarizes my relations in the field, my experiences as a patient-supplicant, and my approaches to an interactive "engaged anthropology" that goes well beyond treating Siberian interlocutors as "informants." Despite a few tantalizing invitations, I have thus far stopped short of shamanic apprenticeship (compare Castaneda 1968; Jokić 2006). I suggest that all effective ethnographic research must be collaborative in various degrees. Although I fear extremes of reflexivity as "belly-button anthropology," I have accepted the premise that readers deserve to know up front that I respect shamanic thinking as more than metaphor.

Theory and methodology are interlinked in any project, especially one as fraught with issues of subjectivity as the study of shamans over time. This is a topic that, as with all sensitive engaged anthropology, demands delicacy, cooperation, and friendship with local interlocutors. I write without pseudonyms because most of my conversations and experiences have been with those who want me to express what they have related, and give them accurate credit. Where discretion and privacy is appropriate, I have tried to be protective, using a coded initial in one case, and masking identities in several others. I write assuming that some Siberians will read my work in English and I have facilitated several translations back into Russian or Sakha.

The second chapter is comparative and historical, using the history of Russian Orthodox missionary activity in Siberia and Soviet repression of religion to make larger points about Siberian indigenous responses and cultural resilience. I feature the Ob-Ugrian Khanty of Western Siberia (also called Ostiak in European ethnographic literature) and the Turkic Sakha of the Far East (also called Yakut). I move from chronological description to a framework for analyzing what kinds of religious, medical, and spiritual repressions were most devastating across the Siberian and Far Eastern North. This then becomes a base for understanding the contexts for relative and differential degrees of later post-Soviet revitalization. Historical contexts are relevant for readers interested not only in Siberia and shamanic studies, but also more general problems of colonialism and empire. Psychological ramifications and transcendence are major themes (Chatterjee 1993; Asad 2002; Comaroff and Comaroff 2004). The (near) destruction of many cohesive shamanic communities, whether colonial, postcolonial, or neocolonial, is acknowledged.[5]

Chapter 3 tackles crucial issues in medical anthropology, focusing on the Khanty. It uses historical perspectives to reveal the dynamics of curing, stressing how social context, the changing body politic, is crucial for medical effectiveness in indigenous communities (compare Boas 1930; Levi-Strauss 1963; Kleinman, Das, and Lock 1997). Negative implications of shamanic power, cursing and abuse of spirituality are also explored (compare Brown 1989; Whitehead and Wright 2004). As many courses in medical schools now validate, social context and political receptivity are worldwide prerequisites for stimulating environments conducive to individual healing or contributing to its debilitating opposite.

Few scholars today might claim that shamans are themselves psychotic, crazy to believe themselves in touch with spirit world, but many recognize the importance of a "shamanic illness" that must be transcended for a shaman to become an effective healer (Vitebsky 1995; Basilov 1997).[6] Many stress the multiple ways shamans can reach "altered states of consciousness" for their diverse purposes, whether through drum beats, slowed heart beats, sleep deprivation, astonishing endurance, or seemingly more prosaic psychotropic substances (Furst 1972; Krippner 2000; Winkelman 2000). Since the first missionaries became fascinated with shamans as their adversaries (Taussig 1987; Flaherty 1992; Znamenski 1999, 2003), assumptions of "truck with devils," deception, and charlatanism have given way to grudging respect or sometimes full-fledged awe (Narby and Huxley 2001; E. Turner 1993, 2006). Myriad conferences, and the U.S. National Institutes of Health take indigenous medicine seriously, in a flood of credibility that is almost incredible for those of us who remember when shamans and charlatans were synonymous for many Western as well as Soviet doctors.

Chapter 4 examines the séance as a spirit calling feat of space, time, body, and language manipulation and mediation. Siberian séances and annual summer solstice ceremonies (*yhyakh*) are described with special attention to the poetic language of rituals, prayers, and epics.

In the process, interethnic relations between "Tungusic" (Éven and Évenk) peoples and the Sakha are analyzed, with an eye toward exploring fuzzy ethnic boundaries and mutual influences. My approaches to language and ritual bridge classical and current scholarship.[7] Historical description segues into personal, experiential description, playing havoc with tense changes.

Chapter 5 builds on my interactions with shamans and my observations of shamanic revival in the Sakha Republic. Its metaphorical title "Flights of the Sacred" plays on the significance of birds as shamanic spirit helpers and soul manifestations throughout Siberia. I describe sacred trees and special ritual-imbued groves in the context of specific local cultural revitalization as well as theories about shamanic "world trees." Discussion features laughter therapy, as well as other séance techniques. I also explore the extraordinary pain that becoming a shaman entails, mentioning criteria to determine who is a "true" healer- ritual authority and who is enacting a dangerous game, perhaps playing with fire.

Siberians themselves puzzle over who is a contemporary shaman and who may have become one in another time or place. Chapter 6 on urban shamans contrasts the careers of four Sakha, exploring the interrelationships among shamanic creativity, healing and divining (compare Hoppál 1992). One interlocutor, a theater director, became the Minister of Culture of the new Sakha Republic after the Soviet Union fell apart. Another founded the "Association of Folk Medicine." A third, with shamanic ancestry, founded a "Center for Communication." A fourth has become a popular diviner, commuting between Yakutsk and Moscow. Through their influential lives and their dramatic self-descriptions, readers can feel the power of political, social, and spiritual change as the republic was redefining itself in the optimistic 1990s and as people have coped with scaled back expectations of the 2000s. This chapter also signals a crucial theme in my work: the nexus of nationalism and religion.

Chapter 7 analyzes multiple generations of Sakha healers as they change their styles of dealing with supplicants, while maintaining their spirituality. Profiles of some of the most famous shamans in Siberia are featured. Analyzing three sets of older and younger generation practitioners and their communities, I argue that sustainable faith has been passed on in flexible, innovative ways. Issues of nostalgia, "constructed culture," and authenticity are revisited.

Chapter 8 asks a question many Sakha and some other Siberians have been asking, "Why can't we have our own true and cohesive religion?" To explore this, I examine the nationalism-religion nexus in the Sakha republic by outlining attempts at organized religion on the basis of shamanism. I then compare other burgeoning "shamanic movements" in the Buriat and Tuvan republics in an effort to understand the potential birth of new religions out of older spiritual vocabularies and practices. Highlighting the interconnection of spirituality and ecology, my analysis fits into globalization and "glocal" literature on New Religious Movements (Lindquist 1997, 2005, 2006; Lester 2002; Daschke and Ashcraft 2005).

My conclusions are reflections on spirituality, identity, religion, psychology, and shamanic studies. I argue that awareness of shamans and shamanic thinking can and has opened our society to new approaches to mental health, community building, indigenous wisdom, and ecology. Many debates explained and outlined elsewhere about shamans and shamanic practices (Balzer 1997) have been transcended or rendered banal by the kind of multilayered approach I am urging. We can use a huge arsenal of terms creatively without acrimony: shamanism, neo-shamanism, shamanship, shamanic, shamanistic, shamanisms. Mihály Hoppál (2007) and Juha Pentikainen (1997) suggest using "shamanhood," derived from the Russian "shamanstvo," to focus on what shamans do. We should also pay closer attention to what they say that they do, while gaining collaborative insights from their patients/supplicants and their communities—as the best anthropologists have done for years.[8]

Only a few worry about the origins of the word "shaman" or the site of the first "ur-shamanism" practice, although I am among those suggesting that "šaman" comes from the Évenk language via Russian.[9] Ironically, exceptions to lack of concern about origins may be some Siberian nationalists competing among themselves for first rights to the world's "first religion" (Kenin-Lopsan personal communication, 2005 Kyzyl, Republic of Tuva). Other exceptions are archeologists who have found bioneurological explanations useful for tantalizing theories concerning the origin of religion and Lascaux Cave art (Whitley 2009).

A more crucial concern centers on the significance of shamans and shamanic studies. Is shamanism an eclectic and quaint set of folk beliefs and practices, a technique of altered consciousness, or a full-fledged religion with relevance for the future? If we call it a "popular religion" with many worldwide manifestations, its relevance becomes obvious. Why quibble over the word "religion," as long as we reserve the word "cult" for only the most extremist, coercive groups? It has been over two decades since I suggested that the significance of shamanism was an "ultimate debate" (Balzer [1990] 1997). Today, many recognize its significance, though we may place our understandings at diverse levels of analysis, derived from various increasingly interpenetrating field contexts across the globe. Shamans, far from dying out, have adapted to our explorations, and invited a few of us in for lessons in humility.

Photo 1 Sakha (Yakut) musicians Maria Osipova, German and Klavdia Khatylaev, with the author after Glen Echo Town Hall concert. Photo by Harley Balzer, 2008.

Chapter 1

Sacred Trust: Ethnography as Renewed Relationships

"My littlest abaaghy *is a real predator. When did you realize you were in danger?"*
                    V., Sakha shaman attempting to provide me
                                with a ritual purification, 1997

"I'm writing my new book on Yakut [Sakha] values. What can you recommend to me concerning the values of other peoples'?"
                              Uliana Vinokurova, August 2009

Cultural changes within indigenous communities, especially regarding their sacred traditions, are as sensitive and volatile as changes of sacred practitioners' relationships with those who study them. Sometimes, these phenomena are interrelated. In our times of increased interactive influences and intensified cultural and identity uncertainties, many of us have learned to expect the unexpected in our attempts to connect with, respect, and understand practitioners of the sacred. "The politics of healing" has long been acknowledged as an important issue in social-cultural anthropology (Johnston 2004), as have debates concerning "who owns Native culture" (Brown 2003) and concerning "authenticity" (Carter 1996; Lindquist, Coleman 2008). In this environment, I argue, along with many of my colleagues, that all responsible ethnographic research must be collaborative in various degrees, although I also acknowledge many different kinds of collaboration and "engaged anthropology."[1]

Reviewing my field experiences from interactive research in Siberia and the Far East since 1975–76, supplemented by sometimes dramatic meetings in other venues (including other continents) with Native friends and colleagues, I suggest in this chapter multiple diverse yet intersecting roles that anthropologists can potentially integrate in studying constructions of the sacred and the politics of identity. One role that has an honorable record in Siberian ethnographic literature is "anthropologist as patient." Another, made only recently possible with our expanding global networks, is "anthropologist as impresario and public translator." This easily leads, at least in my case, to the role of "anthropologist as hostess." Open-ended reciprocity augments the classic, tacitly collaborative yet sometimes problematic roles "anthropologist as friend" or "adopted family member." These all enable cultural interpretation of sacred realms not usually discussed with variously defined "outsiders," and all rely on data and multiple perspectives discretely bestowed. Another role, made notorious by Carlos Castaneda (1968), is "anthropologist as apprentice." I have not been in a position to play or live this role, although it has been offered. One of the most culminating and mature roles, not common enough, is "anthropologist as colleague," including mutually negotiated joint projects and coauthorship. A much less satisfying activity, yet increasingly common and occasionally productive when combined with some of the other relationships, is anthropological tourism.

I begin with my relatively early entrée into shamanic worlds as a patient and then turn my focus on the relatively new "impresario," "hospitality," and "colleague-coauthor" interrelations. These combine the emotional and analytical salience that has enabled many of us to shift to multivocality in our writing and to mutually beneficial collaborative research. They can lead to cotheorizing and to lifetimes of synergistic activism. They transcend the implications of the word "role," with its unfortunate association in English—role-playing—by stress on multivocal constructed interrelations. However, before we congratulate ourselves on twenty-first century ethical sensitivities, we should also acknowledge legacies of superb anthropologists who combined roles of family member, friend, coauthor, and translator effortlessly enough to make a mockery of parsing their "roles."

Anthropologist as Patient

In 1992, I became a patient in a diagnostic séance with a young Sakha healer, L., who claimed to be the great granddaughter of one of the most legendary female shamans in Sakha history, Alykhardaakh.[2] L. was too shy to call herself a full-fledged shaman, yet she described a series of spirit tortures that she had experienced before changing careers from theater arts to folk curing. She covered my body with movements that Russian healers call "non-contact massage," part of an "extrasense" examination. Uncannily, her hands hovered around a spot where only recently my doctor had seen something abnormal, deep inside, using sophisticated technology. Tactfully asking if I had consulted with modern Western doctors, she described what she saw with her X-ray–like vision. Impressed, I asked a range of Sakha consultants if X-ray vision had been part of "traditional" shamanism. Yes, they confirmed, special shamans had such abilities, thought to be passed on in certain families. But my case to build L. into an inheritor of Alykhardaakh's talents and into a research collaborator hit an obstacle when a senior shaman with knowledge of Alykhardaakh's family tree explained she had no direct descendants. A possibility existed that I had been gullible, yet spiritual kinship, or reincarnation, in Sakha eyes could justify the link, and L.'s powers were hard to deny. I was left with a sense of ambiguity, caught in a confusing state of simultaneous belief and disbelief, something perhaps more common among anthropologists than they usually care to admit.[3]

Belief, or at least trust, was also important for my next encounter with a shamanic healer as a patient, in 1997. Though not an alcoholic myself, I was visiting a healer famed for curing alcoholics who come to him from all over the Sakha Republic. He and his large, friendly family were based in a region far from the capital, which for reasons that will become apparent, I am not specifying. V. was a healer who had gone through the "spirit torture illness" (*ettéétén yald'ar*), as he put it, using the full term crucial for shamanic initiation, and who also had shamans in a known lineage reaching back seven generations to an ancestor named Tokunai *oiuun*. V. was pleased when I and others called him a genuine *oiuun*. I arrived with a mutual friend, and we were both sincere potential patient-supplicants. V. warned appropriately: "You need to have a reason before you can do a séance. I cannot perform for show, though I have sympathy for researchers into shamanism and feel myself to be one also."

My first contact with V. was through a family member of one of his "patients." Their story pulled me beyond the everyday tragedy of drinking into a mystical vortex of spirit retaliation. After a history of "very noisy and obstreperous" drunken behavior, the alcoholic was persuaded to turn to V., but accounts differ as to how much he believed in the process. One relative explained: "He did not have the willpower to last out even his agreed time period [of promised abstention]. And his violation cost him dearly. After a binge, when he was sleeping soundly, some neighboring children, who often ran and played near the house...took some boards and just beat [him]...on the head. For no apparent reason." Afterward the children insisted that they had no idea what they were doing: "They just got this strange urge. It was really uncanny."

V. uses this story as a morality play: "At first [he]...did not really believe in either me or the spirits. He laughed behind people's backs, at everybody, thinking he was above it all. But you see the power of the spirits and what these séances can do to people." The alcoholic has been in and out of jail, with a sad history of relapses. V. became more selective, choosing supplicants with strong commitments to change and be counseled. The core of his practice is a spirit-invocation séance of several hours: "Sometimes alcoholics are very frightened when I start. The power of the drum and the idea that maybe spirits really are here after all frightens the hell out of them. Some jump up and run."

Later I was able to talk to some of V.'s patients. A relative of a supplicant confirmed: "Yes, one guy got so scared he fairly flew out of the *balagan* [traditional cabin V. uses for rituals] and went stumbling down the path and then fell flat on his face, arms outspread." I realized that V. was using techniques of Alcoholics Anonymous (binding vows of abstinence, collective reinforcement, multiple therapy sessions) combined with shear fear.

V. has an intense, small, tanned face, muscular runner's body and crinkle-eyed smile, and wears a bear-tooth talisman. He has lost many lower and some upper teeth, as if one of the alcoholics he tries to cure may have hit him. But he gets up from any of life's boxing rings for another round. He received me generously, having "seen an eagle the other day, as I was escorting a patient from the *balagan*....The eagle, mid-sized, had flown down and raised a right leg, as if in greeting....Well it turned out to be a female eagle. Your country has eagle as a symbol doesn't it?"

V., my local Sakha friend, and I headed in a jeep to the woods, stopping at his grandfather's large abandoned fort-house homestead, where we kindled a fire in order to offer bread and pancake thick with butter to his grandfather, via the fire spirit (*iot ichchi*) residing in an old smoky, rarely used hearth (*chuval*). They did not let me sacrifice chocolate, saying it was too modern. Further along, a path leading into the forest was dominated by a large larch tree, where Sakha had left other offerings, especially ribbons and strips of cloth.

When we finally entered his *balagan*, recently built deep in the forest, V. gave choices. He could try to cure me of my specific health concern, attempting a major, private, multiple spirit-calling séance. This would entail banishing our mutual friend to the jeep for possibly as long as five hours. He could provide a shorter, more general "purification, a defense against the evil attempts of others to thwart your work." This would allow our friend to join the séance, and help with firewood. A third possibility was that our friend could be the focus of a three-person séance. We agreed on a rare combination of the last two, and so V.'s two patients settled onto benches softened by horse furs, opposite the old-fashioned hearth.

V. began warming his drum. The fire was roaring, but still not "fed" when he went behind a panel in the back to change into his cloak. He emerged and darkened the room with a black curtain that blocked nearly all the outdoor light. V.'s opening was a deep resonating prayer to *iot ichchi*, as he fed the fire with what seemed to be nearly a whole bottle of vodka. The fire flared dramatically in the perfectly funneled *chuval*. He offered pancake and butter while praying for our well-being. Through the fire, he appealed to many enumerated sky spirits for our health, work, creativity, productivity, and long life. V. rose and began a low chant with the tone of the drum deep and sonorous. He moved his body slowly, the metals of his spirit helper images clanking and swaying all over his fringed skin cloak. Spirit calls were accompanied by whistling and whirling, shifting and shuffling. One of his main bird spirits, the Northern white owl (*mékchirgé*), was called and at once caught my eye, for a huge, fluffy, stuffed one was in the back left corner of the room.[4]

Suddenly he broke into Russian, as I realized with a start that I had been lulled by his magnificent Sakha *algys* and had not responded to a question. "Do you want to feel the hot dank, foul smelling breath of my *abaaghy*? Should I call my *abaaghy* to you?" he repeated. He wanted me to answer. I nodded OK, in surprise. Ah, I thought, he is an *abaaghy* (usually glossed as evil spirit) shaman after all, one who uses predator spirits to do good. This helps explain why missionaries and others have called such shamans "black" or "evil." On another level, it helps reinforce the message that nothing is purely black or white.

The spirits came, whistling and whirring. He blew shocks of wind against me, from his mouth. At first I did not smell anything but the pleasant scent of the *balagan* wood, but then I detected a new element—his skin cloak of reindeer perhaps, sewn by his wife, or the drum beater thrust nearly in my face. He chanted and danced, and again I was alerted with a start to his next question, "Will you let my *abaaghy* eat your heart?" I had nodded a few minutes earlier to letting the *abaaghy* come close, but this new suggestion, it finally dawned on me, was not funny. I shook my head "no." He backed off relieved, and later said that he had prompted me to say "no," but I did not recall this. Somehow, I had realized in the nick of time that I must not let the spirits eat me, that I must protect myself, that I was also being made responsible for my own well-being. He went dancing on, this time more lively, triumphant, and I watched as he crossed the room and began blessing my friend, who had helped only once with some wood.

After more clanking and blowing, whisking away the air around each of us, the *oiuun* retreated to an area where he could sit, still drumming. He chanted more prayers, including for my well-being, my unhindered work, and for my future children. After his intonations and incantations, he ended with a definitive "I have said" and "Dom"—"Let it Be So." Then he launched into a lovely haunting lyric song, "a song of the soul, an ancient Sakha melody," he said later. He opened the curtains and, gently stroking my back, told me to "get back to yourself. Come into your normal state of mind. Return to our time." Indeed, I had lost all sense of time. The séance had lasted about an hour but seemed beyond temporality.

The crux of V.'s therapeutic séances is a dynamic between the healer and the patient-supplicant. This is not a simple performance of a chanting, dancing shaman, but rather a means to trigger a sufferer's body/mind integration. The supplicant's participation, active acceptance of spirit action, is required, and is key to the séances of past generations as well. After our séance, V. commented: "You know, I was easy on you. I could have frightened you very badly.... You could have smelled my spirits and far worse. But you really were in danger, when you did not answer at first about letting the *abaaghy* [spirit] eat your heart. There is a strange energy working here, that I myself do not understand. But if you had answered the wrong way, it is possible that within the next six months your heart might have stopped, for no apparent reason. You could have given yourself up to the spirits. My littlest *abaaghy* is a real predator. When did you realize you were in danger?"

V. was eager to reflect on my reactions and his motivations, in a mutual education of new cross-cultural friends. I mentioned my sweat lodge experiences with Native Americans. He suggested that they use heat, smoke, herbs, and an energy circle to make the shaman's work easier, whereas in a Sakha séance, nearly all the energy, attention, and power must be on and through the shaman. Concerning the purpose of the séance, V. concluded: "My protection will be as good as any other.... I am not saying that I am a great shaman. But the power of what we did, though just a minimal séance...was enough to keep you from the ill will of others [especially other shamans]."

When I next saw V. several years later, our earlier two-day bout of conversation, rituals, and growing rapport was dramatically changed. I arrived with another friend, an artist from Yakutsk who was originally from V.'s home territory. They were cordial, but it soon became apparent that V. was acting oddly jealous. He insisted that to continue our conversation, he would need to take me alone to his new summer *urasa* (a large conical structure) in his back garden, an excellent venue for his burgeoning healing practice. Once there, he began a combination of flattery and intimidation, suggesting that I was fated to be his apprentice, to cure myself of my illness by becoming at once a shaman (*udagan*) and his lover. Such relations may have been a pattern in the past, but I doubt it. I certainly knew that shamans were notorious for using their charisma and ability to travel for philandering, but I had never considered that shamans who were in apprentice relationships were also lovers. On reflection, I realized this was probably an aberration since most apprenticeships I could recall were single gendered. I fled fairly quickly, but discovered that my artist friend had already retreated to another home in the village. It took several more years to learn that this gentle, married artist had been badly scared by V., who threatened to bring spirit retaliation on him if he continued his friendship with me.[5]

A more successful experience as a patient and friend has been ongoing for over 15 years with Aleksandra Konstantinova Chirkova, already mentioned as the healer famed for heritage from her father Konstantin *oiuun*, and also respected for her training in biomedicine. In her childhood, her seer-father explained that she had inherited his shamanic healing gifts and should not be constrained, as he had been, by Soviet persecution. Therefore he urged her to get a full education in European medicine. Her hands radiate heat, and her deep chanting voice generates confidence, in me as well as in many of her very satisfied patients, some of whom I have interviewed for confirmation. She is the star of my next section. Since my collaborative, engaged relationship with her is well-known and she is a published author, I use her full name (Chirkova 2002, 2009).

Anthropologist as Impresario/Translator

Aleksandra Chirkova wears a cross rather than a bear's tooth around her neck and has a Moscow medical degree as a fully accredited surgeon. Yet, after spiritual guidance, she has stopped cutting into peoples' brains, and, like V., she considers the bear one of her guiding spirits. I first met Aleksandra Chirkova in 1992 when she presented an excellent paper on her father during the first conference on shamanism in Russia after the breakup of the Soviet Union, the conference controversially called "Shamanism as Religion"(Gogolev et al., 1992). Aleksandra was emerging from familial secrecy into a public forum with information about Konstantin's seemingly miraculous curing abilities and his quiet practice of medicine during the Soviet period. My first extended visit to Aleksandra, at her invitation, was in 1993, to her home in Belaia Gora, when we also travelled to nearby villages of the Abei region.

In 2000, after living with and/or working with Aleksandra periodically since 1993, I invited her to participate with me in a large public conference on "ethnomedicine" in Germany. The organizers were asking anthropologists to produce "their" shamans, in a way that made me somewhat uncomfortable. Consulting Aleksandra, we decided that she need not bring her famous father's shamanic cloak (necessitating an assistant on the trip), nor did she need to perform a séance "for show," even if organizers were hoping that she would. She is a healer, not an entertainer. In a stadium-sized hall, she articulately explained (through me as her translator) her background and complex philosophy of culturally appropriate patient-centered healing, while wearing a well-tailored suit. Throughout the conference, she was inundated as much or more than other healers, who had come from all over the world, by would-be patients. She accepted a few, and began intensively curing in hotel rooms.

Within days, her reputation spread. Finally she agreed to do a small smudging and chanting purification ceremony one evening in a workshop-like atmosphere. It was announced late, but over 100 people appeared. We sat in a circle and were blessed with smoking herbs she had brought from home, as she slowly circled the group while chanting. She then invited those with medical problems to come forward, and worked with a few in an improvised interview-prayer session. She constantly warned that this was not a "real séance," and made no claims to cure anyone in one session.

At the conference, many were dazzled by the concept of a combination Siberian Shaman/ European Doctor, and trusted her therapeutic abilities over some of the more colorful shamans from Tuva, Mongolia, Latin America, Australia, New Zealand, and elsewhere. While she and I had some tension over the degree to which she should be taking on private patients and missing some of the cross-cultural opportunities of the conference, we agreed that the hunger for shamanic healing and spirituality in Europe had reached proportions approaching the level of cult enthusiasms. While it is a cliché to say that healing is often based on faith, this was well illustrated by the conference interactions. The follow-through continuity of healer-patient relationships that is a hallmark of Aleksandra's medicine was sorely lacking.[6]

The German mega-conference forced me to ponder not only my relationship with Aleksandra, but also changing international approaches to shamans and spirituality. Given the exponential international interest in "traditional" spirituality, often unrealistically romanticized and ahistoricized, what are the obligations of those of us who mediate among cultural worlds? Do those like Aleksandra, who mediate among many worlds in their healing practices, have the most potential to become twenty-first century shamans par excellence? Or are cutting-edge leader-healers in danger of losing their own souls and cultural moorings in the process of international cultural communication and adulation? I suspect any answer requires contextual and contingent perspectives, sensitive to specific, charismatic individuals.

Anthropologist as Hostess

Another foray into the impresario role came in 2008, as I helped with the organization and hosting of two brilliant, innovative, and shamanic Sakha musicians, the husband and wife team German and Klavdia Khatylaev, students of several close Sakha friends. We did two adult and one children's concert in the Washington DC area, with the Khatylaevs living with me during a very hectic week, combining tourism and mutual "fieldwork." (I definitely got some of my own medicine as the lead in a highly ethnographic video on steak grilling.) I learned much from translating and introducing their exquisite performances, but much more from wonderful breakfast conversations about their dreams, literal and figurative.

Klavdia has been having lucent, sometimes predictive dreams most of her life and this has caused consternation amongst some in her family, uncomfortable with her shamanic tendencies. Klavdia, one morning without prompting, mentioned she'd had an important dream the previous night. The dream was that an old woman spirit, very kind, dressed in traditional Sakha clothing, had come to her. She was possibly an ancestress, though not Klavdia's own grandmother, who had been a female shaman (*udagan*) and a major influence. The woman said gently that Klavdia was playing shamanic music, shamanic songs. "No, no," Klavdia had protested in her dream. "We are just playing ordinary songs, traditional Sakha *touk*, traditional melodies on the *khomus*." "No," the ancestress gently responded, "your music is shamanic."[7]

For years, I have been thrilled when people volunteered their dreams to me while I was in the field in Siberia. In my home, I had further insights, highlighting the power of dreams to dramatize key issues and yet, at least partially, be disassociated from their cultural context. Klavdia opened floodgates of passionate perception concerning her mixed feelings about her shamanic heritage. She recalled another dream that had nearly derailed her life, just after she moved from a remote village to the capital of her republic: "I lived with an aunt in Yakutsk. I was training to be a nurse, worked in a hospital. One day I had a horrible dream about that aunt, how she would die. I made the mistake of telling her the next morning. She was angry, told me I could not live there any longer. She cried 'You are an *udagan*. You are dangerous. Don't tell us your dreams. You'll have to go live in the dorm...' I understood that she was scared, but I was confused. This all happened very fast. I packed up and went to live in the dorm. Incidentally, my girlfriends at that time also wondered how I could see so much in my dreams. That same aunt showed up at the hospital a week later, with her daughter. She apologized and asked me to come back. I was young and flexible, and not easily offended. So I came back."

As I reflect on the depth of interaction that was stimulated first by rapport because of my help with the concert tour, and second by my role as a hostess, I consider that the opening of our "global village" to mutual hospitality has enhanced the quality of interdependence. These days, an anthropologist need not just get "adopted" by a family in some exotic field, and then go home. Rather, several families I have lived with in Siberia now can come to me, and can and do send their children. In one case, this turned awkward when a young Sakha woman repeatedly stayed out late and nearly drove me, her unwitting *in loco parentis*, mad with worry. But usually, reciprocity is more possible and seems to mean more. This has gotten me wondering about how many anthropologists of previous generations sustained their "adopted family memberships" and truly transcended their initial status as temporary guests.

Anthropologist as Friend, Family Member, Cultural Interpreter

The complex personal approaches encouraged by my cultural anthropology training stressed the sympathetic if not empathetic participant observer. Here I should acknowledge that my anthropology mentors of older generations were indeed the kind of wonderfully charming, open, and collaborative human beings who took their "fictive kin" relationships seriously. In the case of Jane Goodale, this led to court testimony on indigenous land claims in Australia. For Frederica (Freddy) de Laguna, it meant being given her own potlatch by Northwest Coast Tlingit. Many years later I was welcomed into Cordova, where Freddy had done her early fieldwork, in part on the strength of her excellent reputation with the dwindling Eyak community.

For me, and I have done nothing yet that matches Jane and Freddy, worldview shifting rapport has been possible only because I have gotten close enough to a few Sakha families in several villages and in the capital to be treated more as a family member than a guest. The only way to do this is to keep returning, and to understand the friendships and kindred spirit familial relations as something to be earned, not taken for granted. In this, fictive kinship is not quite the same as the relationship that a prodigal child who is reaccepted might have. I can affirm that this classic form of field relationship is especially enriched if it begins on the basis of intellectual rapport and mutual respect. Thus art historians Vladimir Ivanov-Unarov and Zinaida Ivanov-Unarov (2000), whose art book on shamanic images I helped publish, became family friends.

Living in the small town of Belaia Gora with Aleksandra Chirkova, I learned as much from her intellectual analysis of her traditions, values, and healing practices as I did from observing and benefiting from her rituals. The full deconstruction of a ritual should ideally involve multi-staged dialogues resulting in mutually worked through analyses over time. I constantly returned to Aleksandra, sometimes after over a year's separation, with questions she found exasperating, because she thought she had already explained various Sakha terms for souls and séances. But the repeated interactions are what have given me some depth of understanding of her full powers and worldview. I am not looking for contradictions, but when they emerge, they provide fascinating insights into sacred knowledge and its sometimes bumpy, inconsistent reproduction across generations.

This leads me to my field presentation of my own beliefs. If something is too sacred for me to know, I tell my interlocutors, then I do not want to know it, or to publish it. But because I explain that I have an open mind concerning the possibility of spirits and animals outside of, yet related to, our own social communities, many of my interlocutors feel comfortable that I potentially share their beliefs. I did not start this way, nor did I develop my noncritical techniques to deceptively elicit information. My approach evolved as I perceived unexplainable coincidences, telepathic moments, and complicated synergistic relationships that seemed to be outside of myself or my ability to influence a given situation in the field. By confessing my own incipient spirituality, I learned far more than I ever expected to about traditional shamans, shamanic worldviews, and the imperfect transfer of shamanic beliefs into the twenty-first century.

Part of my ability to collect information about the sacred was enhanced by my reputation for collecting stories of how shamans were repressed in the Soviet period, and how they occasionally transcended that repression. Because people knew I was sympathetic, they sometimes came to me with such stories, before I had requested examples of this fascinating, morale-boosting genre of anti-Soviet popular lore (see ahead).

Another example of ethnographic sleuthing of the continuity of shamanic world views revolves around the 1998 reburial of the *udagan* whose mummified body had spent the Soviet period in the Muzei im.Yaroslavskogo. While I was not in the country during the reburial ritual, I began collecting accounts of it, and what it meant for people. Sponsored by the republic's Ministry of Culture, it was led and blessed by the revered ecology activist and shamanic healer Éd'ii Dora [Elder Sister Dora], featured in Chapter 8. She had warned participants and nearby villagers to later avoid the site, and under no circumstances to kill any animals near it. She also cautioned that the dead shaman's spirit might be tempted, due to her unsettling, to take a few people or animals with her. In 1999, while passing in a bouncy jeep along a dirt road somewhat near the burial site, I was chilled to notice that a horse was improbably caught in a downed telephone wire in a field. I urgently asked my (Sakha) traveling companions to stop the jeep, and two of them ran to the horse to investigate. They returned distraught, as the horse was recently dead. Soon the story spread like wildfire that the buried *udagan* had taken a sacrifice, just as Éd'ii Dora had said she would. Other animals had also died since she was reburied, and their deaths too were attributed to the shaman, as was the illness of a hunter who had ignored Dora's warning not to hunt near the grave.

Return trips, sympathy, and the "willing suspension of disbelief" have helped dispel what have undoubtedly been concerns about my sincerity and sanity since I began working in then-Yakutia in 1986.[8] This hardly means that I have had full access to everyone I have wanted to visit with and learn from. I have been chasing Éd'ii Dora for years, and she keeps promising me that someday when I am ready, she will talk more openly with me. When she does, I will do the same with her that I have done with others: share what I have written about Sakha cultural revitalization, knowing that critique can make my work deeper and more accurate, even if it hurts. In the meantime, I am grateful that some of Dora's (and Vladimir Kondakov's) teachings are in a wider public domain.

Dora's own special voice comes through in a biography of her by Nina Protopopova (2003), as does the voice of the late founder of the Association of Folk Medicine Vladimir Kondakov, in his works utilizing several genres (1992; 1997; 1999). We are living in a fascinating post-Soviet moment when articulate healers can explain their worldviews with access to not only literacy but relatively broader audiences beyond their original communities. As yet such sources are predominantly in the Sakha language; they raise interesting questions concerning the transference of knowledge, the role of text in changing shamanic perceptions, and new stimuli for "live and direct" spirituality (compare Engelke 2007).

Anthropologist as Colleague

To give my fieldwork better context, I depend for perspective on a panoply of sources by Sakha ethnographers (in Russian and Sakha).[9] This was one of the reasons that I transferred my field interest to then-Yakutia in the mid 1980s. The "emic," or "insider's," views that these colleagues' research represent are endowed with richness that I can only hope to emulate. Amongst themselves, some differentiate degrees of "insiderness," just as I differentiate variations of the "etic," or "outsiderness" when evaluating my Western colleagues. Like the word "role," the terms "etic" and "emic" break down when closely examined in the muddiness of context and perception. Newer terms "perspectivism" and "controlled equivocation," as used in Latin American studies, also require sensitivity to incomplete if not insincere connections.[10]

One of the closest collegial and friendship relations I have developed over the years is with the couple Vera and Zhargal Solovyev, who are based in the Washington DC area, and have organized the group Sakha Diaspora, with its superb website www.sakhaopenworld.org. We share news of the republic, visitors, and opinions concerning mutual friends and acquaintances in the republic. They read much of what I write and critique it with tact but without self-censorship. They help me with my students, lectures, and with difficult *algys* (prayer) translations. When Vera's mother, Ekaterina Pavlova, visited in 2008, it was particularly exciting for me to be able to consult with someone I first met in a village, but then came to know as the mother of a friend.

When possible, additional dialogues and informal seminars with Sakha colleagues create an ongoing "reality check." However, "reality" is mediated by interpretation, sometimes leading to awkward awareness of debates among my Sakha colleagues and friends. As much as possible, I try not to choose sides, but rather present debates, including in publications, as usually healthy manifestations of changing and contested cultural values and symbols (Balzer 2005).

In 2003 I learned that in 1986, when I first began Yakutia fieldwork, one of the deans of shamanism studies, Nikolai A. Alekseev (1984, 1997), himself nicknamed "Oiuun," was furious that I seemed to treat him as an "informant." At the time, I well knew the analytic distinction between a published ethnologist working in the Academy of Sciences and a village elder who knew wonderful folklore. I am mortified that I caused offense, but the real difference, ironically, between 1986 and 2003 was that I had become less a student of Alekseev's and more a (still junior) colleague. By 2008, he had been elected director of the premiere Institute of the Humanities in Yakutsk, itself a boon for scholarship on shamanism.

In addition to issues of seniority, issues of collegial rapport are key to working as an ethnographer outside one's own cultural milieu on topics as sensitive as the sacred. One of my guides into Sakha cultural history is the enormously respected ethnographer Anatoly I. Gogolev (1983, 2002), whose insights and hospitality I have benefited from since 1986, when he was my official cultural exchange "adviser." Our less formal work together in his hometown of Viliuisk in 2002 was a highlight of my fieldwork. In one memorable session, the Sakha blacksmith elder Ivan Zakharov confessed to us that his notorious rivalry with the revered shaman Niikon during the Stalinist period had not only been on the level of Komsomol enthusiast persecution, but also on a shamanic spiritual competition level.[11] I have often wondered whether Zakharov's confession would have been made without Anatoly. That trip is an example of one of my preferred styles of fieldwork, returning to the native village or town of friends or colleagues.

The Sakha colleague with whom I have published work is Uliana A. Vinokurova, a sociologist, and former republic parliament deputy (Balzer and Vinokurova 1996). Uliana has become one of the friends from whom I have learned the most about Sakha cultural values, politics, and cultural revitalization. When I first met Uliana in 1986, and for many years after, her wisdom concerning shamanism and folk healing amounted to the phrase "I have a healthy respect for the power of shamans, and therefore I want to stay as far from the subject as possible in my academic work." This included her approach to the path-breaking 1992 Sakha Republic conference "Shamanism as Religion"(Gogolev et al. 1992). But by the mid-1990s, Uliana was ready to survey the most prominent folk healers in the republic, and public attitudes toward them (Vinokurova 1997). One summer, when she was unexpectedly busy as a parliament deputy, she considerately sent me back to her family in Srednaia Kolyma (where I had visited before) with her husband Petr so that we did not have to cancel the research trip.

By 2003, when we were working together on a more broadly defined project concerning changing Sakha identities and "ethnonationalism," Uliana initiated our joint interview with Mikhail Chashkin, folk healer and son of the well-known deceased shaman Foma Chashkin, of the Taata ulus, described in Chapter 7. After a revealing session in his home, Mikhail pointed us to the woods, where a huge "shamanic tree" (*kérék mas* [sacrifice site tree]) that Foma had secretly used lay prostrate on the ground. This larch was an important symbol, for Mikhail had made clear that a major difference between his own herb-based practice and the fuller spiritual healing techniques of his father was that tractor driver Mikhail does not expect spirits to speak to or through him. Uliana was not only distraught about the demise of the sacred tree but also about my failure to photograph the tree as a symbol of cultural decline. Why had I failed? We discussed my overly optimistic spins on Sakha cultural revitalization quite painfully.

Periodic fieldwork for nearly 20 years with Uliana, including in 2010, has centered on issues of Sakha sovereignty, identity, and religious consciousness in light of changing political relations within the Russian Federation. As Russia was recentralized under President Putin, it became "federal" only in name. Uliana senses a patterned danger in the Sakha situation, the volatility of enabling an indigenous group to have tasted an unprecedented degree of self-reliance and political dignity in the 1990s, only to have those rights and hopes taken away. We have together been watching alarming trends of polarization and ethnic conflict. By working with her in the Sakha Republic, in my home, and in several international venues, I have been able to hone and change my own approaches. Uliana's contacts have also enabled us to have access to many diverse groups within the republic, rural and urban. Our symbiosis and friendship has created opportunities for co-theorizing that have allowed us to transcend collaborations that limit indigenous intellectuals to data gathering and reserve analysis for the outsider anthropologist.

Anthropologist as Ethnographic Tourist

The depth of my relationships in the Sakha Republic has never been surpassed anywhere else. Ever since my first fieldwork on the cultural exchange in 1975–76, and my first foray into Siberia, to the Khanty-Mansiiski Okrug in 1976, I have wondered about American standards of friendship in view of the intensity of my family's friendships in Russia. However, this is a matter of degree, and I jumped at the chance to travel in 2005 and 2010 to new regions, especially the Republic of Tuva (Tyva) and The Republic of Buriatia, including Lake Baikal.[12] I had never seen these most beautiful lands, famed for tourism and shamanic pilgrimages, because I had always traveled farther North to less touted (though often equally magnificent) regions. While I knew that chances for independent interviews and personal friendships would be limited, travel also provided opportunities to reconnect with Tuvan and Buriat colleagues I had met or worked with over the years outside their home turf. Because of my personal ties and the nature of each trip's sponsorship, I felt that problems of potential exploitation and "hit and run" fieldwork were lessened, if not mitigated. In addition, the economy of Russia was such that locals in the areas visited were welcoming all the foreign dollars and support for shamanic studies they could get.

To prepare for Tuva, I reconnected with a former Fulbright Fellow who had worked with me at Georgetown, the Tuvan sociologist Zoia Anaiban, who met me in Krasnoyarsk, our group's first Siberian stop. Once in Tuva, in the capital, Kyzyl, I was delighted to find that our translator and local guide was a Tuvan scholar who I'd already befriended several years earlier at University of Virginia, Aldynai Seden-Khurak, who had become a professor at the Teacher's Training Institute of Tuva. She and her young daughter gave us marvelous entrée into Buddhist and shamanist communities. My past connection with ethnomusicologist Valentina Suzukei, coauthor and collaborator with my friend Theodore Levin (chair of the department of music at Dartmouth College), also eased access to academic and music circles.

Most significant and fraught with drama was my important reconnection to one of the Siberian ethnographers I have published, dean of Tuvan shamans, Mongush Kenin-Lopsan, described in Chapter 7. While some foreigners have simply trouped onto the premises of the two main (and competing) shamanic healing centers, *Düngür* and *Tos Déér*, and gotten interviews or treatments, that was a less desirable approach with only a week in the republic. The packed, nearly delirious, week was filled with joyous throat singing, a trip to a nomadic family with horses and sheep, a sacred spring séance, an afternoon with the prescient head of the parliament (Bilchidei, once the leader of the Tuvan nationalist movement *Khostug Tyva*), museum tours, and revealing conversations in Buddhist temples and well as the healing center *Tos Déér*. Tuva is at a stage in its tourism industry where foreigners, especially ones respectful of local culture, are desirable and not (yet?) overwhelming. Outsiders have already, however, played inadvertent roles in the competition between *Düngür* and *Tos Déér*, something I think I managed to gain insights into without becoming a pawn in local political games.

A particularly delicate cultural issue in Tuva, laden with political implications for foreigners, is the opening of religious opportunities in general, and the perceived invasion of Christian missionaries in specific. Our group arrived at the one decent hotel in Kyzyl, overlooking the Yenisei on one side and the old KGB building on the other, just after several American Protestant missionaries had left. Their presence in the republic was tolerated, but clearly had made some of my interlocutors uncomfortable, and by proxy our group was at first viewed with some suspicion. "Could we tell our compatriots to back off?" one Tuvan friend asked me. We also found ourselves the recipients of a fervent, albeit futile, plaint from the distinguished head of the Buddhist community: "Could we influence someone in Moscow to let the Dalai Lama come back for a visit?" Leaving Tuva was difficult, but the gerrymandered homeland of Mongolic Buriats was our next enticing stop, first into Irkutsk Oblast, and then, briefly, the Republic of Buriatia itself.

When our small prop cargo plane, flown by hotshot Russian pilots who bragged they had fought in Chechnya, landed perilously close to the sacred "Shaman's Rock" of Olkhon Island, my heart sank. "Could they really not have found another spot to put the noisy plane down?" I thought, but it was too late to say anything. Our local mixed background Buriat-Russian guide and greeter seemed to think nothing of it, a bad sign. I was not particularly surprised when the chief shaman of the region, the controversial Valentin Khagdaev, stood us up. For me, this was the closest the trip came to a personal pilgrimage, and I decided to be as privately respectful on the island as possible, careful to avoid areas that I knew were off-limits to women, careful to talk to as many female elders as I could in our short time on this island that had only just gotten its first electric lines. I will never know whether Valentin, with whom I have several mutual friends, did not appear because of the plane's location or because he was under pressure from fellow villagers to stop seeing so many paying and polluting foreigners. In any case, gossip about him was magnified because of his absence. Our group spent a day with a multigenerational Buriat family with centuries of residency in one of two villages on the island. They were cordial and forthcoming, but afterward I spent considerable time reflecting on the frustrations of being out-of-control of one's own schedule.

In 2010, in Buriatia's Tunka Valley, I was able to attend a daylong shamanic *tailgan* ceremony in the context of a conference on shamanism, partially sponsored by the local Buriat association of shamans, called *Tengeri*, as well as the Academy of Science. All three trips to Tuva and Buriatia made me appreciate the luxury of the way I have come to do fieldwork in the Sakha Republic with close friends.

What Does Trust Mean?

It is especially due to Uliana Vinokurova's insights that I have increasing trouble separating the political context of interethnic relations from the more tantalizing and ethnographically challenging realms of the sacred. I also have become more attuned to how cultural and spiritual recovery is interlinked. Clearly, sacred shamanic knowledge that could have been passed on from elders to their children has been lost. We should be neither naive nor romantic about the potential for full esoteric shamanic wisdom recovery after the Soviet period.[13] Yet many of my interlocutors, including the perceptive dream-telling Klavdia Khatylaev, feel that for receptive individuals and communities, the chance for spiritual revelations continues, whether through séances, dreams, or conscious spirit quests. Some, recovering concepts of reincarnation, see their grandfathers in their grandchildren's openness to a parallel spirit dimension. Others see their best hopes for recovery of cultural values in a new Yakutsk temple called *Archy Diété*, or Purification House, or in its rival spiritual center, called *Aiyy Diété*, Spirit House, on the edge of town. These are discussed in later chapters.

My methodology as a socio-cultural anthropologist has been to combine many of the relationships outlined here, and others as well, to publish materials that the Sakha and other peoples of the North want published. Mutually congruent goals have included depiction of the dynamic, changing cultural richness of Sakha Republic (Yakutia), too often famed merely for its natural (diamond, gold, and oil) resources or its ecological problems. I also publish the work of some of my Siberian colleagues, in the M. E. Sharpe translation journal *Anthropology and Archeology of Eurasia* that I edit.[14]

A challenge for anthropologists involved in truly collaborative, "engaged anthropology" projects has been to balance interpretive, reflexive, postmodern fascination with subjects like shamanism with the hard-nosed reality agendas of indigenous activists worried about land claims, non-material "cultural property" exploitation, and ecological devastation. This tension is beautifully analyzed in the activist work on land rights by Charles Hale (2006), who explains that court testimony in Central America demands presentation of self as "objective," and "scientific." Similar dilemmas are described by Paul Nadasdy (2007) for Canada.

Some of my colleagues and friends in the Sakha Republic, including some politicians and ethnographers, now make occasional pilgrimages to ancestral graves, and speak openly about their pride in ancestors who were shamans. Yet some of the last esoteric knowledge kept hidden from outsiders (however defined) is the knowledge of local shamanic grave sites. These have sometimes become secret shrines, kept from nonlocal Sakha as well as more removed non-Sakha. I have visited only a few of these sites.

In this century of increasing globalization and encroachment on lands for energy and mineral exploration, keeping sacred sites secret may become an impossible luxury. Throughout the North, indigenous peoples have needed to share with trusted outsiders some of their sacred knowledge so that it can be kept for posterity (compare Novikova 2004; Kasten 2004). At times, development incursions can necessitate court cases involving ethnographic expertise, as in the U.S., Canada, and Australia. They can necessitate painful paradoxes, buying into "global systems" to protect local systems (compare Tsing 2005).

The lands, rivers, and forests that are the manifestation and roots of spiritual connectedness and yearning are best protected by indigenous activists, local ethnographers, and healers in the broadest sense. But sometimes open-minded sociocultural anthropologists with Western, European, or Russian backgrounds can mediate and moderate misunderstandings concerning attributed "primitiveness" or the outmoded nature of shamanic beliefs. They can defend indigenous rights to sacred land and can give credibility to interconnected folk healing and ecological philosophies. In this context, anthropology becomes a sacred trust fertilized by ongoing relationships of many kinds. You do not have to become an apprentice shaman, an arduous path not to be taken lightly, to communicate respect for shamanic knowledge.

Photo 2 Historical anti-shaman election poster - "Vote Workers for the Native Council. Do not Allow Shamans and Kulaks." Artist G. Khoroshevskii, 1931.

Chapter 2

Spirits Under Siege: Shamanic Communities of the North

"Shamans... are made to act as the shock absorbers of history."
Michael Taussig (1987: 237).

"Three times the drum jumped, and three times people retrieved it and put it back on the bier."
Sakha elder I. F. Volkhov to M. M. Balzer, Srednaia Kolyma, 1994.

On the eve of the 1917 Russian Revolution, shamans and the communities that supported them had already experienced the missionary might of the Russifying Orthodox Church for at least a century, and often much longer. Many indigenous people of the Russian North, Siberia, and the Far East publicly identified themselves as Russian Orthodox, while privately practicing complex, syncretic rituals that outsiders labeled as shamanic and animistic. The missionary zeal of Sovietizing atheists reached many of these remote communities late, and in distorted, uneven forms. Yet this second Russian ideological and demographic onslaught had more far-reaching consequences for indigenous peoples than Russian Orthodoxy.

This chapter explores early Christian and Soviet ramifications of repression for indigenous believers in shamanic worldviews. Experiences of groups throughout the North are considered, but the resonance of Christianity and Sovietization is discussed primarily for the Khanty and the Sakha. They provide a productive comparison, given their widely dispersed geographic positions and their contrasting demographic and political circumstances. The Ob-Ugrian Khanty, whose Khanty-Mansi Autonomous Okrug was designated in 1931 as the Ostiak-Vogul National District, are among the smaller and less politically established of the Siberians, while the Turkic Sakha, with their Yakut Autonomous Republic born in 1932, are among the most numerous and strong. The 1926 census revealed the Sakha (Yakut), at 240,709, to be only relatively better able to withstand demographic pressures of assimilation and social pressures of acculturation than the less numerous Khanty, who numbered 17,800. In the 1926 census, all 26 of the officially termed "small peoples of the North" numbered a mere 122,792.[1]

Generalizing about responses to Christian and Soviet atheism campaigns for even two groups is risky, given the haphazard and diverse nature of individual and community interactions with Russian newcomers. Patterns emerge, however, through diverse written accounts, oral histories of local leaders, and various voices of pain and confusion that reach across the generations. Stories about shamans and their communities are conducive to uncovering interconnections of personal, cultural, and political processes and values.[2]

One such story, from early Soviet period Far East, illustrates dual themes that provide an interactive tension in this book, that state antishamanic propaganda and policy were both brutally effective and ultimately undermined by the faith and behavior of indigenous believers. A Sakha grandmother recalled the 1930s drama of her brother's death:

> One time in my childhood, my brother became ill. I did not notice at first, but then it got very bad, so that he was screaming in pain. In the emergency, my mother invited an old woman to come. We did not call her an *udagan* [female shaman], but she was known for doing the things that the [outlawed] shamans had done. She came, looked at my brother, and took down a frying pan. Her name was Matrena. She licked the eyes of the child, the boy, my brother. She took up the pan and beat it with a wooden spoon. After a while she said "In your family, someone killed a big animal. The spirit of that animal has come into your boy." And indeed he did not live even four more days, until the arrival home of our father [who had been hunting].[3]

The Sakha mourner who told this tale did not condemn the would-be curer for the death of her brother, nor did she question the spirit possession interpretation of his death. Rather, she was resigned that the fate (*d'ylgha*) of her brother had been sealed by forces larger than herself. Matrena's efforts, augmented with a frying pan rather than a drum, only extended to diagnosis. Even if she had a full set of shamanic accoutrements, that had been confiscated and burned during

Soviet campaigns against shamans, she might not have been able to cure the boy. But in other cases, shamans continued their practices with newly made or old, hidden drums well after their drums, cloaks, and reputations had supposedly been taken. The larger story that emerges is thus one of tentative human resilience against forces of spiritual and social change that began well before the Soviet period.

Icons and Idols: Syncretic Religion Before Soviet Rule

A Khanty legend tells of ancestors who fled north to the Ob River from the steppes of Permia, precisely when Bishop Stephen tried to convert them to Russian Orthodoxy. These ancestors, called Ugrians (Ugra), reportedly carried with them a gilded "idol" called Christ which they carefully protected, along with carved images of patrilineal ancestors. Their mixture of Christian symbolism with Khanty religion exemplifies a syncretic approach that many Khanty practiced unapologetically over the centuries.[4]

In Siberia, as Orthodox missionaries established churches near Russian trading centers, they had not only the backing but the decrees (*ukazy*) of the tsarist government behind them. Some of the first missionaries, such as Filofei Leshinskii from 1712–14, cut a swashbuckling path through West Siberia, baptizing Natives (called, ironically, *inorodtsy*—aliens) in huge numbers and burning their ancestral images. Under Peter the Great, exemptions from the fur tax were given to baptized converts. But when their new Russian family names were entered into missionary rolls, they were also recorded for future tax obligations.

Native responses to Christianity reveal that the act of baptism itself rarely meant full conversion. In the unfriendly competition between priests and shamans for the respect of many indigenous followers, shamans often won. Russian Orthodox allegations of shamanic collaboration with the devil, excessive greed, and quack doctoring did little to dispel Siberian Native, and sometimes local Slavic (*Siberiak*), fascination with shamanic curing séances. The 1920s ethnographer Georgi Startsev reported with unconcealed amazement on dramatic mixed ethnic séances that had little in common with sedate Orthodox church ceremonies.[5] Nonetheless, some Khanty shamans had images of the curer St. Nicholas painted on their drums, essentially adopting him as a kind of helping spirit.

For several centuries, the Khanty and many other Siberians were influenced by Russian Orthodoxy, but not nearly to the extent that might be expected, given the length of time that was involved.

Explanations include the strength yet adaptability of pre-Christian religion, and the haphazard, undermanned and at first brutal nature of missionary actions. In addition, the relative scarcity of effective Russian Orthodox models among Slavic settlers of "peasant" backgrounds played a significant role. The homestead faith of Slavic colonizers was often a blend of pre-Christian belief, lapsed Orthodoxy, and awe of indigenous shamans.

Much farther to the East, the Sakha (Yakut) too accepted aspects of Christianity and wealthy Sakha merchants occasionally sponsored church building, without losing the underpinnings of faith in spirits and a very complex hierarchy of sky and underworld gods. Respect for the extraordinary abilities of shamans to communicate with these gods and to predict the future was maintained into the twentieth century. In 1920, a Sakha elder proudly recalled the shaman-prophet Khaas [Goose], who had long ago warned of the coming of Russians and the building of "a terrifying construction 10 times bigger than an *urasa* [huge conical summer tent]."[6] He had seen a vision of a Russian Orthodox church.

For the Russians, the most visible aspects of Sakha religion, as with the Khanty, involved shamans. The whole complex Sakha religious and ritual system was collapsed into the term "shamanism" (or sometimes "black faith"), seen to stem from the totemic beliefs of ancient hunting and clan cults. Sakha and other indigenous terms for male and female shamans and for diverse medical and spiritual specialists were masked by the wider term *šaman*.[7]

Far Easterners benefited from their geographical and demographic position in relation to Russian expansion and missionary policy. Some of the worst excesses of the eighteenth century mass baptism campaigns were avoided by Yakutsk Orthodox authorities, who learned to be more patient in their approach to conversions. Concerted efforts to convert indigenous peoples were organized later, with the impressive priest-scholar of native languages, Innokentii Veniaminov (later Metropolitan of the Orthodox Church), playing an important role. Another contrast involved the arrival in Yakutia of some sectarians, such as the Skoptsy, who presented Christian models that were relatively more fervent and communitarian than those of the Siberiaki.[8] As in West Siberia, priests competed with shamans for the attention of believers, although some priests applied to shamans for cures when they became ill. One of the most famous and powerful of the Sakha shamans, the beautiful Anna Pavlova (Alykhardaakh), was also known for helping the Russian governor of Yakutia entertain St. Petersburg visitors.[9]

Prerevolutionary repression of shamans was mitigated by a popular folk conception that shamanism and Orthodoxy were not mutually exclusive. Yet repression occurred, particularly around Yakutsk, the center of the Eastern Siberian Russian Orthodox eparchy from 1868. Here, shamans cut their hair and usually hid their profession from Russians. The shaman "Man-Who-Fell-From-Heaven" told the Polish exile Sieroshewskii: "We do not carry on this calling without paying for it. Our masters (the spirits) keep a zealous watch over us... we cannot cease to practice shaman rites. Yet we do no evil." This shaman had "several times been condemned to punishment; his professional dress and drum had been burned; his hair had been cut off, and he had been compelled often to make obeisance and to fast."[10]

In Northern Yakutia, at the turn of the twentieth century, the exiled ethnographer I. A. Khudiakov (1969) reported local Sakha (Yakut) and Éven to be very poorly Christianized, often by corrupt priests who preferred to stay with rich Sakha and send others to make grueling priestly rounds. "In the first stages... the Yakut completely misunderstood the new religion and took Christian rituals as a new form of government obligation." Sakha occasionally lodged official complaints, for instance against a priest who had beaten a "sleeping Yakut" with a metal cross, and then claimed: "It is not I who am beating you, but Christ."[11]

By 1917, most Northern Natives were officially Christian with Russian family names. They added aspects of Christian ceremonies and symbolism to shamanic and life-process rituals, with syncretism itself becoming a matter of degree and diverse taste. Repression of shamans was haphazard, with excesses at times combated through official channels. The antishaman propaganda war was only begun, and rarely won, despite some genuine converts to concepts of Christian peace, brotherhood, and humility.

From Kul' (Spirit) to Kul'tbaz (Soviet Culture Base)

Throughout the North, when indigenous communities learned that Russian Orthodox priests and believers were themselves condemned by Bolshevik leaders, many temporarily returned to more open practice of their indigenous religion. A few also protested the removal of their local Russian priests, but to no avail.[12] In the turmoil of the civil war, and the confusion of revolutionary construction, shamans were especially in demand. Curing the ills of the body politic, as well as the body-mind, had long enabled a least some shamans to be revered as moral authorities.[13]

Individual and community catharsis occurred in troubled times through séances, intense emotional dramas, usually involving trance (of the shaman and sometimes others) with poetic chants, drumming, dancing, and group participation. Shamans, as intermediaries among cosmological worlds, regained lost souls of the sick, found lost objects, predicted the future, and suggested lucrative hunting routes. They coached people guilty of indigenous concepts of sin into confessions. They used hypnotism, ventriloquism, and tricks to astonish, often believing their techniques would not work if the spirits were not helping them. Eyewitnesses claimed to have seen shamans, while in trance, withstand cold, walk on hot coals, stab themselves without leaving scars, disappear and reappear, escape the bounds of ropes, and induce or control floods, winds, and storms. Shamans sometimes promised the spirits animal sacrifices and their "favorite" coins, Paul 1 rubles with crosses.[14]

As Soviet power became consolidated and entrenched, the repression of Orthodoxy and pre-Christian religion by atheist agitators meant that many aspects of faith and religious ritual were under unprecedented siege. Shamans, symbolizing what Russians perceived to be backward "darkness" and superstition, were blamed for any Native reticence concerning Sovietization. The party tactician I. Suslov warned that missionaries had tried and failed to eradicate shamanism, and that Soviet propaganda and medicine must be better.[15]

The mechanisms enabling Sovietization to be marshaled were "culture bases," establishing schools, clinics, courts, and councils in a few main village centers; "red tent" campaigns that carried activists into the tundra; radio, film, and newspapers, some in indigenous languages; and collectivization. The orchestrator of Soviet policies from 1924–1935 was the "Committee of the North."[16]

Activists calling themselves "cultural workers" and "militant atheists" tried with varied success to disprove and discredit local shamans, sometimes with amusing tricks. One used an eclipse of the moon to shame a shaman in Chukotka, another shot at the sky to show there were no spirits lurking there, while a third pretended to be a devil and gloated in triumph when a local "Eskimo" (Yupik) shaman on Wrangel Island did not catch his deceit. Yet such stunts usually had only a temporary effect, discrediting specific shamans without changing whole belief systems. In a few cases, they backfired entirely and it was the cultural workers who were made to look foolish by "impudent" shamans. The famed Sakha female shaman Alykhardaakh allegedly sexually embarrassed the men who came to arrest her, so that they fled in shame.[17] Some activists, like priests before them, appealed to shamans for help in personal emergencies.[18]

Collectivization and the establishment of Soviet schools influenced Northern Natives, but not always in the direction that planners hoped. Russian newcomers, sometimes called "Red Khans," had basic problems of translation. For instance, when the *kul'tbaz* at Kazym was established, local Khanty identified the Russian word "*kul't*" with one of their words for evil spirit, "*kul'*"[19] This disinclined many Khanty, particularly reindeer breeders who wished to remain with their animals in tundra communities, to allow themselves to be herded into forced village sedentarization. In addition, a red banner at Kazym proclaiming "Integral Cooperatives—the path of natives from darkness and from kulak-shaman hegemony" was allegedly mistranslated as a warning for Khanty to run away (Sergeev 1955:112).

Shamans at Kazym, Iuilsk, and Numto played an active role in a notorious 1933 Khanty "rebellion," that led to the arrest of most of the Khanty men in the community.[20] While details are disputed, Khanty friends, including the writers Eremei Aipin and Maria Vagatova, stressed it in 2010 as a defining moment in Khanty history and self-awareness as a people. Maria recalled: "We had a war in Kazym. But we lived through it and have come out able to talk again about important spiritual things." It was a last-ditch effort to assert some Khanty control over a frightening new Soviet order. Four Khanty fathers had been arrested for refusing to allow their children to go to the new Kazym boarding school (*internat*). Compounding local outrage over this, schoolchildren taken by force from Khanty homes had been housed in the boarding school when a tragic smallpox epidemic erupted. The children were not allowed, for health reasons, to return to their homes. Their families converged on Kazym and prayed to an important female ancestress, housed in a sacred grove nearby, for deliverance of their children and themselves from incomprehensible Soviet policies. A Soviet "brigade" of seven elite Communists, sent to quell the disturbance, was taken to serve as hostages, thus escalating the tensions. In official reports, as many as 300 people were involved in the kidnapping, initiated to release the four Khanty fathers, as well as the children. Rumors abounded in the local Russian community that the kidnapped Soviets (who included the first Khanty "Chekist" Z. N. Posokov and one Russian woman) had been sacrificed in a traditional shamanic ritual. Three hostage deaths, at an island known for sacred rituals, did occur. Some of the first planes ever used in the Soviet North were sent to track the culprits, and massive, indiscriminate arrests resulted.

The Khanty writer Eremei Aipin (1990: 24) has described how Khanty secretly passed on stories of this "so-called Kazym war," which lasted into 1935. Attributing the main cause to the "devastation of collectivization," he explained that Khanty leaders "wanted to reestablish full electoral rights, change the punishments against kulaks, recreate the Native Council, change the basis on which furs were given to the government, close the boarding school." Most of all, "Khanty wanted themselves to orient and control their own lives," according to their own spiritual beliefs.

Khanty activist Tatiana Moldanova has conveyed the suffering and embitterment of her people during and after the uprising, considered a "rebellion" from Russian authorities viewpoints, and a defensive, desperate resistance from Khanty perspectives. It was nearly impossible, after the massive arrests, for the remaining women and children to survive the winter. When men of her family were arrested, "two came into the yurt: one armed Russian and one well-dressed nonlocal Khant in furs. Already on their many sleds two by two Khanty sat tied up" (Moldanova 1990: 24–25). As Tatiana explained to me in 1991, her grandmother had premonitions of trouble when their clan spirits had refused an offering.

Traumas such as the Kazym resistance pitted many Khanty against Sovietizers. But eventually the sheer power of in-flowing Russians organizing new reindeer, fishing, and hunting collectives overwhelmed Khanty resistance. Shamans who were incapable of combating these processes, and the diseases that accompanied the Russian newcomers, lost authority as much from within as from direct propaganda against them.

In contrast, the more numerous Sakha of the East had their own revolutionary intelligentsia. The major Sakha revolutionary hero, Platon A. Sleptsov, tapping into the power of shamans, took the revolutionary pen name Oiunskii from the Sakha word for male shaman, *oiuun*. His influential poem, "The Red Shaman, " pitted benevolent forces of the revolution against the "dark forces" of superstition and exploitation. Yet it also drew on Sakha spiritual and aesthetic traditions, as did his charismatic oratory. Oiunskii received his prerevolutionary education from the Yakutsk seminary (reading Tolstoy and Dostoevskii), and then became a leading member of the Union of Yakut Workers, advocating the transfer of all church lands and property to "the people." His plays mocked the idea of an earthly god (the Tsar) and the effectiveness of priests, but he and most of his colleagues were later themselves caught in Stalinist purges.[21]

Rich "kulak-shamans" were challenged in Yakutia by playing on a mixture of fear and admiration that had also earlier been part of community perceptions of local shamans. Propagandists called shamans greedy charlatan deceivers, who took people's savings, daughters, and last horses for their own pleasure. Activists also accused shamans of being leaders of anti-Soviet opposition, although organized leadership as occurred in Kazym was rare.[22] Accusing shamans of demanding too much for their services was usually unfair, for shamans mostly took only what their supplicants chose to donate. Through the North, most shamans were hunters, fishers, reindeer-breeders, or cattle raisers, like the rest of their communities, with their shamanizing only supplementing other income.[23]

The Soviet Union's Russian Federation legal code was used to prosecute shamans for swindling, although at first Native people's courts (*tuzsudy*) rejected such attempts. A 1924 Yakutia version of Soviet laws condemning shamans typified the groundwork for repression:

> Shamanism in the IaASSR is deemed an especially harmful phenomenon, undermining cultural-national rebirth and the political growth of the peoples…along with all religious cults…the activities of Shamans are thus considered to be under the jurisdiction of the criminal code of the RSFSR, for instance concerning extortion, deception for profit,…irresponsible curing claims…."[24]

By 1928, a section was added to the Russian Federation code called "Crimes that Constitute Survivals of Tribalism," outlawing activities perceived to be sponsored or condoned by shamans, for example animal sacrifices, polygamy, and "bride price/wealth" (*kalym*). Shamanic activity also fell under the strict 1929 antireligious propaganda and education law.[25]

In the late 1920s and early 1930s, through the North, hundreds of shamans' drums, cloaks, and other accoutrements were either collected in forced "donations" for museums, piled in storage and left to rot, or burned by overenthusiastic activists. Some of these were young Komsomol members who were Native converts to Communism, rather than newcomer Russian revolutionaries. In response, many shamans indeed curtailed their practices, promising to reform themselves into "more productive" members of Soviet society, while others continued shamanic healing in secret for predominantly grateful and discrete clients. Noisy drumming, dancing, and chanting in night-long séances in villages called too much attention to shamanic practice, so some séances came to be held at remote cabins and campfires in the woods. A few shamans who continued practicing were hauled off to jail, where some died. The full scope of this repression is unlikely to be known, even with open archives, for some shamans were charged with other offences, when their true "crime" was the practice of shamanism. The elderly Sakha former president of the Suntar village Soviet, Tatiana I. Alekseeva, justified the repression to me in 1986:

> You should put this in perspective. We were doing important things in the 1930s. First there was the liquidation of illiteracy...[then the campaign] for sanitation and elementary hygiene. This was crucial for people who had spent their lives in impoverished *balagan* [low winter dwellings], with animal stalls attached. Further, there was the struggle for Atheist Truth. And the campaign for Rights of Women....If shamans still tried to sneak séances with patients, or if they tried to hide their drums, then their voting rights were taken away. This meant they were without any rights to land use or to membership in the collective. They were outcasts, class enemies, kulaks.

From this kind of attitude came familiar epithets of the period, terming shamans "charlatans" or "shaman-kulaks" [rich exploiters]. If in the early 1930s only 7 culture bases existed through the North, by the end of the decade, 18 had been established, as well as over 70 boarding schools. By 1934, cultural workers claimed that over 60 percent of indigenous Northern children were in school (Sergeev 1955: 382; Gushin 1980: 352, 358). Schoolchildren were enlisted in the fight against shamans. In the Srednaia Kolyma region in 1994, the elder Innokenti F. Volkhov recalled:

> The main purge against shamans was in 1929. In our region, the activist Iuban Gavrilovich Tretiakov took nine drums. He then invited us, the schoolchildren of the area, to help him burn the drums. So we schoolchildren burned the drums in a big bonfire. My uncle was a shaman, and his big white drum protruded obviously from the pile. There were plenty of adults present as well as children. And many of us saw this big drum jump out from the fire. Three times the drum jumped, and three times people retrieved it and put it back on the bier.

Tretiakov, after burning so many drums, was reputed to have died an unpleasant early death from a mysterious bloated stomach illness that villagers attributed to his persecution of shamans. The place where the drums had been burned later became a Soviet festival site, but that did not stop people from fearing both the site and the curses of repressed shamans.[26]

The next period of crisis, when indigenous peoples, along with everyone else in the country, suffered extraordinary hardships was "The Great Fatherland War." A poignant story related to me in the Sakha Republic in 1994 by Sakha historian Egor Spiridonovich Shishigin illustrates the degree to which spirit beliefs, emergency reactions, and flexible thinking about gender are linked. During World War II, in a time of starvation, a Sakha man was left with his bawling baby, after his wife died in childbirth. Far from any human help, he prayed desperately to the spirits to be given milk in his poor male body. Suddenly, milk appeared in his breasts and the child was saved. According to several Sakha consultants, the man, though not a shaman, had tapped into the crucial life forces of the opposite sex, as shamans do, using this sometimes ambiguous, sexual power for salvation.

The ambiguity of shamanic reputations and the diversity of approaches to local shamanic heritage are reflected in a curious geographical and emotional coincidence in the Sakha village of Kachagatsa, Kangalask *ulus* [district]. Two women representing very different sides of Soviet shamanic history have lived uneasily next to each other for many years, one the daughter of a deceased local shaman (Duolan *oiuun*), the other the daughter of the village soviet president who arrested him. One saw her father, the shaman, as a long-suffering martyr who had died in jail, but had cured many people. The other saw her father, the soviet official, as a strong, righteous leader, who had arrested his neighbor for stealing meat from the community storehouse. By the 1990s, villagers were divided over these versions of local history, though sentiment had tipped in favor of the shaman.[27]

In sum, whether reacting with open rebellion, subtle resistance or self-restraint, shamans and their communities endured unprecedented devastation of their ways of life. Shamans, as quintessential symbols of tradition and conservatism, became a focus of repression. Many reindeer breeders were settled, and far-flung villages were consolidated into collectives. Demographic disaster, defined by local peoples as forced settlement or resettlement, rapid Russian influx and increased illness, meant that even the strongest and most revered shamans could not cope with compounding crises. In many places, shamanic worldviews survived better than the shamans themselves, or their clothing and drums. Repression was hardly the most effective way to win hearts and minds in a struggle for rationality, hygiene, and Soviet-style atheism.

Responses to Repression: Analysis of the Spiritual and Political Underground

The adaptability of shamanic practice has led to its survival and diversity over the centuries. Its nonmissionizing eclecticism has provided fertile ground for debates within shamanic studies over whether shamanism is truly a cohesive "ism," a religion, or a set of folk-healing premises and practices. One way out of this familiar, even stale, dilemma is to more closely examine patterns of shamanic responses to major social-cultural upheavals, such as Soviet repression. This can provide context for better understanding the diversity of what shamans do, in and for their communities, as well as what they and their followers say about it. I suggest here diverse shamanic strategies for survival under difficult circumstances. While the strategies build on each other and to some extent conceptually overlap, their order is not fixed, and no one model or response style is a prerequisite for another. I argue that how shamans responded to potential and often very real devastation in Soviet times influenced the uneven 1990s recovery of shamanic practices and beliefs.

One model of shamanic response, interethnic cooperation, may surprise readers accustomed to thinking of shamanic complexes within one "culture" or cultural area, as well as those aware of the often-justified reputation of many shamans as competitive and territorial. Interethnic solidarity is exemplified by the friendship of the famed Sakha shaman Tokoyeu with the Yukaghir shaman Kurilov during the 1920s, and their mutual aid in crisis. Because Tokoyeu and Kurilov had the same spiritual teacher, they were close enough for Kurilov to hide Tokoyeu's drum when authorities tried to confiscate it. Another example is the cooperation of one Sakha shaman with a Russian doctor, whose daughter the shaman cured in the 1950s. The Russian doctor gave the shaman his village's first television, and helped protect him against Soviet authorities, who allegedly condoned his shamanic healing practice, despite its illegality. More recently, those shamanic curers who have also acquired Soviet or European-style medical degrees, such as Aleksandra Chirkova, exemplify a trend in shamanic resilience that may well be the cutting edge of twenty-first century interlinked medicine and spirituality.

A contrasting response style is organized shamanic protest, far more widespread across the North in the 1920s and 1930s than official Soviet literature led us to believe. The most dramatic example is the Kazym resistance of 1931–3 mentioned above, culminating in the hostage taking and probable ritual killing of members of a Soviet brigade. It was led by Khanty shamans, and also included Nentsy leaders. My field interviews on the protest and its brutal, massive aftermath enable indigenous views of this painful, destructive-on-all-sides, interethnic conflict to be heard. A serious ramification of the protest was the arrest and killing not only of most of the shamans in the community, but also of most of the men. Families were scattered and little was left of those aspects of healing traditions that were most linked to séances and an "altered consciousness" appeal to spirit helpers. Demoralization was rampant, with women, less likely to be arrested, carrying on what had been considered in earlier times "lesser" healing arts associated with herbal knowledge and dream interpretation.

Soviet period protests can be compared and placed in the context of classic and more recent theoretical literature on cultural revitalization movements and attempts (Wallace 1972; Golovnev 1995; Trott 1997). These cases all point to the important role of shamans as not only healers and psychologists, but leaders of their communities in times of social, cultural, and political strife. Less blatantly, Spiridon, of the Viliuisk region, became a village soviet president, whose Sakha community hid his continued shamanic activities from higher authorities for many years. Thus a range of politicized responses can be seen as keeping alive an active sense of subversion, similar in social process and personal psychology to what James Scott (1985) has famously termed "weapons of the weak."

A further, and particularly common, kind of shamanic response can be termed the ad hoc, or situational response. It is beautifully illustrated by an account concerning the famed Sakha shaman Konstantin *oiuun*. In the 1960s, he reputedly managed to divert a military plane flying near his village so that a young girl with appendicitis could be transported to a regional hospital. In this period, the aging Konstantin was forbidden to practice his widely acknowledged healing gifts. He went into "altered consciousness" communication with his spirit helpers in secret, in emergencies. In this case, according to the niece who helped him, he used every ounce of his energies, donning his cloak and drumming solo by his hearth in order to cause the plane to need an emergency landing over their village. Konstantin collapsed after sending his niece to village leaders, warning them to be ready with the girl at the landing field well before they saw the plane.

Descriptions of shamanic competitions with Soviet doctors also fall into this "ad hoc response" category, as do the semifantastic, seemingly miraculous accounts of shamanic resistance to arrest and incarceration. In one Khanty case, a Soviet doctor himself fell ill, after he had played with and mocked a shaman's drum without permission. This clearly enhanced the reputation of the shaman, while sidelining the terrified doctor.

Escaping jail using ancient arts of shape-changing is a constant theme in stories I have collected in the Sakha Republic. In one popular account, a shaman was said to have flown out of jail as a bird. In contrast, the revered Niikon of Viliuisk worried about the safety of his family if he absconded entirely. Therefore, he simply proved he could escape his bars by constantly removing himself to the street in front of the jail, where his jailers could see him calmly reading. Another relevant and humorous story about the revered Niikon, before he served his jail sentence, tells of an early, foiled attempt to capture him. He was once led away in handcuffs by a policeman, intending to take him to court. But on arrival "instead of an old shaman, there was just a piece of tree branch left with the policeman, attached to him. The policeman was accused of being drunk, but he cried: 'How could I have gotten drunk?'"[28]

A related, yet analytically separate category may be called the "show-off on demand" shamanic response. Far from a superficial "pokazuka" (a favorite Russian term for a fake-out), shamanic séances performed on demand or under duress are famed throughout the North. In relatively traditional contexts, shamans of some communities needed to prove themselves on demand for their first séance, their debut after "shamanic illness," their initiatory calling by the spirits. But more hostile show-off contexts developed during competitions with Russian Orthodox missionaries. And in the Soviet period, especially but not only in Yakutia, believers repeated with awe reports of séances held in Komsomol halls, where conditions were set for shamanic failure. Konstantin *oiuun*, in the Abei region, along with other captured shamans, reputedly "hypnotized" an entire room full of skeptics into believing they saw first snow and then a bear (or a group of bears, depending on the account), inside a community center. The shamans, the story goes, were released due to a healthy respect mixed with fear for their powers.

The moral of these popular tales, even when jail terms are documented, is that at least some shamans were more spiritually powerful than their captors, that captives could become captors of the mind, and that victims could transcend victimization. The lore serves to reinforce folk respect for shamans as curers and miracle workers. At minimum, accounts are couched in the language of science: that powerful shamans could hypnotize audiences of skeptical Soviet atheists into believing the shamans had turned into bears, for example. At maximum, the accounts become symbols of ethnic pride and rekindled spirituality. I maintain they are subversive narratives that enabled Siberians to claim, at least among themselves, that their shaman leader-healers could outwit even the Soviet-Russian authorities.

A particularly astonishing variation on this theme is the shaman who went all the way to Moscow to try to recover his confiscated drum. On arrival at a Russian bureaucrat's office, he was challenged to prove his powers. "We have not seen meat for months," the bureaucrat allegedly said. "Could you produce some?" The shaman "conjured" a live pig running around the office. But still the bureaucrat balked at finding the drum. So the shaman blinded the pig and mentioned that he could inflict the same kind of harm on the bureaucrat. The stammering man managed to promise he would try to find the drum, not an easy feat, given that many drums were burned.

In Siberia, spiritual prowess is expected to be low profile. Shamans are not supposed to boast of spirit control or communication, lest they lose their powers. Thus another common shamanic strategy in the face of Soviet repression, ironically in harmony with shamanic values, was the modest "go underground" response. In extremis, this led to séances in the forest or spirit invocation without drums, after drums were confiscated, hauled off to museums, or burned. The Sakha curer Matrena, mentioned above, had to improvise a frying pan for a drum, and her solution was quite common. The "underground" response is exemplified by the belatedly valorized career of Niikon. His gentle laying-on-of-hands healing and quiet chanting became renowned throughout the republic, on a need-to-know basis. Unlike previous practice, he had to develop his following with a minimum of information about his patients, to envelope them and himself in a careful veil of secrecy.[29]

A related ramification of secrecy led to the feminization of shamanic practice in the Soviet North, yet another widespread response model. Because the more high-profile, famed "big-man" shamans were more likely to be arrested or pressured, it was often the women who carried on the basics of shamanic traditions within their communities. This "gender transfer" response meant that much esoteric and important knowledge was lost, in cultural environments where male shamans had previously passed on their clients, prayer chants, and sometimes specific spirit-helpers to male protégés. Beyond what had been common for women in the past, and women were indeed often strong healers plus dream interpreters in many communities where curing divisions-of-labor were refined—women took over shamanic practices on an unprecedented scale in Northern communities, certainly including Khanty, Sakha, Yukaghir, and Amur River ones. This kind of gender transfer needs to be further and better investigated in diverse areas, for it concerns both changes in gender status, and the question, crucial for recovery of shamanic knowledge, of whether human apprenticeship needs to be part of the inheritance or acquisition of spirit power, supplementing the usually involuntary calling by spirits.

In sum, many continued living in a shattered and shaken, yet viable and shifting shamanic cosmology. Shamanic responses and folklore accounts of shamanic prowess kept alive beliefs and faith that softened the mundane and often harsh daily activities of the human "middle world." Shamans and their spirits, in the middle, upper, and lower worlds, could counteract and subvert Soviet-power cruelty. Nonetheless, a Sakha ethnographer who has become a leader of traditional ceremonies himself, has cautioned that it is unwise to romanticize the few hero-shamans who survived, or whose reputations survived, repression.[30] For many shamans, their ultimate despair was the inability to find and train worthy successors. A Komsomol boy who was courted by a shaman, but who ran away from shamanic training, expressed bitter regret over his decision years later. His life story of thwarted shamanic practice was repeated through the North.

By 1941, most children in Siberia and the Far East had been herded into schools where their beliefs were ridiculed and their languages little used in the higher grades. They were taught that their relatives who were shamans were "enemies of the people." In one school, a teacher insisted that students tempted by shamanistic beliefs write "shamanism is the opium of the people" 50 times. Such punishments ensured outward compliance but inner turmoil, reflected eventually in alarmingly high rates of suicide and suicide attempts among youth.[31]

Negative aspects of belief in shamans as capable of curses and destruction of enemies was reinforced in the Soviet period. Fear of shamanic curses in families whose members were involved in Soviet repressions has been repeated across the North, and through generations. Several Sakha have confided that their families attribute premature deaths and various serious illnesses or accidents to shamanic curses against relatives who led aspects of the Soviet antishaman campaign.

Pitting indigenous peoples within a given small community against one another was one of the most insidious legacies of the

Soviet campaign against shamans and their rich "class-enemy" kin, "kulaks." An additional legacy was that shamans who continued their practices despite all the pressures against them were marked "insane." Within Soviet logic, they were dangerous egotists to pretend to commune with the supernatural, and still more dangerous deviants to flaunt the rules of an increasingly rigid new system. The insanity accusation laid the groundwork for what was to become full-blown policy after World War II—the incarceration of shamans, with other political and religious dissidents, in physically and mentally debilitating psychiatric prisons, nicknamed *psykushka*. A middle-aged Khanty man confessed in the 1990s to me that he had resisted all his powerful spiritual urges to become a shaman, following in the footsteps of his ancestors, because he desperately feared landing in a *psykushka*.[32]

Partial Recovery of Shamanic Knowledge

In the post-Soviet period, and for about a decade prior to it, at first cautious and then exuberant revitalization of shamanic traditions occurred throughout the Siberian North and Far East. Recovery has been spotty, seemingly haphazard or capricious. It has depended in part on the accident of particular strong personalities living in certain areas and not others. Yet some clear political trends and cultural patterns emerge on closer examination. Analysis of early Sovietization in the North must be viewed differently from a post-Soviet perspective than from the premature hindsight of the mid or late Soviet period. Aspects of shamanic belief and practice that were proclaimed dead have been reincarnated. Kernels of belief that were nurtured in private have blossomed in public. In some places, shamans and shamanic reputations have experienced a post-Soviet reversal so profound that some indigenous intellectuals fear too much folk reliance on Native doctors will be harmful to their people's health. Thus the purported successes of antireligious, antishamanic propaganda were in some measure illusory, although the suffering of shamans and their communities was not.

In West Siberia, especially in Northern Khanty territories, recovery of shamanic knowledge has been slow and halting. This is precisely the territory of the Kazym "rebellion," with its widespread, chilling resonance. One young reindeer-breeder, who later became a folklorist, mourned to me in the early 1990s that he felt the urge to explore his shamanic roots, but still feared the psychological dangers and community suspicions that séances entail. He went periodically into the forest to drum by himself, and had the potential to rekindle his family's curing legacy. But he had no viable teacher nearby, and was leery of training with the few shamans still left in the more remote Eastern Khanty territories. By the mid 2000s, when I saw him again, he was less conflicted in his loss of a shamanic path.

Shamanic knowledge in some particularly repressed communities has continued at a more subtle, philosophical level. For example, Siberians of the Far North, such as the Ob Ugrian Khanty and the Yukaghir, have kept alive a variant of belief in reincarnation and multiple souls (compare Willerslev 2007). This consoling belief has specific ramifications. The Khanty of Kazym kept secret their practice of the ritual of *khentykhlaty*, or divination for the names of newborns, through the Soviet period. When senior male shamans were not available to practice this ritual, Khanty women took over, in a dramatic example of maintaining and reviving the essence of Khanty beliefs for the perpetuation—survival—of their people. A Khanty school teacher explained in 1991 that she was proud of those who were continuing this age-old tradition "that determined whose reincarnation soul (*l'iaksas*) has come into the child." By 2010, enthusiastic Khanty folklorists were asking questions at a conference in Buriatia about other peoples' reincarnation beliefs in the North, seeing common patterns.[33]

A less esoteric complex of rituals honoring slain bears in order to encourage their return survived in changed form in numerous Khanty communities, and other areas of Siberia. These "bear ceremonies" derive from shamanic cosmology and mythology, yet need not be dependant on shamanic leadership. They have been significant especially among the Ob-Ugrian and Tungusic (Amur River) peoples.[34] Soviet propagandists of the 1920s and 1930s were horrified by the time and energy expended on this perceived wasteful and sometimes bawdy exercise in feasting, drinking, and singing. Satirical plays that constituted part of these marathon rituals captured the spirit of whining Soviet propagandists, just as they had mocked tsarist authorities and missionaries. Today they mock new politicians, among others.

In the Far East, especially the Sakha Republic, prospects for shamanic recovery have been much better. An explosion of interest in shamanic healing, spirituality, and séances has occurred, to the point that in 1992, some in Moscow proclaimed that shamanism had become the official "state religion" of the indigenous-led Sakha Republic. This was far from accurate, but several groups advocating a return to indigenous philosophy and shamanic healing have been vying for popularity.

One Sakha group sponsoring cultural revival calls itself *Kut-Siur*, meaning heart-soul-mind-body (Afanas'ev et al. 1990; Afanas'ev 1993; Utkin 1996). It has been active in performing specific public rituals, advocating integrative medicine, and promoting a program of self-defined Sakha traditional philosophy, *aiyy yoreghé*, roughly glossed as benevolent spirit(ual) teaching. For almost a decade, from 1993 to the early 2000s, concepts of multiple souls, of a multileveled cosmology inhabited by specific gods of the upper and lower worlds, and of kinship, ecology, and morality were taught under the rubric of a republic-wide *aiyy yoreghé* elementary and secondary school program. Success depended on the skills and enthusiasm of specific teachers. While children enjoyed it, reactions of their elders ranged from pleasure to shock and even anger. With the Putin administration's centralization of education programs, standardization pressures curtailed this culturally specific program.

Other groups have been more specifically oriented to recovering shamanic medicine. The Association of Folk Medicine, founded in Yakutsk in 1990 by the late Vladimir A. Kondakov, has focused on curing by broadening and integrating its repertoire of techniques (Kondakov 1992, 1993) and is discussed ahead. Shamanic practice itself has historically been highly syncretic, so Kondakov's followers can and do argue his innovations are within a shamanic tradition of creativity and flexibility.

A multitude of other healers and groups have also formed small clinic practices, working in what can loosely be considered Sakha shamanic traditions, Russian-influenced folk medicine, and Eastern medicine philosophies and practice. For example, the sports medicine trained Yuri Prokopiev founded the Center for Traditional Healing, outside Yakutsk. Until it was closed in the early 2000s, his center made room for acupuncture, acupressure, and other aspects of Eastern curing traditions, with his healers discussing "chakras," "chi," mineral baths, homeopathy, aromatherapy, "vito-therapy," and "bio-energy" with the passion of the converted.[35]

Several indigenous shamanic practitioners focus on the use of the Sakha *khomus* (jaw harp) for curing, while others far from the capital use the more renowned drum and chanting of relatively traditional séances. Some are specialists in herbal cures, massage, or bone-setting, while others practice telepathy and counseling. Traditional Sakha healers also were specialized, so such divisions are not new. What is different is that they are being revitalized in a politicized context of rekindled confidence in the potential of such cures, after intense propaganda to the contrary. Unusual, too, is the group orientation, for traditional healers often jealously guarded their community turf and competed with each other, a phenomenon also known today. Nonetheless, in times of crisis, such as epidemics, some Sakha shamans historically worked with each other to communicate with a greater number of spirits (compare Gogolev 1983:44–73).

Thoughtful Sakha warn not to be overenthusiastic about the revival, for they are aware of aspects of shamanic knowledge that have been lost. One shaman of the Upper Kolyma area was reputed to have been able to cure TB. A young Soviet doctor accidentally stumbled on evidence that this shaman was helping patients that the doctor could not cure. But in the 1930s, they were forbidden friendly contact, much less rapport. Years later, the doctor returned to the village hoping to work with the shaman as a colleague, but it was too late.

Analysts today are in an exciting, though bittersweet, position to review a broad range of shamanic responses to cultural repression and shamanic stimulation of cultural revitalization. More models can be generated, and mere categorization should be augmented with understanding of their interrelations and mutual synergy. In the post-Soviet period, increased potential for the abuse or faking of shamanic knowledge must also be acknowledged, as should increasing strains of Moscow-based policies, involving recentralization of medicine and education. Yet cautious conclusions can be suggested concerning which historical shamanic strategies met with the greatest success, and provided the best conditions for a recovery of shamanic practices, when post-Soviet spiritual revitalization became politically possible.

Those groups with greater numbers of indigenous leaders, greater numbers of indigenous philosophers, and more diverse historical responses to repression (especially the quiet, modest "underground" responses, the creative ad hoc responses, and the interethnic cooperation responses), eventually were able to bring shamanic practice out from underground, into public display and discourse more easily and more quickly than those where violent protest was met with violent reprisal. Thus it is no surprise that shamanic healing and reconfigured cosmologies have become part of an adapted, eclectic, popular cultural revival in the Sakha Republic, while in most Khanty areas, shamanic practices have been harder, but not impossible, to recover.

Neither shamans nor their oppressors should be seen as solely "black" or "white." Rather, engaged analysts can recognize the ambiguities of shamanism and its checkered history, without trying to homogenize its colorful lessons and tales. Soviet rule introduced significant health and education benefits to Northern peoples.[36] In the process, each generation constructed and reconstructed perceptions of shamans to fit their fancy, their ills, and their political lives. Shamanism, as part of a vast and diverse pre-Christian philosophical complex, has become synecdoche for and symbol of the richness of selected pasts. My Sakha friend Uliana Vinokurova, reflecting on the history of widespread repressions, yet the lingering, indeed "permeating ideology" of shamanic beliefs, explained "perhaps it is just a matter of seeing what is still alive to be valued rather than moaning over what has been lost."[37]

Photo 3 Maria Vagatova, Khanty (Ostiak) poet, daughter of a shaman, with her grand-daughter. Photo by Marjorie Mandelstam Balzer, 2010.

Chapter 3

Doctors or Deceivers?

"How can people say there aren't shamans? Of course there are."
                                                                Tegy consultant, 1976

"I dreamed I ran in the image of a bear."
                                                                Khanty friend, 1991

"Khanty healing was done with many techniques, but key was that a supplicant saw and felt electricity, and the curers believed in their own powers."
                                                                Tatiana V. Voldina, 2010

In a new spirit of respect for indigenous medicine in the 1970s, the United Nations World Health Organization instituted a policy of training traditional medical practitioners in hygiene and midwifery, while at the same time encouraging certain ancient "folk" herbal and shamanic cures (Bannerman 1977: 16–17). By the 1990s, the United States National Institutes of Health (under pressure from Congress) created its first research division devoted to integrative medicine, becoming in 1999 the "National Center for Complementary and Alternative Medicine." Without denial of the real benefits of modern psychiatry and medical technologies, health problems are increasingly studied in their historical, social, and symbolic contexts.[1] It is especially appropriate to undertake such studies in Siberia, where "classical" shamanism has long and diverse roots.[2]

This chapter examines multiple ways that illness is cognitively and behaviorally coped with by the Khanty.[3] As stressed in the previous chapter, Khanty ideas about illness changed with the arrival of Soviet doctors and European medicine propagandists, although some traditional ideas about health and how to obtain it survived underground. Shamanic trance journeys have enabled a few Khanty to believe they can communicate with and control spirits perceived as hypernatural rather than "above" nature, as implied by the term supernatural. Khanty concepts of health as essentially spiritual help to explain shamanic curing and some contemporary distrust of biomedicine. Shamanic cures are directed at spiritual ailments of patients, usually believed to take the form of lost or stolen souls. In treating such afflictions, shamans have sometimes managed to get at the heart of interlocked biological and psychological problems. The success of shamans in doing this, however, depends on their stature in a given community and that stature has declined dramatically.

The Relation of Souls and Morality to Health

Khanty souls have contrasting named functions and locations, leading to categorizations of souls as "dual" or "multiple," depending on the researcher.[4] The Soviet scholar Chernetsov argued that it is impossible to squeeze all Khanty concepts of the soul into a dualistic framework. I would add that we have yet to understand the scope of soul belief, given indications of "souls" or soul-aspects residing in many parts of the body (head, hair, skin, liver, heart), plus indications that souls guide human conscience, dreaming, sickness, and reincarnation.

Chernetsov (1963: 3–45) classified four main Ob-Ugrian souls as those representing material being, sickness/health, dreaming, and reincarnation. He suggested a fifth soul, representing physical strength, is exclusively the province of men (1963: 5). Souls associated with sickness and health (*iləs; ort; urt*) can leave shamans' bodies in trance. According to Khanty consultants, most of the dangers that can befall a soul are considered unavoidable by the unfortunate victim. Soul theft is often attributed to a recently deceased relative longing for the company of the patient. Nonetheless, some examples of soul loss have been related to a patient's morality. Such concepts were common through the 1930s and have some currency today.

Khanty considered themselves safe from spiritual and therefore bodily harm only when ancestral images or soul keepers (*itarma*, misnamed in the literature 'idols') had been treated well, when rules regarding ritual purity had been obeyed, and when ceremonies had been performed properly. Ancient concepts of well-being merged good health and fertility with fishing and hunting gains, since success in these goals reflected oneness with propitiated ancestors. Ancestral patrilineal clan spirits, called *menk* and *mis*, were believed capable of chastising Khanty for sins of disregard by soul theft. Ob-Ugrians believed smallpox epidemics resulted from grave disrespect for spirits, possibly incurred by too much contact with Russians (compare

Gondatti 1887a: 84); Nosilov 1904: 14). Traditionally defined sins worthy of bringing on illness thus concerned human-to-nonhuman transgressions and interpersonal human relations. Serious crimes such as incest or murder were especially liable to invite retaliation by ancestral spirits (Bartenev 1896: 85, 95).

Health also was thought to depend on maintenance of rapport with shamans. Revengeful shamans were believed capable of sending disease in the form of a physical object—like entrails, a worm, or hair—into their victim's body (compare Shashkov 1864: 99; Startsev 1928: 93). But shamans, especially those known personally in a given community, were usually considered to be more doctor than witch. A popular late-nineteenth century shaman assured Alexander Brem (1897: 378) that, although his spirit helpers could be used to do evil, the shaman himself endeavored only to cure and to protect his community from "unclean powers."

Shamans were able to attribute illness to a supplicant's own behavior, to someone else, or to a dead relative. To accomplish this attribution, shamans solicited confessions from patients and family members. Such a confession was itself believed beneficial to health, and may indeed have had psychological benefits (compare Frank 1961: 51–2).

Definitions and Classifications

Since shamans determined the nature of illness and were major actors in séances to recover lost souls, Khanty considered them crucial for their personal well-being. But Khanty shamans, like most Siberian shamans, were more than medical practitioners. As mediators between the natural and hypernatural spirit worlds, they made predictions, provided spiritual shields for the living in times of danger, acted as intelligence agents in times of interclan rivalry, and behaved as psychiatrists, entertainers, and judges.

Ugrian names for shamans reveal many nuances of meaning. The Northern Khanty call the shaman *semvojan*, or "seeing one," with suffixes *ku* or *ni* to denote man or woman. *S'art-ko (ku)* or *s'art-ne (ni)* are fortune-tellers. *Tsepanən-ku* connotes a sorcerer as well as a medicine man in Vakh River dialects, while on the Vasyugan River a shaman is referred to as a great or little magician, *jol [ëlta]* (Hajdu 1968:170). This correlates with a more precise gloss for the *isyl'ta-ku* (or *-ni*), soul crying man or woman, who have reputations for curing people by "eating" their illnesses and taking bodily harm upon themselves (Kulemzin 1976: 56). Karjalainen (1927: 245–305) mentions also *multə-ku* ("praying man") and *t'arttə-ku* ("prophet") for Tremyugan River shamans. Still other widely used terms denote those "who fall into trances," with notions of heat and narcotic drunkenness as intrinsic to the trance state, as well as shamanic drumming (Balazs 1968: 53–57).

Certain categories of shamans could traditionally only be men. One, termed *arəkhta-ku*, or legend-singing man in the Vasyugan region, received his strength through his ability to play a stringed zither-like instrument, the *narsus* (also called *panən-iuk*). In 1976, in the Northern Khanty village of Tegy, the one remaining player of this instrument, a cheerful and charismatic decorated war veteran, was revered for his memory of legends and his knowledge about spirits. While he kept any curing practice secret from prying anthropologists, others openly associated the instrument with curing and prophesy. Those attempting spirit contact through this sacred instrument went to a grove or promontory far from human settlement.

Another shamanic practitioner used dreams for diagnosis and curing. This specialist was and is likely to be an older woman, well-versed in relating dreams to personal or social realities, through long experience. She is called *ulom-verta-ni* (dreams-doing-woman) in Eastern Khanty dialects (Kulemzin 1976: 52–53) or *olum-verta-ni* in Northern dialects (Moldanova 2001: 7, 13–14).[5] Specialists in dream interpretation are attuned to multiple meanings behind their own dreams, and also to those of supplicants. This sometimes requires dreaming in an evening session while lying next to a patient, so that the dreams-doing-person can visualize the spirit carrier of a particular illness requiring attention. If that illness-spirit is under the control of the curer, through past encounters, further measures can be taken, involving séances or medicinal cures.

The pre-Soviet Khanty shaman was often a community leader, by virtue of personality, spiritual knowledge, and proven ability as a conductor of souls. A classification of Khanty shamans should be based on their reputations and the range in which they operate, rather than on distinctions of "black" (evil) and "white" (pure, good) identity.[6] An apprentice shaman "graduated" to practice first in the family, then the locality (defined as extended patrilineal clan affiliations), and finally in villages not affiliated by clan. However, gradations of power were undoubtedly not so systematic.

A Lifetime of Training

Questions of shamanic power began with the apprentice. Potential talent was believed inherent from birth, although it was often not discovered until the teens, when it was revealed in nervousness, dreaming, and illness (compare Dunin-Gorkavich 1911: 48). While shamanic status was not necessarily hereditary, usually close older relatives who were themselves shamans discovered and informally coached their sometimes reluctant candidates. Training stressed learning how to send one's illness/health soul into the world of the spirits. Shamans were taught drumming and how to use dried mushrooms, *Amanita muscaria* (mukhomor). Alcohol and physical exertion later became less effective means to alter consciousness.[7]

The apprentice learned to control specific, often totemic helper spirits appearing in trance as animals, birds, and anthropomorphic ancestral clan forest spirits (compare Sokolova 1971: 224; Ridington and Ridington 1975: 190–204). Through dreams or trance, the shaman also discovered how to obtain magical accoutrements, such as reindeer-skin drums, felt hats, and iron or brass ornaments for swirling cloaks. The most structured aspect of training involved memorizing songs and prayers, passed down by the shaman with whom an apprentice eventually worked as an assistant. Service to a master shaman included maintaining séance equipment and sometimes translating the shaman's trance exploits from mumbling into a dramatic story for the audience. This gave an assistant considerable power as well as practice.

While no formal initiation or fixed training time was required, part of the shamanic trance process involved the symbolic flesh cutting and bone reorganizing torture of an apprentice by spirits, to signify death and rebirth (Eliade 1974: 62–75; Nachtigall 1976: 320; Siikala 1978: 22). This well-known and widespread process of rebirth was agonizing, with spirits believed to strip a shaman to the skeleton or to pierce a shaman with arrows. Suffering from spirit torture by the shaman could then be reenacted during curing séances. The message of pain probably reassured onlookers of a curer's sincerity. More important, it convinced fledgling shamans of their own seriousness and value, instilling in the best of them a kind of empathy. When a master considered an apprentice ready to perform, a small extended family séance was arranged for curing or prediction. Word of success spread rapidly, making for a flexible system.

Family shamans, "people with sensitive nervous systems," were on call for relatives and were rarely felt to be spiritually threatening to members of their community (Hajdu 1968: 147). This kind of shaman had some herbal knowledge, but little séance paraphernalia. Most shamans through the Soviet period functioned on this level, and many were women (compare Durrant 1979). One example in the 1970s was a Tegy woman considered by several Russians as well as Khanty to be a shaman. She had little contact with Russians, refusing to learn their language, and was well-versed in shamanic lore.

A more powerful shaman, operating at the local level, had a reputation for prediction and healing through trance with helping spirits. A 1970s example of a shaman with a local reputation was a Tegy recluse in his 40s, who lived in the forest and was feared by many but summoned by a few Khanty believers. A more recent example is the late, honored elder Ivan Sopochin of the extended Eastern Khanty Sopochin family.[8]

The true shaman of wide reputation and power did not develop in every community or in every lifetime. This "big man" wonder-worker traveled widely, in both this world and the spirit world, with many helping spirits (Hajdu 1968: 147). On the Vasyugan River, such helping spirits were consistently of the opposite gender to that of the shaman (Karjalainen 1927: 282). With spirit guidance, Khanty shamans were perceived capable of visiting both the upper and lower worlds of Khanty cosmology, of manipulating in one séance as many as seven spirit helpers including the bear, and of controlling the emotions of a large audience for two or three consecutive evenings.[9] They acquired many professional secrets, enabling them to perform logic-defying feats of physical endurance, ventriloquism, and dancing.

A "big man" shaman was a true man of iron, wearing a cloak filled with dangling metal ornaments calculated to attract helper spirits (Businskii 1893: 35; Prokof'eva 1971:5-10). He beat an enormous drum(*koim*) believed to be transformed in trance into a horse or reindeer (Roheim 1954: 49; Diószegi 1968: 260–61). He rode his drum into mountainous upper and lower worlds, sometimes depicted in symbolic form on the drum (Czaplicka 1914: 222). Often the back, handle, and beater of the drum were decorated with iron rings and figures representing spirit helpers gained over a lifetime of spiritual training. Iron, as a multifaceted symbol of strength, longevity, and spiritual power, was particularly appropriate for the shaman.[10]

In the 1960s, the great Eastern Khanty shaman named Jorgen was buried by his clients, mostly old men who came from 150 kilometers around (Sokolova 1971: 224). In 1976, I heard of one shaman reputed to have been a phenomenal miracle worker operating out of Beriozovo, the father of a less respected forest recluse Tegy shaman. In addition, several Salekhard shamans had wide reputations for curing. In the Far North around Salekhard, where Khanty and Nenets shamanic traditions are mixed, the greatest potential for current shamanic apprentice-style revival in the post-Soviet period can be found (compare Golovnev 1995).

A powerful Eastern Khanty *isyl'ta-ku* named Aleksei Kunin described his initial call to a Russian patient, the anthropologist

Vladislav Kulemzin (1976: 56): "The person destined for this has a dream with orders from Torum himself [the Chief Sky-God]. The future *isyl'ta-ku* must sew eight identical cloaks out of white material. Seven of these are to hang in the forest on the east side of a birch tree. The eighth is to stay with the *isyl'ta-ku*." The long white cloaks served as a constant symbolic connection between the curer and his forest-dwelling helper spirits, while the birch tree was associated with particular patrilineal groups. The curer wore the eighth cloak during curing sessions, as a mark of purity and readiness for contact with spirits. The Sky-God relayed explicit directions concerning methods of curing only after all paraphernalia were ready. A second message could take two to three years, to ensure that the chosen person "doesn't appear just crazy" (Kulemzin 1976: 56 quoting Kunin). An *isyl'ta-ku* claiming to have powers from the Sky-God without a specific dream message could die, or could be hounded out of the community. The shaman became skilled in coaxing helper-spirits, often in the form of a snake or lizard, to devour offending spirits. Otherwise, spirits of illness were dangerously immortal.

Inherent in Khanty medical thought has been a fatalism defined by the general belief that the Sky-God, or, in some areas, the Birth-Mother, controls the length of one's life. Nonetheless, Khanty shamans tried to ensure that clients did not die before their time. For some, this required extraordinary measures and preparation. They trained early to do arduous self-inflicted harm to their bodies, or to display sleight-of-hand skill, which, in classic accounts, left audiences and patients gasping. Cleverness in learning sleight-of-hand tricks (such as appearing to cut oneself), to impress audiences and patients, did not diminish a shaman's basic confidence in the spirit system: the tricks would not work if they were not meant to. Similarly, endurance drumming for a full-night séance could not produce results unless the particular helper spirits evoked by the drumming cooperated. Action reinforced belief, except, perhaps, for the most cynical shamans.

Séances: Cosmological Dramas for Translating Belief into Action

Complex beliefs enable performances of séances and help shape not only the personality and power of individual shamans, but also the culture of curing in a given community. Many researchers focus on the psychology and "miracles" of a shaman, rather than on the reasons these "miracles" are or were impressive to supplicants.[11] During a séance, an enormous amount of communal energy was directed at solving a spiritual emergency, with an extended family often actively participating in chants and dancing (Startsev 1928: 94–96). Khanty shamans, whether male or female, were and to some extent are, able to fulfill mediating roles and to manipulate important Khanty symbols of communication by being an artist and impresario, transforming a small hut into a scene of moving dramatic action.

A shamanic cure often has two stages. The first is a diagnosis stage, involving confessions and the summoning of spirit helpers to the cabin of a sufferer to discover the causes of illness. The second stage consists of the shamanic trance (altered consciousness) journey into the upper or lower world. Such an arduous journey may not be necessary if helping spirits are able to accomplish a cure or suggest a sacrifice in the first stage.

The Russian scholar Shashkov (1864: 97–99) witnessed a Khanty séance that culminated in a sacrifice. The shaman's helping spirits directed him to order several reindeer from the patient's family as their price for a cure. The reindeer were dragged directly into the yurt of the patient: "To the leg of one deer they fasten one end of the rope, the other end is held by the patient, and when the latter pulls the rope, they kill the deer. The head and horns are laid on the floor, the flesh is eaten and the sick man is anointed with fat" (Shashkov 1864: 98–99).

This sacrifice is significant because the patient took an active part in his cure. Anointing the patient is itself similar to the smearing of ancestral images with fat and blood during shaman-led offerings to the ancestors. Thus this patient was given the same kind of concerned attention that sacred ancestral images were given. In the Soviet period, because of Soviet restrictions against killing collective animals, animal sacrifices for curing, burial ritual, or ancestral grove worship, were rare but sometimes surreptitiously practiced. They have become more common and more openly acknowledged in the post-Soviet period, as my fieldwork and a film by Finnish ethnographer, Juha Pentikainen, vividly demonstrates.[12]

Patient participation during curing sessions was, and to some extent still is, also accomplished by confessions. Obdorsk resident Bartenev reported that during a difficult childbirth, female relatives of a Khanty expectant mother sent for a renowned shaman in panic and concern. The shaman entered the darkened, ritually prepared birth hut and beat his drum, asking the unhappy patient in what way she had "sinned." She first said that she had "masturbated," then that she had a "relationship with a dog," and finally that she had "slept with her father" (Bartenev 1896: 85). Only after this ultimate confession was the shaman satisfied, and the mother safely delivered of her child. This shocking, probably exaggerated, story may have served as a morality play, demonstrating graphically the necessity of full confession.

While confessions of culturally defined "sins" by a patient or family members might help clear the air for a cure, further information regarding sources of illness was acquired hypernaturally. The Finnish ethnographer, Karjalainen (1927: 310–15), witnessed an impressive summoning of helping spirits on the Vasyugan River. At nightfall the shaman placed himself in the darkest corner of a low, crowded yurt and began to play the *narsus*. First he contacted a fierce and somewhat impertinent flying messenger called "Stern Woman with a Handled Stick." When she arrived, he began to shake and ordered her to summon underground spirits. With each helper's arrival, the shaman sang to his audience about the journeys the spirits had made. He announced a bear spirit, claiming, "I hear the hairy humped beast of the Great Earth coming from under the first layer of the earth to the water of the second" (Karjalainen 1927: 313).

Karjalainen (1927: 318) stressed that the Vasyugan shaman was not possessed by spirits, but rather was inspired by their whispering in his ear. During séances, shamans were likely to sing praises of special spirits, to challenge them, and to advertise control over a range of spirit types. A song fragment collected by H. Paasonen on the Konda, at the turn of the twentieth century, brags, "I spirits (*tonxet*) a hundred, forest goblin (*menk*) a hundred have conjured" (Vértes 1968: 119). Two kinds of classic song-myths were folk models for shamanic trance, one enabling the shaman to rescue a lost soul from greedy, fighting underworld spirits of the dead; and a second in which the shaman either flew by horse or turned himself into a white-winged bird to negotiate with sky deities (Karjalainen 1927: 245–331; Senkevich 1935: 158).

In an Eastern Khanty séance on the Tremyugan River, the shaman, after taking the hallucinatory mushroom *Amanita muscaria* and warming his drum over a fire for an all-night session, sent his soul via a dead man past various guardians of underground river crossings, until an offending ancestor who had stolen a family member's soul was found (Karjalainen 1927: 305–82; cf. 1921: 84). The shaman's proxy promised the deceased "keeper" of the patient's soul an appliqué shirt and a meal from a reindeer sacrifice. Deception was necessary, using a helper bear spirit hidden on the shaman's breast for the journey. The bear engaged the deceased in conversation, until it suddenly sprang for its quarry and frightened the thief into releasing the soul. The shaman then grabbed the soul in his fist and finally blew "the soul into the right ear of the patient" (Karjalainen 1927: 305; Siikala 1978: 224). In the 1920s, despite the Russian Revolution and subsequent civil war, Khanty séances were widely believed capable of solving spiritual problems. The skeptical Soviet propagandist Startsev (1928: 94–96) saw a Vakh River séance intended to recover the lost soul of a young child. The tightly packed session continued until five in the morning, with seven séances. During breaks, the shaman told his audience which spirits had come to him. With each séance, he became more energetic and "ferocious," while dancing, reeling ,and tossing his drumsticks to his anxious followers. He brought himself and his community to a fever pitch with the ever-louder intensity of his drumbeats.[13] "Characteristic moments occurred when the shaman put the edge of his drum on the small of his back, on his left leg, and on his torso. He would touch family members [of the ill child] and yell" (Startsev 1928: 95–98). When the sessions were over, the shaman barely had enough strength to promise that the child would be well.

In crises of illness or of poor fishing and hunting, lost possessions and general community malaise, shamans were expected to judge what kind of séance could benefit individual sufferers and the community. Given political tensions and shamanic competition, this was often compromised, but it remained an ideal well into the Soviet period. Helping spirits, usually in the form of spirit birds, horses, bears, hares, or snakes, guided the shaman toward battle or mediation with spirits in multiple realms: layers of the underworld, dimensions on the earth (including the forest, the graveyard, the village, and the body), and levels of the sky.

The loss of the soul called *lil* (breath and reincarnation soul) was and is considered cause for the greatest alarm, since it keeps a person alive. While its loss could lead to fainting or death, people hoped the *lil* could be recovered by a shaman before it settled in the underworld. A practicing curer explained to Kulemzin (1976: 59) that people can fall into the hands of the God of the Dead *Kallokh-Torum* earlier than the Sky-God decreed. In one case, to "revive the dead" the shaman emptied the victim's house of relatives, closed the door, and covered himself with the "deceased`s" shroud. He laid beside the deceased for three days, since the journey to the underworld lord took one and a half days. The curer "asked *Kallokh-Torum* to release the deceased since his life's term, designated by the Sky-God, had not ended ... [The dead man slowly revived and began to talk.] But relatives were not allowed back into the house until he could speak coherently and with his full voice" (Kulemzin 1976: 59).

After such a recovery, as can well be imagined, great rejoicing occurred, with food, clothes, and wine given to the healer. Shamanic preoccupation with revivals of the "dead" was known throughout Siberia (Nowak and Durrant 1977). This, and third day burials, may have been an adaptive response to the problem of premature burial (Balzer 1980: 77–90).

The ultimate shamanic mediation occurred in the realm of the Sky-God, called the Supreme God (*Numi-Torum*) or more metaphorically the Greatest Elder (*Allə-Iki*), and his pantheon family. When a crisis of illness persisted, or when crucial community decisions were required during famine, the strongest available Khanty shaman sent his soul, along with a helper spirit, through seven layers of the sky.

On the Vakh River in 1926, the Soviet ethnographer Shatilov (1931: 120–130) interviewed three shamans. One powerful and elaborately dressed shaman, Andrei Prasin, consented to perform a séance for Shatilov and an audience, to consult the Sky-God about the future of the Khanty.[14] This séance fit a pattern: along the way through "many suns," the shaman encountered various difficulties with "evil spirits" who tortured him into cries and contortions (Shatilov 1931: 125–129). But in this case the patient was the Khanty people.

During the séance the shaman sat on his eagle-spirit (*egkoer*) and flew to the edge of the sky. He passed a birch tree stretching through the sky, and tricked seven evil wolverines into opening seven doors to the upper sky. In many repetitive flights, the eagle and shaman visited six suns and moons, avoiding hunting and fishing traps set for them. Each bright sacred level of the sky became more splendid, but encounters with successive elders in the sky houses did the discouraged shaman no good. In a meeting with a sympathetic mythical couple, *Iki-Vanin* and *Imi-Vanin*, he explained, "I am a...Khanty-ku (Khanty man), and I live on land where everything is bad, [where there are] few fish, few animals. We probably should find another land" (Shatilov 1931: 127). Near the sixth level, the shaman asked: "What if everything is in vain?" A voice told him to go on, and they continued searching (Shatilov 1931: 128):

> We fly. We fly.... Reaching that place where brightness is nowhere better. Seven suns shine, and seven moons. Silver flows like a river. A house of gold stands there. In this house sits the great elder *Allə-Iki*, the Eldest Elder, looking like the White Snow Elder *Nagi-Iki*. Dismounting from his bird, the shaman sits on a stone. He gathers his courage and enters the house, with bows and prayers. Having prayed and prayed, he says "There, where our land is, it is bad to live. For

some, there are no fish, birds, or animals. Some are ailing and some have actually died. The Russian elder (*Rut-Iki*) has sent me here to learn where we can live better." Bowing on all sides, he continues: "*Allə-Torum* I have come to ask you, since on our [Khanty] land it is difficult to live, [since] people are ailing, could you, *Iki*, become aware of us?" *Torum* then answers: "I myself know who lives how, who suffers, who is healthy, and what you have told me. Go back home and tell the people that everything will be fine." [They fly back]...faster than an arrow shot from the tautest bow [and land on a sacred island of the swamp hair people].

This marathon séance is based on a traditional legend that the performer had learned from his shaman father. It is filled with widespread shamanic symbolism like the "world-tree," the number seven, the eagle guide, and the many suns with gold and silver. Yet aspects were adaptive. The source of his commission, the "Russian elder" Shatilov, was unconventional but easy to accommodate, since their mutual concern was the well-being of the Khanty. Most Russians were not perceived so sympathetically. Implicit in this séance, and others of its time, is an opposition between Russians and Khanty, with indications that the local Siberian-Russians, newly granted access to Khanty hunting and fishing sites, were living better than the Khanty. Such complaints are sadly resonant today. The need to attain the highest level of the sky was merited by the gravity of the changes in social, economic, and political life. Andrei asked for new land, as a way out of the poverty and starvation of a people already pushed northward by Russian colonization. This must have been similar to earlier periods when shamans used séances as a way to lead their people to new sites, legitimizing the authority of risky decisions. On their return from the sky, shamans usually became peddlers of hope, rather than prophets of doom.[15]

Theories About Shamanic Cures

The importance of patient-sufferer and audience-extended family participation in séances reveals shamanic practice to be potentially effective for community cohesion as well as individual health. Sergei Shirokogoroff's monumental work on Siberian Tungus psychology stressed the responsiveness of shamans to community stress. He called "the treatment of psychic troubles...the practical aim of shamanism" (1935: 422). His analysis can be compared with that of Victor Turner on the African Ndembu (1964: 230–63), particularly because each saw curing complexes as aiding adaptive responses to tensions produced during cultural change (Shirokogoroff 1935: 393). For both, major benefits of Tungus and Ndembu séances were assumed to stem from improvements in community relations that result from confessions and symbolic enactments of emotional group solidarity.[16]

This applies to Khanty curing, although it is unwise to attribute to shamans control over all latent social problems. Social control varied with the personality, experience, and stature of a shaman. What the nonlocal shaman gained through reputation as a "big man," he lost in intimacy regarding local affairs. To compensate, shamans' assistants and in-laws acted as informants, explaining marital problems, hunting shortages, and extended family tensions in a community.

While traditional séances were clearly a form of group therapy, successful treatment of individuals was more problematic. The intense communal and spiritual activity of séances provided a psychological boost by increasing self-confidence and jolting a sufferer out of depression (Gillin 1948: 387-400). Creatively handled symbols of common cultural experience, whether coded in shamanic paraphernalia or speech, could also help define and channel individual problems, beginning with diagnosis of problems, peaking in altered consciousness journeys, and ending with prescribed post séance tasks. Whether this psychological effect, reinforced by a shaman's "radical empathy," was enough to unblock mental or physical anguish depended greatly on the patient and the complaint. Psychological techniques that may apply to Khanty shamanic practice include shock therapy (during sorcery object removal), hypnosis (from repetitive shamanic recitations of spirit arrivals), dream interpretation and channelling (during diagnosis and in shamanic training), and social reintegration (showing to a supplicant group concern).

Levi-Strauss (1963), stressing the value of repetitive, emotion-laden symbolism in shamanic Cuna Indian chants, has provided an explicit discussion of how individual cognition may be shaped by cultural assumptions in the curing process. The crux of curing is that a chaotic and painful experience is reorganized by the shaman for the patient, through processes of abreaction and transference, and fitted into a comprehensible familiar mythical system. This reorganization "induces the release of the physiological process" (1963:198). While Levi-Strauss suggested that polynucleids in brain nerve cells could be affected, newer research indicates that brain chemicals such as endorphins (enkephalins) and neurotransmitters such as acetylcholine may be triggered in the brain to willfully control pain and adapt dream patterns.[17]

Detailed metaphors that Khanty shamans used to regale their followers may have had a focusing effect on patients. As the shaman overcame an obstacle-filled topography of the lower world, with a power bear spirit as a guide, the patient anticipated recovery of a lost illness/ health soul. When the shaman finally confronted a spirit of the dead with soul theft and offered the spirit food, money, and valuable cloth, it must have been an enormous relief to the sufferer to know that the soul was pinpointed. If a battle ensued between shamanic helpers and spirits of the dead, this battle may have been mirrored in the mind of a patient struggling with pain or drowsiness. Finally, when the shaman flew back to earth with the prized soul clenched firmly in his fist, the patient probably sensed a renewal of energy and confidence, made concrete when the shaman blew the soul back into the patient's ear.

Generalizations about what goes on in a patient's mind are highly speculative. But in traditional contexts of faith and communal concern, some shamans were able to cure at least temporarily a respectable portion of their patients, probably beyond what can be accounted for with the "placebo effect." Relief was accomplished with the aid of symbol manipulation, perceived telepathy, clairvoyance, synesthesia, and more. Shamans themselves may have had no inkling of specifically how their altered consciousness journeys, including but not limited to "ecstacy" and "trance," produced bodily cures. They were just as likely to go into trance for the lost soul of an infant, who could not mentally follow their exploits, as for an adult, who could. Thus, I am not attributing clairvoyance of scientific principles to shamans, but emphasizing that the effect of their journeying was sometimes positive. We may well acquire better scientific knowledge and vocabulary concerning the effects of journeying, spirituality, and health, augmenting explanations of placebos and endorphins, as more researchers keep open minds.

Although Levi-Strauss's thesis is furthered by the discovery of endorphins, aspects of his structural assumptions are questionable. As his articulate critic Jerome Neu (1975: 285–92) has pointed out, there is no direct homology, for the Cuna and others, between the physical body and the supernatural world, so that universal structuralism cannot be proved by reference to either physical or "fantasy-physical" parallels with shamanic mythology. Similarly, "limited laws" of symbolism cannot be derived from physical correspondences.

Assuming that processes of abreaction and transference do occur during some shamanic cures, they undoubtedly are managed in different ways. For Khanty, abreaction could result from confession of cultural or clan-specific taboos; from adroit removal of bloody hair out of a patient's body as evidence of sorcery; or from the blowing of a lost soul into a patient's ear. Transference could be accomplished not only during séances, but throughout a sufferer's potentially lifelong relation with a family or local shaman (Beck 1967: 317, 321).

Worldviews reaffirmed in séances are also significant. The cosmology of a soul's journey or a shamanic initiatory trance may be similar for a number of Siberian peoples, but it differs considerably from that of the Cuna. Thus a modest analytical balance should be kept among awareness of similar widespread and effective forms of psychotherapy, an understanding of the multiple symbol systems tapped in the process of therapy, and an open-minded possibility of shamanic access to intense, hypernatural healing spirituality.

Indigenous views of health and of shamanic behavior may vary in their congruence with interlocked psychological and biological curing. Success rates for groups where mythological chants are loudly dramatized and shamans are widely respected may be greater than in cultural contexts where shamanic cures are secretly mumbled away from the patient.[18] Since cultural contexts for curing also vary in social orientation, ranging from the more individually oriented to the more communal, further scope opens for variations in effectiveness. This in turn can change over time, as our own psychiatry reveals. Crucially, various kinds of illnesses may lend themselves differently to symbolic manipulation. Difficult childbirth may be more conducive to cure through psychologically triggered release of brain chemicals than tuberculosis.

In sum, shamanic approaches can cure certain kinds of social and personal ills, working at once on the body politic, ancestral relations, and the culturally influenced mind of a supplicant. Cultural influences may go deeper than what anthropologists mean when they stress consciously socialized values. However, they are susceptible to cultural change and should not be reduced (essentialized) to overgeneralizations about whole cultures or their representatives (Koss-Chioino and Hefner 2006; E. Turner 2006).

Cultural Change

A prerequisite for an effective shamanic cure is faith, and this is difficult, but not impossible, to find today. Much belief in shamanism that currently exists in Northern Khanty villages seems to be a negative belief in the power of shamans to do evil. Whereas many Khanty shamans were traditionally thought to be restrained in misuse of their spirit powers, heightened community tensions—with increased Russian contact and antishaman propaganda—seem to have exacerbated Khanty ideas of the shaman as sorcerer. This trend was particularly marked in the 1930s through the 1950s.[19] Any previous ability of shamans to restore community equilibrium in times of trouble was often overwhelmed by Sovietization, accusations against shamans as traitors, serious losses in World War II, displacement of Khanty communities, and efforts to settle nomadic Khanty reindeer breeders. This does not mean that Khanty cultural values completely changed or disintegrated, but rather that new emphases came to be stressed in other areas of cultural life, including rituals (Sokolova 1976, Balzer 1999).

By the 1970s, many Soviet officials denied the existence of Khanty shamans, and, indeed, belief in shamans as either healers or sorcerers had waned. However, I was able to get the following account of a curing attempt in Tegy:

> There is a shaman, about 41 years old, who lives not far from here, separate, with his family. He has daughters who study. He is always drunk, and has been in jail. He came to this house one time and tried to cure an old woman who was living here. Everyone ran away when he came, except one woman who was very drunk, and a small child. The shaman cut the sick woman who had called for him. He cut her on the side of the neck, and blood ran down to her stomach. He stood at the door so no one could see just what he did. He raised his hands and motioned to the sky, to call his special evil spirits. You can tell he is a shaman by his evil eyes. Everyone knows he is a shaman. He takes an ax and shakes, when the spirits come to him, as he crouches on the ground.

There is much that is unconventional in this account. Shamans are not known for extreme bloodletting or for covert séances. Like the shaman, the helping spirits are referred to here as "evil," whereas once only a few in uncontrolled contexts were considered frightening. A medium of divination (the ax) has become a weapon, while other crucial symbols of shamanic power (the drum, zither, iron ornaments, special clothing) are missing. The story of this disreputable shaman continues:

> This same man, earlier, lived in this very house. He tortured us. He was always drunk, broke furniture. He speaks in shaman's tongues, and knows all the old shaman songs. He sometimes did not let us into our own home. He stood straight at the door, and stared, and said: "The spirits are helping me." The police chase him. He lived in Beriosovo, and his father was a big and very famous shaman. He is a swine shaman. He was kicked out of the Beriosovo collective and so he came here. His wife's brothers lived here ....He lived there but after a month and a half, they kicked him and his family out of their house. He cursed them, and I heard it: "From now on in this house,

you will not live well, may there be blood on your floors." And after this, the brother of the wife shot himself and died... Then he moved in here... and finally the police chased him from here.... He aided so many deaths.... Probably one of his daughters too will become a shaman. How can people say there aren't shamans? Of course there are.

It is hard to measure how common such stories of shaman misbehavior and Khanty condemnation were, since in the 1970s a few shamans were still revered and protected from prying ethnographers. This Tegy shaman was disillusioned to the point of despair at the ridicule of his knowledge, but some shamans in the Arctic town of Salekhard had reputedly not lost their confidence. In general, the Soviet-spurred cycle of hiding and distrust broke many of the mutually reinforcing bonds previously maintained by followers and shamans. Private séances were not necessarily effective, because an important aspect of curing involved the communal support given to supplicants and shamans.[20]

The decline of shamanism among Northern Khanty began in the 1930s, with collectivization and agitation against shamans as "deceivers" (Sergeeva, Ankudinov, and Dobriev 1939). Soviet officials destroyed sacred "idols," often of ancestral shamans, and took away drums and other equipment of shamans in raids. They used each illegal offense of shamans, for example, drunkenness, or "kulak" offenses of wealth and hoarding, as a reason to put them in jail. More positively, the government also initiated "red tents," with which doctors, nurses, and medical assistants traveled, giving modern medical aid.

Judging by Startsev's accounts (1928: 88-97), shamanism was alive and popular with both Khanty and Siberian Russians in the 1920s. Senkevich, ten years later, had a much harder time trying to record shamanic songs: "The clever shamans not only don't want to sing them, but also in general hide their profession" (1935: 158). In the 1930s, under the leadership of the shaman Yarkin of Narikarsky, a huge sacrifice of horses was organized, in an effort to prevent collectivization (Kartsov 1937: 120). Such activism was especially great on the Kazym and Sosva Rivers, where some shamans advocated destruction of Soviet encampments as well as boycotts of schools, as seen in the previous chapter.

By the 1970s, local log-cabin hospitals were available in villages as small as Kazym. Hospitals were relatively accessible—even to nomadic breeders of reindeer—by helicopter and Ob River hydrofoil. Focus for curing was and is on hygiene, drugs, and surgery.[21] Although modern medicine was introduced, psychological roots of illness were rarely explored. The shared worldview on which shamanic legends and cosmology were based was nearly discredited, or turned into an ethos of suspicion that made "nocebo reactions" as likely as "placebo effects" (compare Kennedy 1961). Communist ideology precluded most psychological explanations of illness, whether Freudian or Native, and thus many indigenous people were left in a dangerously incomplete limbo. In the context of modern diseases, Khanty and Siberian Russian villagers came to realize that European-style medicine often is more effective than shamanic séances. Yet modern medicine was not always chosen by the Khanty, and in the post-Soviet period some of the village hospital facilities were curtailed for financial reasons throughout the North.

Hierarchies of Resort

The first point to stress about Khanty responses to European-style modern medicine is that choices of cures are open to experimentation. If a local healer is more accessible than a hospital-based doctor, the healer might be tried before the patient bothers to apply to a clinic or hospital. If a modern medical cure has failed, a Northern Khanty family may send for a nonlocal Salekhard shaman with a wide reputation. In 1976, I learned of a blind woman who, having been treated unsuccessfully by both Russian and Khanty practitioners, was putting her final faith in a new laboratory-derived medicine that she had heard cured reindeer of eye problems. Today, recourse to shamans continues to be difficult, given how few are actively curing and given renewed Christian propaganda against them. A progression of medical alternatives for a range of sufferers could theoretically be mapped, leading to a systematic study of shifting "hierarchies of resort" (Romanucci-Ross 1977: 481–87).[22]

A second factor, concerning contrasts in the curing milieu, partially explains Khanty difficulties in adjusting to European medicine. In hospitals, the family is confined to formal visits, and patients are likely to feel isolated. They feel an unaccustomed discomfort in the clean white rows of beds and the unfamiliar faces of other patients and staff. A modern cure entails the reverse of concerned group solidarity, engulfing the patient in goodwill in an otherworldly, darkened, and impassioned atmosphere. It involves the crisp professional relationship of the patient with a usually Russian doctor and a few medical assistants of diverse ethnic backgrounds.

In 1976, I met a young woman in Kazym who was awkwardly waiting out an illness of her mother in the hospital, while her reindeer-breeding father stayed behind in their reindeer-skin tent. She told me she longed for the tundra and for her family, and that her mother also wished to go home. They disliked the "noise of civilization" that they found in Kazym, although Kazym is a large village, not a city. They, like most Khanty, had some confidence in the ability of modern doctors, but they resented the family's situation. It was hard for them to understand why a cure for the body had to be divorced from cures for the souls of the mother and her family. It was likely that, when they returned to the tundra, a shaman would be asked to make sure that not only the symptoms but also the cause of the illness had been treated.

Third, it took a long time for any level of confidence in European medicine to develop. When Soviet doctors first came to the north, they were resented as part of the collectivization effort. They were confusing foreign figures, curing without communal ritual. They were also actively opposed by Khanty shamans, who believed sincerely in their own abilities. In the early Soviet period, shamanic self-assurance was still nurtured with community approval, in a complex feedback system (Boas 1930: 20–41; Levi-Strauss 1963: 186–205). Any defect of Russian doctors became a victory for shamans. Polarization then prevented shamans, often especially intelligent and creative individuals, from becoming "culture brokers"(mediators) in the new political and medical atmosphere (Landy 1977: 468–81).

Modern European (Western) medicine also requires some faith to be effective, particularly if cures entail the regular taking of carefully prescribed drugs. The transfer of faith can involve an intense conversion with a successful cure, or more commonly a slow process of trial, suspicion, pain, and reward (Frank 1961: 76, 81, 98; Csordas 2002: 5). Failures of "foreign" medicine when Russians were trying to win over the populace could not have helped the Soviet cause. Just as "red-tent" programs were beginning to be accepted, World War II, with its terrible losses of Siberian Natives, occurred. "Why couldn't Russian medicine have saved more Khanty soldiers?" Khanty asked.

The issue of change in medical faith leads to a hypothesis concerning how some Khanty may think about medical problems. Ward Goodenough (1963: 152) long ago noted that Pacific islanders coping with acculturation cognitively divided illness into white man's and indigenous categories. When they had a white man's illness, it could be treated with white man's medicine. Otherwise, indigenous cures would suffice. Khanty, by the mid-Soviet period, similarly differentiated choices about cures, but not all illness was so easily pigeonholed into "Russian" and Khanty categories. Thus in practice, Khanty came to combine European and Native cures. Illnesses likely to be treated with Native medicine continued to be menstrual, birth, and sexual difficulties, as well as depression, lethargy, dizziness, blindness, soreness, and arthritis.

Today, when many Khanty combine respect for modern surgery with belief in lost souls, they are demonstrating an underlying awareness that illness involves the whole self—body-mind and social context. In the twenty-first century, this underlying awareness is itself widely acknowledged by modern international, internet-using doctors, usually using different vocabularies to express the acclaimed return to holistic, integrated medicine.

It is too simple and dangerously romantic, to claim that either Westerners or indigenous Siberians have returned full circle to ancient medical wisdom. Shamans' versions of theory and their accompanying symbolic actions are relatively impossible to prove valid in a scientific "falsifiable" context. But shamans with "healing gifts" and extensive traditional apprenticeships may have reached important realms rarely glimpsed by modern medical practitioners of any ethnicity. For some Khanty, these realms are based upon specific sacred correlations, such as birds and hair with souls; bears, horses, and reindeer with spirit messengers; and iron with strength and longevity. These Khanty symbols are at once multifaceted and pervasive, rendering them flexible and long lasting, with potential to take on new meanings (compare V. Turner 1977: 77). Representations of the sacred that seemed to have lost value for the Khanty during the Soviet period, such as reincarnation souls (*lil*) and clan-related forest spirits (*menk* and *mis*) took on renewed and relatively more public meaning when the Soviet Union collapsed.

This chapter began with a 1991 quote from a Khanty friend who has become a post-Soviet leader, whose ancestors were shamans. It relates to her own dramatic rekindling of shamanic abilities after she had been diagnosed with a tumor. Her experience and jolting honesty raises important questions concerning the level of self-healing, body-mind interaction that shamans could trigger, in themselves and others, as well as the role of dreams and ancestors in the curing process:

> I cured myself, to the point where I was supposed to have an operation but then did not have to have it. Doctors thought I had a tumor and then could not find it. A month before, I had gone into the same deep, multileveled worlds, dreaming as I had as a child. And I think

that when I was in that state, I cured myself. In modern terms, maybe I used bioenergy on myself. I do not know. In Khanty terms, I turned into a god. Or rather, I used a spirit helper to help me find my way. [*Shyly and hesitantly*] I dreamed that I ran in the image of a bear.

It is difficult to determine the degree to which ancient shamanic techniques have meaning and power in new post-Soviet curing contexts. Khanty of younger generations rarely express such faith in shamanic ability to turn into bears, birds, or other spirit manifestations. Memory of marathon legends dealing with the travels and powers of shamanic ancestors often is divorced from curing contexts, so that the connectedness of ancestors, animal spirits, and health expressed by this perceptive Khanty leader is rare. In the Soviet period, I was told a legend about a shamanic ancestor with animal transformation abilities who founded the sacred grove that secretly continued as the site of Kazym Khanty sacrifice rituals. In the post-Soviet period, that same site has become a venue for the bear festival revival and occasional reindeer sacrifices. But Khanty mourn that the potential of their rituals and healing wanes with the death of each shamanic elder.

Like some of the Sakha featured ahead, the Khanty elder Maria Vagatova, granddaughter of a shaman, has channelled her heritage into singing and poetry (2007). She explained in 2010: "I only do the rituals that are given to me to do. I don't do healing like my grandfather. But sometimes I feel strongly that I must sing prayers and write poetry. It is a strength that seems to come from the earth, from the very ground, from Nature and its energy."

In sum, Khanty communities have increasingly turned to modern medicine and continually lost their miracle-producing "big man" shamans. The communal atmosphere required for effective symbol-manipulating, spirit calling, spirituality stimulating shamanic séances has been undermined by Soviet persecution of shamans, the advances of modern medicine, and renewed Christian (Russian Orthodox and other) missionary activity. Faith in shamanic power has sometimes curdled into fear, making failure of traditional medicine as self-fulfilling a prophecy as success once was. As in many parts of the world where indigenous communities struggle with contradictory "globalizing" trends, changing and competing worldviews have brought awkward cognitive dissonance, some syncretic creativity, and increased choice.[23] A combination of factors governs Khanty choices about cures, including issues of convenience, finance, family attention, shamanic reputation, Christian conversions, and definitions of illness as Western or Native. Khanty consider shamans to be both doctors and deceivers.

Photo 4 Line dance and chant "okhuokhai," Suntar 1986 *yhyakh* summer solstice ceremony. Photo by Marjorie Mandelstam Balzer, 1986.

Chapter 4

Poetics of Sacred Language Through Time and Space

> "At the place where she [the Éven shaman] had been, blood flowed for three days into the river..."
>
> Philip Tretiakov, Sakha elder
> (Khatingaakh village, 1994), legend

> "After the melting of snow/ When life arrives through dripping rivulets/ We greet the beginning of summer with joy/ When living berries uncover themselves/ When the cuckoo confirms summer with song/ From the original hearth of our people built..."
>
> Evdokiia Semenova Likhanova, Sakha curer
> (Nemegiuntse village, 1993) sung prayer

In 1991, I made a personal and professional pilgrimage to the young yet already famed Sakha shaman Fedot Ivanov in the Viliuisk region of the newly sovereign Sakha Republic. He had mixed feelings about seeing a foreign anthropologist, but agreed through mutual friends to meet at his parent's cottage in a small, remote village. After hours of talk, during which we discussed many aspects of my pilgrimage, including a medical problem, I confessed that I was also interested in the aesthetic power of shamanic chants as poetry. Expecting him to dismiss this as absurdly isolated from the core of his curing purposes, I was delighted by his broad grin. Ironically, it was this, rather than my medical problem, that convinced him to bring out his drum. He agreed to sing parts of an introductory séance song, although not to call his helper spirits in a true séance at this stage of our relationship.[1]

The young shaman, removed from specific intellectual trends of the urban Sakha intelligentsia, was nonetheless also caught up in the cultural and political revival of the Sakha people. Some Sakha then and now believe that this healer's powers are so extraordinary that speaking his name calls his attention to them, wherever they are. He was both pleased and wary that some urban Sakha have rediscovered the beauty and power of shamanic practice, and that texts of memorized yet sometimes improvisational chanting could be appreciated and touted as aesthetically worthy. His own view of the séance as a performance on many levels, for many listeners (spirit and human, Sakha and non-Sakha), meant that he is fully aware of the dramatic and poetic value of his art. With neither cloak nor fire, he sat in a straight-backed chair and produced a low, moaning, repetitive, and intense song describing himself, an *oiuun*, as having two loyal helper spirits, a dog and a raven.

Sakha consultants readily recognize multiple genres of sacred poetry: legends and epics (*olonkho*), especially those with shamanic heroes; shamanic séances (*kyryylara*) as multilogues with spirits for diverse purposes; summer ceremony prayer-blessings (*yhyakh algys*); participatory recitatives (*uokhar*) during the sacred dance called *okhuokhai*; blacksmith chants (*timiri uuha*); and household prayers (*algys*). They are conceptualized more on the basis of their spiritual functions than their content, which has much symbolic and tropic overlap. Despite distinctions among genres, the Sakha who discuss such matters believe only spirit permission and guidance enables singers of these genres to flourish. Indeed, interlopers or headstrong youth are thought to incur spiritual danger from abusing the tradition. Guidance can and should come from spirits and ancestors, as well as from elders known for specific talents passed from generation to generation.

The power of sacred language is illustrated by a Sakha saying that "words have spirit," *ichchi*. Such power is manifest in many creative directions, through curses as well as blessings, as seen in the previous chapter. Language is at once a celebrated marker of cultural identity and an ironic mocker of cultural difference, as well illustrated in regions such as Northeastern Siberia, where diverse indigenous groups have lived together and competed with each other for centuries. The multiple powers of Siberian shamans extend across space, time, and language barriers. Shamans mediate not only cosmological worlds, they also bridge interethnic relations.

Using excerpts from legends, epics, séances, chants, and prayer-songs culled from the literature, archives, and from my fieldwork in the Sakha Republic, this chapter attempts the impossible: to convey the aesthetics and power of ritual language through mere text.[2] Along the way, I build a case for the impure and complex legacies of Tungusic, Turkic, and Mongolic cultural traditions. Issues of spirit-uality also are explored, through the ways Siberians discuss in-spir-ation with charm and humor. As shamans have long known, speaking in tongues and with spiritual guidance is an ancient art.

Darkness and Light, Competition and Power In Legends

Debates concerning the interethnic relations of Tungusic (Éven, Évenk) and Sakha (Yakut) ancestors often revolve around the degree of assimilation of Tungusic peoples and the extent of their early interethnic warfare, described in poetic yet quite violent epics and legends. Initial Tungus-Sakha contacts included the spirit-fighting competition of shamans, women and men, acting on behalf of their peoples. However, strong influences flowed in multiple directions. In the previous three centuries, Sakha acknowledged that Tungusic shamans were stronger, more attuned to spiritual connections and healing powers. Particularly interesting and understudied is the phenomenon of language transfers during shamanic séances, when, for example, Sakha shamans chanted and sang in Tungusic languages.

The great Konstantin *oiuun* (Konstantin Ivanovich Chirkov) of Abyi region provides a Soviet period example of the use by a Sakha shaman of Éven (Lamut) spirit power. Occasionally during séances, he confounded participants by breaking into the Éven language, although he did not know this language well, according to his daughters Aleksandra Chirkova and Matriona Chirkova. They thought one of his spirit helpers had come from a deceased Éven shaman. His cloak (now sometimes worn by his daughter Aleksandra) has elements of Yukaghir and Éven symbolism, and his own background included some Yukaghir. Until he died in 1974, his reputation was strong enough to have semisecretly drawn patients from all ethnic groups of the region (including Russians) in his far-flung, broadly defined mixed ethnic community.[3]

Sakha today often repeat the historical wisdom that Évenk and Éven shamans are stronger in both curing and cursing than their Sakha counterparts. Certainly this was reinforced by the positive reputation of the late, revered female shaman, Matriona Petrovna Kurbel'tinova, who secretly helped supplicants regardless of their ethnic identity. It is also manifest in the way people of diverse backgrounds currently revere the Éven shaman Sobei.[4] Ideas concerning the spiritual power of Tungusic shamans may date as far back as the period of first contacts among the ancestors of the Turkic Sakha and indigenous Tungusic peoples, and were enhanced by the classic works on Siberian shamanism of Sergei Shirokogoroff (1935) and Arkhady F. Anisimov

(1958; 1963). As with shamanic encounters in the Americas (Taussig 1987), newcomers in Siberia were frightened of the spiritual prowess of the local shamans they met. Shamans were perceived to know more deeply their local, natural, and spiritual landscape. They were at once "wiser" and "more primitive" in a particularly threatening way.

In 1994, the Sakha elder Philip Tretiakov of Khatingaakh village told me a long legend concerning the early contact period in today's Srednaia Kolyma *ulus*. The legend, "Yréuguchchéléékh Yeulék" [Triumph of Yeulék], detailed warfare between Urangkhai Sakha and Tungusic peoples in pre-Russian or early Russian times. An alternative name is "Køruu orochuottaakh" [Seeing ahead to success]. It related the competition of two shamans, a Sakha *oiuun* and an Éven (Lamut) *udagan*, who used their extraordinary powers to defend their communities from death and destruction. The Éven female shaman eventually was captured, tortured, and completely defeated. Her group had to retreat, with their river running bloody, giving way to Sakha in the area. The Sakha incursion was allegedly sparked after an earlier retreat of a Sakha man, Yeulék, who had lost two friends to Éven warriors years earlier. He had returned to central regions of the Lena River until he was able to come back with greater numbers to wreak revenge. P. Tretiakov's rhythmically paced tale concluded:

> The Éven *udagan* had said that the Sakha would have arrows from the bones of deer, and that they would have smoke coming out of them. And so they did. Each time an arrow was shot, an Éven would die, she predicted. And so they did. The people of Oro [Khoro?] left in spring, especially to attack, though some of the Éven ran away to Birigei. During the struggle, many were hurt, some on both sides. But on the side of Yeulék, only three were killed. And the *udagan* was captured alive. They tied her to a post, on which they had earlier tied a dog. They put a sharpened pole through her. At the place where she had been, blood flowed for three days, into the river. The place was called Omok Sena, river of a foreign people. The place was also called Krivoi [Crooked] in Russian, or Kéltégei in Sakha. They tried to bury the *udagan*, but each time her skull came back up through the earth. The Sakha became masters of this place. Thus ends the arrival of the Sakha to this place, more than 300 years ago. My father told me this.

This legend makes many uncomfortable today for its highlighting of interethnic conflict and the bloodiness of war and torture. Yet it also reveals the significance of how shamans, including *udagan* were used as clairvoyants in war, and as proxies for their people's competition. The Éven were defeated as much through the capture of their *udagan* as through the battle with fire arrows. In the tale, the Sakha shaman's group clearly triumphs, at least temporarily. Variations on this legend probably have been passed through Éven communities, perhaps emphasizing the refusal of her skull to be buried, living on. To confirm his version, P. Tretiakov mentioned "when we tried to create an ice preserve pit for food, we found the remains of axes where the battle had been."

In the Kolyma region, some shamans maintained competitions well into the twentieth century, both in their actual deeds and the resonating tales that built their reputations. The Sakha shaman Parilop, usually known for such benevolent acts as putting out forest fires and curing people, was said to have taken such offense at an insult of a local Évenk shaman that he took the form of a wolf and devoured much of the Évenk's reindeer herd.[5] Legends of interethnic competition between shamans spread well beyond Kolyma. In the Abyi region, the village Suturukhaakh on the riverbank opposite the current town of Belaia Gora was founded when a Sakha shaman vanquished an Éven "mother-beast."[6] In Viliuisk, one Sakha shaman, taking the form of a wolf and the other Tungus, taking the form of a bear, defeated a third shaman Biutee-Ilii, just after he had warned his wife of impending doom.[7] Their mastery has become an (en)chanting example of poetic justice transcending ethnic competition.

The Évenki writer Galina Varlaamova Keptuké's touching memoir (1989: 54) gives insights into Évenki values that help children cope with unfairness after competitions (worldly and shamanic, inter- and intraethnic) have been lost.[8] Her father explained, after the unjust arrest by Russians of the Évenki shaman Cherikté, who had saved her leg: "We must be patient with all in this poor struggling land of ours, for every person is from the land, her children. And remember, daughter that all the bad people are the ones who live longest. They have long lives because they drink the blood of good people, they extend their lives with that of others."[9]

A dark side of shamanic power runs through Tungusic and Sakha legends, and is partially responsible for the somewhat artificial yet popularly proclaimed division of shamans into "black" (evil spirit calling) and "white" (prayer blessing giving) categories.[10] In practice the same shamans could use their extensive, multitasking powers for good and bad deeds. However, many accounts, particularly those from nineteenth and early-twentieth century Christians, tended to emphasize their abilities to curse using elaborate, deadly language. The Tungus shaman Semen Popov Kékén, who died in 1860, was held in awe by both Tungus and Sakha as an "iuer," a kind of avenging ghost, well after his death. People said that "from his grave they heard the sound of a drum and the rattle of his [metal ornamented] clothing" (Khudiakov 1969: 412).

Two other shamans were Sakha sisters, Chuonakh and Manchikai, who had been captured as brides by Tungus near the river Yana in the late eighteenth century (Khudiakov 1969: 407–9). "Two of the best Tungus" became their husbands, having killed their parents to get them. When their adopted Tungus nomadic community had trouble due to people and animals "going crazy," the elder sister Chuonakh was asked to shamanize [*jajaəld'ən*].[11] She sang to her deceased father:

> Father mine, Kiktei-shaman! When you were on this earth,
> you were renowned far and wide, and you had quite a memory.
> Those Tungus spilled your dark blood, cut your thick skin.
> Turn their place so, that it would seem no one has been
> here, that grass will grow on the place they live.
> Lower their high reputation, shame their white faces;
> Wipe them from the face of the earth! [*Imnéritténsalghaa!*]
> Treat them just as they treated you!

After this séance-curse, everyone in the Tungus community of seven yurts reputedly died. The girls returned to their homeland to live. Chuonakh later was baptized as Agrafena, and lived in Yakutsk. Manchikai became Nastasiia. But both maintained reputations as shamans, including after death, with local Sakha and Tungus. Out of fear, no girl of either group wanted to be baptized with the names Agrafena or Nastasiia.

Shamans and Singers of *Olonkho* (Epics)

While debates exist about the timing and origins of *olonkho* (Gogolev 1986, 1992, 1993a, b; Nikolaev [Somogotto] 1992), it is likely that these great epics were created in part as narratives about the formation of the Urankhai Sakha people *in relation to* other peoples, Turkic, Mongolic, and Tungusic. Relations were both warlike (F.F. Vasil'ev 1995) and cooperative. A delightful passage towards the end of the *olonkho* Kyys Debeliie describes a multiethnic *yhyakh*, the annual summer solstice ceremony (Burnashev et al. 1993: 276–7, lines 4738–59):

> In three big circles guests gathered,
> for the celebration of the Yakut [Sakha] *omuk* [people],

to honor the upper benevolent *aiyy* spirits,
to the table came the Khoro *omuk*,
the Chukotsk people were treated,
the Russian people were feasted, as at a wedding,
to honor the upper gods,
to pacify the lower spirits,
an unending feasting-festivity,
a deep whirl [of activity] was created,
people's heads were spinning here,
the best heads [brains] were collected here,
everyone gathered together, on each other's heels,
people came as fast as their legs carried them,
in seven places the calls of song rang out,
in eight places the celebratory blessings were heard,
in nine places the sounds of *olonkho* tellers were heard,
here the fat became fatter,
the hungry ate their fill,
the sickly became well,
the thin took on fat...

At this wonderful festivity, the identities of Chukotka ancestors and Russians, who may have been added in later versions of the epic, are clearly marked. But the identity of the "omuk [people] khoro" is less clear, and may be linked to the Mongolic ancestry of both Tungusic and Sakha groups.[12]

In the *olonkho* Kuruubai khaannaakh Kulun Kullustuur [Obstinate Bloody Kulun Kullustuur] another passage clearly links Sakha and Tungus, their shamans, and the issue of interethnic marriage or wife capture (Mirbatalaeva with the singer Timofeev-Teploukhov 1985: 249 [Sakha], 509 [Russian], lines 9760-79):

Your older brother sent me to you
He said "A Tungus shaman
by the name of Ard'amaan-D'ard'amaan
took from your uncle Toion Niurgun his wife;
In deep suffering,
with great vexation he is coming.
See if you cannot find the shaman,
Follow him,
Correct the wrong done to your uncle!
You meanwhile sit here [reassured the hero],
Do not leave your place,
And I will set out,
I will try to follow and defend
I will ask the gods to help your captured wife.

> I do not know, where I will find [them]
> With what kind of [spiritual] help
> I will be able to out-maneuver, to overcome, the clever Tungus shaman
> And extract your elder aunt!
> Farewell for a long while!
> Urui, aikhal!" [Salutations!]

Here, the hero is chasing after a Tungus shaman, to outsmart him and get his stolen aunt back. Because this is *olonkho* told from a Sakha point of view, a plan to recapture her is successful. It involves tricking the somewhat "naïve" Tungus hunter-wife-stealer by having her nearly seduce the disrobed Tungus, and turning her into a golden ring. The passage shows the degree of intimate interrelations between Sakha and Tungusic ancestors, and the whole *olonkho* reveals mutual influence.[13] Dialogues elsewhere in the epic confirm the Tungus were indigenous, and the Sakha ancestors were newcomers to the whole Lena River region.

The Kulun Kullustuur epic is replete with Sakha sacred symbols, the color blue, the numbers nine and seven, the crane. The hero is described as having come from a warm ancient Sakha homeland, bounded by an unfrozen sea, possibly today's Lake Baikal:

> This person grew up and became rooted
> In a bright-blue country,
> So great that it could not be encircled in flight
> By nine waves of white-headed cranes
> Even in nine full years...

Within such epics, once sung in marathon sessions that could last each night for over a week, are parts for many voices, including hero and heroine shamans. An example of a beautiful and less well-known *olonkho* that includes a female shaman (*udagan*) is Mas Batyia Bogatyr, a story of an orphan stranger who becomes a Sakha. He is blessed toward the typically happy end of his tale by the *udagan*, who reveals hopes for the whole Sakha people:

> Never let in the course of three centuries
> The spirit of death appear
> Protect yourself with the water of immortality
> Let two Sakha become many
> Let three Sakha be praised
> Let five Sakha become famous
> Let from century to century

The Fate of the people be bright
Let his heroic deeds in life never die
Let in this Middle world
All good things and riches come to him. Aikhal![14]

Proud Sakha folklorists compare the *olonkho* to the Iliad, the Odyssey, the Manas, and the Mahabharata. This delightfully patriotic claim is confirmed by the best-known examples of the genre, the published and annotated epics Niurgun Bootur (Oiyunsky 1975) and Kulun Kullustur (Mirbatalaeva with the singer Timofeev-Teploukhov 1985). At an international folklore conference hosted in Yakutsk in 1994, one of the last of the great *olonkho* singers, Maria Tomskaia, performed a version of a little known epic she had learned in childhood. She explained that her whole being had absorbed the chanted phrases, as she lay in a semi-awake trance-like state in her bed, listening to a traveling *olonkho-hut* regale her family by the hearth in their small home. When she enjoyed a tale, she explained, by morning she could perform all the parts, to the amazement of her parents, who recognized and feared her powers as shamanic.

Although *olonkho* is an ancient and waning art, chanted today in excerpted forms in ceremonial contexts, in school programs focused on memorization, or at conferences analyzing the tradition, an intimation of how it could be revived came to me through conversations in 1994 and 1995 with the late Asen Zverev, a well-known TV journalist, related to the famed shamanic performer and singer Sergei Zverev. Asen explained that he did not begin to reveal his poetic talent until after age 50, for fear that ancestral spirits would disapprove. He then became popular at summer solstice festivals, where many commented how well he was carrying on the poetic dance chant heritage of his esteemed ancestors. Winning prizes and gathering acclaim paled for Asen in comparison with a compelling spirit muse that was pointing him to compose a whole new epic, in the genre of the huge *olonkho* that were once part of traveling master-singers' repertoires. He confessed that multipersonage stories telling of shaman travails in the Soviet period were buzzing in his head, but sadly, he died suddenly before this great talent was able to be revealed. By 2010, some of his ideas were taken up by none other than the Minister of Culture himself, featured later in this book.

The Séance as an Art Form in Sociopolitical Context

In Spring 1991, a sensation was caused amongst the Sakha intelligentsia when a newspaper interview appeared, entitled "She comes in the Form of a White Horse." The interview was with the renowned Sakha female shaman (*udagan*), Zoia Duranova, whose helper spirit, the white horse, is one of the most powerful multivocal symbols of Sakha rituals. Zoia explained that she becomes one with her helper spirit during curing séances, and when she senses friends are in need. She also related how she had found her husband when she arrived in a particular town for a public séance (sometimes broadcast on local Sakha language TV). She had been invited to a banquet in her honor. Near her was an empty seat, and she decided to see if she could sense who was missing. She sent one of her souls to a nearby house, where she saw a man lying drunk on a couch. When she came to herself at the table, she apologized for having seemed out of the conversation and requested that someone go awaken the man two houses down and bring him to the banquet. He became her husband, as she knew he would. In 1992, she showed me that he had the proper mark on his forehead, just under the hairline, that confirmed he was her destined husband.

People who read or heard this story were divided as to its validity. Many believed Zoia can turn herself into a horse, and a few told further stories about the harm she reputedly had done to a Russian doctor who doubted her power. Some, including one who came from her home village, scoffed and said she has always been crazy, even as a little girl. But no one could deny the sensation she caused with her public séances, during which people were supposed to feel better after auditorium-sized bouts of communal solidarity with her, and with her spirits. Some attending these all-purpose, unconventional séances claimed they were indeed healed of various illnesses. After many years of practice, and then a lapse into alcoholism herself, she was back with a small healing booth at the "Us-Khatyn" (Three Birches) Republic summer solstice festival in 2007, itself a violation of Sakha customs that kept healers from working at the festival.

As stressed earlier, spirit-guided journeys to upper or lower worlds must be used for specific, usually benevolent, purposes. Only the most powerful of the Sakha shamans are able to reach the highest, ninth heaven, common in the cosmologies of Siberian Turkic peoples. To reach these heavens, the shaman goes into "a kind of religious ballet...a combination of dance, song, and extempore poetry, together with a considerable amount of mimesis" (Chadwick 1942: 16–17). Such a disciplined frenzy of motion and words is possible only through an enormous amount of control, energy, and training. As with all art forms, a degree of impromptu, inspired loss of full (ordinary) consciousness is also quite common.

A true (not simulated) trance, with spirits perceived by the shaman and the séance audience to either be inside the shaman or escorting the shaman, may result in a lack of conscious manipulation by the shaman. Shamans exhibit degrees of control and letting go, just as they have degrees of skill by which participants judge a séance. Chanting may be both a way into ecstasy and a manifestation of it. The poetry and speaking in tongues that emanate from a shaman at the height of a séance are not premeditated, although they are usually based on a shamanic repertoire of learned songs. As Dulam (2010: 38–39) has explained for Mongolian shamanic rituals, different "degrees of ritualization" are expected (including for the same shaman in different contexts) as well as different degrees of intension in ritual language.

The chanting can be so overwhelming for shamans that they are transported into a state from which it is difficult to return. For instance, one twentieth century northern Sakha shaman sang in the Éven (Lamut) language and then could not remember his native Sakha when he returned to consciousness. He was so disoriented he fell into a pile of sawdust. And he only gradually reacquired the Sakha language, like a child.[15]

Another dramatic Tungus-Sakha encounter occurred with the nineteenth century Sakha shaman Tius'piut. He told Polish exile ethnographer V. L. Seroshevsky [W. Sierozhewskii] ([1896] 1993: 605) that he had gained a main protector spirit (*ämägkät,* also *émégét*) unexpectedly: "when I was traveling in the North, in the mountains, I stopped at a wood pile for dinner. I used some of its wood for the fire. It turned out a famous Tungus shaman had been buried there; that is how his spirit came to me." Tius'piut's *ämägkät* spirit was easily distinguishable during séances when Tius'piut "muttered Tungus words and [enacted Tungus] gestures." Other, lesser beings who visited his séances included a capricious, vodka-demanding "nuchche tangaralakh"—a Russian spirit. The spirits themselves did not seem to put much effort into ethnic boundary maintenance or language barriers.

Different levels of skill, of ability to create heart-stopping shamanic performance, have been noticed by almost all researchers of shamans. Seroshevsky (1901: 105) explained:

> Observation justifies the division of shamans into great, middling, and petty. Some of them dispose of light and darkness in such a masterly fashion, also of silence and incantation; the modulation of the voice is so flexible; the gestures so peculiar and expressive; the blows of the drum and the tone of them correspond so well to the moment: and all

is intertwined with such an original series of unexpected words, witty observations, artistic, and often elegant metaphors, that involuntarily you give yourself up to the charm of watching this wild and free evocation of a wild and free spirit.

Seroshevsky's description is quintessential romanticism. Yet he captures a tone of abandon that not only shamans, but their audiences have shared in the past, and occasionally continue to share. Together they enter an alternate consciousness that makes both more receptive to creativity, more real than the "willing suspension of disbelief" of great theater.

The séance in Sakha is sometimes called *kyryylara*, or travel to the edge. Symbolic meaning is combined with phonics, so that a synergistic spark stimulates the aesthetic imagination of creative initiators and audience-participants alike (compare Friedrich 1991). Nonetheless, not every moment in a séance must have specific decipherable semantic meaning. Some shamans use animal calls, rhythmic vocal sounds, and a kind of jazz-like scat to enhance their performance. This was one of the hallmarks of Sergei Zverev, a Sakha shaman's assistant (*kuturukhsut*) who then became a performer of séances on the stage. The channelling of neighboring, imperfectly known languages, and the speaking in a kind of "tongues" or seeming gibberish, is consistently explained as stimulated by the spirits. The spirit world that shamans are tapping into is one they themselves perceive as having wide-ranging, cross-cultural commonalities, reaching well into North America and India.[16]

Feats of entertainment and wonder occurred in the séances of the renowned Sakha shaman Konstantin, whose use of the Sakha and less familiar Éven (Lamut) languages enhanced their impact. In 1993, one of his séance assistants, Maria Ivanovna Rebrova, then in her eighties but a young (premenstrual) girl when she helped him, regaled me and her close family with descriptions she had kept secret for decades:

> In Arlakh, one woman had a psychological illness. Konstantin was invited. She had been sick for a long time...Again I warmed the drum by the fire, and his clothes, and got everything ready, especially the *dépsé* [white horse skin]. He started to dance. Well this sick woman had on a red dress and was completely bedridden. He was dancing furiously. All of the sudden, the red dress was outside—not on her body but walking outside along by itself, without any person in it. So the *abaahy* [evil spirit possessing the woman] was sent away in the dress. And Konstantin kept dancing.

Maria's family (and I) dissolved into laughter at this story, which was, according to Maria, even funnier at the time. The woman was discretely slipped a new dress by the end of the séance, when she had "completely recovered." Laughter therapy as well as Konstantin's dialogue with the *abaaghy* was undoubtedly part of the benefit of this séance.

Whether they used momentary inspiration, bawdiness, or blatant ventriloquial performance, shamans could not produce a fully effective or satisfying séance unless they also had reputations for spiritual depth. Within their own cosmological-philosophical systems, shamans were and are respected as wise spiritual advisors and keepers of a huge range of sacred knowledge, not just religious ballet masters, crazed prophets, or charlatan actors. In Sakha reasoning, a truly powerful and effective séance performance is the very mark of spirituality. In other words, the medium gives the message of spirituality.

Séance Poetry

A séance from the late nineteenth century observations of Seroshevsky ([1896]1993: 618–20), probably featuring Tius'piut, gradually intensified with drumming "in an entire waterfall of sounds" that ended abruptly with two strong beats. The shaman fell to his knees in "deathlike silence" and then began a low, "darkly toned" song, a spirit-calling chant in a new beat:

> Powerful bull of the land...horse of the steppe!
> I, a powerful bull...call you in!
> I long for you...horse of the steppe!
> I am a person dedicated from above!
> I am a person gifted!
> I am a person created by the One on High to be the Most Powerful of the Powerful!
> Horse of the Steppe, Appear!...Teach Me!
> Magical bull of the land, Appear!...Incant!
> Great One, Instruct!
> Everyone, who is coming together, let them listen with their ears! Let there be no one behind me to whom I must say "Go!"
> As you come forward, do not stand closer than you should! Let everyone see sharply! Let everyone hear quickly! May you protect [us]!
> Look well! Let everyone be well-behaved...all united...
> Let all come, as many as you are!

92 SHAMANS, SPIRITUALITY, AND CULTURAL REVITALIZATION

> You from the left side, ruling with your staff, if you turn aside
> somehow on the wrong road, I beg of you, correct yourself! Collect
> yourself!
> Show us, ruling mother mine any mistakes we have made, show us
> the road!...
> With care, fly to us! Let the way be wide-open!
> In the South, in the nine forested [sky] hills where live the spirits of
> the sun, mother of the sun who is the envy of all, I ask you all...
> Let come to stand, three of your high shades!
> In the East, on your mountain, my ruling father of great strength
> and broad shoulders— Please be with me!
> And you, gray bearded, miraculously honored one (fire),
> I beg of you, please agree to answer and accept all my thoughts, all
> my requests, without exception!
> Listen well! Do everything! Everything, Everything—Let it come to be!

Again the shaman drummed until he reached an apogee of sound. Further prayers and requests were made to specific helper spirits, and the shaman, exhausted, fell. If he fell front forward, it was a good sign, but if on his back, a negative indicator.

Another shamanic chant from a séance opening, illustrating the synergism of phonics, semantics, and polytropy, was collected by the talented Sakha native ethnographer Gavril Ksenofontov in the early 1930s:

> Kunum kunum kötördörö
> Kunum kunum suurérdéré
> Béttékh- béttékh buoluts éré
> Kha, kha, kha... Khaakh-Khakhak
> Khuuk khuuk kush tik
> Chek chekh chekh

My very rough translation, allowing for all that has ever been said or written about the impossibility of translation, and more, is:

> Drive, drive, like a raven rise
> Drive, drive, open the way
> Closer, closer, come, appear
> Kha, kha, kha... Spit, cackle
> Khuuk khuuk Sting, bite
> Chek, chekh, chekh

When this first helper spirit arrives, a lively dialogue ensues between it and the shaman, with the shaman voicing both parts.

Later a significant and typical moment occurs when the *oiuun* enjoins multiple spirits:

> To this middle world homeland of our people
> Bring lasting good fortune
> Spirits purify us.[17]

During another séance from the 1920s, Ksenofontov recorded the calling for an evil female spirit, in order to banish it from a specific patient in great pain:

> Arise now, show yourself
> Even to your slender waist
> Because I with the shaggy head
> The stallion shaman
> Sing and perform the ritual
> Do not dare to pluck away and carry in
> From the hallowed earth
> A piece the size
> Of a goodly island
> Relax, then, the burning bout of pain
> Turn away your jagged fangs.

In this, a key metaphor involved human flesh, by definition precious, being likened to sacred earth from which not one bite may be taken. There was also a sexual tension here between the stallion shaman and the female spirit. The séance builds intensity, enabling ecstasy and inspiration, until the shaggy stallion shaman dance-rides and thus unifies himself with his sacred drum-horse.[18]

Broader purposes, combined with symbolism of the familiar horse and an ancestral spirit snake, characterized another historical chant attributed to a séance performed by the great Spiridon of the Viliuisk region:

> Breathe into and strengthen the land
> Make its expanses inhabitable
> Multi-colored circular snake
> Do not crush the wide retinue of your ancestors
> With cries bring me forth
> Open the doors of the homeland for this horse rider
> Mother of our homeland fling wide our entrance

Place the homes of our homeland in safety
Protect our home hearths...[19]

In Spiridon's poem, the shaman seemed reborn with birth cries during the séance, out of the womb of the mother of the Sakha homeland. The focus on the hearth was significant, for many Sakha prayers are addressed to the fire spirit, and the fire spirit is the intermediary through whom other prayers are sent. In the 1930s, Spiridon's secret shamanic practice was never given away by his community, and he himself became a Communist Party official. Indeed both roles were perceived to be potentially community-protecting, and both were fraught with danger.

Prayers for well-being were and are part of the health-stimulating continuity implicit in the Sakha multi-vocal word *chebdigir*, to become "cultured and healthy." Shamans, however, were often far busier averting or coping with individual or community disaster than supplicating spirits as a prophylactic measure. The dire circumstances of World War II especially brought out this crisis orientation, despite earlier Soviet attempts to discredit the shamans. For example, a famous, creative, and goodwilled shaman nicknamed Kuruuppa (from the word "always") held a séance in 1941 to combat a familiar tragedy that plagued many Sakha communities:

> Spirits by pairs from the forest
> Following our family
> Banish the bitterness descended...
> Honored one circling
> Well-being it seems fleeing
> Apportioned fate
> Growing up warm
> Now internal misfortune
> Has crept in
> My human speech beseeches
> Let the people's good fortune return
> The tree there grows and protects
> Show me the road to fight hunger...[20]

In this chant the slippery concept of fate was introduced, in order to be dispelled. The word used here, from the root *tölkölön*, is less definitive than another subtle Sakha term for fate, *d'ylgha*, which can be glossed as destiny. The very soul of a shaman's mission was exposed in this poetic and poignant moment, for the *oiuun* is supposed to be able to thwart, adapt, or counterbalance individual or community fate through proper intercession with the spirits. The costs of interceding can be high in a cosmological world believed to have intertwined and balanced good and evil energies, which, once set in motion, are difficult to stop. Spirit intercessors, usually called *aiyy*, must fight with evil spirits, *abaaghy*, and yet the intercessors themselves are far from predictable. The shaman appealed to forest spirits, who, like humans, came in pairs, and he evoked the growing, nurturing cosmological tree, linking his world with the upper heavens and lower levels of spirit existence. Through the tree, he must find the road, which for him and his audience was literal, to travel to ever-greater spirits in search of food, plenty, and health for his people. This sacred tree, widespread in shamanic symbolism, is very much alive in the twenty-first century, in séance imagery and in a network of groves scattered through Sakha territory. Such groves, dominated by one particularly striking tree that is bedecked with ribbons, coins, and other prayer offerings, are explained further ahead.[21]

In 1993, a special outdoor fire was built in a particularly beautiful field near the Lena River, representing the future hearth of a folk medicine clinic for the village of Nemegiuntse. It was blessed with a shamanic chant/prayer by one of the oldest, most revered of living Sakha curers, Evdokiia Semenovna Likhanova. Turning gracefully in multiple directions and tossing fermented mare's milk (*kumiss*) and bits of sacred farmer's cheese (*iéd'égé*) into the fire, she evoked multiple spirits, including the fire spirit (metaphorically called beautiful bright gate), the female sun spirit (called the changing sun master), the major sky spirit master (our aged father), and a three-headed horse spirit that may represent concepts of a first shamanic ancestor as part human and part horse. She then danced and chanted:

> After the melting of snow
> When life arrives through dripping rivulets
> We greet the beginning of summer with joy
> When living berries uncover themselves
> When the cuckoo confirms summer with song
> From the original hearth of our people built
> So that we could sound your name
> We have found our way to you
> To become close neighbors
> To become close soul mates
> We have come to you
> Adorning ourselves with a garland of horse mane
>   Standing and neighing to you in greeting
> Like a standing bull
> That touches and nudges its mate

> We appeal to you...
> We appeal to you
> With the same appeals as in ancient times
> When there had been born only three Sakha...[22]

Evdokiia's purpose, to bless a new clinic where she would be the star, was unconventional. It was the Sakha version of laying a cornerstone, although the funds needed for the clinic were in doubt, as became apparent much later. Evdokiia, who at the time was a healthy 91, was careful to modestly call herself a curer, massage specialist, and prayer singer, but not to use the Sakha word for a female shaman *udagan*. While she danced, she neither drummed nor went into trance. Rather, her *algys* had an underlying similarity to the ceremonial language said for fertility at the beginning of summer pasture season.

Ceremonial Prayers and Dance Chants: Celebrating the Summer Solstice with *Yhyakh*

One of the institutionalized Sakha ways to influence and insure a balance of cosmological, including ecological, forces is the once-a-year fertility festival celebrating the opening season of fermented mare's milk (*kumiss*), summer plenty, youthful strength, mating, networking, and community solidarity—among many other things. This exuberant two-to-four day *yhyakh* festival is opened with chanted shamanic blessing-prayers, *algys*, preferably by a priestly *oiuun* dressed in white, from conical headdress to beaded boots, with a "white," or at least generally benevolent reputation.

A particularly lengthy and lovely opening *yhyakh* prayer was recorded by P. Fedotov in 1920, in the Western Kangalask region. Verse 17 links the ceremony to the first Sakha shamans:

> From the White-Light Creator Blessed
> From the country of blessed and lucky inhabitants
> And of water-filled lakes
> Via the first shaman ancestor
> We joyfully bow in prayer
> Fulfilling the thankful ritual
> Of the Summer Festival.[23]

While the festival declined in most places through the 1930s and in World War II, it had a dramatic comeback just after the war, when returning soldiers were feted at mass revival *yhyakh* ceremonies. The ceremony was kept alive particularly well in the Suntar region. In

1991, the festival was declared a national holiday of the Yakut-Sakha Republic, and this was formalized by the local parliament in 1993. I first participated in this thronging, magical ceremony of light, color, and horses in 1986, when I was privileged to drink my first *kumiss* and dance *okhuokhai* at Suntar. I had to be dragged from the joyous festival near midnight when the sun was still bright. Through years of seeing over 25 festivals in numerous regions, I have found them to have varying degrees of theatricality and spirituality, not necessarily correlated to their size.

At the 1991 Nam regional festival, at midday by a bonfire in a field, Vladimir Kondakov poured *kumiss* from the sacred carved wooden chalice called *choron* (shaped as a woman's breast with horse hoof legs) onto the sacred living earth in the four directions. He beat a special inherited drum while chanting these time-hallowed lines:

> Spirits of our homeland
> Spirits labor for us
> Five-fingered spirits
> Sacred head of the horse
> Unified with this shaman
> Spirits of the homeland
> Riding horseback
> To you spirits I give prayers
> My tongue speaks for us
> Understand my speech
> The Sakha person
> Strains to ask an important favor
> That the spirits bring good fortune to our people
> Assuage and banish evil spirits and enemies
> From our homeland
> Dispel the darkness
> Dispel all knowledge of terror.

In this poem, the archaic word *urangkhai*, is used for "person" in conjunction with "Sakha." Since this word is sometimes substituted for "Sakha" in epic tales, it evokes in Sakha participants feelings of cultural longevity and continuity. Enemies of the Sakha have of course changed over time and are not specified here, but there is a strong sense of an us/them division being cultivated—one that the Sakha notice and the few Russians attending the festival might miss.[24] In the chant, learned from a now-deceased shaman, there is little room for improvisation. However, new meaning is easily read into the old text. Kondakov told me later that something special had happened as he sang, when a light gentle localized rain descended on the field where the ceremony took place, as a mark of the spirits' acceptance of his ritual.

One of the most exuberant moments of the *yhyakh* festival is when, after communal sampling of sacred *kumiss* from several large *choron*, previously passive observers are invited onto the central field of sacred territory to sing and chant with the ritual leaders and performers. In the larger regional festivals like Suntar, Viliuisk, and Nam, hundreds of people spontaneously form huge circles of song and dance. In more intimate family, "clan," or village ceremonies, smaller circles of 10 to 20 smiling people are also compelling. This stems from a palpable sharing and spreading of electrically charged spiritual experience through the intense rhythmic beat of *okhuokhai*, from the roots *os*, and *us*, meaning all-protecting. At *yhyakh* ceremonies, it can last for many marathon hours into the white nights of summer's peak. It has become an integral part of many weddings, and, in the post-Soviet period, is performed by a group of club member enthusiasts weekly, unconventionally through the long winter. Inspiration derives from the spirits during the recitative of *okhuokhai*, as I have been told many times. This is the form of sacred poetry most conducive to improvisation. It also traditionally and currently can incorporate greater numbers of participants than small familial séances.

The dance consists of large circles of gracefully bowing and stepping people, rocking forward and back, moving in the direction of the sun, linked to each other in tight but comfortable hand-to-elbow clasps. Each dancer repeats phrases of chanted poetry called out by male or female leaders, who spell each other. As a phrase is chorused by the crowd, the leader has a chance to think of the next words. This recitative is called *uokhar*, a word also used by Tungusic and Mongolic peoples. Themes can be current, situational, or traditional, often evocations of nature and of cultural heros, including shamans. During the 1991 white nights *yhyakh* of Viliuisk, with children dancing in their own circle within ours, we repeated after a vibrato-voiced female leader:

> A woman has come to the dance...
> A youth has come to the dance...
> An old man has come to the dance...
> How can we learn the future?
> How can we avoid becoming the sacrifice of circumstance?
> A person oneself must learn
> Okhu okhu okhuokhai[25]

My experiences joining in mesmerizing hours of chanting during Sakha circle dances may be relevant to the issue of the creation and reception of meaningful sacred poetry during trance. As I repeated phrases of a dance leader's improvisation, the power of the words poured over me, so that I absorbed the vocabulary more deeply, in a near-sun-stroked condition. The almost addictive feelings of communal solidarity and group-trance-like unity are particularly strong when the leader is clearly in an altered state of consciousness. This comes naturally, and may be hampered by current competitions (complete with official judges) during the republic-wide festival that limit the time a leader can sing.

The revival of this great improvisational art has been one of the most powerful sources of optimism for the survival of Sakha cultural values and language in the post-Soviet period. Some Sakha say they hope for prayers and chants that can somehow rebalance (ecological rebooting?) human-spirit relations through the inspiration of dreams, trance, intuition, and inherited talent, guided by the spirits themselves. An intimation of this strength for me came from Mikhail Mikhailevich Evseev, a ponytailed elder-okhuokhai singer of the Suntar region, whom I first admired in the 1990s and refound in 2007, at an *yhyakh* ceremony bringing the Suntar diaspora of Yakutsk together outside town. He explained:

> Sure singing talent comes from the ancestors...mine were singers, and white shamans. But really, it is from Nature, from the energy of the place I was born. It is natural, you can't teach it. You certainly can't memorize it. Many Tiubés villagers have made it in the republic....It has been going on for generations. A little village and many talents. Including in the old times, warrior strength. I think it comes from the place itself. We think of this as coming from God, our god, Aiyy Aar Toyon, in the ninth sky...Well the energy is also across Suntar, and I think it was also in Turkic peoples. We all feel the power of the Sun. The sun energy radiates its powers differently in different peoples, places.

Fire Power: Blacksmith Ritual and Household Prayers

In Sakha lore, only one human can compete with the prestige of a shaman, and that is a blacksmith. His power comes from knowledge of the same spirit world and cosmology as the shaman's, and he too has a tradition of using poetic songs as a way to reach this spirit world. The Viliuisk blacksmith, Ivan Zakharov, bragged to me in 1991 that he had continued his sacred family smithing traditions into the especially sacred ninth generation, maintaining knowledge of sacred songs sung to the fire spirit. The popular and cheerful Zakharov in his youth was also a shaman's helper. By the 1990s, he reforged himself into a performer, simulating shamanic drumming and prayers for *yhyakh* festivals, museum openings, and other events. He chants his family "forge prayer" with a drum, dancing in full shamanic dress:

> Strong beautiful
> Unbroken hammer
> With Flame complete the task
> Noisy frightening
> Grandfather spirit
> Oh chief ancient one
> Leader tall and great
> Of wondrous fate
> Do not mistake this prayer
> Be fair to this master
> Seven centuries you have come to us
> Preserve me.[26]

This self-protection prayer has taken on greater meaning as I have learned more about Ivan Zakharov's life. In his youth, he became a young Communist (Komsomol) activist, repenting for his first career as a shaman's assistant. He clashed directly with the most honored shaman of his region, Niikon, and allegedly once came to physical blows with him. Locals also say that the two engaged in vicious shamanic spirit helper fighting, leaving them both personally harmed. Each attributed tragic family losses to this warfare via the spirits. In 2003, when I visited him again in Viliuisk, he admitted that he regretted his persecution of Niikon in yet another repentance.

In general, prayers (*algys*) for personal and household protection and blessing are said or sung to the fire spirit (*iot ichchi*) during life passage rituals, at important moments in one's professional life, in crises and when new visitors arrive. Such prayers are usually accompanied by small offerings of *kumiss*, alcohol, or choice bits of food to the fire spirit. A particularly poignant one is a prayer-blessing sung by a bride's father before she left her husband's home, recorded by the Sakha ethnographer A. A. Savvinov in 1938:

> Today, when the white sun has risen,
> I want to sing of your happy life,
> To wish you a great future!
> When you light the fiery hearth,

> raise the coppery horse post,
> create a bright, cozy home, then remember
> the upholding support on your right of nine strong young men
> the upholding support on your left of seven beautiful maidens!
> May you be protected forever
> by the creator of the Sakha people
> Honored White Aiyy Toiun!
> Be for the horse—his goading lash,
> for the person on foot, his guiding hand!
> Always treat the traveler with hospitality,
> warm the frozen,
> comfort the unfortunate!
> Be for the blind, with your eyes, his eyes,
> for the lame, his well-jointed support![27]

This prayer combines elements of spirit appeal with more direct blessing and advice for the daughter-bride. The ritual support of maidens and youths during the wedding ceremony is evoked to remind the bride that her wedding should become a memory of more general family and community support. The Creator, the highest God of all Sakha, is evoked to sustain the bride. But most of all, she is enjoined through bodily tropes to herself sustain others.

Algys live on, for they are the most direct and simple means of communication with spirits. In 1993, after being told I was in the household of a family with long and revered lineage, that of the Zverev family, my hostess, the artist Anya Zvereva, encouraged me to repeat one such prayer, in effect introducing me to the household spirits as a friend. As we gave the hearth fire a few drops of champagne, we said:

> To all household spirits
> We salute you
> Sending warm feelings into your cavernous realm
> Through the sacred hearth spirit to all others around
> First of all give us plenty
> Take away all our greatest fears
> Feed us and let us feed you
> Give us fine tastes with your flickering tongue
> Dear spirits of the house
> Sacred fire spirit
> We treat you so that there shall be no want
> We salute you with cheer
> Be joyful
> Dear spirits of the house.

Do Shamanic Arts Require Shamans?

As the very definition of "shaman" shifts in the post- Soviet period, local emphasis is on shamanic heritage and talent, rather than on full-time "professional" shamans. Form and content, purpose and symbol are intricately mixed in Sakha shamanic poetry, as in many well-developed arts. Sakha poets and consumers of poetry are well aware of this, and revel in the variety of inspirational, improvisational, yet rule-bound genres that have flourished in their past. Some forms are more formulaic than others, with the simple *algys* prayer perhaps the least spiritually demanding but most accessible of the forms, and the shamanic séance the most demanding and least accessible to the Sakha themselves, much less to outsiders. The complex and flexible tradition of sacred poetry composition can be glossed as "shamanic," if considered broadly as a Sakha spirit-calling and coaxing tradition that has much in common with shamanic practices and cosmologies of other Northern Siberian peoples, for example Éven, Évenk, and Yukaghir, as well as other Turkic peoples, for example of the Altai mountain region and Central Asia (compare N. Alekseev 1984, 1997; M.B. Kenin-Lopsan 1987; Basilov 1992; Gogolev 1993a,b).

In contemporary, crisis-sensitive anthropology, the concept of "Culture" as belonging to a single people through time, or through some specific process of "ethnogenesis" has become impossibly muddied, impure, and elusive (Fox 1995; Golovnev 1995; Appadurai 1996; Jackson 2009). People in groups, and individuals, have cultural values, socialized standards of behavior, and politics concerning these, without all adhering to the same things in the same ways, whether now or in the past. This is especially true when hundreds of years of intensive and problematic interethnic mixing has occurred. Ethnographers have for years committed the not-so-minor sin of overgeneralizing about peoples, and their cultures, or describing whole peoples as "winners" and "losers." One way to mitigate past pretension is to look at language processes, including sacred language: interpenetrating, adaptive, and constantly taking on new life with new vocabularies and forms, within both conscious and subconscious cognitive frameworks.

In this chapter, I have tried to reveal the aesthetic and semiotic power behind a small sample of poetic words, in their changing sociopolitical contexts. While historical grounding is crucial, Sakha themselves, involved to various degrees in shamanic concepts and practices, often place high value on continuity of shamanic beliefs and images. I have purposely shuffled time periods within the thematic sections of this chapter. Through attention to both continuity and change, local meaning(s) and text-based approaches can be used to better understand that fascinating locus of shamanic poetry, the séance, as well as other poetic genres, especially the highly public summer festival prayers and the more domestic personal prayers.

Some ancient chants, such as the smithy and festival ones given above, are less improvisational and more specialized than others. Smithy (*timiri ukhanar*) and festival (*yhyakh*) prayers, considered together with multipurpose séances (*oiuunna, udaganna*) and recitative during *okhuokhai* dances, represent four Sakha genres of sacred poetry with relative degrees of improvisation and trance permitted within and among them. Yet this review does not capture the full extent of sung Sakha poetry related to shamanic practice and cosmology. The enormous semisacred epics, *olonkho*, have become a famous symbol of Sakha cultural pride, although they recently are performed only in fragments. When President Yeltsin visited the Sakha Republic in June 1993 as the honored guest at the Tatta regional *yhyakh* festival, he was treated to a small girl reciting parts of *olonkho* poetry with remarkable composure and charm, a pattern of public display that intensified after *olonkho* was made a UNESCO world "intangible heritage of humanity" in 2005. Another less sacred genre is the improvisational song [*toiuk*] in which shamans are sometimes featured.[28] Perhaps most significant of all for the transference through the generations of Sakha cosmology are the modest Sakha prayers [*algys*] quietly maintained in Sakha households with or without shamans throughout the difficult Soviet period.

By the 1990s, new style shamanic poets, including some talented women, had tapped into the shamanic symbolic, lyric (effusive and musical) tradition in a secularized, highly literate way. This relates particularly to a group calling themselves "White Horse." They merge allusions to sky, light, sun, and stars, along with more prosaic images of cities, violins, bloody meat and foreign countries. Direct references to shamans and spirit helpers are also part of their syncretic style, expressed in print and at fashionable poetry readings. A few are so successful that literate practicing shamans themselves admire their published work, acknowledge the shamanic roots, and even joke about their sexual shamanic metaphors.[29] Yet these usually young poets do not pretend to be composing "sacred" or spirit-induced prayers, dialogues or epics. They do not claim to be mediating between their audience and a spirit world for a specific purpose. They write in both Sakha and Russian, and they see their creativity, while rooted in traditional images and concepts, as deriving from their own personalities, minds, and eclectic experiences. The best of these, however, are celebrated for having *kut-siur*, that mystical, intuitive sense of the soul-reason nexus (or heart-soul-mind-body) that also permeates new genres of film and art. A few artists interested in post-Soviet community psychic curing are struggling with entirely new media, including rock music, theater, and film, into which ancient shamanic myths, prayers, and poems may be syncretized.[30]

In séances, too, we have seen there are degrees of inspiration, degrees of the sacred, and degrees of dramatic participation. In the 1990s, one curer was accused of taking advantage of Academy of Science archives, via a friend, to learn traditional chants for more effective curing séances. If this is true, it shows not spiritual "cheating" (as some gossips claimed), but rather a flexible approach to recovery of traditions perceived as valued and urgently useful.

In a séance, poetic metaphors become real to all those involved and the easily metaphorical Sakha language comes alive. The spirits are believed to appear: the poetry would not work without them. Shamans are believed to become one with their horse-drums: they could not travel without them. Here one of several Sakha terms for the séance itself, *kyryyr*, or travel to the edge, becomes relevant. The beloved Sakha actor Afanasy Fedorov, who often played shamans on the Sakha-language stage in Yakutsk, had a frightening insight into the nature of "the edge," as he had experienced it. He had a superb reputation for having done solid research into shamanic séances, texts, dancing, and music, and by the 1990s began using rhythmic breathing and drum therapy on supplicants, working in conjunction with a trained psychologist. He became popular as a prayer singer and folk curer, but confessed to me in 1995 that he stopped doing full séances because he nearly "slipped over the edge" several times into such a deep trance and such a compelling spirit world that he felt he might not return. When he performs, he gets carried away with the poetry he has memorized, sometimes using it as the core of further improvisation. He fears for the health of his family, since those who make mistakes evoking helping spirits of dead shamans sometimes find that these spirits come back to haunt them or their loved ones.[31]

The multiple tropes and multivocal symbols that form the basis of Sakha poetic construction are drawn from a deep, archaic, and rich cultural reservoir of Sakha ideas, philosophies, and cosmology. Horse-drums, shaggy stallion shamans, fermented mare's milk, multicolored snakes, sacred trees, five-fingered fire spirits, cranes dancing, eagles circling, and paired forest spirits all come from a three-part cosmologically complex world that resonates with many Sakha. One concept recurring often in the poems, and in the thoughts of Sakha intelligentsia and villagers is the concept of homeland [*doidu*]. It is as tangible as flesh, and just as precious. It has become the basis of an evolving Sakha nationalism consciously being stimulated by the society *Kut-Siur*, stressing social life forces, discussed further ahead.

For participants, shamanic poetry is a mode of transport, not just beyond the mundane and into the sacred, but into other realities and dimensions where capricious spirits may possibly—nothing guaranteed—be harnessed to help humans out of very ordinary and concrete problems such as illness and hunger. The way the poetry is produced, and precisely its inspirational nature, in a disciplined frenzy of symbolic codes, clues both human and spirit audiences into the spirituality, or depth, of *kut-siur*, of its creator.

In sum, Siberian shamans have become symbols and conduits of alternative ways of thinking in the Soviet and post-Soviet periods. Poet shamans of the Sakha Republic are today tentatively traveling into the realm of hard-won spiritual knowledge and inspired creativity along accepted ancient paths, the séance, and totally new ones, rock music, written verse, drama, and film. Some of the ancient paths have become overgrown with disuse, but shamans like the young Viliuisk healer mentioned at the outset say they have rediscovered the paths with the guidance of elderly living shamans and the spirits of deceased shamans. Both old-style and new-style shamanic poets have in common the root of the Sakha word for shaman, *oiuun*, possibly from *øi*, meaning intelligence and conscience together, or from *oi*, meaning to jump.

Photo 5 The late Vladimir Kondakov, founder of the Association of Folk Medicine, holding a photo of legendary shaman Niikon, Photo by Marjorie Mandelstam Balzer, 1993.

Chapter 5

Flights of the Sacred: Birds, Trees, and Open-Body-Mindedness

> *"I wanted to be a bird, a lark, and sang of this, and of flying. It was wonderful..."*
>
> Aida, in Belaia Gora, Abyi region healer relating her first séance experience, 1993

> *"If a scientist... rejects the right of his people to a spiritual culture, then are we [that people] alive?"*
>
> N. Bugaev [Bugay], *Molodezh Yakutiia* August 6, 1992, p. 8

During the summer of 1994, in a small Sakha village in the Far North of the republic, I visited the grave of a famous Sakha shaman and had what can be called an "altered states" experience. Since altered states—of consciousness, politics, and conditions of life—were quite common in the former Soviet Union in the nineties, let this story be an allegory for the disorientations and new connections that many experienced in post-Soviet times. The morning I walked out of the village to search for the shaman's grave was a gift of time, for I had just learned that the plane that would take me away would be a half-day late. I had wanted to visit the grave of Tokoyeu *oiuun*, but several Sakha friends tried to dissuade me, saying, "It will be your responsibility, you can go there by yourself if you like." They had shown me the appropriate path through a field, leading out from a rutted, muddy, Soviet-style road strewn with garbage. Visible in the distance was a hillock with a Russian Orthodox cross astride a long, low miniature house. The grave was separate, for the much revered and feared resting places of shamans are kept apart from others and usually hidden even deeper in the woods or taiga. When I reached the site, I passed its fenced grave in silence and tied a few horsehairs onto a nearby low bush-like tree, feeling somewhat awkward yet hopeful this was the proper behavior, as in sacred groves, to show respect. I turned back to look at the grave, and though I cannot say that a huge black raven literally flew out of it, I suddenly sensed his presence near the grave. The raven silently flew to a larch tree nearby and stared at me for long minutes that seemed to stop time. I remembered that one of the helper spirits of Tokoyeu was believed to be a raven (*suor*). And so I looked at him calmly and said, in my mind, "If you are who I think you are, please help your grandson."[1]

Meeting Tokoyeu's grandson had been one of the most jolting and significant experiences of my fieldwork. He was a downcast and disheveled young man, with long straggly hair and a black leather jacket. When the Sakha friend with whom I was traveling went to ask if this grandson would be willing to talk to an American, he had responded somewhat sulkily, "I guess I will have to talk to her. I dreamed about her before she came. But I thought she was Russian." Later, while the grandson, born in 1959, choked out his chilling life story, I turned off my tape recorder with tears streaming down my face. Tears were streaming down his, too. When he had been a teenager, he experienced all the signs of a shamanic illness—`éttéétén yald'ar*—a tormenting and testing by the spirits. In another age, he would have accepted the spirit helpers of his grandfather and become a leader and spiritual healer of his people. Certainly his grandfather had been such a leader, before Soviet repression of shamans had made him an outcast.

In the Soviet period, "shamanic illness" in a young man was taken to be an extreme mental illness, both politically and socially dangerous.[2] And indeed, the grandson admitted with a wry half-grin, it was probably a little scary for his fellow villagers when he rode a motorcycle around the graveyard and then came down a hill toward the village with no hands on the handlebars. He was twice taken to psychiatric prisons, where horrendously painful and debilitating drugs were administered within a system famous for its institutionalized sadism. Far from becoming a healer, the young man had become a mess, although he still showed signs of shamanic talents and had a loving family. Ironically, I was able to help him understand some of his options for potential curing in more "traditional" ways, since he felt isolated from knowledge of living Sakha shamans and from the activist cultural revitalization in republic cities and towns. I suggested that he might travel, despite long distances, to Fedot Ivanov, the young shaman of Viliuisk, one of whose helper spirits was a raven.

The raven figures in many shamanic narratives and séances throughout Siberia and in North America. In Sakha tradition, the raven is a spirit mediator par excellence but also a controversial bird, still believed by many today to appear as a harbinger of bad news, especially death. Shamans whose main spirit helpers are ravens are particularly powerful and revered, yet also feared and even pitied for the troubles this paradoxical spirit helper can bring.

This chapter focuses on the significance of birds and trees in shamanic cosmologies and in specific historic and current sociopolitical contexts. I feature Sakha ideologies, making comparisons among Siberian and other peoples, and exploring various interpretations. Birds and other shamanic animals, as powerful tropes, are used here not to fly in the face of existing theories but as a way to work through them, to achieve complex, locally adapted matches among various theories and diverse data. Birds are the anthropological helper spirits of this effort, a mediating starting point for traveling into conceptual spaces that cannot and need not be homogenized.

Two key concepts suggested by comments of Sakha consultants, including shamans and curers, provide a framework for initial discussion: birds as helper spirit-mediators and birds as souls or soul manifestations. In discussing these concepts, I shuttle between ideas that are in the esoteric domain of shamans, passed on as special knowledge through generations, and ideas that are in the wider mainstream of belief for many Sakha. These domains overlap, especially since shamans shared and still share their knowledge with supplicants. Both domains are changing in ways that are not easily predictable. I am particularly interested in the eclectic shamanic worldviews expressed by non-shamans, which continue despite all the efforts to suppress them.

Birds and Beyond: Spirit Mediation and Soul Beliefs

Birds and other helper spirits were and are today summoned to solve personal or community problems through the séance, that crucial dance of poetry, full of sound and fury, intensely involving, at once frightening and fascinating. Sakha use several words and phrases for séance probably due to their eclectic heritage, as well as their sensitivity to its varied purposes: *kuturar* places emphasis on shamanic chanting and songs, including calls of birds; *aptaktaakh* refers to everything in the séance, songs, dances, trancing, tricks, and miracles. *Turuk* is the closest Sakha come to a word for trance; and *kyryyr* (travel to the edge) emphasizes shamanic risks in nonordinary reality, as we have seen.[3]

Some of the most compelling séance descriptions in all of Siberian ethnographic literature come from the turn-of-the-century Russian exile Ivan A. Khudiakov (1969: 303–55), who recorded, in Sakha and Russian, dialogues between shamans and helper spirits. One such dialogue, between a Verkhoyansk shaman and an eagle spirit, involved the radical changing of the shaman's face and voice as he took on the persona of the spirit:

> He stood, and bowing to all people present, said, "Hello! Why have you called me here? Why have you bothered me? With what will you reward me? My steps are heavy, [though I trust] it is not for nothing that I have reached you. My sharp, fast eyes are piercing, my fiery tongue pours over and surrounds you all, my eagle talons capture and pin you, I will squeeze anyone who clutches my tail! Why have you asked me here? Tell me now, oh why?"

The shaman, feeding morsels of food to the spirit through the fire, drumming, shaking, and twirling in his iron-laden cloak, replied: "We have bothered you for a great reason. Please be kind. Please soften your skeptical heart, calm your boiling blood, look with pity. We disturb you for the sake of a sick one: cure our sick one here. And all that you demand, we will fulfill."[4]

In séances, including some that still occur, the sounds of animal and bird spirit helpers are not so much mimicked as embodied by the most effective shamans. Some iron ornaments of the Sakha, Éven, Évenk, and Yukaghir shaman's cloak symbolize bird feathers, certain bird bones (especially the humerus), and, often, full bird forms of various bird helper spirits. In certain séances, depending on their purpose and context, the shaman, instead of bringing spirits to the bedside of an ill patient, must travel to upper or lower worlds of the shamanic cosmos. Bird spirits are so salient that the Russian ethnographer Waldemar Jochelson suggested that the full shaman's cloak "represents a bird's skin, with the help of which the shaman is transformed into a bird...he is a bird-man...supposed to rise to the upper world by means of his coat" (1933: 111).[5]

As birds help shamans ascend through difficult, multilayered cosmic terrain to capture lost souls or find spirits of illness, they loan shamans their qualities—for example, the eagle's piercing eyesight and endurance. An illustration of the degree to which shamans were identified with their helper spirits is the nickname of one of the great deceased Sakha shamans of the Kolyma region, Kuba-*oiuun* (Swan-shaman). A current example is Kytalyk-*oiuun* (White Crane-shaman), whose name is significant because many revere the crane as a sacred, rare, and protected bird, long associated with femininity, blessing, and seasonal balance (I. Gogolev 1987).

The identification of shamans with their helper spirits is confirmed in numerous stories of shamanic exploits. When the shaman Bahylai of the Sredn'aia Kolyma region was blamed for starting a forest fire soon after World War II, "the militia came searching for him, either to arrest or fine him. But he got away. He swam into the water and became a loon. As a loon, he was able to create a heavy, wet snow that stopped the fire." When he died, his family burned his mattress and clothes: "Out of this fire came a raven, which flew toward his home village."[6]

Parilop, a popular, wise, and kind shaman of the Sredn'aia Kolyma region, was said to be uncannily accurate at predictions and diagnoses of illnesses and troubles, although he supposedly stopped his curing séances after Soviet repression. He foresaw the burning of an electric power station a week before it occurred, but people did not take him seriously enough. Parilop had a wood grouse as one of his helping spirits. "One day Parilop decided to visit his friend Kharkha in the village of Khatingnaakh. He came as a wood grouse and sat right on Kharkha's roof. Kharkha came out of his house, saw the wood grouse looking at him, and grabbed his gun ready to shoot the bird, who got away." In a few days, Parilop arrived by plane. He "went to Kharkha's house, somewhat miffed but smiling, and said 'You nearly shot me the day before yesterday. Why did you try to do this?' "[7]

Tokoyeu, Parilop's contemporary, controlled the difficult and dangerous raven, whose uncanny abilities in identifying and transferring souls made them logical messengers and helpers. Tokoyeu was, by his own modest account, a shaman of merely middle-range power, capable of some curing, predictions, and finding of lost people and objects. As a young man, Tokoyeu had stopped at a hunter's rest spot near Sion Kiuol'. Suddenly, he fell into a kind of enchantment:

> I was surrounded by five human-looking spirits, who decided to test me at this place. What kind of séances could I do? What kind of spirits, *aiyy*-benevolent, *abaaghy*-evil, would I control? What kind of attributes [e.g., dress, drum] would I have for my séances? Then they said, "You will be a medium-level *oiuun*, a kind shaman. You will salve people's grief." At that moment I came to myself. I was on my back, with my hands to my aching head. I woke up, and from that time I started to do séances.[8]

Another shaman of Kolyma, reputed to have a raven and an eagle as his helper spirits, was Sémën Gul'aev, who died in 1965. Before he died, he searched desperately and fruitlessly for a successor. One promising candidate was a young man, Vasily A. Kudrin, who later regretted that he had rejected Gul'aev's overtures. Kudrin explained to me in 1994:

> I was a Komsomol [young Communist League member] in the 1950s and was taking a sled with horses from Khatingnaakh village to Sredne Kolymsk. Suddenly I saw a raven swoop down and scare the horses. I calmed them down and went on. The next day, Gul'aev found me in the street and said, in the most fond, affectionate voice, "I've been looking for you and finally found you. I was petrified. He had seen me react with the horses when he was in the form of a raven, and wanted me to then become his apprentice. [Did you know who he was?] Yes, I knew who he was. Everyone knew who he was.

Kudrin's fears were derived from concern over Soviet repression of shamanic activity, but he had what was perhaps a greater terror of the spiritual trials required to become a shaman. Such birth-pain trials differed according to the type of shaman the neophyte was destined to be and the personalities of a given shaman and mentor. But in the ideology of generations of Sakha shamans, they involved a complex tempering of various kinds of souls. Through this tortuous process, lasting from one to nine years, shamans received multiple helper spirits that could troubleshoot at a shaman's will. These mediating spirits ranged from the raven and eagle to such birds as the loon, hawk, crane, wood grouse, swan, lark, cuckoo, and sandpiper, and included bears, wolves, foxes, bulls, and dogs. They were beasts of prey as well as more domesticated animals. They were rare, larger-than-life birds of great soaring power, as well as commonly seen birds of modest abilities and size. A great shaman could have as many as 47 helpers, but more typical numbers ranged from three to nine, and could change over a shaman's lifetime.

The Sakha ethnographer Nikolai Alekseev (1984: 79–81) makes an important distinction between situational spirit helpers, who can be spirits of specific localities or specialized disease alleviation, and major tutelary spirits, who are more like alter egos or "doubles" of a shaman. The most important of helper "doubles" is the "mother-beast-spirit" (*iié-kyyl*), sometimes also termed "primary-form-beast" (*kép-kyyl*) (Ksenofontov 1992: 69; Seroshevsky 1896: 626). Such spirits are incorporated into cosmologies and iconographies that are alive and well in the lexicon of folk medicine practitioners and believers. My interlocutors constantly reiterated that spirits in general are called *ichchi[ler]*, benevolent spirits are *aiyy*, and evil ones are *abaaghy*.

Shamanic tutelary spirits and the images they are housed in are both *émégét*, mistakenly glossed in Christian-oriented ethnographies as "idols." Wooden *émégét* usually take human or bird forms.[9] Sakha of diverse regions and backgrounds explain that they have three main souls: the *iié-kut* or "mother soul," *buor-kut* or "earth-clay soul," and *salgyn-kut* or "air-breath soul." This concept of spirituality is crucial in philosophical teachings called *kut-siur*, glossed variously and taught in Sakha cultural heritage classes in the republic. Although the 1990s group of Sakha intelligentsia calling themselves *Kut-Siur* no longer meets regularly, their popularization of the term remains significant. As mentioned earlier, this crucial but slippery concept can be glossed as soul-mind-life force or soul-reason or heart-soul-mind-body.[10]

In Sakha concepts prevalent among elders and members of *Kut-Siur*, the key to Sakha fertility and the transfer of souls to human mothers is the sky goddess, Aiyyhyt. Various shamanic rituals of earlier times helped assuage problems of infertility or child deaths by convincing Aiyyhyt to transfer souls from the sky (especially from the main sky god Aiyy Toyon) into a suffering woman. Shamans considered capable of leading such rituals were often, but not necessarily, women. In one case, a young woman asked the shaman Sémën Gul'aev for help because she had lost many children in childbirth or soon after. He prepared a small bird's nest that was placed on a sacred tree in the forest to attract the souls of a potential newborn. A child was born soon after and lived until adulthood.[11] After I became interested in this ritual, I learned that similar rituals were performed for women in forests near Yakutsk in the post-Soviet period.

A far more esoteric ritual of fertility, linked to horse power rather than birds, has almost definitely not withstood the test of time. Provocatively called "ritual for the enhancement of sexual power," it was reported in the 1920s by the Sakha ethnographer Gavril Ksenofontov (1992: 203–5). This ritual aphrodisiac was for women, led by a vigorous male shaman with nine maidens and nine youths assisting him, dancing to his drumbeat. During the ritual, *dzhalyn ylyyta*, a small group of target women were captured by the shaman's frenzy, dancing with abandon and neighing like horses "innesasakh." "With their neighs they threw themselves on the shaman and performed various bodily movements," pushing him to the ground until men standing nearby took them off him. "The shaman, rising, whistled and made a circle with his drumstick. Then the women came to themselves, calmed down, and sat [with blushing faces]." The procedure was repeated three times, and provoked an observer to remark that "the most respectable women simply did not come to such a ritual."

For future shamans, including those with shamans in their family trees and those who are reincarnated shamans, the three souls have special fates (*d'ylgha*) and require special training. Knowledge about this, like the sexy ritual above, is esoteric and mystical and thus controversial, personal, and less susceptible than other beliefs to generalization. Yet a few patterns emerge. The earth-clay soul becomes a fish for its training, acquiring knowledge of water-based diseases and illness caused by shamans. The air-breath soul, nestled in hollows or nests at ranked levels of a great larch tree, is fed raven or eagle eggs. Sons and daughters of one of the Sakha sky gods, Âry Darkhan, take the form of either the raven or the eagle and "teach the soul diverse shamanic tricks and cleverness" (Popov 1947: 283). This soul could take the form of a cuckoo or sandpiper. If it has trouble, a nurturing double-headed eagle (*öksökiu*) dries its soul wings and fattens its body.[12]

A shaman's mother soul is spirited away to a land parallel to earth in the middle world, where it becomes the *iié-kyyl* (mother beast). It lives physically separate from the shaman, who sees it and/or takes its form—some say three times in a life, others once a year, others when it is critically needed. Yet its fate is intricately tied to the shaman's, for when it dies, the shaman dies, and when the shaman fights with other shamans it can be in the form of the mother beast.

Stories of shamans fighting in the form of their mother beast are still popular and believed by some. The Viliuisk shaman Niikon is said to have vanquished the blacksmith Ivan Zakharev, whose repentance I described earlier, by taking this form and killing the blacksmith's wife. The theme of ethnic competition weaves back in here as well. The Kolyma shaman Parilop, allegedly sickened by a local Évenk shaman, took revenge in the form of a wolf and gorged himself on a herd of the Évenk shaman's reindeer. A village on the Abyi riverbank was founded only after the site had been made safe by a Sakha "white shaman" who vanquished in a mother-beast fight a "black shaman" who may have been a local Évenk.[13] Typical shamanic mother beasts of the central and northern Sakha are the eagle, raven, crane, bull, elk, deer, and bear. Stronger shamans have a bear or an eagle, and weaker ones a wolf or dog.[14] One of the Sakha curers with whom I have worked considers herself "especially close to the eagle." Her patients confirm they have seen an eagle during her séances, but I have not managed this.

In 1991, the main yearly Sakha festival (*yhyakh*), which celebrates fertility, fermented mare's milk (*kumiss*), the advent of summer, and (on this occasion) the legalization of the festival as a state holiday, was declared in honor of the eagle. Based on enlarged horse hitching posts, special carved wooden posts called *sergé*, topped by eagle images, were raised at several festival sites in the republic. In 1995, I attended the raising of an enormous eagle post placed on a peak at the homestead site of one of the earliest known Sakha ancestors, Tygyn-Darkhan, said to be a warrior shaman. The ceremony, organized by members of *Kut-Siur*, included prayers to Tygyn. The sacredness of the eagle is reflected in beliefs about serious supernatural punishments for the hunting of eagles, said to be children of the sky-god Khotoi-aiyy. While the eagle's origins may be forgotten by some today, reticence to hunt eagles remains. A foolish Sakha eagle hunter could go crazy, acquiring the sounds of an eagle and ultimately writhing in death. (This might not happen to a Russian, however.) Poetic epithets for the eagle, used in shamanic séances, in prayers, and in sacred epics (*olonkho*), include "talons sounding like metal, screaming [into the] stone sky, with all seeing eyes, encircling shoulders, sharp tail, metal paws, dappled wing-feathers, encircling-wide wings, huge circular eyes, hooked-nose eagle-master."[15]

The famed interpreter of shamanism Mircea Eliade, relying especially on legends collected by the Sakha ethnographer Gavril Ksenofontov ([1928] 1992), attempted to squeeze various Sakha (Yakut) ideas of souls, shamanic initiation, and torture by spirits into his comparative framework. In Eliade's summary, a bird-of-prey mother, with her iron beak, hooked claws, and long tail, transports the shaman to the underworld to be torn apart by spirits of disease and then reborn. Alternatively, training takes place in a giant pine "world tree" of the sky, where the bird-of-prey mother, with the "head of an eagle and iron feathers," hatches "great, middling, and lesser shamans" by sitting on eggs containing their souls for "respectively three years, two years and one year" (Eliade 2004: 36–38). The beauty of the Ksenofontov collection is its rich diversity and historic specificity. Some narrators discuss the mother beast as a large bird with iron-like claws seen at birth and death by all shamans, while others insist only great shamans have mother beasts (Ksenofontov 1992: 50, 55–56).

Eliade's bird-of-prey mother is overgeneralized and simplified even as Yakut, much less for all of northern Asia, although certain Sakha concepts of the mother beast resemble those of their Tungusic neighbors, the Éven and Évenk.[16] The Ksenofontov accounts reveal the significance and range of bird-shaman tropes. The shaman Séménchik, for example, "during his shamanic torture, somehow rose to the sky, and there, sitting in the heights of a great tree, was made to call like a cuckoo-ku, ku." Platon Pavlov, from a family of Tiit-Aryy island shamans, explained that "the old people say that the shaman, or rather, his soul, endures torture in the lower country, at the hands of nine clans of evil spirits. When they have done enough they ask, 'Has not a flying bird yet appeared, have wings not yet sprouted, has fluffy bird fuzz not yet covered the body?'"[17]

A comparable narrative of shamanic illness and "emergence as a curer" comes from Aida, a young woman of Belaia Gora in 1993: "I had trouble sleeping and felt sick...but then I slept fitfully and thought I had woken. I felt I had guests. I saw my mother coming out of the grave, and [deceased shaman] Konstantin *oiuun*." Konstantin introduced Aida to a spirit helper, who said: "You will be curing people, but you must not be greedy." "How could I cure people?" I ask, "when I don't know how?" Aleksandra Chirkova, hearing this vision of her father, invited Aida to a séance in the local hospital, during which Aida could not stop dancing:

> People were even a little scared of me...but I went home in a mood to cure....I started singing in the old Sakha song style [not known before]....I wanted to be a bird, a lark, and sang of this, and of flying. It was wonderful....Once I saw a road, long and hard. On one side was Konstantin *oiuun*, with a drum, and a bear, dancing. On the other was my mother, in traditional Sakha dress. I went home on this road to get a bird I had there, a lark. I clasped it to my breast to give to Aleksandra. Then I said to all the animals, to Grandfather, to the bear, to my mother, "Stay, stay behind."...I see so much now. Who has darkness, who has energy, light. I always have the urge to fly.

This lovely, lively young mother became part of a folk medicine team, helping Aleksandra Chirkova, then head doctor of Abyi region, who was just beginning to incorporate curing techniques of her father.[18]

A contrasting version of soul flight was encouraged in the 1990s by the head of the Association of Folk Medicine, Vladimir Kondakov, exhorting potential Sakha healers as follows:

> In spring or summer, rise early in the morn with the sun; as the song says, "Friend, stand early to greet the sun on a high mountain." Climb a mountain or hill, where all around is silence, and observe nature everywhere. Fear not, empty your head, feel the earth, the water, the height from which to see grazing cattle grounds; rejoice, go forward, feel yourself one with nature. Let the first rays of sun and the first songs of birds give you strength and energy. Then, together with the

golden rays of the sun, rise higher. As the sun rises, so shall you fly higher. Fly as high as the clouds. Feel the height of the Sky. Fly until your head blanks out the sparkle of light and your body loses strength. Look from above down to the green earth. Perhaps the warmth of Aiyy [kind spirits] will come to you and will reach your land and help people. Slowly come back to earth. Calm yourself. Breathe! At first it will be hard to walk, but soon it will be possible. If everything has gone well, it means you have a special Gift.[19]

This courting of spiritual experience is not typical of standard portrayals of Siberian shamanism, in which a shaman resists the call of the spirits until given little choice. Rather, it is closer to the vision quests of North America, although the voluntariness of North American training and the involuntariness of Siberian training each may have been overstressed in the ethnographic literature.[20] Kondakov's exhortation represents a democratization of shamanism. He has tapped into a yearning for spiritual fulfillment prevalent in post-Soviet Siberia by reaching deep into what he perceives to be past traditions. His flight training is meant to be more than a metaphor, becoming also a means toward the ultimate goal of helping his people out of a spiritual void and physical-ecological devastation.

In the political and social climate of the Sakha Republic in the 1990s, only about seven Sakha, Éven, and Évenk men and women were reputed to be shamans. With recent deaths of major shamans in the republic, this number may diminish further and is easily disputed, with some believers emphasizing that no "true" shamans are alive today, while others claim many folk healers are undergoing shamanic illness and using shamanic techniques. Far more people have made aspects of shamanic thinking, especially prayers, soul, and spirit beliefs, integral to their ways of defining themselves and their environment.

Sacred Groves: Thinking Beyond the World Tree

A particularly enduring and flexible manifestation of shamanic beliefs is the maintenance into the twenty-first century of sacred groves, in the Sakha Republic, and elsewhere in Siberia, the North Caucasus, and Central Asia. The powerful trope of the "world" or "cosmic" tree as a grand mediator among sky, earth, and underground worlds has been suggested as key to shamanic thinking by many, most famously Mircea Eliade (2004: 269–274). Whether shamans are newly "hatched" in a tree, or use tall, well-rooted trees as a route to fly to the sky or travel underground, the repeat patterning of tree symbolism is so striking that researchers stressing its universality can easily miss fascinating and rich local nuances. During the Sakha *yhyakh* festival, young sapling birches, representing the promise of new life, line the festival entrance. Birches were also chosen for the grounds of the *Archy Diété* [Purification House], the shamanic urban temple built in 2002 in Yakutsk. In Sakha rural areas, major trees, especially cedar, larch, and birch, have long been the focal points of clearings near villages and homesteads (*alaas*) where people give to local spirits small offerings of ribbons, coins, and food along with prayers.

One of my first magical moments of feeling accepted by Sakha friends and colleagues, when I knew I was being let in on indigenous sacred knowledge, was when I was taken on a road trip to the Nam region in 1986 after several months of begging to be let out of the capital, Yakutsk. The proximate cause of permission to leave the city was that student protest demonstrations had occurred, and paranoid authorities were debating whether to send me home or send me to villages. Permission to stay was a psychological turning point for the friends who defended me, and thus I traveled in a celebratory mood with the ethnographers Anatoly I. Gogolev and his student Platon Sleptsov. While the discrete and secular Anatoly read a mystery novel in the car, Platon and I found a path through the snowy woods and into a sacred grove with a prominent larch near a lovely, yet chilly cliff overlooking a valley near Nam. For Platon, our arrival was a homecoming to a local sacred grove of his ancestors, and he made offerings and said prayers of thanksgiving (*algys*) quite reverently. Platon showed me how to fasten the ribbon and suggested possible prayers to enhance our work and health. His reverence was a revelation that was to be repeated each time in many years of stopping at such sacred groves. That year alone I saw eight others, and I lost count after traveling with friends through numerous Sakha regions in the 1990s. Many Sakha drivers say they stop because they fear something will happen to their car or themselves if they do not. Stories abound of people in too much of a hurry to stop being sorry later when they fall ill or endure a flat tire.

After seeing over 20 groves, some in well-kept condition and others with sad hulks of dying trees strewn with trash, I began wondering what sustained a community's maintenance of these groves, how they were picked as special, and whether any of the groves were completely new, post-Soviet manifestations of renewed faith in spirits and spirit power. Most were established in clearings that went back before the Soviet period, where large, impressive trees or a single major tree, had survived the ravages of time. Some of the trees were fully draped with ribbons or colored cloth that had turned to rags, showing that they had grown with offerings that were now hanging far out of reach. Coins were stuck into the bark, and placed below. Sometimes whole busloads of people would come to pay homage to the local spirits, and picnic nearby. Some of the trees had small fences around them, demarcating sacred space and in effect warning people to be careful as they entered the tree site.

Across the Lena river, in the late 1990s, I was finally taken to several trees that looked relatively young. They were only beginning their careers as sacred trees, set off a local road but within sight of the road. Surprised, I asked how they had been chosen, and who was doing the choosing. A local sports coach explained they had been established by one of the new, younger healers, the shaman V., who was rapidly gaining his reputation for curing alcoholics. His followers were placing ribbons on trees he had selected, but the followers of another local healer, Kyta Baaly, were in effect boycotting these trees. Kyta Baaly later told me that he could not see the effectiveness of showing respect to trees chosen by his competitor V.

As my awareness of the politics of sacred trees grew, so did my sense that these trees were becoming emblems of contested cultural revival as well as personal rivalry. In one satellite village of Yakutsk in 2001, a small rowdy and reputedly drunk gang of Sakha youths cut down an ancient larch, considered by many to be sacred and untouchable. The community was shocked, and the scandal set off a campaign to teach young people why the trees were important manifestations of ancestral honor and ecological harmony, even if one did not believe in spirits inhabiting the trees themselves. Another community's young people took upon themselves the task of cleaning up a sacred grove (near Nemegiuntse) that had trash strewn too close to its huge but dying tree. They saw the difficulties of the tree as a kind of metaphor for the neglect they had been showing to their spiritual life. A group of folklorists and ethnographers from Yakutsk, led by William Yakovlev, also launched a project to catalogue the sacred groves in that *ulus*, resulting in a precedent setting, if limited distribution, toponymic, geographic, and religious guide (Gogolev 2000). By 2007, a conference and website was devoted to the sacred groves, although debate about revealing their exact locations was ongoing.[21]

Showing respect for dominant larch, cedar, willow, and birch with small offerings and short prayers was only a part of community sacred tree tradition. Perspective is provided by a related but more secretive practice. Individual shamans often had their own sacred trees, near their homes, either huge and natural or carved into fantastic shapes. I've been shown several of these trees, one said to have been pivotal in a shaman's ability to stimulate fertility by the baby symbols left in the tree with incantations. More abstract spirit trees were made of posts and poles with wooden birds carved to look as if they were flying off them. My closest look at one of these came during a visit in 1986 to the former shaman's helper-turned-choreographer, Iakim Izbekov. Izbekov and early ethnographic sources correlate such sculptural poles with shamanic *ämägkät* or *émégét*, wooden spirit holders that were enlivened by ritual to become imbued with spirit helpers, often but not only birds (see cover, compare Gell 1998).

A search for further insight takes us back to a moment recorded in1890 about a desperate, devout Sakha man whose wife had left him, and he wanted her back. Recorded by the People's Will revolutionary exile V. M. Ionov, who married a brilliant Sakha folklorist, the following account of a "reversal of fortune incantation" said in a sacred grove answers questions about how sacred trees were selected and why their power was and is believed to be so potent.[22] The man found in the woods a double trunked larch, seemingly separate trees facing each other, but united by a common root. Since this was clearly a sacred grove, he appealed to the trees, offering three birch bark containers filled with fresh butter. Touching the trunks, he incanted:

> Spirits-masters of these trees, tightly and joyously bound to each other, growing in this center of our middle earth, in the eight-leveled and eight-sided world, covered with a coat of green, cleansed by your kinship!
>
> Kind and all powerful gods made you O Trees, so that you could never be torn asunder from each other, neither in life nor in death!
>
> Here am I, unhappy, standing before you, separated and eaten by sorrow, with a faltering stomach covered loosely by a shirt, that hides the pain of a lonely heart.
>
> If you ask, "what is the reason for my presence, for coming from so far, with such full grief, spilling from me like a river?" I will answer, will hide nothing.
>
> Since that terrible moment when my spouse decided to leave, for a whole three years, I have counted the days.
>
> My strong spirit has weakened, I sleep with my head on a saddle, awaken with a wicked impatience; I feel that my very bones could break.

Due to nights on hard boards, my bones seem to visibly protrude—my hands are like sticks between skin.
Since I've been in bed alone, I freeze without my spouse—
This is why I have come before you today!
Besides all this, I've got other sorrows; my milk cow has lost her calf, wanders about and possibly will cease to give milk.
I stuffed the calf skin, thinking I could fool the cow into providing milk.
But it didn't work, the cow stomped the stuffed animal, ran away and has not returned.
And here, I have my last request, that some herb can reverse my broken soul, put back together my soul and heart—and liver too!
To you, all seeing and protecting, I recall a saying of my ancestors:
"Those who have only an underground hut will seem lucky to those who are without a home entirely."
You, strong through the centuries, through your branches can see, that I am still more bitter, jealous, and crying.
With tears I request, teach me how to reach Aiyhyyt and the Goddess who is her elder sister, so that we can live with love and harmony!
Humbly I request, beg of you to teach us how to reach Iéiékhsit, so that people could live with each other in union and happiness!
If you, Tree Spirit, could gift me with your sap and strength, then give me in the left cup the means to soften a female heart!
In the right cup, give me the means to let my cattle prosper!
In the middle cup, give me the means to myself become strong!
There, this is why I've come, appealed to you, All -Powerful Tree Spirit!

Ionov's account continues, that the suffering man knocked on the tree trunk and that three times the tree bowed and three times made a kind of "trrr—trrr" sound. When he looked down at the cups, he saw that in each had fallen a bit of red sap. Mixing this with butter, he surreptitiously found a way to get his wife to ingest it. She instantly came back to him and they lived long and well, with thriving cattle. This poignant tale is compelling for me in part because the shamanic pleas tapping into the sap of spirit power are not said by a shaman. This power, evoking the goddesses of fertility and fate, is accessible to the desperate and humble.

Multiple Interpretations Revisited

The attraction of shamanic stories and the experiences behind them can inspire flights of fancy about flights into the sacred. As suggested throughout this book, this material is rich but difficult to understand without direct experience. Yet readers gain a sense of substance through the voices of those with shamanic worldviews. Modes of interpretation need not compete; they can augment each other synergistically.

An interpretive mode that is widely explored in Siberia is that of historical diffusionism. Ethnographers such as Anatoly Gogolev (1983, 1986) and Nikolai Alekseev (1984), who are themselves Sakha, have traced their roots and found sometimes unexpected links. Native anthropologists who are interested in family trees as well as shamanic ones can help us reconsider the implications of close examination of cultural influence through time (Balzer 1995).

The striking reverence for the raven and eagle across north Asia and North America is relevant here, but analysis can be refined to describe variations on the theme.[23] For example, intense respect for the raven as a god-spirit among peoples of the Bering Sea area wanes when focus is further inland on the latecomer Sakha, who stress the eagle. Turkic ancestors of the Sakha, traveling north from an area around Lake Baikal, encountering and intermarrying with Tungusic, Yukaghir, and Chukchi groups, found their shamans to be especially frightening and powerful. Reverence for the raven was adopted or adapted with mixed feelings, accounting for the association of the raven with death, the underworld, and evil spirits. Indeed, as mentioned earlier, Sakha continue to claim Éven, Évenk, Yukaghir, and Chukchi shamans are more powerful and more dangerous than Sakha shamans. In keeping with the logic of these reputations, a rich cross-fertilization of shamanic traditions continues. For example, a famed Évenk shaman in 1995 summoned a promising young Sakha shaman for a pilgrimage and apprenticeship.

Another mode of interpretation, mischievously mixing Malinowski's (1945) functionalism with that of Shirokogoroff's *The Psychomental Complex of the Tungus* (1935), focuses on the heuristic, underlying usefulness of shamanism for personal, familial, and community-wide healing. Bird-shamans within this context become one of several powerful means of communication to convince local human audiences of the shaman's otherworldly abilities. Here, whether shamans play tricks or produce real miracles makes no difference; what is important is that the community of active shamanist believers perceives that the shaman becomes a bird for their benefit. All the symbols of the shaman—cloak, drum, and émégét- become stage props toward this end. Skeptics were and are subdued by a cycle of reinforced belief, as each story of a cure confirms shamanic power and each story of failure is deemed exceptional. This cycle was never fully undermined, despite Soviet repression.

Stories of shamanic curing abound in current Sakha discussions. These are stories Sakha tell each other, not just visiting ethnographers. This book opened with the story of Fedot Ivanov, the young Viliuisk shaman who I recommended to Tokoyeu's grandson, who reputedly cured a Russian woman doctor of cancer by conducting full-fledged séances with a raven and other helper spirits. One diabetic patient, grateful for Fedot's alleviation of chronic symptoms, explained that Fedot loves manipulating the theater of séances. He directs his patients and their subsequent therapy, "playing psychological games with us for our own good.... I do not understand how he does it but it works."

Claude Levi-Strauss's (1963, 1966) dualist structuralism can be combined with insights of the Russian Siberianist Elena Novik (1984) to build on the analysis begun earlier on more precisely how individual and community healing works. The shamanic world is divided into familiar realms of the sacred and profane, white and black, good and evil, upper and lower cosmos, male and female, wild and tamed. The eagle, raven, crane, loon, and lark become mediators, valued for their specific talents, absorbed by the shaman-mediator, and protected—not hunted—by those who revere them. Birds and bird-shamans serve as particularly effective mediators among cosmic worlds, since they perch or swim on earth, dive under water, and fly through the sky. Further, they are associated with world-mediating trees, rooted in the lower world, flourishing on earth, and branching into the sky. The intricate cognitive capabilities of humans, combined with close observation of and kinship with the natural world, make birds appropriate intensifiers to express and promote personal and ecological harmony.[24]

To deepen the understanding of birds, Siberianists may follow the leads of Victor Turner's multivocal symbolism (1969, 1977) and the work of Mary Douglas (1970, 1975) on implicit and explicit meanings, together with the poetic beauty of Steven Feld's Kaluli monograph (1990) and nuanced approaches to Siberian data by the Finnish scholar Anna-Leena Siikala (1978; Siikala and Hoppál 1992: 87–106). Shamanic ranking in nests or hollows of trees appears to change over a lifetime of periodic spiritual testing. It may be only from an outsider's point of view that one shaman becomes a privileged interlocutor with an eagle, while another is stuck with a wood grouse vulnerable to shooting. The personalities, talents, and emotions of shamans resonate with specific birds, as hunters (eagle), scavengers (raven), singers (lark, cuckoo), divers (loon), and flitters (wood grouse). Shamans hone their skills through helper spirits in a mutual courtship more subtle than most ethnographic accounts portray (compare Willerslev 2007: 132). In Yurok (Native American) shamanic thinking, "The Hawk is not just a beautiful bird who has certain physical characteristics; it is a spiritual source of power. It can be used for seeing because it is a good seer; it can be used for protection because it is a strong fighter; it can be used for soul travel because it can fly long distance against great odds and the forces of nature" (Lake (Medicine Grizzly Bear) 1991: 4). Sakha believers similarly describe a range of power properties for helper spirits.

Birds should be placed in the context of multiple, interpenetrating symbolic systems that are replete with contradictions, as complexities of the Sakha mother-beast suggest. Birds are only one part of the shamanic calling, as the existence of multiple spirit helpers, including shamanic ancestors, reveals. The shamanic drum, in the Sakha and other Turkic and Mongolic peoples' symbol systems, often represents a horse. In some séances, a dancing bird-shaman can ride a horse-drum and wear iron reindeer antlers in a headdress. Such virtuosity is more common in historical depictions than today, however (Kulakovskii 1979; Seroshevsky 1896).

A thesis of this book is that the séance is more than a tidy liminal ritual system that returns community participants to some status quo ante. Séances can confirm, consolidate, and stimulate changing relationships. Spirits, animals, supplicants, and shamans are interwoven within a constantly adapting, interactive communication system (compare Nadasdy 2007: 35–36). For example, when Konstantin *oiuun* had gifts that grateful patients had given him sewn onto his shamanic cloak, he was adding the spirit of their love to the bones and metal ornaments symbolizing his connections with helper spirits, including the raven and bear. These spirits could not have chosen him without his respect for and offerings to the animals themselves.

The slippages of metaphoric and allegoric meanings and beliefs are immeasurable, also constantly changing or being (re)invented (Basso 1996; Fernandez 1991; Taussig 1993, 2009). This leaves all shamans and other fast-thinking symbol manipulators vulnerable to accusations of inauthenticity. As I have said to surprised Sakha audiences, each generation recreates its own traditions, and none is in full solidarity with itself. While some members of the Sakha intelligentsia rail against "superficiality" and "artificiality" in ritual (re)creation, others, for example members of the group *Kut-Siur*, have revived rituals they learned from archives and have repopularized the powerful concept that words themselves have spirit (*ichchi*), especially when used in prayer. Shamans themselves say that they are far more than symbol manipulators.

In 1991, at the urging of a Sakha friend, I read a paper on the interconnection of the popular Sakha national instrument, the *khomus* with shamanic healing, for a conference in Yakutsk. I had only circumstantial evidence, but the argument was well received because members of the revitalizing Sakha intelligentsia wanted to believe in the link and in the curing powers of this small resonating "jaw harp." In the hands of a master, the eerie yet soothing sounds of this forged vibrating circle become ways to call spirits, and, for some, to feel the spirit manifestation of birds. In Ksenofontov (1992: 56) is confirmation that an obsolete word for some of the magic of shamanic séances is *khomusun*. This puts in marvelous perspective Sakha assertions that the *khomus* at its uncanny best sounds like and becomes a loon or a cuckoo.

By 1995, Sakha experiments in group and individual therapy with the *khomus* had been launched by the International Khomus Center and expanded by two well-known and respected curers, Klavdia Maksimova and Piotr Sleptsov. I watched as one group of about 20, in their tenth and culminating therapy session, danced and tranced in a field to *khomus* music, played by Spiridon Shishigin and Matriona Il'ina. Many of the patients, who had been quite ill before they joined the program, danced with bird and other animal movements, jumped, contorted, and rolled on the ground. At the end people stood in the field, raising their hands to the sky and pulling solar energies toward their chests, chanting after Klavdia Maksimova: "I am well. I am Sakha. I am here, in and with this land." They then related their experiences and feelings in testimonies about released creativity, physical recoveries from paralysis, ecstasy through trancing, and joy at finding community in each other. They had (re)created the kernels of the séance experience, democratized it, and made it actively theirs.[25]

Can this compare with "new age" shamanism in America and Europe (Harner 1973, 1990; Goodman 1990; Mehl-Madrona 1997; Jakobsen 1999; Francfort et al. 2001)? The two have in common a straining to get at some inner core of human affect, to break the bonds of received distinctions between reality and unreality, and to touch people spiritually and aesthetically. Belief that sighted ravens are more than ravens can take place only in a psychological climate of openness to altered states—of consciousness, of politics, and of conditions of life. Such beliefs can come through deep involvement in a particular shamanic cosmology, provoking for anthropologists what Piers Vitebsky (1993: 256) calls bisentience, and what I think has the potential to become multisentience. They also can come through trance or dream experiences, and can transcend various field sites. As we open ourselves to diverse "realities," our sensitivity to multiple ways of understanding fieldwork influenced dreams or hard-to-explain but difficult-to-dismiss "mystical" events may become better attuned, beyond our often-evoked fallback of Jungian (1965) "archetypical symbol" analysis. Such learning opportunities can be interpreted with the help of experienced elders, so that they become more than simply flights of fancy.

Sakha believers, like other contemporary spiritual searchers, are balancing personal and more universal claims as they broaden the scope and venues of their spiritual quests and expressions. Art produced by one of the participants in the *khomus* séance was filled with images of her human-bird, free-flying soul soaring heavenward. Such art continues to be popular in the republic (Ivanov-Unarov 2000). By 2009, art videos proudly shown on Sakha TV integrated shamanic themes, including a technical marvel called "My town Pokrovsk," featuring a shaman turning into an eagle and flying off a cliff.[26] Some Sakha healers are turning to Slavic-style new age seminars for "extrasense" training in Moscow and Kiev, whether or not purist ethnographers approve. They find it feasible to add theories about energy transference, auras, and Indian chakras to their shamanic heritage. Some call them charlatans, and indeed their curing abilities vary widely. But one patient's charlatan can be another's curer. One of the most interesting and reputable healers with whom I have worked is an ethnically mixed rural woman who combines Sakha and Russian folk healing traditions.

The best shamanic séances somehow manage to combine serious, cathartic exploration of family or personal traumas with good old-fashioned bawdy fun through dialogues with spirits (compare Kendall 1985, 2001, 2009; Vitebsky 1993). Focus on expression of strong feelings in specific shamanic rituals fits with interpretations that stress the anthropology of emotion (Lutz and Abu-Lughod 1990). It also renders more understandable a Sakha tradition associated with childbirth ritual (and the goddess Aiyyhyt) that has been resurrected in certain recent shamanic séances. The ritual involves laughter therapy, an all-out guffaw-til-you-drop communal or familial mirth session provoked by shamanic or helper-spirit clowning.[27]

A few Sakha cases involve the working out of recriminations over the death of a child in families with a practicing shaman. These are hard cases to report and analyze. Confidentiality is a serious problem for ethnographers of personal tragedy. In Siberia, and I suspect elsewhere, pseudonyms are thin disguises so far as the communities involved are concerned. Some Sakha believe that shamans cannot begin their practice without the sacrifice of family members. Siberian shamans have reputations from the Christian and Soviet literatures as being quite capable of terrorizing patients, families, and communities. But several Sakha believers made it clear to me that shamans are not truly great unless they evoke mixed feelings of both love and fear. Analysis of family dramas allows us to see shamans in this more nuanced light. In addition, a strong barrier to the ability of shamans to do harm is the widespread belief that a shaman's ill will or abuse of spirit power can redound against the shaman's loved ones. The force of this local interpretation is precisely why stories about Niikon and Zakharov's rivalry (and other shamanic rivalries) are so compelling and possibly prophylactic.

The contexts in which people who turn into birds are defined as sane and can become community leaders were diminished but not fully demolished in Soviet Siberia. Stories of Sakha shamans escaping from Soviet jails in the form of their helper spirits, including birds, were told through the Soviet period and became popular in the 1990s. Analogous stories of shamanic subversion of Soviet power are told in Buriatia as well (Anya Bernstein, personal communication Sept. 16, 2010). Confessions of both young and old that they regret not having been able to meet the potential of their familial shamanic backgrounds are poignant. But there is a tendency to romanticize "true traditional" Sakha shamans as totally benevolent, priestly, and "white." A fuller historical perspective must confront the implicit menace of Sakha stories about continually avoided shamans' graves, about ravens as bad omens, and about shamanic curses against Komsomol enthusiasts that are said to have affected some families for several generations.

Shamans, healers, and charlatans are all making a living and building reputations in post-Soviet Siberia. Sometimes a prospective patient, anthropologist, or combination of the two, as I have been, has trouble telling them apart. Ancient shamanic techniques, as yet defying "scientific" explanation, are being used in new sociopolitical contexts (compare Atkinson 1989). One modern female shaman reputedly used spirit power to fix a broken bus on the way to a meeting with Native American visitors. Another has built a reputation for finding stolen cars, and still others have been remarkably successful in helping the police find missing people, as we will see in the following chapter. A friend confided that one curer had used "X-ray vision" to discover she was wearing an IUD, this at a time when such contraceptive devices were rare in the republic and my friend had given no clues to its existence. Some healers are also ecology activists, building on their fabled shamanic harmony with nature through helper spirits, meditation, and telepathy.

The eclecticism and openness of current Sakha shamans to other cultural traditions mitigates against any simple correlation of Sakha shamanic revival with Sakha nationalism, another theme explored ahead. Ethnic purity has not been an expressed shamanic goal and efforts to build an official, republic-sponsored "house of purification" in Yakutsk took much spirited negotiation. Shamanism is far from being a "state religion" of the Sakha republic. Nonetheless, shamanic idioms and practices are part of politically salient, conscious cultural vitalization. A new and determined iteration of ethnonational pride is reflected in the romanticism of the focus on "white" priestly shamanism, as healers try to salve the wounds of past cultural and political repression with public prayers and private séances.

Members of the Sakha intelligentsia are debating the degree to which spiritual revitalization should be tied to their ethnicity. As seen in the previous chapter, folklore about competitions between shamans of different ethnic groups, through spirit-helper proxies, makes some Sakha uneasy, revealing past sociopolitical and sometimes warfare-level cleavages among indigenous peoples of the north that they would rather forget. Ethnicity is about selective memory and selective forgetting (Grant 1995; Balzer and Vinokurova 1996; Cruikshank and Argounova 2000). The democratization of shamanism can mean expansion of its appeal beyond ethnic boundaries without rejecting the richness of specific cultural traditions. Sakha writer N. Bugaev (1992), rebutting criticisms of local "neoshamanism" as empty, artificial, and potentially chauvinist, pleaded in a newspaper article, "If a scientist...rejects the right of his people to a spiritual culture, then are we [that people] alive?"

Open Body-Soul Mindedness

Sakha refer to a person who is susceptible to spirit belief, particularly one who could potentially become a shaman and thus mediate among spirit, animal and human worlds, as *ahaghas éttéékh kihi,* or "person with an open body." The urban Sakha scholar who first discussed this with me was an Institute director with a self-identity as a scientist. He expressed surprise that others had not explained the concept sooner for he considered it key to shamanic practice. This is a way of discussing altered consciousness, but "consciousness" is perceived as coming through all pores into the center of one's being, one's *kut-siur*. While few aspire to such a state of simultaneous strength and vulnerability, many Sakha have renewed respect for those who do. Social and political disorientation means increased potential for (or vulnerability to) open, intuitive body-minds.

Anthropologists coping with their disorientations, open-minded to various degrees, could benefit from this tantalizing version of openness, correlating it with anthropological appeals for greater emotional, aesthetic, and experiential sensitivity.[28] My purpose is not to "go native" in some unrealistic or absolute sense but to be part of shifting degrees of mutual, interactive influences that leave their mark in deeply felt, occasionally tearful, multicultural exchanges. As I sacrifice scientific presumption, I gain multisentient rapport and engaged analysis. Syncretic modes of interpretation based on rapport help alleviate the urge to elevate any one theory or model to the realm of the sacred.

Photo 6 Laughter therapy after a *khomus* séance, led by Klavdia Maksimova. Photo by Marjorie Mandelstam Balzer, 1995.

Photo 7 Andrei S. Borisov, Minister of Culture, at epic poetry performance, Gornyi *ulus*. Photo by Marjorie Mandelstam Balzer, 2010.

Chapter 6

Urban Shamans? Unmasking Leadership and Creativity

"I was teased recently for having said to some journalist that we are pregnant with talent. But we are pregnant with talent."
Andrei S. Borisov, Minister of Culture,
Sakha Republic 1992

"People must think and make their own choices, not logically but intuitively."
The late Klavdia I. Maksimova (Saiyyna),
founder Center of Communication 2000

"The aiyy [benevolent white/light] shaman cures people with prayers, with algys, through the help of the gods."
The late Vladimir A. Kondakov,
founder Association of Folk Medicine 2004

Klavdia I. Maksimova, the Sakha leader extolled in the previous chapter for laughter therapy, went on to call herself "Saiyyna" (Summer) and create a group-oriented healing center in an old wooden house at the seedy, industrial edge of Yakutsk, the capital of the Sakha Republic. Over the doorway is a banner "Séhén-séppén bihigi–Kømøluøk," or "We cure with talk-aid." Her Russian gloss, also on the door, is "Tsentr Obshchenie," or "Center of Communication." She is one of four urban leaders highlighted here, as I explain themes of contrasts and convergence in rapidly changing and interacting political and cultural processes. To do this, I branch beyond the usual definitions of "shaman" to explore various styles of creative self-making in the urban spiritual cacophony that is Yakutsk. The leaders profiled each proudly proclaim shamanic ancestry as part of their Sakha "national" identities. However, in conversations with me they have all been leery of being perceived as chauvinist anti-Russian, and only the two who recently passed away (Klavdia and Vladimir) called themselves "shaman."

Political context is crucial. During my early fieldwork in then-Yakutia (a fraught half year in 1986), the concept of nationalism was anathema and cloaked in discussions of "ethnic consciousness." By the time of my fieldwork in 1991 and 1992, however, open political expressions of nationalism were not only acceptable, but fashionable, simultaneously despite and because of the legacy of Soviet propaganda and policy.[1] Sakha nationalism then centered on the formation and consolidation of a new "sovereign" republic, within the federal framework of Russia. In 1992, the Sakha legislature passed a new constitution confirming their identity as the Sakha Republic. In doing so, they were rejecting the compromise "Yakut-Sakha" title they had proclaimed in 1990 by omitting the term "Yakut," which Russians and others had called them for centuries.[2] Their mood was exuberant, but it turned more sober by the 2000s.

In the 1990s, the first leader profiled here led the movement that became the political equivalent of a Popular Front, called Sakha Omuk (The Sakha People). This was Andrei Savich Borisov, the ongoing Minister of Culture of the Sakha Republic and, by 2008, the director of the feature film *Taina Chingis Khana* (*The Secret Chingis Khan*, or in English advertising, *The Mystery of Chingis Khan*). He was an elected deputy to the All-Union Parliament in 1989 until it imploded. His politicization began well before the Gorbachev era, incubating when he was a young acting student in Moscow, and emerging when he became the star director of the main republic theater. In 1986, Andrei's sensitivity to his own culture was evident in the confession that he surely would have been a shaman, a medical and spiritual intercessor for his people, if he had lived in another time. I agreed, for shamanic practice had been the most creative, dramatic outlet for leaders and non-conformists in pre-Soviet Sakha life. Andrei later helped subsidize Saiyyna's center and gave moral support to the Association of Folk Medicine, led by the second Sakha leader featured here, the late Vladimir Alekseevich Kondakov, who died in 2009.

When I first met him in 1991, Vladimir Kondakov had recently moved to Yakutsk from a remote area of Northern Yakutia filled with poverty, hardship, and illness. As a Sakha shaman, he traveled widely to perform curing séances, and he was renowned for his difficult campaign for the legitimation of shamanism. His self-defined mission, to bring shamans together as professionals, pool private and republic resources for revival of faith, and create a school so that shamanism can be passed to future generations without fear, was paradoxical on many levels. Most shamans are loners, competitive, and wary of political activity after long years of experiencing persecution. Vladimir's claim to be a "true" Sakha shaman was controversial among urban and rural Sakha. Yet many believed not only in his powers to cure individuals, but also in his ability to help rejuvenate the Sakha people themselves. For Andrei, Vladimir, and Klavdia, this has been the ultimate goal of their new brands of urban shamanism.

The fourth spiritual activist is a more modest diviner who I met in 2010. With a blossoming reputation, she has become friend, therapist, and prophet for diverse and grateful clients who include Russian police, Sakha elites, and rural poor of various ethnic backgrounds recently moved to Yakutsk. Working from her well-appointed two-story home on the outskirts of town, she met me with trepidation but eventually gave permission for me to write her remarkable story. I begin, however, with the "high-profile" minister.

The Minister

I first met Andrei in 1986 at the Sakha language theater, just before a glittering performance of one of his daring, edge-of-political-acceptability plays. The theater was easily the largest, most impressive building in Yakutsk, with modern sleek white architecture serving as a frame for huge wooden doors carved in ancient swirling Sakha fertility symbol patterns. The play was equally disconcerting, by a well-known Sakha writer, Dmitri Konovich Sivtsev (pen name Suoron Ommolon), set in South Africa about Black revolution against apartheid. It ended in a burst of rock music and dancing, with a rich White girl brandishing a machine gun, after joining the revolution. Ostensibly about a remote Third World rebellion against capitalism and racism, in which issues and people were literally black and white, the play could also be construed metaphorically as depicting complex relations of Russians with their nonwhite indigenous peoples. At least some of the Sakha audience "read" the play this way, but it was 1986, the tentative dawn of the Gorbachev era, and such analysis of Russian colonialism in Siberia was not stated directly.[3] By 2010, Andrei's theatrical exploration of this was more direct.

Andrei's spirituality came from multiple sources, as he revealed in 1992: "When I was born, my grandfather, the one who had taken me in, fed the fire spirit, and at the same time crossed himself and prayed to God. And when I was born, a reindeer was killed. Well, sacrificed. So they fed the fire, sacrificed a reindeer, and prayed to God for me. And so the line of faith, of belief, comes to me from mixed ancestry. This is in general empowering...I was even recently baptized...and I fed the fire before I traveled to America."

Soon after we first met, Andrei proudly called my attention to a symbol he had chosen as the emblem of his theater: a shamanic mask face with three antlers coming out of its crown, taken from the ancient pictographs found on Lena River cliffs. For Andrei and many other Sakha, this exciting cliff art, including runic writing, has revealed ancient Turkic roots of their culture, plus more local shamanic traditions (Gogolev 1986; Okladnikov 1970). "The three antler prongs are reminiscent of old shamanic crown headdresses of iron," Andrei, turning ethnographer, reminded the ethnographer, "but I chose to put different colors on them, white, black, and red...I read somewhere that in ancient Asian theatrical arts these colors stood for the three major emotions of the stage—laughter, tears, and love." The three prongs can also be seen as "tragedy, comedy, and satire," but, Andrei grinned, with wry dig at the Soviet establishment, "we really do not have true satire here." Adding further subtlety to his symbol, Andrei called my attention to the "ambiguous" gender of the face: "The face is male, rimmed with a tiny beard, but it is also very soft and female-like."

Andrei's own mustachioed face is white, kind, and gentle, not as round or dark as that of some Sakha, with almond, but not heavily lidded eyes, framed by long, dark, extravagantly thick curly hair. Given his over six-foot height, he might pass for a European, yet he also looks Sakha. His discussion of gender ambiguity was the first of many times when I found Andrei's thinking or choice of emphasis dovetailed with popular foci in Western anthropology. Clearly I was running a risk of attributing to him concepts that stem from my own philosophical roots, but I used his constant indications of sensitivity and intelligence to explain how kernels of his ideas fit with Western ones. His thirst for cross-cultural comparisons and new slants on old ideas was great. Thus I described the fascination of anthropologists of Melanesia with hermaphroditic symbolism (MacCormack and

Strathern 1980), and I outlined Victor Turner's (1982) ideas of multivocal symbols in the African context. I was rewarded with a further discourse on the multiple meanings of the mask as an *émégét*, a spirit holder-protector. For Andrei, the mask image he chose embodies the spirit of *kumiss*, and of celebration, festival, creativity, beauty, improvisation, and, "above all, Sakha identity."

When Andrei's actors were "struggling over something really hard," he would promise them "we will do *olonkho*." This was a crucial assurance, for actors and audiences alike, since *olonkho* had become a marker of Sakha-ness well before the Gorbachev era. The most famous was *Niurgun Bootur*, mentioned earlier, recorded by the folklorist-poet-revolutionary named Platon Sleptsov, whose pen name Oiyunsky mixed the Sakha term for male shaman with a Russian ending. The epic, featuring a quintessential Sakha hero-warrior, could take one animated storyteller weeks of near all-nighters to enact. Its *olonkho-hut,* often male, changed his voice to take on multiple male and female roles, as tiny attentive audiences gathered round the hearths of isolated Sakha farmsteads.[4] *Niurgun Bootur* was staged by the Sakha theater several times in abridged operatic forms, with much local success and Russian suspicion, but never was done justice in Andrei's eyes. Andrei was searching for a new, less well-known *olonkho* to render into soul-rattling theater. He described why: "*Olonkho* is not a fairy tale. It is not even an epos. It is *olonkho*. It is beyond...simple depictions of good and evil." Instead, "*olonkho* captures details of the beauty of traditional culture, the way a saddle was decorated, the magic of improvisation." For Andrei, *olonkho* had become a synecdoche for Sakha culture itself, and its flexibility.

Andrei was still looking for an *olonkho* to satisfy his own and others' spiritual thirst in the early 1990s. In 1992, he confidently promised actors that he would go into the woods where horses could come up to the windows of his cabin to write a scenario adapted from *olonkho*. Even in the 1980s, his plays became mass séances, and, at their best, they were able to lift the spirits of his predominantly Sakha audiences with a special brand of Sakha identity consciousness-raising. He continued this into 2010, with an inspiring play *Ice Break Up* (*Kømuøl*) mourning intelligentsia repression and celebrating Sakha elite cultural leadership.

By the late 1980s, as perestroika began to take hold, and the first remotely democratic elections for an all-union parliament approached, the theater of "real life" captured Andrei's imagination. He decided, after urging from his audiences and from networks of kin back home, to run for deputy to parliament representing a Viliuisk district. He was easily elected, going to Moscow to become a "liberal" deputy.

Despite the 1989 election, Andrei kept a few theater projects, working with participants at odd hours, including at night. And he eventually agreed to take on the daunting role of republic Minister of Culture, hoping to "change from within" a stultified system. But perhaps his most dramatic and uncharted new role was as one of the founders and leaders of a mass political-cultural movement for the revival of Sakha consciousness, euphemistically called an "informal group" in post-Soviet parlance. The group organized as *Sakha Omuk*, the Sakha People, in 1990, and helped to push through the "Yakut-Sakha Declaration of Sovereignty" in 1990 and the constitution in 1992. Though it started with a base of Yakutsk intelligentsia responding to the ineffectiveness of a local Popular Front, its following quickly spread beyond the city.

Sakha Omuk was not born smoothly, nor was its short life easy. Andrei's satisfaction at the large turnouts for early meetings was mitigated by subsequent ebbs of enthusiasm. "I work from inside, and so I can see how far we are from a real movement. People are still conservative. We seem to be used now to fighting against something, but not fighting for something. The psychology of our people is still too slow." But beyond concern about pushing people toward diverse reforms, Andrei also worried in 1991 about something less tangible. He puzzled over the 1920s history of his people, feeling as if their struggles for a national identity were being repeated in similar terms and debates. He even knew whose role he had taken, as if he were outside of himself, looking on as he himself was "making history": "I seem to be [A. I.] Safronov. It is uncanny. Safronov was responsible for the Sakha theater in the 1920s, and went on from there to lead the national movement. We have the same concerns. And yet, when I look back on the debates, I see that people were too insistent in their positions—so black and white [about revolution versus tradition]...when both positions are correct..."[5]

I was able to observe Andrei's new leadership responsibilities in 1991, after he became Minister of Culture under the first Sakha president M. E. Nikolaev. Andrei was constantly giving awards with speeches, and presiding over prestigious exchanges and conferences. I asked to attend the next meeting of *Sakha Omuk*, and later was included in an excursion across the Lena River in the homeland of Manchari, a Sakha nineteenth-century Robin Hood. Andrei and others explained their people badly needed some relaxation, and that they wanted to do homage to Manchari (with whom I had long been fascinated). Along the way, our bus abruptly stopped in a field at the edge of a forest, where we got out at a sacred tree that had been one of Manchari's refuges. This was the local grove where people leave offerings of ribbons, money, or food. Whenever I was taken to one of these places, I felt awed, grateful, and ready with a purple ribbon to tie on a tree branch. People milled around the tree, a huge, gnarled larch covered with offerings, set inside a wooden fenced area with a neat gate (to keep out animals and make intruders think twice before violating the spot). Nearly everyone placed ribbons on tree branches. The atmosphere was festive, not hushed.

Our destination for the night was an outdoor historical museum complex, next to a small village by a pond, with fields filled with horses and grazing cattle. The privately run museum, partially funded by donations from *Sakha Omuk*, had traditional Sakha houses: an oblong, low winter *balagan* with a thatched roof and mud walls; and a tall, spacious summer *urasa*, the Sakha version of a huge tepee. We feasted in the village clubhouse on fish, meat, pastries, and traditional dairy delicacies at a u-shaped banquet table. We toasted (with *kumiss*, wine, and liqueur), sang, gave speeches of joy at being together, sang, toasted, and feasted some more. The group, with Andrei presiding but not monopolizing, included some of the musicians, actors, and writers who have been the backbone of the Sakha cultural revival movement, and thus the level of singing and poetry was quite stunning. Guitar and accordion were incorporated into rotating performances, as was the jaw harp. Andrei had me listen closely to a song written and sung by Anastassia Varlaamova in honor of her brother who had died in Afghanistan, about grass and its rejuvenation each year, the timelessness of the ecological cycle, and about death and reincarnation. After the banquet, we headed for the more traditional buildings.

It was dusk, and near midnight; we were far enough North for nearly perpetual day at midsummer. Our excursion had acquired the spirit of a midsummer night fest, better than a dream. A fire had been laid in the center of the *urasa*. Andrei and several other *Sakha Omuk* leaders, including our local host, lit the fire and gave the fire spirit an offering of alcohol, with a prayer. The rest of us were seated on the comfortable fur-covered benches built along the rounded wall as people discussed problems of organization and, as the historian Egor Alekseev complained, the lack of reverence most Sakha pay to their own culture and language.

We poured outside in time to see a sunrise on the heels of a sunset, and walked across a field to the smaller *balagan*, where we crowded around the central hearth, and lit another fire. This time, after several other people had made offerings of alcohol and prayer to the fire, it was my turn. Sprinkling liqueur, I said a few words of thanks, but Andrei and others would not let me get away with standard ritual phrases of good wishes. I was asked to comment on *Sakha Omuk* and the republic's newfound sovereignty, and to my own surprise, I found myself mentioning my sorrow at what I had seen of their infighting as well as approval for their strong efforts at language and ritual revival. We walked back across the fields to the club house, for more drinking, feasting, and, since the sun was up, for outdoor *okhuokhai* dancing, celebrating summer, led by a young man with a magnificent undulating voice, who had recently won the *okhuokhai* poetry championship of Suntar at their famed annual *yhyakh* festival.

Weeks earlier, at another *yhyakh* festival by a lake in the distant Viliuisk region, Andrei had asked why I thought *okhuokhai* was so magical, sacred, and persistent through the "ages of Sakha culture." I discussed, like a student searching for the correct response, the beauty of improvisation within set poetic rules and the communal solidarity of hours-long, arm-linked dancing. Not until I mentioned my own feelings of near-mesmerization in the group experience did his eyes light up. "Yes this is it. It provides us with a trance that lets us feel at one with our surroundings and our people."

We constantly returned to the multiple meanings and philosophy of *kut-siur*. Andrei noted, "It is our source, our way of trying to reach the *aiyy* [benevolent spirit forces] inside and outside of us." Andrei has tried to capture a creative manifestation of *kut-siur* by producing *olonkho*. "But it is easy for us to get sidetracked. Re-creating *olonkho* is not enough. We need to take the essence of *kut-siur* and leap with it into the avant-garde... *Kut-siur* is inherent in the nuances of the Sakha language, its many channels, its density. We have an expression that words are more than the person who says them. And that words can come from many winds." Andrei trusts his intuition to understand *kut-siur* as the essence of Sakha-ness.[6] "Sometimes I feel that this comes from here," he smiled, touching the back of his spine. The following year, he elaborated: "It comes close to [Gabriel] Marquez. Not just because life seems like a montage. But also because there is such a strange feeling of premonition. [Premonition?] Well, intuition.

Yes, that. It is called *kiusym karaha*—hidden eye. [Like the shamanic eye?]...No, although it is true the shamans dance with metal attributes on their back, the shamanic eye is more like the eye of reason. And for me, this is the eye of intuition."

Andrei often revisited issues surrounding *olonkho*, Oiyunsky, shamanism, and the theater. Both his interpretation of Oiyunsky's *olonkho*-like "The Great Kudansa" and a separate theatrical biography of Oiyunsky closed with audience-shocking decapitations of his heroes. "The rolling skull is a metaphor of life and death together, and intertwined. Oiyunsky himself was a simple revolutionary. He stood on soapboxes in town squares and beat the drums of revolution. But the poetic language he used, and his style, came straight from shamanic tradition, and it was incredibly effective. He thought he could change the world, but he brought his death on himself...and he very nearly killed the source of his own talent, shamanism."

Andrei's devotion to *olonkho* continued as his marathon stint as Minister stretched into 2010 (as has our friendship). He was able to bring a new version of one of the greatest Sakha epics, Kyys Djebelije, whose heroine is an *udagan* (played fabulously by Andrei's wife Stepanida), to an original Noh theater venue in the Japanese town of Nara, using my friends the Khatylaevs for live shamanic music accompaniment.[7] Before they left, during a rehearsal /break, Andrei took a mystical turn that reminded me of the thwarted Asen Zverev's hopes for composing a rejuvenated epic: "I had a real insight into how the actual technique of *olonkho* works. I was sitting on the riverbank of the Lena with a friend, and yes, we were a bit drunk. Just enough to be in an altered state of consciousness, and I myself started singing *olonkho*. I was singing words I'd never known I knew. Something was pulled up from deep within me. There are entry words with this...D'éé boo is not just a simple sound, but an entry to another world. Same with Dom Dom at the end. Well I sang some of the ancient words and suddenly before me, as if hovering over the lake, was a vision and I barely had time to sing the description of what I saw. This was like a film—it was happening before my eyes. And I think that is what happens with the best of the real singers. So this is our chance to recover it."

In sum, Andrei has long been trying to help resuscitate both shamanic language and shamanic practice itself, as a way to cure the Sakha *kut-siur*. This is why he earlier helped support the Association of Folk Medicine, founded by the shaman Vladimir Kondakov.

The Curer-Historian

Andrei was elected President of Sakha Omuk after a dramatic speech railing against those he considered too bitter, chauvinist, "deformed," and nationalist. He explained in 1991:

> There is another very important nuance here. My heart was beating very fast. When I went onto the podium, I thought I would fall over. [Even you?] The crowd was massive, and in its center sat, I saw, Kondakov. [Ah.] Well, we are relatives. You did not know? I thought you knew. Even very close relatives, very close. And so this uncle was sitting there, and from him, I felt a warmth, a very warm energy. He looked at me—so. And suddenly out from me came a really strong voice. I spoke so that it was impossible not to listen, with such a voice, and such words, I amazed myself. Everyone looked straight at me...[So Kondakov. Did you ever mention this to him?] Yes, he just looked at me and laughed knowingly.

Vladimir Kondakov was a man driven by his curing mission, and unused to being courted by the cultural elite. A Ministry of Culture invitation to join a delegation of scholars—to an international conference on shamanism held in July 1991 in Seoul, South Korea—made him hesitant yet intrigued. The invitation represented a kind of legitimacy that he had wanted and that had been elusive in the Soviet past. Sadly, in this case too, satisfaction was elusive. After agreeing to travel with his drum, perhaps even to give séances in Seoul, he was forced to give up the trip when "higher authorities" in Moscow deemed his visa request too late. The group left without him, thus, so many said, without the one person who would have truly been able to offer international audiences, fascinated by shamanism, a taste of "the real thing."

With shamanic practice, and indeed with most folk curing anywhere, judging "reality" and "success" is a difficult task. In the 1990s, Vladimir asked only that his patients be satisfied, and did not worry too much about his general reputation. But the Sakha grapevine, called the "fur boot telegraph," touted his successes and decried his lack of a visa to Seoul. Vladimir threw himself deeper into activities for the Association of Folk Medicine, the fledgling organization of shamans he founded in 1990. He explained: "Our association should be a loose organization of true curers. We want to build on diverse traditional methods, and also to be able to create new methods of curing...But there are many dangers. We have our own internal conflicts. There is an effort for the association to be taken over by the simple massage artists. Traditional Sakha folk medicine is much more than this. And then there is the alternate danger that the association could be taken over by the adventurists, the con artists. The association has become my struggle."

Vladimir named his organization, which received its government charter April 29, 1990, "from the Presidium of the Supreme Soviet of the Yakut-Sakha Republic," the Association of Folk Medicine, in order to diffuse potential lingering public prejudices left over from harsh propaganda against shamanism. But he called himself a shaman, explaining, "First and foremost I am a Sakha *oiuun*. I am also what the Russians call an 'extrasense' [psychic]. I am both. I like to think of the word *extrasens* in its literal Russian meaning. Someone who has extra feeling. That is what a true curer has. Sometimes I envy those who do not feel very much."

Vladimir tried to establish conditions for curers that would enable them to easily connect with appropriate supplicants and cure in an organized and effective manner. He bemoaned lack of facilities in Yakutsk, and concentrated much of his organizing and curing activities on rural areas. He hoped to impose a new social order on a traditional profession that has been, to outsiders, quite chaotic and competitive, but that has had its own set of customary rules and hierarchies. He pleaded to any who would listen:

"For the growth of folk medicine, we need new and better conditions. We must have a traditional atmosphere, including a hearth, and the ability to have contact with earth. We must be on the ground floor, if we are going to be in a modern building. It is better for us to build new large stone yurts or *balagan*, as was traditional—even in the city. An *extrasens* or *oiuun* on a second floor just does not work. A shaman needs access to upper and lower worlds."

Vladimir agreed to talk to me after mutual Sakha friends called him and explained my interest in his new organization. He generously invited me to an *yhyakh* ceremony the Association of Folk Medicine was sponsoring in the Nam region. Our first meeting was at the home of the Sakha art historian friends with whom I lived, for Vladimir confessed to them over the phone that he did not feel his ramshackle wooden house on the seedy outskirts of town, with outdoor plumbing in the courtyard, was a place he wanted to show to foreigners. The argument that I already had seen plenty of such places did not dissuade him. When I opened our door to him at the exact appointed hour, I was in the role of co-hostess, helping to serve tea and later supper, and Vladimir was in the role of honored guest.[8]

Vladimir discussed the basic goals of his Association: "to establish, study, and put into practice the best traditions and methods of Sakha curing." To test my previous knowledge, and to guarantee that I understood the wide range of traditional Sakha specialists, he asked if I knew that as many as 14 different kinds of doctors, or categories of doctoring, had existed in Sakha communities before the arrival of the Russians in the seventeenth century. We discussed some of these specialists, for instance, the *otohut*, or bone-setter and herbal specialist, from the root *ot*, meaning grasses; the *algyshut*, or prayer and incantation specialist, from *algys*, prayer-blessing; the *kuturukhsut*, or shaman's assistant, who literally helped the shaman not to fall into the fire during trance; the *ilbiihut*, or massage ritualist; and the *ohko køtørkhøørchchu*, or elderly midwife, from the phrase "lifting the child out." Each had continued practices at various levels of secrecy but often in losing competition to Russian or Soviet doctors.

Vladimir emphasized the linguistic gender distinction between male and female shamans, that a man is an *oiuun*, while a woman is an *udagan*. More subtly, he explained: "shamans can tap into and balance energies from the opposite sex." Truly skilled shamans use their gender and that of their patients to counterbalance gendered spirit forces. Thus certain trees, for instance the birch, are considered female, and are used in the curing of men. *Oiuun* and *udagan* move through different levels of skill over their lifetime, and often, but not necessarily, begin as *kuturukhsut*, shamanic helpers. Ranking is informal. Thus lesser *oiuun* are likely to practice bloodletting, bone setting, and predictions of the future. To be an *oiuun*, they should have at least one helping spirit. Middle level *oiuun* have a greater range of skills, and a greater number of helping spirits, acquired through spirit journey trances to both upper and lower worlds of the complex Sakha cosmology. Great *oiuun*, who have always been rare, have wide reputations for knowing hundreds of techniques and controlling numerous animal and other helper spirits. The fire spirit is the crucial entrée, during a séance, to the spirit world.

The goal of this rich shamanic "philosophical system" was, and is, to try "to balance forces of the three worlds, and of evil and good." To help people live in proper balance within the middle world, earth, the shaman must travel (potentially) to nine levels each of the upper and lower worlds. The directions, east and west, are also associated with balance between middle world forces of good and evil. Thus, the West is related to relatively evil spirits and dark forces (*abaaghy*) and the East correlates with relatively benign forces (*aiyy*). "The danger today is that the middle world is destroying itself, and the balances are out of kilter," bemoaned Vladimir. Shamans use the *abaaghy* and *aiyy* for their purposes of balance, to correct local ecological problems, find lost objects, predict the future, see into the past, or to cure an ill patient.

Vladimir's careful explanations of shamanic specialists, hierarchies, and cosmologies correlated well, although not exactly, to what I had learned from others, and had read in works of Sakha ethnographers (N.A. Alekseev 1975; Kulakovskii 1979). I was eager to proceed to more controversial questions, such as how he rated female shamanic power in relation to male. Women were more likely to be lesser shamans, in his view, although certain *udagan*, both historically and currently, had great powers. "I called the well-known female shaman, Zoia Duranova, to try to help take care of my sick daughter," he noted, with sorrow in his voice that I did not understand until later.

On the debate over whether shamans can be divided into "white" (benevolent) and "black" (malevolent) categories, Vladimir answered:

> Few shamans are purely white or black, today or in history...A purely black shaman is especially rare. Most shamans are mixed in the forces they use and in their purposes. They themselves must feel the balance. If they do evil, they will be punished themselves. An evil shaman will be judged at death. This is not only in Christianity. All of nature punishes people who are evil. The Sakha person has always tried hard not to do evil or truck with evil. Sakha are frightened of *sét* [retribution]. This was not their Christianity. This was before Christianity.

Vladimir nonetheless considered the "white shaman" a key to the history of the Sakha people, and a legacy of their roots in Turkic and Mongolic cultures farther south. In this, he agreed that he was following the ethnographer N. A. Alekseev (1975), nicknamed *oiuun* Nikolai. One of Alekseev's main points, quite popular with the Sakha elite, was that the Sakha originally had only white shamans, but gained more evil-doing "black" shamans from neighboring Évenk (Tungus) influences, after Sakha ancestors traveled north. Vladimir's view of "black" shamans was more complex and personal, but he too speculated:

"The white shaman was governmental. He was the leader of his tribe. He opened the *yhyakh* festival with *algys*. He performed white shamanic rituals in service of the cult of the Sky God Uluu Aiyy Toyon, and he was the messenger of this greatest of Sky Gods. He cured, but this was not the main issue. He advocated when to go to war. He was skilled in diplomacy. He predicted the weather; he knew how to save his tribe in emergencies. He was the main advisor to whomever was the main tribal leader, if he was not this leader himself. The first shaman was probably white. His power was from Uluu Aiyy Toyon. But the black shaman was local. Not because he was evil did he become a black shaman, but perhaps because of tragedies and suffering in his life that he tried to counteract. Perhaps a white shaman had hurt him, and he turned to darker powers for help."

This last statement turned out to be revealing, for Vladimir later confessed that he himself had once used "darker forces" for revenge. He had done this in his youth, when he was testing the limits and confusions of his own powers. Apparently, someone had insulted him quite severely. "I did not want to hurt him," Vladimir assured me, "just to scare him a bit. It was one of my first attempts at a séance, and I was by myself. I started near my hearth, dressed in [traditional] clothing and using a drum I had made myself. I did not know what would come of it, but I started beating on the drum and chanting. Soon two beings, exactly, definitely two, appeared on either side of me. I did not know what to think. I even asked myself: "Am I normal?' Most shamans are perhaps abnormal, so the thinking of many people and some scientists goes. But this is just an illusion. My mind was sound. My logic was intact. Indeed I am always psychologically healthy. More than most. So I looked and I saw I was very far from my hearth. It was receding and I came into the house of the man who had insulted me. He was very frightened. I am not sure what I or the spirits did. The next day I came to him in person. He looked at me in horror. I laughed and walked out. To this day, when I see him, he turns away. We do not greet each other. (Laughter.)"[9]

The same evening Vladimir decided to help my friend the musician, ethnomusicologist, and director of the Museum of Music and Folklore, Aiza Reshetnikova, who had a headache and was tense from a very traumatic period of nursing her seriously ill mother. Gently, he asked her to close her eyes, and he stood over her, counting her into relaxation. He slowly moved his hands along her head, spine, and legs, and then around the rest of her body, always keeping them about three inches from actually touching her. He was doing the basic "bioenergy" movement that has become popular among Sakha and Russian folk curers and "extrasenses." He removed "impurities" from her, repeating this process, as I quietly counted, nine times (the most sacred number in the Sakha belief system). He also had her lean way back into his arms twice. With small, and then more expansive hand motions over her chest, he waved away ill "energy." With one hand lightly placed over her eyes, he leaned into her neck, sucking at something, but again not touching her. To bring her out of what was a semihypnotic state, after about 15 minutes, he began rubbing her sore legs, and then had her continue this for herself. He counted with her to bring her back to full consciousness.[10]

While Vladimir's soothing use of "bioenergy" did help Aiza feel better that evening, something he had said to her earlier disturbed her greatly. She described the agony her mother was going through, after what seemed to us all to be a botched cancer operation and late diagnosis. Vladimir's contempt for the local Soviet-style medical establishment was blatant and understandable. Among many other things, standard procedure in Soviet hospitals was refusal to tell patients they have cancer. In this case, the doctor also had to repeat a procedure that he admitted to Aiza had been done improperly the first time. "Poisons" had been building in her body, without being properly "drained." On learning the horrendous specifics of the case, Vladimir said: "Why didn't you bring her to me in the first place? We cannot do anything now. She has already been cut. They have already botched it. We generally do not take cancer patients who have had operations. Most of these so-called modern operations in Soviet-style hospitals fail." He added: "When we have a patient with a tumor, depending where the tumor is and how far along it is, we often effect a cure without any kind of cutting. We dissolve the tumor. We have our ways. This is the sort of thing 'modern' medicine could study from us."[11]

In 1991, the shaman most famous for miraculous cures, including of cancer, was Fedot. Vladimir was in awe of this young man, who he described as potentially becoming one of the "greatest of Sakha *oiuun*," capable of regaining lost credibility for shamanism. Already, said Vladimir, this young man had surpassed him in skill. He was needed for the Association, but was hesitant to join. "He says he has his own territory, and he does not want any conflicts. This is how he has operated from childhood. He does not want anything to do with the city, or the Association." I should travel to him, Vladimir urged, and see for myself, as I subsequently did.

In later conversations, Vladimir, a tall, heavyset, lightly bearded, imposing man, told his dramatic life history: "I was born in the taiga, near a big lake. We lived not far from a village, but separate, as the Sakha used to do. We did not even drink tea, but only *chaga*. Nearby was just one other *balagan*, besides our own solid little house. I had only one older sister. Our family lived very isolated, and I was very separate, alone, as I was growing up." Still in childhood, Vladimir became fascinated by a shaman who lived nearby "in the next field." "D'anna was a middle-level shaman. He did *ilbii* (massage) and knew his herbs. In the Fall, when many were hurt with eye trouble from the dust, he would help them. He also said incantations." Vladimir was encouraged by this neighbor. But he was scared and unsure.

"When I was only four years old, and my elder sister read out loud [the epic] *Miuldu Bege the strong* by Kiuniuk-Urastyrov. I, not knowing how to read of course, completely reproduced the text, in full verse form. People thought I had learned to read."[12] At first, said Vladimir in a newspaper interview (Senkina 1991: 5), "I thought that everyone had such talents, and so it was not really until I was into my thirties that I realized my abilities to hypnotize and to be an 'extrasense.' But even in childhood, I could project and transfer my thoughts onto other people. They did not notice. For instance, I could walk behind a comrade, will him to fall, and have him fall." Vladimir gave up such pranks, but recalled that in childhood, "it seemed as if the trees were breathing, and I could telepathically communicate with them."

Vladimir, feeling the pull of the Sakha past in many directions, decided to become an historian. Through history, he could at least fulfill a love of "the ancient material and spiritual culture of my own people." He studied history and became a schoolteacher, his official occupation for many years of harsh life in northern Soviet villages. As an adult, however, he was inspired by two great curers, especially Igor Gerasimov:

"In 1968, I found Igor Gerasimov...An old woman sent me...People laughed at this, at his kind of curing. It was forbidden. But still, many came...I entered, and many, about thirty, were already there. His *balagan* was stuffed. Only spines were visible. But I heard his voice, a low bass voice, saying: 'Well, it seems a big man has come in.' It took me a minute to realize he was talking about me. The crowd parted and people stared. They waved me to him, and he looked at me with joy in his eyes. 'You are not sick,' he said, 'you will help cure the sick.'"

Vladimir recalled that Gerasimov's homestead was set up to serve many patients. They stayed in a large tent, near his *balagan,* and were served tea at outdoor benches and tables by an elderly woman helper. "I could not sleep that night. The mosquitoes were bothering me, and much else. I saw the old man in the morning, curing a group of people, one after one. I watched him all day, calling his spirits in front of the fire. He asked me to stay, ten days at first, and later in longer sessions." Vladimir, as had many shamans before him, learned that to cure his own ills, he needed to cure others. "Gerasimov showed me everything ... he was a natural hypnotist, a natural curer... But he too suffered from his own powers. If he had been a scientist, he would have been a great one. He managed to cure even tuberculosis, bone diseases, and other serious illnesses. Venereal diseases, even."

Given the atmosphere of repression surrounding shamans in the Soviet period, Gerasimov was careful not to term what he was doing shamanism, or to do extravagant tricks, as was done in the old days. "He lit his fire, and he called his spirits. There was nothing complex, with lots of fancy dances. He did not even have a drum-- they [Soviet activists] had taken it." Gerasimov was also cautious in his relations with patients, who were mostly old and very ill. "He figured out what was ill, where the pain was, and he cleared it up. Afterward, he only asked his patients 'where are you from,' and sometimes he was lazy and did not even ask this. But he also told them to call for him, if they really needed him." Gerasimov himself had been seriously ill only three times, each time associated with an increase in his shamanic powers. "By the end of his life, he had become very powerful, and was making very important predictions about the eighties. But he did not live to see this.... He told me what to do, but to keep it secret. Do not tell anyone until you are forty years old. Then it is your business. Tell your true patients, but do not tell anyone else. Many will be against you. Some will be jealous. Do not take any money. Many will tell you that I am not a shaman, but this is temporary. Indeed, sometimes my own spirits do leave me. And I feel deserted, but each time I get stronger... There will come a better time for shamans, but I am afraid by then there will be few talents left."

Vladimir, while working with Gerasimov, followed the advice of his own spirit helpers and made a shamanic cloak, with dangling iron ornaments to signify the spirits, and a drum. He was never satisfied with the drum that he had made, however, and was thus thrilled when another shaman, Maxim, passed on his own drum to Vladimir, "with appropriate *algys*" and spirit transfers. This inheritance of a drum is not traditional, since drums and clothing of dead shamans are said to belong with these shamans in the afterlife. Some Sakha even voiced suspicions that Vladimir's acquisition of Maxim's drum was possibly dangerous. But Vladimir was convinced of the blessing of the transfer. The drum shortage would not be so critical, of course, if shamans had not been persecuted so severely.

Vladimir's life had its share of tragedy, from official discouragement of his initially covert curing practice and from more personal causes. When I met him, he was grieving for his nineteen year old daughter, who died in 1991, after the family had moved to Yakutsk, where she had been a student at the university. "She was much more talented and wiser than I. She criticized me, and rightly so. She felt her strength, even when she was very young. She had a great mind, and she always made great grades in math. When she decided to go on to Yakutia State in the Russian division, she got great grades there. She read the classics of Russian, knew the Greek classics, and also the Sakha classics: from the Iliad to Ellei."[13] Vladimir called upon the *udagan* Zoia Duranova to cure her, but regretted that he had not called Fedot.

Vladimir's daughter had shown some shamanic tendencies. Thus his sorrow was doubly severe, given how few potentially great shamans were left in the republic. Vladimir blamed the horrible conditions of their Yakutsk housing, including traipsing to an outdoor toilet in the winter, for exacerbating her illness, possibly a liver ailment. By 2004, he was cryptically referring to the inadvertent involvement of "one white shaman" in his daughter's death, blaming a ritual gone wrong. Rumors abounded. Some Sakha suggested his daughter's well-known death could have been the price Vladimir paid for his shamanic practice. Perhaps he had offended spirits in some way (for instance, with Maxim's drum), or he had misused his own powers. The death of family members of shamans, one scholar pointed out, was something that occurred rather frequently in traditional lore. "Once one enters the realm of the *abaaghy*, one pays for mistakes with the lives of loved ones," a frightened would-be shaman declared. Could this be the chilling meaning of Vladimir's daughter in a dream saying to Vladimir, "You yourself know why I died?" I, as outsider-ethnographer, have not been in a position to know, but have been shaken by diverse indications that belief in the dark side of shamanism is very much alive.

Vladimir stressed the long-ignored beneficial aspects of shamanism, with me and in press interviews, although he also warned: "Shamanism requires great study. To use its' power, one must be very careful" (Senkina 1991:5). Calling shamanism "the experience of many generations," he enumerated successes. One heart patient turned out to be the father of Fedot: "I cured his father, and then he believed in his own son." In 1991, with a small "brigade" of folk healers, Vladimir had traveled to the Kobiaisk and Ust-Aldan regions. There they cured four people of painful kidney stones, using a combination of "non-contact massage," and "hypnotism," to "liquidate" the stones (Senkina 1991: 5). The group also used "shamanic secrets," including understanding the natural properties of magnetism, to cure many nervous illnesses. Vladimir explained: "Each folk curer must help everyone toward the good and the sacred, and must fight any powers that interfere with this" (Senkina 1991: 5).

Over the years, I visited the Association's several clean, sparsely decorated clinics. Vladimir's office was adorned with portraits of shamans, including Niikon. I also saw displays in huge bottles of "passed" kidney stones, and observed the use of acupuncture as well as shamanic therapies. Patients seemed pleased, though interviewing them on the spot was awkward. By 2009, the Association's website listed many successes, although problems persisted concerning payment for services and members' dues to the Association.

Vladimir, in the last decade of his life, consolidated his Association of Folk Medicine of 75 members with five shamans, moved its headquarters, wrote many books and novels featuring shamanic healing, and performed in concerts with his wonderful, sonorous, booming voice. Some joked that one ancestor may have been a Russian Orthodox priest, since his singing persona seemed to evoke Christian spiritual style. He was proud that an ancestor, the white shaman Tumus Mékhélé (Mikhail Pavlov), had in 1897 blessed a new Orthodox church in the Viliuisk village of Khampa. His last interviews, and his Association website, constantly stressed his "benevolent spirit shaman" identity, as did his obituaries, for example one that blared: "Vladimir Kondakov Aiyy Shaman has Left Life." He had a degree in psychology and was a licensed hypnotist, to help legitimize his Association. Through the Association, he promoted respect for nature, for Sakha "ancient spiritual traditions," and for Sakha family values. The Association's long list of curing services continues to include "incantations for phases of the planet," and enlistment of help from "the cosmic strength of Aar Aiyy and benevolent earth spirits." In a 2004 interview, he rather sensationally implied that he, as a true *aiyy* shaman, could go beyond the ninth Sky level (where branches of shamanic trees end) to reach the "tenth, eleventh, and twelfth heavens" in an emergency.[14] When Kondakov died in 2009, one of his *algys* was broadcast on the radio:

> Supreme God Urun Aar Toyon looking with magnanimous eyes,
> Always protect; with clemency, good calling,
> Our Body-blood strengthen, cure, brains educate,
> Heads, our brain's every "fiber," long veins of blood vessels clear,

Protect our spirit filled with light, preserving dark breath,
Award with a long life, with opened opportunities
Let life in our Homeland-Middle world be long lasting,
Breath endure! Happiness-well-being come to us!
Generations continue in posterity! Dom! Dom! Dom!

Vladimir compensated for the pain and sacrifices made as perhaps the most famous-notorious shaman in the republic with a sense of mission and balance with the "universe of nature." His confidence in shamanic practices and worldviews was honed by persecution from those he called "little people," those, whether Russian or Sakha, with questionable moral qualities, and those who think shamans are crazy. Somewhat defensively, he reminded: "Shamanism is a great philosophy. Shamans are not stupid. They never were." He made it his life's mission to affirm this, as did the next healer featured here, Saiyyna, whose "Center for Communication" extended Sakha curing philosophies beyond Vladimir's level of experimentation with tradition.

The Curer-Communicator

Klavdia I. Maksimova took the name "Saiyyna," she explained to me in 2000, because she wanted it to evoke fresh summer breezes of renewal and light. She placed healing emphasis on personal intuitions, as my chapter epigraph shows, and yet she wanted her clients to learn to do this first in group, community-building contexts. They needed to reach back to their Sakha roots with pride, and reach into themselves for special Sakha abilities to go into trance (*turuk*) to heal themselves. Her own abilities and charisma, I learned after her death, derived in part from her Suntar heritage as one of shamanic singer Sergei Zverev's many "illegitimate" children.

Saiyyna's small office-therapy room in her center had a mirrored floor, cut into a mosaic river pattern, with river rocks along the edge. The walls were gauzy purple and blue, part paint and part material. The effect was a disorienting, yet calming space that she augmented with soft taped Sakha music. Saiyyna called this her "room of psychological unburdening."

Stories often swirl around successful healers with powerful personalities, and Saiyyna was no exception. Several friends, learning of my interest, mentioned a rumor that Saiyyna had managed to get her problem son exonerated from a murder accusation in the mid-1990s by the unlikely conjuring of a judge, and similar gossip haunted her reputation even after death. An important aspect of Saiyyna's reputation is that she herself became ill in the late 1990s. When a curer cannot cure herself, people start to gossip, but in Saiyyna's case she recovered beautifully (until 2009). When we talked in 2000, Saiyyna was wearing a long traditional brocade dress, with an elaborate headpiece. She was on break from monitoring a group trance session. Having recently celebrated her fiftieth birthday, she looked a bit more gaunt, and more regal than she had in the mid 1990s.

Saiyyna explained that she had been leading courses since 1989, with about 3,000 selected students going through some version of her séances, for which she usually charged a small fee. Her mostly Sakha students resonated with one of her main messages: "I strive for the self-awareness of my own nation: for us to understand and utilize the full potential of what is given in our genes, from our ancestors. Every nation should be a product of self-being according to their own direction."

Saiyyna consistently made the case for special Sakha conditions of spirituality, based on the "Triad of Cosmos-Person-Land": "This land, the medicinal herbs, the food, the water, this wonderful Nature of ours, is what gives us our special energy." For Saiyyna and many of her loyal followers, this energy derives from the natural beauty, resources and ecological balances of the North. Followers acclaim that "the interrelationship of energies is especially potent here."

In 2000, I encouraged Saiyyna to brag about her curing successes: "At the finale evenings [of our two week courses], I see joyousness. They come in dark, with burdens, closed and depressed. At the end, they are all lit from within. Their souls are lightened. It is wonderful to talk with them. I think there is a potency here, from...what they do for themselves with my help. They say they have a better microclimate in the family, more communication...better creativity, and some have grandiose plans for new creative projects. They have better health. They begin to test themselves, in poetry, in drawing. They have better dreams, and remember them better."

Saiyyna offered to let me hear such testimonies directly, escorting me into a large cheerful room trimmed with freshly cut wood, with a Sakha hearth in its front corner. A séance of *turuk* was just ending for 28 people, in their ninth of ten therapy sessions. The *turuk* was not a drum-induced trance, but rather a "visualization" on a theme, with discussion afterward of what people had envisioned in a "waking-dream" state. The group of mostly women was effusive in their praise for the sessions, their morale, and their enhanced, interrelated creative, psychological, and physical health. One striking therapy was that they were drinking sun-drenched "energy water" from jars on the windowsill, but had no afternoon meal during their daily sessions. Many had lost weight and were feeling refreshed. No one mentioned feelings of faintness or panic during a session, though I had heard from outsiders that this occasionally occurs. Later, Saiyyna's assistant said that if anyone had trouble during visualizations, the group, or Saiyyna, was usually able to calm them down.

During *turuk*, some uncover reincarnation histories, a phenomenon better known among the far northern, indigenous Yukaghir than the Turkic Sakha. "I have lots of reincarnation cases," Saiyyna explained. Examples included "a man who had been born in England in another century. And a woman who had been with Napoleon as some sort of general." ["She was a man?" I asked.] "Yes, a man, a warrior. Though she had no interest in history, she knew amazing details."[15] Saiyyna mentioned that one person remembered living several times, with different genders. "Some lived here in Yakutia, some lived in the North, one lived in Vietnam. In this life, sometimes something ties them back... Also, those who had drowned in the previous life are scared in this life of water. Or those who experienced fires are scared of fires. When people are freed of these traumas during our séances, they are cleansed. Then normal orientations can grow."

In a striking case, "one woman was a very loud snorer. She also wanted to sing, and had trouble singing, with her throat somehow constricted. But during our sessions, she found the core of her darkness. She saw her own home from another time on fire, and her close ones were in the house. She understood that the fire had been set, specially, and then she was shot in the neck. This scene of terror was a reenactment of something she had been through in another life. So our reincarnation theory helped her, and she already has not snored in her sleep for an entire year. And she has regained her voice, she can sing."

Back in the office, I reviewed patient comment books and several photo albums, and interviewed two more satisfied consumers who had arrived [spontaneously?] to register for advanced courses. They did not include reincarnation experiences in their narratives, and I realized that, while Saiyyna had intrigued me about this, I had a very incomplete sense of their proportion and significance in the therapy.

The photo albums included pictures of Sakha celebrities who had taken the course or visited the sessions. Some of the funniest posed pictures were of people clowning on a bed of broken bottle glass that I had seen in the courtyard. They walk, lie, and even pose in acrobatic groups on the glass chunks. On my way out, Saiyyna's assistant and an elderly female client were very happy to show me how they walk on glass in bare feet. "You can do it too," they encouraged. But I declined, feeling a bit off-balance.

In sum, Saiyyna's discourse was more blatantly nationalistic than most of my friends, but was a strategic morale builder. She included among her supporters in the past ten years not only Andrei but also the Khatylaevs. I continually found people who had taken her courses and felt "opened up" by them. By 2010, her followers had been awarded a prime spot near the gates of the city *yhyakh* grounds, and during the two-day celebrations were purifying all who entered their compound with birch wands, prayers, and smudging. Her Center lives on without her.

The Diviner

Natalia Dmitrievna Ivanova is a popular diviner who represents both a growing trend and an ancient aspect of shamanic talents. According to her eclectic clientele, she is particularly successful at prophecy and individual-oriented therapies without performing full-fledged "séances." I had heard of her for several years, and was able to meet her through her friendship with the Khatylaevs. Interestingly, her home and work base is near the state-of-the-art Austrian-built modern medical complex at the most accessible edge of Yakutsk. It is a big renovated wooden house filled with paintings and a yoga-meditation room; a separate bathhouse with small swimming pool adorns the courtyard, as does a ceremonial *sergé* and a colorful *ger* (felt covered yurt) mail-ordered from Mongolia.

Rapport came easily as I noticed a photograph of the legendary shaman Niikon in the front room, and a painting of the Himalayas imitating a Roerich. Natalia and her husband came from the Tatta region, and moved to Yakutsk in 1989. But her opening to spiritual life did not occur until 1998, when their home near the Lena embankment flooded and they lost everything. Earlier, she had stomach troubles, went through an operation that left her weak, and had other strange illnesses. But she never associated this with "shamanic illness," and did not understand real spiritual trauma until 1998. I asked if she thinks of this as *éttéétén yald'ar*, and she demurred: "I don't know what it was...but spirits are helping me. I don't know who or how."

She emphasized that she came to healing late, and without real training by a living shaman. She had been an orphan with a difficult childhood, and later a postal worker. "I consider myself not an *udagan*, but a healer (*émchité*) and seer (*kørébété*). I don't feel comfortable being called a shaman. People are scared of shamans." Only when pressed did she admit: "People do call me now, from everywhere for help. And much of my work is in Moscow." As others had mentioned, at least some of her clients in Moscow are from the Ministry of Internal Affairs and the ordinary police, trying to find missing people. We were talking in the bathhouse, away from her bustling household, when she received a phone call from a local Sakha family who wanted her to identify the killer of their relative whose body had just been found in Yakutsk. I found this intriguing in light of recent local paper headlines blaring that crime was down in the republic. She would not generalize but said she would try to help them. She confessed that she worries some of her clients may be trying to stay one step ahead of the police: "I try not to take jobs where I think missing people are mixed up with the mafia. But sometimes it cannot be helped—it just turns out that way."

One missing person case was particularly vivid: "a guy who had been drinking and sleeping around had completely disgusted his wife, who wanted nothing more to do with him. And his brothers were out of town, probably in Moscow trading or something. So he disappeared without a trace and it took months to find him. His brothers returned and could not find him. Because of his lifestyle, people thought he was probably off on a drunk or with some woman. But the brothers finally found me...I visualized that he was dead and told them to go to the police station of a particular place. There they indeed learned that the body, in a terrible state, had been found, no one had claimed it, and thus it had been buried in an unmarked grave. The brothers dug him back up and took him to their own place."

Natalia said that she had long been scared of "spiritual things" and way too poor to take training courses in Moscow as an "extrasense," as Vladimir Kondakov had done. Later in the courtyard, I asked about techniques of her healing and visualization work, and she replied: "I cannot tell you everything. I cannot even explain it in words. But I see columns of air canals." She jumped up and motioned to the air and nearly hugged it, gesturing as if there was an invisible *sergé* before us, not just the wooden hitching post. "It is as if paths to the sky or other worlds are open to some people and not to others, that others do not see with ordinary eyes...It is not a trance, and definitely not hypnosis...It is just a different way of seeing and being in the world." She described a kind of telepathy, aided by spirits that enable her to see into people: "I just know that I can see things in people. Sometimes I can tell people that their worries will go away, and they do." I recalled a mutual artist friend, worried about an upcoming trip to America, who Natalia had reassured. Suddenly Natalia grinned: "Or I can predict future wealth." I recalled another friend, whose restaurant business was just beginning, being flabbergasted when Natalia predicted it would flourish—and it has. This friend had described Natalia's odd preferences for scheduling "prophecy sessions" only at certain times of the month and certain days of the week. Natalia confirmed: "Some things I can only predict on Fridays—I don't know why."

Natalia stressed that she uses her intuition to decide whether to take clients. She often rejects people, and sometimes refers them to others, including the official medical establishment down the road. I asked for other examples of cases she has taken. "One time there was an unborn child—in her mother's belly already at [an advanced] stage and the doctors said the child was abnormal. The mother panicked, called me and asked if I could visualize it. I said that the child would be fine, and the next day the doctors looked again with their fancy machinery and saw that sure enough the child had turned and was functioning normally. The mother was thrilled." Here, Natalia had not intervened, merely seen, as she explained, the equivalent of a time-dimensional CAT scan.

Natalia's husband of 38 years, V., who supports her in her work and often accompanies her to Moscow, helped orient me to the eclectic symbols of their home, where Russian Orthodox, Buddhist, and Hindu iconography comingled. "All these spiritualities are valid. We've lived with Russians for over 300 years. Most important, we've kept our own, our own sky gods (Tangara), together with the others. I think in the end it is all about one thing—respect for higher powers."

Natalia's roots make her especially respectful of the legendary Tatta shaman Foma Chashkin and his son Mikhail, a tractor driver turned curer: "Foma helped me directly. One time I was coughing and could not stop. It was really bothering me but we could not figure out what to do. I was half-sleeping and felt a kind of kiss on my back. I saw V. was curled on the other side of the bed sleeping—couldn't have been him. I thought it was odd but went back to sleep. The next morning I got up and made *alady* [pancakes, sometimes used in spirit offerings]...and saw in the kitchen window a huge bird—raven-like. I quickly also made porridge to address him and offer it to him but was completely confused...I said: 'My big brother, if you have come to help me, please do. Tell me what you want...' I wasn't connecting any of this to the coughing. But that same morning some friends, other curers, came over... I was happy to see them, and asked if they saw anything unusual in the window... [One] said yes, but I wasn't sure if I believed him, since he didn't describe it. Then I stopped coughing and made the connection—I remembered that Foma Chashkin had a big Raven as his totem. [His *iié kyl*?] Yes, yes, his *iié kyl*. I checked later with Mikhail, describing the bird and its talons closely, and Mikhail said, 'yes, I had probably seen his father, who had come to help a poor countrywoman from his home region.'"

Natalia in one fell swoop confirmed with this story the vibrant significance of birds (especially raven), of the "mother beast" *iié kyl* (see previous chapter), plus the reputations of the deceased Foma and very much alive Mikhail (see ahead). She also correlated the word "totem" to the *iié kyl* with no knowledge of contentious anthropological literature about "totemism."[16] Further, her life history elegantly bridged rural and urban spirituality. My fascination earned me an invitation to her birthday party the following Saturday.

I arrived with the Khatylaevs in time to help with massive preparations for a sit down event of around 50 people, mostly friends, family, and clients of Natalia. As a brigade of women turned out Russian-style salads, a more gender-mixed group of us labored over four enormous bowls of the Sakha delicacy *kerchek*, a whipped cream and berry confection. Raw and cooked fish, Buryat-style dumplings, meatballs, grilled meat, cakes, bread, fruit, and waffles eventually completed the sumptuous table. People of all ages and presents of all shapes began pouring in. Natalia was everywhere greeting guests with glee and directing the placement of huge bouquets of flowers. At the last minute, Natalia, who had changed into Sakha long-gowned finery, decided to scale down the ritual she had planned to greet people. This was directly related to her surprise that one of the guests, a professional TV journalist, had turned up with a cameraman. She had not expected documentation of her "modest" birthday. Instead of a formal, long poetic *algys* and fire feeding by the ceremonial post, she simply welcomed everyone and said she was happy to have such dear guests share her special day, and that her family was blessed by the wealth of so many friends when she had grown up quite alone. After feeding a small open fire with quiet prayer, she turned over the welcome to the professional pop singer Anatoly Burnashev, dressed in a sequined green shirt, and also to a professional toastmaster, Klim Fedorov, a large Sakha man with booming voice, ready smile, wearing a white outfit with Chinese calligraphy on it. Natalia slipped off to change into more simple dress.

The guests were from varied occupations, our toastmaster joked, from cattle raisers to sports and music stars, from elite administrators to "the mafia." Folklorist colleagues also arrived, and as I learned how diverse everyone's birthplaces were, I realized that the "class" and "regional" cross section of Natalia's networks was indeed extraordinary. Only one obviously Russian red-headed client had come, bearing gifts of two huge porcelain animal sculptures (a bear and tiger), and speaking only Russian when everyone was speaking Sakha. He said that Natalia had done a great service to his family without elaborating. I landed next to a retired Sakha judge, his wife, and their lawyer guest. Opposite sat several of the best known musicians in the republic, and their musical toasts and jamming set the celebratory tone.

The judge, a former employer of Natalia from Tatta, had refound her when his friend Vladimir Kondakov recommended her for a personal problem. As he explained in a public-testimony-style toast, "I went to the address I'd been given, and was amazed to find that the Natalia I'd been referred to was my own past employee. I had my doubts. How had she become a seer? She had not been like that when I knew her: just a simple Sakha lady. So I tested her. She said that I had a dent in my car, and said what side it was on. How had she known that? She had not seen the car. So I decided to trust her, and we've become friends ever since."

Others had diverse stories of psychological and spiritual help from Natalia. One journalist from the main republic paper spoke at length of the "spiritual crisis" that we are all facing, "as serious as any economic crisis." She emphasized that people like Natalia were crucial in these troubled times. A friend who had helped with food and brought her extended family toasted her friendship with Natalia as the key to her survival in town, since she had first arrived lonely and confused from her rural home village. Her toast dwelled on our connection with Nature and with other worlds that Natalia opens up for people, enabling them to share in Natalia's spirituality as well as hospitality. A woman who runs the travel agency that Natalia and her husband regularly use, and who runs tours especially to China, spoke of a time when for two days a tour group was stuck in an airport in China because the airport in Yakutsk was closed due to cold, ice, and fog. She had called Natalia in panic, Natalia had calmed her and then called the airport. Soon after the weather cleared.

The toastmaster who was orchestrating people's speeches and keeping the alcohol flowing also kept up a fine banter, sometimes teasing people about their diverse local (*ulus*) backgrounds and their names. At one point a call went out—how many are from Tatta, how many from Churbacha, how many from Verkhoyansk? People enthusiastically raised their hands, claiming their sometimes quite far off homelands and noticing each other.

No one spoke openly of lost and found bodies, but one administrator with serious responsibilities (ministry not named), explained his panic when he discovered he had lost a briefcase of documents, signed and needing to be delivered. He appealed to Natalia, who figured out he had left them on a bus, and helped him recover the valuable papers before his bosses found out. At least two toast narratives concerned Natalia's predictions of political winners. Since elections are no longer held for republic president, by President Putin's notorious decree of 2004, everyone had been in considerable suspense over the Moscow-derived appointment of the newest President in summer 2010, and whether he would be Sakha. A friend related with amazement that the previous New Year's Eve Natalia had named as a soon-to-be President Egor Borisov, the Sakha leader whose inauguration I had only just attended. In January calling him a "dark horse" would have been an understatement since the Russian president of the republic, Viacheslav Shtyrov, had not yet officially resigned.

We grabbed a ride home from a businesswoman of mixed Russian-Sakha background, who was driving a new, gold-colored, four-wheel-drive Japanese car. She had founded her own arbitrage company that negotiates bankruptcies for people. I had not realized such a niche existed in Yakutsk, but recent economic instability has made this not only logical but crucial (compare Kendall 2009). An economist by training, she turns to Natalia for therapy, consultation and help when things get rough. "I don't have any big miracle stories to tell you, like some of the others. But I can say that she has been a great friend and confidante when I need it, including about my children. I come to her for help and purification."

Natalia herself blessed and purified us with a horsehair wand (also used to deter mosquitoes) as we left. She gave me a small birch bark human figure, gender ambiguous, which she spat on, breathed on, and put on the back of my hand, as she murmured an *algys*. The figure has arms raised in supplication, and her prayer was "to ensure you will be well and have success in your work." Natalia's birthday bash is an annual event, a way, she explained, to show her friends and supplicants her appreciation, as well as the other way around. Its reciprocity revealed a stylish, ritualized partying, and *ad hoc* community leadership.

Leadership Legacies

Who shapes the sacred and its interpretations, in the post-Soviet world? The premises behind this question earlier would have been reviled by Soviet scholars and many Siberians themselves. The revival of shamanism in Siberia was laughed at as an impossible dream by some, and a ridiculous nightmare by others. But striving for identity through spirituality has become popular in a society starved for the sacred and its reconstruction. In the broadest sense, new concepts of "sacred" emerged in the 1990s as Siberian leaders redefined who they wanted to be. Many, like the "urban shamans" featured here, learned to derive spiritual and intellectual sustenance from their past, discussed and debated predominantly but not exclusively in "ethnic" terms. Creativity has permeated their vocabulary and their consciousness. They have not been paralyzed by nostalgia, nor have they been sticklers for traditional rules. Because of their adventurous flexibility, these leaders are to various degrees controversial with their own people. Yet this same flexibility enabled them to shape themselves into effective leader-shamans. This unfinished process has been fascinating to watch, yet sometimes painful for participants, seriously painful. Natalia provided insight into the amorphousness and possible spreading of something like "shamanic illness" when I asked her a second time about *éttéénei* and she replied, "Doesn't everyone have *éttéénei* to some extent?"

Leaders inspire. Yet take-me-to-your-leader ethnographers searching for noncontroversial "representatives" of a given people's elite search futilely. Leadership is constantly, refreshingly opposed, unless it is imposed by force or spiritual terror, thus conforming only to the narrowest, least productive definitions of leadership (compare Bohannon 1960; Marcus and Fischer 1986; Smith 2008). Traditional shamans were also controversial. Indeed, labels of "black" and "white" shamans have long had as much to do with who is doing the designating as with particular rituals or intents attributed to these prominent, now legendary, figures. In this context, it is understandable that a diviner would deny the label "shaman" because she does not want to scare well-paying, mixed ethnic clients away. As a "seer," she is also the most nervous about bad publicity.

Although only two of the cultural trendsetters profiled here term themselves shamans, they all have found relatively open and inspiring ways to influence hearts and minds in new and troubling times of mixed ethnic diversity and Russian hegemony over the top political leadership of the republic. No matter how international they have become, each of these extraordinary people have deep roots in Sakha rural spirituality and they have tried to share this through sometimes spectacular bursts onto the urban stage. Not all are healers in a direct sense, but all have sought ways of building diversely defined community in an urban environment of geographically scrambled people yearning for reconnection to their "mini-homelands," their native *ulus*.

Shamanic thinking provides an ideal medium for the message of creative anti- and post- Soviet leadership, given its legacy of being persecuted and its inherent spirituality. The leaders described here have used this medium to further the healing of their people. In over 20 years of public personas, Andrei and Vladimir became more than merely the Minister of Culture (official) and the Minister of Health (unofficial) in a society of victims preoccupied with official face. In the past decade, Saiyyna and Natalia became more than curers helping individual clients or supplicants. As legitimation of shamanic practice and spirituality proceeded, Sakha confidence in their ability to revive their most valued cultural legacies increased. Shamanism, like *olonkho*, for many became synecdoche for and symbol of the richness of the Sakha past.

Can this be translated effectively into today's contexts and terms? I probe this question further in the next chapter exploring generational differences in community and personal curing. The reputation of shamanic healing may have hit a peak by the end of the 1990s, and declined somewhat thereafter. The beloved founding president of the Sakha Republic, the elected Sakha Mikhail Nikolaev, openly consulted healers including the versatile Alexandra Chirkova. By the early 2000s, President Putin's appointed Russian "president" of the Sakha Republic Viacheslav Shtyrov was far more embarrassed than pleased by the reputation of the republic as "shamanic." Sakha are watching to see whether the third president, Egor Borisov, will provide any moral or material support for "traditional" medicine or shamanic creativity labeled as such.

For many Sakha, as for other post-Soviet peoples shopping for diverse models in a politically porous world, it is "potentially a highly creative moment, one whose essential relativism forces us to recognize and reconsider the moral basis of our cognitive outlook that is so often masked by taken-for-granted communicative conventions. It is an equally dangerous moment for it can always stimulate backlash" (Crapanzano 1991: 438). The internal dissent that I rashly criticized at a late-night *Sakha Omuk* ritual was part of an emergent brokering of national images and eclectic spirituality. By 2010, leaders of *Sakha*

Omuk were planning a major celebration of the anniversary of their founding. Anthropologists and national leaders can all try, without homogenization, to respect the spirituality of *algys* and *olonkho* and, as Andrei once suggested, "to take the essence of *kut-siur* and leap with it into the avant-garde."

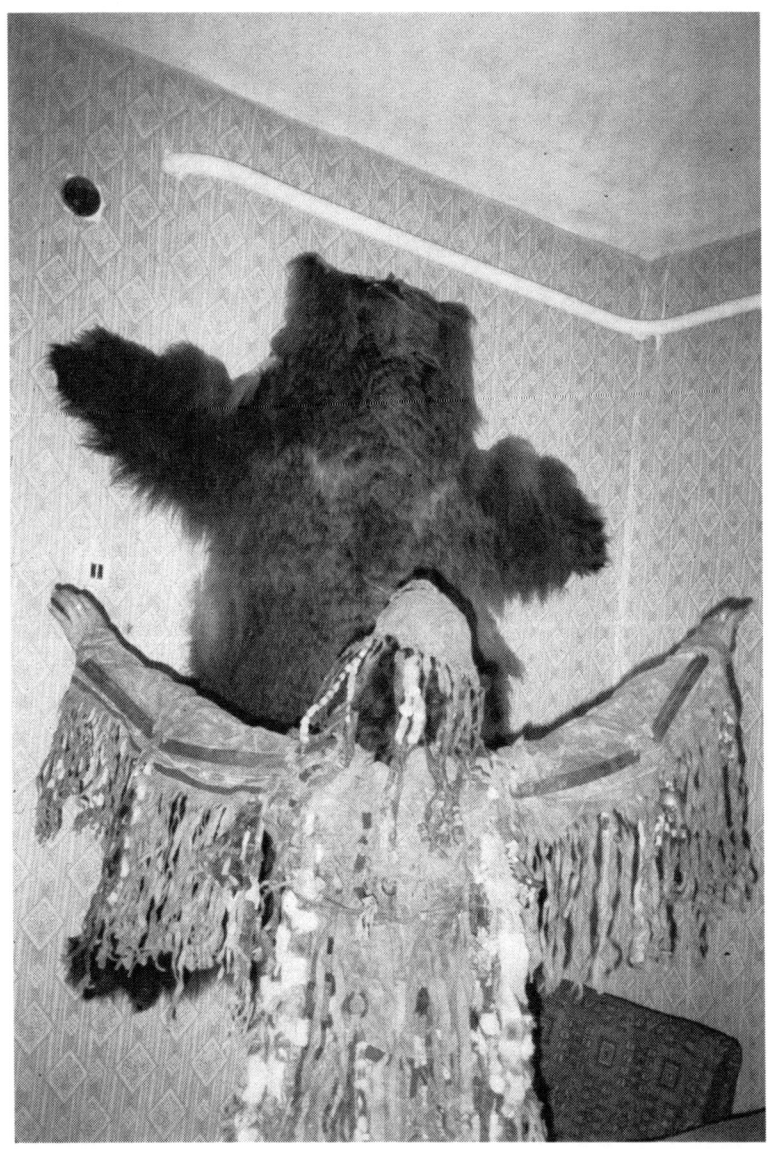

Photo 8 Aleksandra Chirkova, wearing the cloak of her deceased father Konstantin *oiuun*, Abyi *ulus*. Photo by Marjorie Mandelstam Balzer, 1993.

Chapter 7

Sustainable Faith? Multiple Generations of Healing and Spirituality

> *"I had acquired a new gift, the ability to see through a person into their illness."*
>
> Aleksandra Konstantinovna Chirkova, head doctor of Belaia Gora, daughter of Konstantin *oiuun*, 1993

> *"If you really want to be cured... then you must get rid of those two bottles that you hid along the way here."*
>
> Chaashka *oiuun*, in a former patient's 2002 recollection attributing clairvoyance

> *"Niikon taught me a lot. He taught me how to find healing herbs and how to mix them in appropriate doses. He gave me my drum and instructed me in how to gather important components of my cloak [through spirit communication]."*
>
> Fedot Petrovich Ivanov, 1991

While the most creative, forward-looking Siberian leaders publicly may not indulge in it, nostalgia is rife in Siberia for the pre-Soviet days when powerful shamans, in control of a panoply of spirits traveling across multiple layers of the universe, could cure patients during deeply dramatic and transforming community-wide séances. Poignant stories abound of lost knowledge: the shaman who died knowing where a special plant that could have cured his cancer was located, "just at the edge of the village airport," and just beyond the edge of our current medical practices and perceptions. Another depicts the shaman who died several days before a repentant Soviet doctor returned to probe the healer's renowned, yet earlier rejected, understanding of an illness known in the ethnographic literature by the infelicitous term of "Arctic hysteria" (*menerik* in Sakha and Russian). Such stories are told and retold with sorrow by the Sakha, and they can be understood on multiple levels.[1]

For many elders and some youth, such accounts sustain faith as well as place it in distant temporal and spatial perspective. Sakha in numerous conversations yearn for the reincarnation of named hero-shamans of previous generations, who could recognize a medicinal plant from its life-force vibrations, knew as well when to harvest it at its peak, how to prepare it, and, as important, how to ask permission from local spirits for its removal by giving a token offering in return. Yet discourses of disaster are deceiving, for a strong and, I argue here, effective revitalization of shamanic healing has become a crucial part of larger processes of cultural recovery. As we saw in the previous chapter, the post-Soviet period has led to considerable personal and social transformation for many Sakha. While acknowledging the seriousness of Soviet repression of shamans, analysts should also consider that mourning a previous generation's lost esoteric knowledge and spirituality may be a pattern that goes back at least through the nineteenth century, when shamans were hounded and denigrated by Russian Orthodox missionaries.[2]

As a new generation of healers has turned to elders and spirits for guidance, some exciting (for healers, patients, and ethnographers alike) accounts of "miracle cures" have begun to supplant the litanies of loss. This chapter features three sets of healers of two generations. Each set is imbued with human and/or spiritual kinship. All are well known in the Sakha Republic, with varying degrees of controversy, rumor, and confidence swirling around them. In each case, I know or have worked with only the younger generation, since the generation of legendary hero-shamans has passed in the biological sense, though not spiritually. Through examination of generational differences, shamanic approaches to spiritual healing processes and transformation are also analyzed, using specific descriptions and epistemologies of cures in their cultural contexts. A key and often explicitly stated task of the healer is to stimulate a patient's own potential to self-cure, using an integrated body/mind approach, activating that "Heart-Soul-Mind-Body" termed *kutsiur*, as stressed in earlier chapters, through the healer's intuition and "radical empathy."[3]

The first set of healers profiled here is the family of Konstantin Ivanovich Chirkov, who is also reverently called the "Elder of Abei region" and "Konstantin *oiuun*." He is renowned for "miracle cures," and for his empathy and tact under extreme conditions of

Soviet repression. It was at his urging that his daughter, Aleksandra Chirkova, became a Moscow-trained surgeon and the head doctor of her northern region. After age 50, she returned to the shamanic healing traditions of her father, incorporating spirituality into her therapies selectively and creatively, depending on the patient. A second family of healers is that of Foma Petrovich Chashkin, whose two sons have increasingly openly been seeing patients in their rural Tatta region, after years of hiding their inherited shamanic gifts and the spirit-torment that constitutes Siberian shamanic initiation. The third set is linked by apprenticeship and spiritual communication, since the shaman Niikon (Nikon Alekseevich Vasilev, of the Viliuisk region) is said to have passed on his legendary abilities to the young shaman Fedot Petrovich Ivanov, whose fame began this book. The chapter reveals an interplay among Sakha principles of shamanic healing gifts that are inherited genetically, like musical talent, yet activated spiritually and cultivated with training.

Konstantin and Aleksandra: Adapting "The Healing Gift" to Fit the Times

Aleksandra shared with me in 2000 a curing event that she considered best illustrated her father's colossal talent as simultaneously a "white shaman" and "psychotherapeutic master." She later featured the story, related by the son of the patient, in a memoir honoring her father (2002: 211–213). I begin with her voice, told with the authority of a licensed surgeon who later decided cutting into people's heads was unbearable:

> One Spring a Sakha hunter who was a friend of father's went blind, probably from the glare of the sun on snow. Possibly the nerve endings in the brain that guide vision were affected, or it was a kind of spasm. In any case, nearly a year passed and he requested Konstantin's help. Konstantin prepared him psychologically by asking the family to please find an Arctic white owl, within the next three days. Konstantin promised to return with his cloak, drum, and assistants for a séance, if only the owl could be found. "How can we?" fretted the hunter's family, for he was inactive and his son was too young. "Do your best," said Konstantin, "even if it is not alive, we will manage." Soon after, the hunter's wife found that a frozen owl somehow had landed on their sled. They worried that the owl was dead, but when Konstantin arrived with his entourage and drank tea with the family, he said "it will be fine."' They prepared the room for

the séance, placing the owl near the hearth. The old hunter sat near the fire as Konstantin began drumming, dancing, and calling his helper spirits. One moment, he was drumming close to the hunter's ear, and took his drumstick, whooosh, and made a whistling sound nearby...

The account of the hunter's son, a witness, continues:

> About midway through the séance, Konstantin took up the owl and put it on his knees, stroking it and saying incantations. I sat near him and with amazement watched his every move. I saw that the frozen owl had come to life, was scratching, and had taken flight. "Bai, what happened with that bird, look where its flying," exclaimed Konstantin. The owl, flapping its wings, was flying around the cabin, and then flew up the chimney. Konstantin continued long in his singing [in Sakha, *kuturuu*]. His assistants took two frozen boards from the yard and hit him in the kidneys. They took an ax and beat him ... as they held it, the shaman licked it, ran his hands over its blade. It was horrible. ... The shaman licked hot strips of wood from the fire and licked my father's eyes, [then...] bound [them] with a dark cloth. [Konstantin] told him to open his eyes by slowly and carefully unbandaging himself only on the third day. ..."You will at least see your feet..."And on the third day, my father made it to the open door and took off the bandage. Opening his eyes, he cried several times "I can see," and he wept for joy.

Aleksandra explains that the Arctic white owl is sacred, not to be killed. Thus the hunter was primed to be thrilled that his family avoided having to kill the bird: its appearance was a blessed sign. Its revival and flight during the séance created conditions for a still more intense epiphany for the hunter, who so wanted to see, and for his extended family, who all rejoiced at the sharp-eyed owl's recovery. They were in a state of spiritual astonishment, possibly group trance and certainly group solidarity, caused by the drama of drumming, the rhythm of dancing, poetic mantra-like incantations evoking nature, as well as the palpable presence of spirit helpers. All this was compounded by the adrenaline (and endorphin?) stirring excitement of shamanic exploits, aided by Konstantin's helpers.[4] The séance lasted well into the night and was perceived by attendees as a miracle, the epitome of a "benevolent spirit shaman's" negotiation with the spirit world. Aleksandra wonders if the bird was really an owl, and if the group was not under mass "hypnosis." She notes that ophthalmologists recommend waiting three days after an eye injury to remove bandages and that Konstantin's licking probably had medicinal, purifying value precisely because he licked a hot stick first. Yet she too has had her own spiritual epiphany, after moments of self-doubt, "shamanic illness," and yearning to be guided from realms of the dead by her father, who was born in 1879 and died in 1974.

In childhood, Aleksandra had notorious symptoms of shamanic illness, called in the Sakha language *éttéénei* or *éttétén yald'ar* as we have seen. Aleksandra also called it "the Sakha illness" [*Sakha yald'ybyt*] to distinguish it from more "standard" identifiable illnesses of the "European" lexicon. A form of "spirit torture," it often results in painful feelings of being "sick all over," of being torn apart and remade from the inside out by snakes and other animal-like spirits. The goal of this "initiation" is to feel a variety of pains that one's future patients are likely to feel, to gain enough empathy to become a true intuitive healer, tapping into the spiritual potency of oneself and one's patients in a synergistic way. To recover, a potential healer must promise to cure others, in a literally and figuratively enlightening bargain with spirits who become one's helpers.[5] Aleksandra explained to me: "I was young when I first felt the strength. I had visions, forebodings. But I was also headstrong and emotional...Father tried to tell me this was not how to be. I had a dream that I was thrown into a pit with snakes. I heard a voice that said 'She will see it through. She will win.'"

Aleksandra, confirming that various stages of transformation are typical of Sakha shamans, describes a later episode in her memoir (2002: 100–106):

> In 1985, something happened with me that is beyond explanation. It began with a headache and unstoppable vomiting. For three days, I was not able to get up from bed, and then I revived. The whole time I wanted fish...My body was covered with red hives. I had a terrible skin itch, as if worms were crawling all over my body...A woman came to me and said that I was not curing myself correctly, that what I had was well-known...She brought three kinds of herbs and said to burn them in the evening and purify myself with smoke. Also, that I should eat fish...After feeling better, I decided to take the smell of smoke from my body. But again the headaches began, and I realized what I had to do. I had to put on my father's [shamanic] dress [bequeathed to her ten days short of three years after Konstantin's death, as he had directed]...I put on the cloak and immediately felt a lightening. I even looked at myself in the mirror. I felt a tranquilizing

of the soul, and with a great yawn I lost my footing, and fell into a deep dream ...."

After taking sick leave, Aleksandra continued to use her father's cloak to cure herself, as she gradually realized that what was happening was "the ritual of tearing apart." She explains this as "a ritual of suffering through which one is taught." Among the teachers were animal spirit guides, including a bear. Significantly, one of Konstantin's most famed forms was as a bear, the animal associated with his "mother spirit," or *iié kyl*. Her suffering was far from over. During this period, she would sing ancient Sakha songs with abandon in her sleep, jolting awake her confused Russian husband.

After three years, a still greater trauma occurred, the one that led her away from being "the kind of doctor who cuts and sews," as her father used to say. Having performed a brain surgery, she reeled from the operating room, vomited, and was unconscious for three days. She landed in several hospitals, including in the republic capital, Yakutsk. Marks appeared on her face that some said resembled a cross on one side, and a drum on the other. She envisioned the bed she was to have, and was later taken there, near patients who subsequently were amazed when she began understanding their illnesses without their having told her their complaints. She hid her dizziness, blurred vision, and mental state, in great fear that her colleagues would put her in one of the notorious Russian psychiatric clinics, and that she would be inappropriately drugged. Gradually, she realized: "I had acquired a new gift, the ability to see through a person into their illness." She saved one woman from a kidney stone operation by willing the stones into sand. Another, who was to have a leg amputated, was saved when Aleksandra "by thought, with intense gaze, cured her. Soon she stood, felt warmth, and itching in the leg." As Aleksandra cured others, she improved herself, and was finally released, still wobbly, with the diagnosis "illness uncertain."

Back home, donning Konstantin's cloak, Aleksandra finally felt relief and calm that led to her spiritual transference from a surgeon to a healer, guided by the spirit of her father, who sometimes sent messages through an elderly mediator fondly named "Aunt Shura." Konstantin had delivered Shura in a difficult birth, had accurately predicted her future family life, and later began sending her elaborate dreams as a way to contact Aleksandra. Aleksandra herself had saved Shura from going blind in 1991, by Shura's own account to me. When I first met Aleksandra in 1992, she was head doctor of her region, with a large plant-filled room within the Belaia Gora hospital for those patients who wished to be cured in séances that included Sakha chants, incense purification, and mutually reinforcing group prayers. Their enthusiastic testimonies made me realize Aleksandra's *étéénei* had fulfilled a powerful promise, though she still wore her white doctor's gown and inspired confidence in more "modern" ways as well.

Within ten years, Aleksandra resigned as head doctor, and began receiving selected patients in her home, including those she helped occasionally by donning Konstantin's cloak and drumming by a fire, in a special healing hut in her backyard. A patient who had never seen a picture of Konstantin recognized his photograph, an identification that may have involved the "power of suggestion" derived from knowledge of his existence. However, Nikolai, a patient with cancer, and several others, say they have seen a man standing behind her while she chants, as she evokes the beauty of the Northern mountains. In any case, Aleksandra and her sister Maria are well loved for dealing with emergencies, with the traumas of hunting accidents, as well as for curing nervous system disorders and alcoholism.[6]

The Chashkins: From Exploits to Tractors

In the central Sakha region called Tatta, renowned for producing many artists and writers, the family of Foma Petrovich Chashkin felt the same heat of Soviet repression that Konstantin's did. Foma and Konstantin together spent time in jail in the 1930s for their illegal practice of "charlatan medicine," since in those days Soviet antireligious authorities considered the words "shaman" and "deceiver" to be synonymous. Foma first came to my attention not for his reputation for healing, though it was great, but for his exploits with Soviet police. In one account, Foma invited the policeman who had come to arrest him to eat a cooked fish with him, but it wiggled on the plate and the poor man fled. In another, Foma was arrested, but he kept showing himself in the surrounding fields and woods, as if he were everywhere at once. They let him go because they could not be sure where he was. In a third, he was being taken to be shot, but a policeman put the gun to his own temple instead. Finally, they let Foma go home, where he married a girl he had cured of a skin disease. Some said he had sent her disease himself, in order to then cure her.

Chaashka *oiuun*, as he is nicknamed in Tatta, became known especially for curing alcoholics in secret, after the performance of community-oriented Sakha drumming séances attracted too much attention and became too dangerous. One time, recalled a friend of his, Chaashka visited another friend, who was drunk. The drunk evicted them angrily, so Chaashka made himself invisible. Later, at a time chosen for maximum startle effect, he "scared the guy straight out of his drunkenness," and, implied the speaker, his addiction.

In another case, told by a friend and patient of Chaashka's, two men showed up on his doorstep asking to be cured of their vodka habit. But they were not entirely sure that they wanted to quit, so they decided to test Chaashka by hiding a couple of bottles along the way. "If you really want to be cured," he told them, "then you must get rid of those two bottles that you hid along the way here." Impressed, they decided that he could see everything, and that they may as well agree to be cured. It should come as no surprise that some claimed Chaashka had hovered as a bird nearby to pull off this feat. Chaashka's usual method was to get people to guarantee with a ritual oath a particular amount of time that they would quit drinking. "If they violated this, they could be in big trouble," said one of Chaashka's elderly followers. "Sometimes people came back to him asking that the 'spell' be lifted, so that they could go to someone's wedding and drink for just a short period, say, three days. But if they did not get the ritual and tried this on their own, they had terrible repercussions—sickness, dizziness, and even death." Swearing and fear of spiritual enforcement enabled emergence from addiction in these cases.[7]

Two of Chaashka's sons have continued the family healing traditions, one more publicly than the other. I traveled to meet a modest, somewhat jolly, middle-aged Mikhail Fomich Chashkin in his home village in 2003. Large and brawny, he has not given up his regular job as a tractor-driver on an impoverished nearby farm that is part of a former Soviet collective, although he also regularly receives patients from the capital, a full eight hours bumpy drive away. A local patient explained that Mikhail "has a strong tie to the land, and this is where he derives his strength, the human-natural connection that creates the context for the information he uses to heal. This includes deep knowledge of plants, of all their medicinal possibilities. But he doesn't pretend to cure everything."

Mikhail began our discussion with his ancestry. "Doimpo was my ancestor, one of the great shamans of this area. We all probably got our healing abilities from him." In answer to my question about using the heavily charged word *oiuun* for the more recent generations, he replied: "Yes, it is in our line to be *oiuun*. Foma certainly can be called an *oiuun*. He died at age 78, treated like an ordinary person, and was buried that way, not as the *oiuun* of the past were [in special tree platforms in sacred groves]...There is a place named for Doimpo, and a sacred tree *kérékh mas* associated with him. I sometimes go to Foma's grave for inspiration. He died quietly in his sleep. He knew when he was going ..."

Both Foma and Mikhail are perceived as *oiuun* by their supplicants, because they went through the painful process of *éttéénei* to become healers. While Foma probably had some inklings of "shamanic torture" in his childhood, the most striking bout in this process was not until the age many Sakha claim is a key turning point in the revelation of creative and spiritual talent: "When Foma was about 40, he became very sick and was tortured by spirits. He had *éttéénei* for about seven years. For three to four of those years, he could hardly walk. He sang at night....I was born when he was around 50, so I do not remember his *éttéénei*. He cured it the way Sakha shamans do—he drank milk as if it were his life's blood, used milk to purify his system." Rather than stressing a pact with spirits, Mikhail chose to emphasize Foma's "rechanneling of his talents." "Since he could not use a drum...he used other instruments, for example horn tubes for blood cupping." With some sorrow, Mikhail said: "he didn't pass his healing implements to me, he didn't think his children should suffer [by becoming healers]."

Foma channeled his talent into "great herbal knowledge and psychological understanding...He used everything that was in his head, his brain. I myself can figure out who is coming and why. He did this too. It is possible when you are calm and connected. I think that telepathy was more needed then than now. Now we have the telephone." Unlike many rural Sakha, Foma did not keep cows or horses, but rather was a forest-oriented hunter. This helped him avoid too much contact with Soviet authorities in the village, and, more importantly, gave him the spiritual connectedness he needed to open himself to appropriate cures for individual patients. Many of his patients were women with *menerik*, perceived to have psychological problems collectively (mis-) labeled "Arctic hysteria." Quite possibly, such women were themselves frustrated healers, unable to cure themselves by becoming openly respected *udagan*, women shamans. Instead, their "nervous" bouts of dancing with wildly loosened hair, talking in tongues, and singing were perceived by their families and communities as frightening reminders of a "primitive past."[8] Mikhail continued: "In those days, there were quite a few *menerik*. Foma helped them, calmed them, and let blood out of them, from their temples. He also cured depression, back pain, osteochondrosis, stomach ulcers, and fertility problems."

Mikhail's practice has been imbued with the faith that he can eventually learn to cure precisely 41 illnesses. He got this from his own version of *éttéénei*, which he freely admits began with suffering from alcoholism. "It was really through dissipation and disorientation. I was very out of it when I drank, and through this, I suffered *éttéénei* without at first understanding what it was. I too went through this struggle for about seven years. Papa died before he could help me in this [healing] life. He was an *oiuun* and accepted that fate for himself. But now I see him in my dreams. This is how he has helped me." When I asked if he had any urge to take up drumming and perform séances, he hooted with laughter: "How am I going to jump around like that? The most important thing is the results, the cures that you help people achieve, when people believe in you. You can use herbs and the words of a blessing [*algys*] the same way as the drum. The energy of the curing is in the herbs, in all of nature itself." Mikhail's spirituality is inspirational and *ad hoc*, in that his intuition guides him to the right diagnoses, herbs and prayer-chants to use. "The words just come to me, they come from nature, a kind of prayer. I can see a person and figure out their illness. But I only have strength for five or six people a day." We have seen that the Sakha word for nature, *aiyylgha*, stems from the root *aiyy*, benevolent spirit. Mikhail recognizes this, yet hesitated to discuss its implication as inspiration for his prayers.

Mikhail differentiates Sakha and Russian patients, noting that sometimes Russians are more receptive than Sakha, with "softer internal structures," that is, more adaptable and less prone to chronic ailments. With Sakha patients, he is attuned to their three souls, thought by most Sakha to be an integral part of their being. He acknowledges the primary soul to be the "mother soul," or *iié kut*. It is important not to scare it, but rather to let its life force refresh itself. "Most curing, however," says Mikhail, "takes place with the *salgyn kut* [the breath soul]. Nearly everyone has their breath soul spoiled to some degree." This is due to human exposure to the destruction of nature, to human-made ecological imbalances. If a mother or breath soul wanders or is stolen, the task of the great shamans of old, including Foma and Konstantin, was to recover and control it. But Mikhail confessed he cannot do this, nor can he send his own soul in search of another's, as shamans are supposed to do. The third soul, the "earth soul," or *buor kut*, is most identified with a person's shadow, and possibly, in some interpretations, with a person's "aura." Mikhail, like others, sees it as especially relevant in death. All three make up the full harmony of an integrated, healthy person, enabling a balanced *kut-siur* and a pure liver.[9]

On leaving, I noticed patients were waiting. Mikhail apologized for not being able to personally show the local sacred tree where his father had once gone to make spirit offerings and derive inspiration. Mikhail admitted he had not been there for a long time, and felt more comfortable at Foma's grave, rather than Doimpo's tree. To my surprise, he encouraged a pilgrimage, probably because he was charmed by the woman I was with, the well-known Sakha sociologist, parliamentarian, and author, Uliana Vinokurova. As mentioned in Chapter 1, we searched for the tree in a nearby forest, where a stand of larch meets one of birch. But sadly, the most likely sacred tree we could find was a prone larch, an enormous, once-living being lying on the forest floor, abandoned.[10] Uliana, having been ready to make a prayerful offering, stared forlornly at it, and expected me to understand its significance as an index of cultural and spiritual decay. We pondered the twenty-first century ironies of a milk-drinking, tractor-driving healer whose *salgyn-kut* does not fly.

Niikon and Fedot: Transcending the Generations

In the Viliuisk and neighboring Suntar regions, a phenomenal number of shamans were renowned for their healing, spirituality, and ability to counteract or at least hide from Soviet repression. It was precisely in Viliuisk where the head of a "village Council" managed to cover up his shamanic practice because he was protected by his loving community while perceived by the outside world as a good Communist. Probably the greatest of all the Viliuisk shamans was Niikon, for whom a local curing center is now named. One legend about Niikon is that he was shot in the 1930s, having fled into the forest with a "rebellious" group of Évenki trying to avoid Soviet collectivization. When the activists who had shot him came to his body, they found only a dead dog, instead of Niikon.[11] Though hounded, humiliated, and forced to relinquish his drum and cloak, Niikon, believed to have lived 104 years (1880–1984), managed by the end of his lifetime to gain special official dispensation for aspects of his curing practice. In one account, Foma Chashkin himself referred a patient with several ailments to Niikon in 1971:

> Niikon was an open, warm, and hospitable elder, who loved to chat and tell stories. He looked at me and said just what Foma had: "Come next summer when the birches are budding." I came at the right time and found Niikon had moved to his summer camp. With other patients, he took us to a birch grove and had us gather large branches of young birches into a pile. He then instructed us to make a pit for a fire, and when there were only coals left, he lined the pit with them and put birch branches in a bed on top, covering the pit. He had us one by one lie on the branches naked. Then he asked what part of the body felt hot, and added more branches there. During this, he held our hands, taking our pulse, to check our heart. When he finished with one, he'd take another, adding coals and branches as needed. After this healing, I became well and for 20 years have had no illnesses.[12]

This frustratingly spare yet glowing testimony is typical of many recalled by Niikon's admirers. Niikon used prayer-chants during such purification sessions, made spirit offerings, and rarely discussed his own relationship with helper-spirits, hard-won through shamanic initiation. In the darkest moments of his secret practice, he was constrained from taking the life histories of patients, some of whom he barely knew. He occasionally told newcomers that he did not want to know their names, yet his loving empathy came through, especially as he lay his hot gentle hands on their heads, softly blew across their fontanel and prayed for them. He modestly received all supplicants, taking from them only the gifts that they could afford to give.

One of the most haunting of the healing stories associated with Niikon did not concern his direct "laying on of hands," but rather with the ramifications of a terrible accident that befell one of his patients in the early 1960s. The woman had a form of encephalitis that has come to be known as "Viliuisk Encephalitis," although local doctors resent the designation and point out there are cases throughout the republic. The unfortunate woman tried to circumvent a crowd at the helicopter taking people to see Niikon. The pilot, Konstantin Vasil'evich Ivanov recalled some details in 2003:

> In 1962 or 1963 a woman was hurt in my propeller. She was trying an end run to get to the door of the plane and her fingers got caught. She flew up and around, and landed on her back, so her back

was bleeding as well as her hand. She was bleeding profusely, but she was still living.... So I grabbed the prone woman with a cow hide, wrapped her and threw her inside the plane...We got her to the hospital in Yakutsk...After three months of intensive care [involving blood transfusions]... she lived another 35 years ..."

The pilot stressed that he and Niikon, for whom he had enormous respect, both considered that the key to this mysterious encephalitis that has vexed United States National Institutes of Health researchers for years may be found in this remarkable case, due to the nearly complete exchange of blood that was necessary to heal the woman.[13]

Niikon's practice in retrospect is surrounded with the mystery of successful healing using a relatively narrow range of traditional therapies, herbs, bloodletting, sucking, prayers, purification, and counseling. His "healing gifts" were said by local Sakha and a few big-shot Russian patients be "from nature" and inherited within his shamanic line. But to whom could he pass this precious yet dangerous gift? One of the many tragedies of the Soviet repression of shamans is that they only with great difficulty found appropriate youth to bequeath their secret knowledge and practice.

Niikon, however, had several apprentices in his lifetime, including one promising young man who landed in jail for alleged murder after working with Niikon for seven years. By 2010, the young man was released and reputedly healing supplicants, having also aided people in jail. Another was Evresenia Dmitr'evna Petrova, whose practice was focused on cupping with various sizes of cow horns, bloodletting, and knowledge of pressure points. Late in his life, Niikon learned of the extraordinary young man Fedot, who was still in school in a neighboring village.

When I met him, Fedot lived with his parents in a small and isolated village, where many villagers thought he was "just weird, not a healer" and his own mother was terrified of his fame. At the time, he revealed enough telepathic skill to cause me to reevaluate my own assumptions about "shamanism" in relation to "science." By Fedot's own testimony: "Niikon called me to him when I was 16. I felt the pull and resisted. I was ill [with *ettéénei*]. I was confused. And I was different from the other kids and did not want to be. My mother was very upset. But Niikon found me. He sent me signals through dreams and sent me a letter asking me to come live with him, to train with him." Fedot's mother, sitting nearby, confirmed that she had been vigorously against his leaving school and going to study with Niikon in 1981. But she could not stop him, and she became the only one who knew where he had gone: it was kept secret from the rest of the family. Fedot continued: "Niikon taught me a lot. He taught me how to find healing herbs, and how to mix them in appropriate doses. He gave me my drum and instructed me in how to gather important components of my cloak [through spirit communication]. I worked with him for about a year. [As he became infirm] he passed me on to his friend, another shaman..."[14]

Since Niikon's death, Fedot has periodically visited his grave, known to special followers as a pilgrimage site. At the grave, Fedot occasionally has felt comfortable enough to spend the night, shyly saying in answer to a direct question, "Yes, I go to Niikon's grave...I cannot go into details, but you can say we met each other there." One aspect of Fedot's burgeoning reputation with intelligentsia in the capital is that he spends time each year at Niikon's grave, something few have the courage to do.

Fedot outlined more specifically some of the Sakha therapies that Niikon had taught him, while making clear that he was still learning, was at a relatively early stage of his healing abilities. One of the most common, which has striking correlation to the healing practices of some Native Americans, is *boksuruiuu*, sucking illness from the body.[15] Another is a ritualized massage, *ilbiyii*, literally "casting out illness," that includes lengthy incantations. More serious illnesses require *sullérdééhii*, a kind of telepathic operation without cutting the body, and *d'albyii*, removing and escorting ill-willed spirits (*abaaghy*) from a patient, through a séance. For this, a shaman needs a darkened room with a hearth or an isolated spot in the forest where a fire can be lit. Prayers are said to the fire spirit, with offerings of white horsehair, Sakha pancakes, and butter, as is typical of many Sakha rituals. Then, early in the séance while drumming and singing, Fedot evokes his helper spirits, a raven and a black dog. "I use the same song always to start. I cry like a raven, to evoke Raven, and then call to Dog, like a dog....I do not consider my spirits *abaaghy*—they are *ichchi*. They are helpers, not evil spirits. I try to cure people, to be kind, not to hurt people. How effective I am partly depends on what kind of illness is being discussed."

One of the reasons I had found Fedot and been received warmly in the early 1990s was that I was accompanied by a Sakha friend, Ivan Alekseev, who is a linguist from the region, and a virtuoso player of the jaw harp [*khomus*]. As used in Saiyyna's and others' therapies, this deeply resonating small forged-sculpture metal delight is justly famed in the republic for creating calming, sometimes healing, effects. In part due to Ivan, it has had an enormous revival of popularity in the last 30 years. Fedot too plays the *khomus*, and welcomed Ivan with joy. Yet he was not ready to treat either of us for the specific complaints that we arrived with, for he had just performed a risky séance with his own brother the day before and admitted he was feeling unwell himself. He nonetheless managed through some sort of telepathy [called "clear-seeing," *kørbøchur*] to discern what our needs and hopes were as potential patients, before we explicitly mentioned them. He also warned us that he could not simply sing and drum "for show," without immediately evoking his helper spirits.

My respect for Fedot's effectiveness has increased over the years, as he for many years treated a mutual friend, the late singer-songwriter Anastassiia Varlaamova, for chronic diabetes, and stayed with her when he traveled to Yakutsk. When I first met Fedot, I brought a tape of her music as a gift. When it was clear she was dying, Fedot eased her death, playing the shaman's well-known role as mediator between worlds.

Another case was mentioned with sorrow by Fedot himself, who admitted that he could not use "clear-seeing" or a nonintrusive operation to cure patients from afar, although he had tried. One desperate family had brought him the clothing of a loved one dying of cancer. He recalled, "It was too late, but I think I made the pain of the illness easier to bear." As mentioned in opening this book, I first heard of Fedot because of the sensational story buzzed in the capital about the Russian woman doctor who he had reputedly cured of cancer. Her own doctors were furious with her for risking her life by delaying an operation. Similar concerns have been repeated to me for many years by certified Sakha doctors, who point out that the woman in the helicopter accident was saved "not by any Niikon," or that folk medicine on balance represents "more of a risk than a blessing."

Like many of the great shamans in Sakha history, Fedot has been consistently modest and cautious in his contacts with those he defines as outsiders to his belief system, including Sakha like the doctors quoted above. By 2007, he was celebrated in certain Sakha circles for curing rural and urban supplicants in secret séances and for having acted as a psychopomp, conveyor of the soul of the beloved but dying Anastassiia. He was also admired for accepting only those fees or rewards his satisfied patients volunteered, and for rejecting the public glory of a foreign trip that would have involved performing a purification séance on a stage at the United Nations in New York. His efforts to keep his profile low included swearing witnesses of his séances to secrecy and urging them not to say his name out loud, for he would hear them if they did. One elder (an old friend) in 2007 told me that he had recently seen a shaman performing a drumming séance in an isolated dacha outside of Yakutsk, and that the chanting had been as powerful as anything the elder remembered from his youth. Only by implication would he confirm that this was Fedot, since he refused to say his name. He suggested that revealing details of séances was as private as exposing details of lovemaking, something young people were all too willing to do these days. The mystery in both is gone with too much analysis, he warned.

Spiritual Transformation as a Social and Personal Process

Despite the elder's friendly warning, I attempt here a review of some of the issues surrounding generational change. We have seen that stories such as that of the Russian woman doctor cured of cancer by a remote rural Sakha shaman are balm for a recovering post-Soviet society. Such accounts represent widespread affirmation of faith in traditional healing, in revitalizing shamanic traditions, and in transference of shamanic power to a new generation. But in 2003 in Viliuisk, I heard far more striking news from several of Fedot's followers. In the Viliuisk area, forest fires raged especially strongly in 2002, coming perilously close to the village where Fedot's parents are based. Just as the fire was about to engulf the village and force mass evacuation, a strong rainstorm, complete with hail, as some enthusiasts explained, diminished its strength and saved the village. How did this happen? I was repeatedly told that Fedot himself called on his helper spirits, including possibly the revered deceased shaman Niikon, to avert disaster. Further queries produced the admission that teams of forest fighters from the whole Far East had descended on the region. But they were not given the dominant credit for success. This is precisely the kind of narrative told about the great hero-shamans of the past, including Konstantin, who used their abilities not only for healing, but for community protection.

By 2007, I was able to confirm that Fedot's satisfied patient list has been growing. However, in 2009, a more disturbing and less miraculous account was circulating. Fedot had joined the famed Évenk shaman Sobei in an uncharacteristic, even bizarre, mass audience séance in a venue that usually housed the Sakha circus in Yakutsk. This ticket-taking venture had been a necessity to raise money for Sobei's eye operation in another city. Fedot had drummed off to the side, and was probably there as much for moral support of Sobei as for his share of the money. Their performance was held on one day instead of the originally advertised two, and some said that both Sobei and Fedot ultimately had understood that a place where the circus usually performs is the last setting they needed to raise the reputation of folk healing. This made a mockery of community healing by going too big and brassy, rather than too small and secret.

As we have seen throughout this book, post-Soviet life has produced many changes in indigenous Siberian attitudes toward the spiritual and healing potential of "traditional medicine." The decline of 1990s commercial "charlatans" trading on new credibility for religion was hastened by licensing fears plus less official processes of trial and error as people shopped for effective healers. Shamans have long had their own powerful ways to practice "licensing." Yuri Sidorevich Prokopiev, whose Center for Traditional Healing changed its name to the Center for Prophylactic and Sports Medicine, estimated in a 2002 interview with me that about 240 claimed to be healers in the republic, while only 30 to 50 had real talent. By 2010, both figures may well have shrunk.

The healers who have survived the zigzags of enthusiasm and scepticism about "authentic" shamans tend to be those who have shamanic lineages, believable personal stories of spirit torture-inspiration, as well as a many-staged apprenticeship to a knowledgeable elder. If those elders are legendary shamans like Konstantin, Chaashka, and Niikon, then their few, selected successors have an excellent chance of building a viable reputation for "hands on" therapies such as massage, use of pressure points, and bone-setting, plus herbal knowledge tied to ecological care, and intelligent, flexible empathy [*ahynyy*], over many proven years of practice. Such shamans, of various levels of spiritual power, often are practicing quietly in their own communities, rather than the capital Yakutsk. However, as they did earlier, major shamans travel widely. Aleksandra has proved able to move back and forth between Belaia Gora and Yakutsk, seeing old and new supplicants. By 2010, she was living back in Belaia Gora, taking care of her ill husband and a few patients there.

Concerns about "institutionalization" of shamanic practice remain. By 2010, the "Center of Folk Medicine" founded by the shaman-historian Vladimir Kondakov continued to combine Sakha therapies and Chinese medicine. It had survived his death, although only five "shamans" were listed on their roster out of about 70 healers. Yuri

Prokopiev's Center for Prophylactic and Sports Medicine, using scientific language and stripped of most of its shamanic therapies, had floundered for personal reasons, including the alcoholism of some of its own curers. The scourge of alcoholism, lightly introduced in the heading of this chapter, can be seen as a lightening rod illuminating the interconnection of personal and social illness. Treatment for alcoholics can bring out tensions between individuals and their communities, and precisely these kinds of tensions can be managed if not solved in effective, long-term shamanic practice. Foma Chashkin and his sons are far from the only curers who have needed to specialize in helping alcoholics (re)learn how to become productive members of their communities. Mikhail Chashkin himself represents an interesting variation on the shamanic initiation theme—a shaman who cured himself of alcoholism in order to help others. In many ways, shamanic family-based séances and shamanic therapy can be well-adapted to play an important role in mitigating this key destroyer of Siberian life.

The scourges of cancer and of pollution-derived illnesses in the increasingly industrialized North are far less susceptible to shamanic healing, although its potential may surpass our Western science. In what may be wishful thinking and yet may prove "real," new accounts of cancer cures were surfacing in 2010. Anna Vasil'evna Safroneeva is an *otohut* (bone setter) from Verkhoyansk, who also calls herself an *udagan*, and whose ancestors were *udagan*. She has told her patients that she was able to help the dying wife of an *ulus* head in the nick of time, after the local cancer case doctor had given up and ordered a death certificate. The medical worker who arrived to confirm the death was confronted instead with a recovering woman who sat up to greet her. Anna rejects membership in the Association of Folk Medicine, and takes patients only by word of mouth (with individually negotiated payments). I hope to verify her narrative someday, but thus far it can be seen as another case of striving by Sakha to rebuild the reputation of folk healing.[16]

To return to themes of the book, the sharp extremes of hero-shamans versus charlatan-shamans are softened in everyday practices, as people experiment for themselves, whether opening themselves to internet information about diverse illnesses, going to local clinics and hospitals, frequenting a folk healer, or traveling to a prominent shaman. New generations of healers and their supplicants are not only utilizing an increasingly wide range of healing options (compare Lola Romanucci-Ross's famous 1977 "hierarchy of resort") but are also becoming more comfortable with the creativity and energy of cultural revitalization (Vinokurova 1994). Positive self-identity, stimulated by pride in some of the republic's health, education, and ecology support programs, is as yet fragile. If healing is gradual, like planting a seed, as Thomas Csordas (2002: 5) warns, then a full range of healing options needs to be consistently made available.[17] Fresh sprouts of rekindled spirituality associated with traditional healing practices may easily be trampled by formal gatekeeping measures designed to control and monitor shamans. But as we have repeatedly seen, shamanic worldviews are not easily suppressed, even when shamans like Konstantin, Chaashka and Niikon themselves are. An optimistic example of generational change is Aleksandra Chirkova, who sensitively selects her healing methodologies on the basis of what each culturally mixed (and sometimes mixed-up) patient needs.

Photo 9 Tuvan-Russian shaman Natasha at a sacred spring, Republic of Tuva (Tyva). Photo by Marjorie Mandelstam Balzer, 2005.

Chapter 8

Social Medicine? Religious Movements in the Siberian Far East

"We, the Uranghai Sakha, created strong, were born on that very place that the spirit of Nature built his hearth."
Ed'ii Dora, shaman and community activist,
Sakha Republic, 1999

"Tuvans have saved for the world their religion, the archaic religion of shamanism."
Mongush Kenin-Lopsan, founder *Düngür* [Drum] and *Tos Déér* [Nine Heavens], Kyzyl, Republic of Tuva (Tyva), 2005

"Do not speak un-truths, strive for justice and it will find you."
Concluding commandment on the business card of Valentin V. Khagdaev, Orkhon Island, Buriat "Shaman-Böö", 2010

Politicized religious movements, often aborted and local, have dotted the emotional and physical landscape of Siberia without being adequately analyzed or compared. What is their resonance today? Where can we look, beyond the Ob River "Kazym resistance" and Altai Burkhanism, for mobilization that transcends individual therapies and addresses intertwined social, ecological and political crises?[1] As we have seen, zigzags of confidence in public and private spirituality have characterized post-Soviet rural and urban religious life in the Sakha Republic. Exuberance that accompanied initial "glasnost" years of cultural roots rediscovery has given way to soul-searching as people accommodate fragmented moments of dreams, rituals, telepathy, and faith into personal, idiosyncratic strategies for everyday life.

In villages and towns of the Sakha Republic, in greater Buriatia (including its satellite regions), and in the Republic of Tuva (Tyva), shamanic revitalization has taken place at many levels, from annual nationally sponsored ceremonies, to ancestral community offering rituals, to police use of "seers," to emergency curing séances. The diversity of shamanic activities is matched by a variety of shamanic styles, and some publicized disillusion with failed faith-healers. By 2010, friends in the Sakha Republic were self-consciously critiquing this amorphous spiritual striving, and asking, in remarkably similar language: "Where is our own true Native religion? Why isn't our shamanic faith more integrated and coherent?"

I explore here this religious impulse, and the links between individual and community healing in multicultural, multicontentious social contexts. My goal is to reveal fledgling shamanic community activism as it acquires some of the characteristics of "new religious movements." Hopes of indigenous peoples for spiritual revitalization at personal, community and national levels are taken seriously. Nascent shamanic movements are highlighted in three of the Siberian regions best known for their strong shamans, their recovery of shamanic healing, and the popularity of their shamanic culture. In these three regions (as well as Altai and Khakassia), indigenous intellectuals have consciously correlated shamanic activities and national identity. For Sakha Republic, I feature two charismatic figures not yet analyzed, the young, rural philosopher-visionary Kyta Baaly and the more established healer and ecology activist Ed'ii (Elder Sister) Dora. I also mention three attempts at "temple" building in the past decade. For Buriatia, efforts of the colorful Orkhon Island (Lake Baikal) shaman Valentin Khagdaev are discussed and contrasted with those of other Buriats. The section on Tuva features the stimulus and legacy of ethnographer-turned-shaman Mongush Kenin-Lopsan and his protégé Aichurek.

The literature on cultural revitalization movements is burgeoning and eclectic.[2] Revitalization movements are often responses to compelling, conscious ideas of internal social reform as well as to pressure from external social oppression. Many political, social, and religious movements have revitalization potential, despite differing manifestations and end results. Whether called revolutionary, messianic, nativistic, vitalizing, or revitalizing, the psychological-functional vocabulary used to describe such movements often implies mass-level spiritual crisis-easing related to cultural rebirth. Single theories stressing "objective" material causes, charismatic leadership, widespread psychological depression, or relative deprivation rarely do such movements justice.

The Turkic and Mongolic groups featured here have considerable cultural commonalities in shamanic poetry and prayers (*algys, algysh*), circle dances with improvisational chants, shamanic world trees and/or horse hitching posts (*sergé*), shamanic illness conceptions, shamanic heredity patterns, drumming, jaw harp (*khomus*) playing, throat singing, and much else. These cultural correlations, often celebrated by indigenous scholars themselves, make sociopolitical comparisons compelling but not determining.[3]

Two themes are relevant as I compare the indigenous groups selected here: stalled or plateaued movements, and the interrelationship of religious movements with nationalism. Any narrative about the shamanic leaders profiled here as yet has no definitive ending. I use the term "shamanism" carefully, to indicate an eclectic philosophy and cosmology consciously mediated and adapted by shamans in each generation.[4] I extend Thomas Csordas's suggestion (2002: 241) that in studying spiritual healing, anthropologists should understand embodied, emotional experience as "the starting point for analyzing human participation in a cultural world" by stressing that the cultural is also political. Can Siberian communities be stimulated to self-cure?

Sakha Republic: Leaders in Search of Followers?

In the Sakha Republic in the mid-1990s, a young mystic named Anatoly Yurevich Mikhailov, who took the name Kyta Baaly, aspired to the role of a prophet for his people in ways that are somewhat similar to other Siberian religious movements. His movement began in a traditionally sacred heartland area, away from the capital but connected to Yakutsk through kinship and reputation. He stimulated popularity with a hallmark ceremony: a private, annual *yhyakh* ritual performed at his farmstead in a region across the Lena River from Yakutsk. The Sakha ethnomusicologist Eduard Alekseev first alerted me that a rural, poorly educated, charismatic young man had captured the imaginations of a number of followers in his district (*ulus*), in what appeared to be a classic syncretic religious movement. Kyta Baaly was combining aspects of Sakha religion with claims of being the son of Jesus Christ, and his movement seemed, as Eduard termed it, to be an example of "*dvoeverie*" (Russian for double faith). For me, Kyta Baaly's movement provided an excellent opportunity to explore theories concerning the dynamics in crisis times of shamanic revival, multivocal faith, and uneven syncretic processes.[5] I realized that I had been half expecting such a person to surface in the post-Soviet spiritual chaos. However, I did not predict the colorful details of his life, or how fast his movement would fizzle.

Kyta Baaly's assumed name came from the farmstead he had inherited, wrested from a collective farm. His Sakha *alaas*, or rural homestead, came from his mother's side, for his father had been a Russian, whose heritage he had alternately embraced and rejected. Kyta Baaly means place of plenty; thus his personal name was supposed to evoke thoughts of wealth and hope. His personal background fits into patterns of particularly intense faith proclamations coming from those with mixed ethnic backgrounds.

In June 1997, after five hours of driving through swamps and on back roads, I arrived with friends in time for Kyta Baaly's *yhyakh*. The setting was gorgeous, with a lake, forest, fields, and two houses. Eventually over 60 participants formed a procession. Kyta Baaly had transformed himself into a prince, wearing a long beige jacket cut like those of the heroes of Sakha epics, embroidered in symmetrical, curved fertility designs. Women in long satin dresses and heavy, carved silver traditional jewelry followed. Less appropriately dressed visitors brought up the rear. We filed unevenly to a majestic tree that had a huge bull skull lodged at the joint of a lower branch. Kyta Baaly softly spoke a prayer-blessing, *algys*, as he confidently tossed the fermented mare's milk symbol of fertility, *kumiss*, from an elegant wooden chalice in an arc at the base of the tree, "feeding" the earth. We proceeded to a slight rise overlooking the lake. First Kyta Baaly and then a few others sang or spoke more *algys*, as the spirit moved them. The crowd was hushed as the soft light over the lake seemed to shimmer. Later some proclaimed that they had seen bejewelled Sakha ancestors in nineteenth century clothing, mirroring the splendor of the living, emerge from the lake in response to the prayers.

We headed back to the ritual ground where three ceremonial posts (*sergé*) were placed, and where a fire had been laid. Kyta Baaly used a microphone to say another prayer. The fire roared, as the spirits were fed *kumiss*, melted butter, and horse hair through the fire, itself personified as the mediator spirit *iot ichchi*. The offerings were tossed from a particularly huge *choron*, the breast shaped wooden chalice with legs mimicking horse hooves, and a *kytiia*, a squat carved wooden bowl. The elegant chalice of delicious, fresh *kumiss* was passed around our circle, so that all could sip from it in communion.

After a night of feasting, circle dancing, and talking about plans for proselytizing Kyta Baaly's teachings, we stood facing the east in a gentle breeze, as the sun peeked over the horizon, huge, almost blinding. Kyta Baaly said another prayer-blessing, praising the spirits of the directions, and asking for health and prosperity of the assembled group, while he anointed the earth with more *kumiss* offerings.

Later, several claimed the breeze was Nature's approving answer to his prayers, although I thought I felt the breeze before the blessing. As Kyta Baaly said the *algys*, we stood in a ragged arc behind him, holding our arms up, palms out.[6]

The next two dizzying, near sleepless days were spent in conversations with Kyta Baaly's followers, on a long walk and personal but aborted curing session with his mother, and in rambling interviews with Kyta Baaly. After protesting that he had not beaten the drum in a year, and that séances (*kamlanie*) were "more for a black shaman controlling *abaaghy* spirits than for a white benevolent spirit shaman," he agreed to a drumming session in his mother's cabin before the old-fashioned Sakha fireplace. Its purpose, more to please his mother and me than to cure anyone, was left atypically open. Smiling from his fireside stool, he peered sideways at me and said quietly: "I am the favorite son of Aiyy Urung," the ultimate sky god in Sakha layered heavens cosmology, also called Urung Aar Toyon. His low, confident drumming lasted about a half-hour, with a steady rhythm, changing intensity slowly, except at the end when the beats became more intricate, intense, and rapid. He was drenched in sweat when he stopped, and his loving mother wiped his forehead with a towel.[7]

Kyta Baaly used his drumming in part to work through his relations with other spiritual leaders. "He made a crude mistake" said Kyta Baaly, referring to a local *abaaghy oiuun*. He explained that *abaaghy* are capricious spirits, sometimes helpful, sometimes evil, and I encouraged him to elaborate on concepts and people I thought I already knew. The shaman he mentioned, a man I had worked with and admired, lived in a nearby village, and had become a rival for local affections. Kyta Baaly recalled the first *yhyakh* he and his mother had launched several years previously for friends, family, and followers. It had marked the neighbors' open competition, for Kyta Baaly felt the shaman had tried to crash his *yhyakh* with ill will, and that, according to tradition, *abaaghy oiuun* did not belong at *yhyakh* ceremonies.

> I did not give him the road. I made his legs so they would not move. He should not have tried to come like that. Of course he could come, should have come. But not like that. I showed him who was who. He was on my territory. You know how shamans earlier did this? Blocked the path for people?...I sent an arrow.

When I recalled that shamans fight via proxy helper spirits, he vehemently rejected the suggestion, associating this with *abaaghy*. He stressed that while the Russians may view both "white" and "black" shamans as bad, "there is a difference between an *aiyy oiuun* and an *abaaghy oiuun*. I do not communicate with *abaaghy*...only benevolent spirits, *aiyy, ichchi*."[8] He added: "But this is really coming from me, my thinking and my ability to have the third eye...[that] enables me to travel to the Sky God, who gave me the third eye of wisdom, prediction."

Two years later, Kyta Baaly had become more mellow and mature. While he still had a team of healers who travel from village to village, he was trying to fulfill his image of himself as a benevolent *aiyy oiuun*, a ritual leader and moral authority. "My teachings now stress etiquette and love," he explained at a home in his *ulus* center. "People need to live up to relaxing with a drink, and they need to earn the right to have multiple wives...I am for polygamy not just to increase our Sakha people, as Professor Antonov advocates, but to return to Sakha values."[9] He described his concept of "sacred debt," *ytyk iés*, that everything one gains in life should be returned back through "strong love" of one's fellow creatures, human, animal, and especially children. "For the sake of love, you should live fully. But it is not like that with us. Instead we have huge numbers of alcoholics, divorces. It is a big sin to separate from one's loved ones." He said this repentantly, given notorious aspects of his earlier personal life. "The key is to increase, not debilitate, our children's potential. They must learn internal freedom, but within limits."

Kyta Baaly's teachings had resonance for Sakha republic education policies targeted at integrating Sakha values and customs into everyday teaching, although by 2005 such policies were being phased out by standardization orders from Moscow. "Our first goal should be the stimulation of internal renewal, of healing ourselves to the point where reflexive energies radiate out from us, in a kind of sixth sense, *iniir*." Anyone can grow into this gentle sensitivity, since it is more accessible than the telepathic abilities needed for a shamanic "third eye." "*Iniir* is needed to spiritually reharmonize the earth, *aiyy siré*," Kyta Baaly explained.

I asked about his communication with benevolent spirits, *aiyy,* and he confirmed he has "many helper spirits, both small and higher." "Sometimes I wish for something and it has happened just like that, chek chek," he said with a repeated hand chop. He rejected earlier claims to being a son of Jesus Christ and admitted it had been a mistake to make such extravagant claims, especially on TV. He had thought of the Christian God as similar to Aiyy Urung, and was confused by his mixed Christian-shamanic dreams.[10] His adjustments reveal the pitfalls of hasty categorization of particular social movements at one moment in time.

Kyta Baaly's philosophy utilizes a cosmology of spiritual hierarchies similar to those of past Sakha shamans, with spirit personae occupying nine levels of upper and under worlds, plus our middle world. "Shamans are working with spirit-received information. But shamans are not shrines, they do not create centers of religion. Spirits dictate to them sometimes, but spirituality goes beyond this. What we are trying to do is create more of a system, a philosophy, more scientific." He added that his teachings put humans more in control of themselves than shamanic teachings surrendering to concepts of fate used to do. "We take in our own spirit. If it a strong spirit, it will be different from a shaman's spirit, more personalized." Kyta Baaly clarified why he differentiates Sakha traditions of priests and shamans. "Shamans became especially aggressive in the nineteenth century," when they were under siege from Christian missionaries. "They were capable of eating people's souls... their spiritual core was not fully formed. And soon [because of Soviet oppression] there will be fewer shamans able to treat the ill. A shaman without a séance can do nothing. Some percent of shamanic teachings is Truth," he added, "but truth and sincerity come through actions."[11]

In Kyta Baaly's teachings, morality is reinforced not by the threat of hell, but by a threat of becoming a wandering spirit of the middle world, earth. "When you die, you will be asked, 'Did you fulfill your debt?' Otherwise you will become a *yuor* [a kind of Sakha ghost]." Kyta Baaly's message of love, peace, and responsibility in this lifetime had resonance for some Sakha struggling to establish themselves in a world at once opening up and turning to traditional family-oriented values. Yet his uneducated writings and not fully articulate speeches could not sustain the interest of followers beyond his own *ulus*, and even there, his competitive spirit seems to have made people grumble that he should practice what he preached.

Kyta Baaly's movement first rested on a kind of plateau and then stalled before it could be fully routinized into a new religious movement (compare Weber 1947; Lester 2002). In the plateau stage, at the turn of the twenty-first century, his followers knew each other by the wearing of small "sacred world path" pins and pendants that elegantly combined a Christian cross with a tree symbol. When worn on a chain with a circle at its tip, the symbol also resembles a stick figure person. By 2000, attendance at the annual Kyta Baaly *yhyakh* had increased modestly, and some of his followers had decided to become accredited healers by taking courses at Yuri Prokopiev's Center For Traditional Healing, including his mother. By 2007, hardly anyone I asked remembered Kyta Baaly or how enthusiastic they once had been for his teachings. By 2010, I heard he had landed in jail after a drunken brawl.

A more sustainable movement is illustrated by the growing respect for an imposing Sakha "earth mother" named Dora Innokentievna Kobiakova, who nearly everyone in the republic affectionately terms "Ed'ii Dora," Elder Sister Dora. Hers is a contemporary movement for the moral, spiritual, and ecological healing of the Sakha people and lands. She is a real mother, a widow with shamanic heritage from the Kobei region, whose curing "miracles," celebrated anomalies, have become as renowned as her impassioned speeches and mass rituals. Her admirers are legion, including, it is rumored, the founding President of the Republic, Mikhail E. Nikolaev. Some of the same people may be attracted to Kyta Baaly and Dora, for attendance at their rituals has been open. But Dora is far better known; few healers in the republic are considered her equal. I have met Dora (in 2000 and 2004) and talked to her briefly, including one memorable exchange at an *yhyakh* ceremony in the Tatta region when I made the mistake of gesturing toward a large cricket-like bug that had landed on her chest, to the horror of the friend I was with, who was concerned that the bug was Dora's and my gesture was disrespectful.

Dora, born in 1959, has told the Sakha ethnographer Ekaterina Romanova (2008: 315) that she has been growing in her spiritual strength since age 12. A crucial year for experiencing intense bouts of the "shamanic illness" was age 30. As with other spiritual leaders in Sakha conceptions, her strength was further enhanced after age 40, when people feel freer to reveal their full creative potential. By numerous accounts, she has reached levels of success beyond her abilities to cure individuals. Tall and imposing, with a round, kind face and long hair, Dora looks the part of an earth mother-priestess. She has acquired numerous mediator spirits for different purposes and different kinds of cosmological contacts, including birds (swan, crane, cuckoo, loon, woodpecker) for the upper world, elk and bull for the middle earth (*ortu doidu*), and bass and duck for the watery underworld.

Dora has described how she heals in revealing interviews with an admirer, Nina I. Protopopova (1999; 2006), although Dora also has said that she has trouble explaining in words her techniques and the requirements of being "chosen by Nature" to heal people.[12] Dora uses her mediator birds, swan and crane, to reveal who will visit her. She also troubleshoots through dreams and intuitive perceptions at dawn. More profoundly, she taps into the natural interconnectivity of humans, flora, and fauna. She teaches that each human when born is linked in spirit to a gendered tree and an animal, often a bird, living in that person's homeland. "This is my system. Those who come to me for cures have a special protection that derives from their land and their kin [ancestors]." Dora empathetically uses the energy of that connection to restore health, if necessary by flying (Protopopova 1999: 153–155; 2006: 33):

> When I raise myself, I stand straight and go where I am needed. What is traveling is my energy. My vision along the way depends on natural circumstances. Across destroyed earth, I can fly as wind or fog. Over more calm rivers and lakes, I reacquire my own self. I can go anywhere, whether Viliuisk, Japan, America...my body is at home, but my energy is moving [like smoke from a cigarette] to where it is needed, and then returns.

A friend in the Yakutsk intelligentsia was lucky to have Dora as a houseguest when the friend's niece had a bad accident: her face and neck were burned from an explosion of hot milk:

> She was taken to the hospital, in shock...when we picked her up, her face was filled with burn marks, pus, corpuscles...Dora said "Do not worry, we can fix this. Our paths have crossed. It is your fate that the explosion happened, but I am here to help you." She took out a long, thin bone, I think from the leg of a crane, and began to suck and blow all over her face....Pus and blood came out. I saw it all, she sucked it all out, at each spot, systematically all over her face. This is *bokhsuruiuu*, the sucking cure....The face was red, with a whole layer of new skin....Dora then apologized, and took her own spit and rubbed it all over my beautiful girl's face, saying spit is medicinal...Dora also soothed with words, saying "you are lovely and will soon be married and have children." Sure enough, she soon married and just recently had a first child...I would not have believed all this myself, except I saw it with my own eyes.

Dora's cures go well beyond the cosmetic. One family took their daughter out of the best Yakutsk hospital when doctors said they could do nothing for her brain tumor without a risky operation. The girl was fading, hardly able to lift her head or to see. They traveled far to Kobei, where Dora used another kind of hollow bone to suck out the illness and gradually return her to health. The girl later attended a university.[13] Dora also uses six drums (*düngür*) of three sizes, with the two largest reserved for special natural or human emergencies. She more often uses three consecrated wooden spoons (*khamyiiakh*) of birch, pine, and larch, decorated with special symbols, for predictions and help with purification of patients. In addition, she has sacred jaw harps, three for curing and one for communing in nature. Individual shamanic cures, no matter how sensational, constitute neither a movement nor proof of what Edith Turner (1999) calls the collective subliminal, revising Jung (1928), and playing on Victor Turner's (1977) concept of ritual "liminality." But Dora's language, her claims, and her recent rituals suggest correlations of her philosophy of Sakha cultural renewal with major Sakha shamans of the past and with other Native prophetic spiritual leaders who founded new religious movements for their struggling peoples.[14] After flooding of the Lena River in 1998, Dora proclaimed in mass meetings: "The spirit of the earth warns us with fires and floods that we must embrace Nature, that we must not forget that we are Sakha. Nature is giving a signal that each *ulus*, each *nasleg* (subdistrict) should not appeal to others for help but should themselves generate their own beneficial renewal."[15] Although some Sakha have blamed Dora for not predicting the Lena River floods, she in retrospect looked on the flooding as punishing purification of Sakha sins:

> Nature has eyes, a bellybutton, and roots, veins. The spirit of our great earth has east, west, north, and south sides, with a strong foundation. We, the Uranghai Sakha, created strong, were born on that very place that the spirit of Nature built his hearth. We are designated to live in harmony with Nature... yet we, despite considering ourselves a wise people in preserving our language and history, have violated the behests of Nature, and for that sin are being punished. Nature, insulted, has responded with the bitter tears of a flood.[16]

Like many Sakha, Dora considers that a key to healing the Sakha people and their land is the reverent summer celebration of *yhyakh*, preferably on the bank of a river or lake, or on a rise with a great vista. While the republic declared June 21 an official holiday soon after it declared sovereignty within the Russian Federation in 1991, debate continues over the profanation of the festival in Soviet and post-Soviet times. Dora urges return to the original meaning of *yhyakh*, as a ritual stimulating fertility of people and land, as well as seasonal, cyclical balances of Nature. The summer solstice, when people are closest to Nature, is Nature's day of peak flourishing and purification potential. "One should go to the soil of one's homeland on that day, take horse meat, shashlik, and fish, milk products, and pancakes, or even just tea, and sit on the green grass in the circle of one's own kin and friends at the sacred *yhyakh* place (*tyuhyul'gé*)."[17] As Dora explained to Ekaterina Romanova (2008: 320), "We must always honor the sun, and during *yhyakh* we must be especially thankful, for in the summer all nature is awakened and all spirits are alert."

Contemporary young Sakha women sometimes fault Dora for being too "traditional," too worried about sexual "sins," and too oriented toward women's roles as wives and mothers, encouraging large families. But Dora advocates higher education for all, including her own daughters. Her advice to young parents stresses the need to stimulate all children to study well, as well as to be proud of traditions of cattle and horse breeding. Scolding, cursing, and disharmony, she reminds, were always discouraged in Sakha families. To avoid alcoholism and poverty, so rife in Sakha villages, she suggests trying to help children find value in any kind of labor, whether paid or not. Sakha were once self-sufficient, without money, and need not today find meaning in life only through outsider—or state—driven employment.

Dora is no revolutionary, but she does have social messages that she repeats in meetings and interviews, addressed to her own people. Others should not be blamed for Sakha problems, she suggests, even though as a people Sakha may be as much as 50 years behind where they might have been, both morally and economically, without Soviet rule. "With other peoples one should have an open heart and good will. But at the same time, one should not allow inconsiderate behavior." She adds: "It is not in the nature of the Sakha people to protest, demonstrate, and act out." For survival, Sakha have become cautious. Elders who participated in war and experienced starvation should teach young people the perils of interethnic and intercommunity disharmony.

Dora's messages jive well with her times, and she is popular in villages as well as in some corridors of power. Through Andrei Borisov, the Minister of Culture, she has been hired to bless major *yhyakh* ceremonies, as well as the openings of new theaters and sports stadiums. Dora does not call herself either an *oiuun* (reserved for men) or an *udagan* (a female shaman) but rather lets her admirers do that for her. She does recall flying to other worlds, and her lovely, archaic blessings help validate her powers and the very existence of spirits for her followers. Her strong poetic prayers, kindness, and obvious commitment to ecological activism have made her an enduring presence in the republic. And yet Dora herself has been frustrated in translating her ecology movement into a new level of savvy sustained development. She plans a community center/clinic on the outskirts of Yakutsk, but has thus far functioned without a major infrastructure to support her curing practice and larger purification program. Her campaigns to save particular sacred places, such as the whole Tuimaada Valley where Yakutsk is located, have been unable to withstand government plans for development of gas and oil pipelines and the first rail line into Yakutsk. They have been unable to prevent gas pipeline accidents that have occurred at the Lena River near Olekminsk. Political and economic forces "higher" than Dora, or the Ministry for Protection of Nature *(Ytyk Kéré Sirér* in Sakha), or any other ecology activists, have stymied the possibility that shamanic connection with Nature could make an important contribution to the health of all the republic's peoples on the scale that is needed.

Significantly, Dora considers herself the reincarnation of the legendary nineteenth century shaman, the beautiful Alykhardaakh (also called Alykhyrdaakh), whose spirit helper-avatars were a bass and a loon.[18] Sakha who know her well and revere her poetic language believe in her reincarnation identity. Thus she bridges worlds of contemporary and past Sakha spirit mediation at a crucial moment of ecological crisis and national hope for her people.

Other "bridges" have more concrete manifestations but are more controversial. Three competing structures that Sakha sometimes call "temples" (Russian, *khram*) were built within the last decade in Yakutsk. A few affiliates have also sprung up in the regions. In the Sakha language, they are *Archy Diété* [Purification House] founded in 2002; *Aiyy Diété* [Spirit House] built by 2005; and *Tengra Diété* [God House] consecrated in 2009. Their leaders are rivals, and their philosophies, while drawing on Sakha cosmologies and values, are quite diverse. I have visited them all, especially the first two, multiple times, and plan to write more about them. Here, most relevant is their variation along degrees of religiosity and degrees of resemblance to Christianity.

In 2002 the new *Archy Diété* hosted a crowded opening filled with Sakha intelligentsia. It was meant to serve as an urban temple of rekindled Sakha spirituality. Led by friends and colleagues I admire, including its director Nadezhda S. Tolbanova and its advisory committee member Uliana Vinokurova, it was heavily subsidized by the (Russian) mayor's office. Due to city funding, their compromise name was "Purification House" and their approach was to welcome people of all ethnic groups to participate in rituals, language classes and book launches, in order to show off the richness of Sakha culture. However, soon after its opening, several of the core group of *Kut-Siur* members, lead by the linguist Lazar Afanas'ev (Téris, or Organizer), became bitter that the new *Archy Diété* was not a "true *Aiyy Diété*," literally a house of benevolent spirits. They complained that established and relatively secular "bureaucrat-intellectuals" had hijacked their idea to create a Sakha temple in the city. They were also upset that the initial site for the temple, opposite a new Russian Orthodox church with gleaming golden domes, was moved to a less provocative place down the road. The geography of the capital had become a symbolic battleground, with multiple sides and agendas competing for presidential and mayoral favor (compare Balzer 2005).

The magnificent Purification House, opposite a sacred marsh that had been the site of early ecology protests against urban sprawl, has become a popular cultural center, somewhere between a secular community center, a dynamic art gallery, and a temple. Made of white stucco, glass, and wood, it resembles three interconnected tepees on steroids. Some consider it a spacious Sakha refuge for contemporary, urbanized times where they regularly can go to perform either the circle dance *ohuokhai* or to waltz. When commissioned, their prayer-givers (*Algys-chit*) perform life cycle rituals honoring births and weddings, or, recently, mourning deaths.

The rival Spirit House, on the edge of town in an unglamourous area of rundown old log houses, is shaped like a traditional Sakha winter home, *balagan*, with a courtyard for small-scale rituals. Subsidized by the Sakha shop owner who donated their rented land, its leaders worry they are on borrowed time. The walls are covered with the iconography of Sakha cosmology. The main priestess is the articulate poet Irina Uiuskhaana, whose pen name means outcry. A vocal supporter is the nationalist poet-journalist Ivan Nikolaev (2001) or Uhhan, whose pen name glosses as great. Téris's teachings (1993, 2002), called *Aiyy yoréghé*, or benevolent spirit teachings, stress the roles of the Gods and Goddesses of the Upper World, as well as a strict traditional morality filled with prohibitions.

The Tengra House was built well outside of town near the grounds of *Us-Khatyng* [Three Birches], where Yakutsk's annual summer solstice *yhyakh* ceremony is held. The brainchild of Sakha entrepreneur Vasily N. Atlasov, inspired by the mixed Russian-Cossack-Sakha historian Andrei Krivoshapkin, it is a copy of the old wooden Russian Orthodox church Blagoveshenskii Sobor. Filled with icon reproductions as well as a huge central tabletop fortune wheel depicting Sakha cosmology, it has a mix of multiple religious images vying for attention. In 2010, Andrei and Vasily explained they worship the main Christian God and the Trinity, but that God is really also the ancient Turkic dualistic God of Light and Darkness. A follower in the nearly empty temple attempted to coax me to offer the fire spirit some chocolate while twisting my body into the shape of "an ancient Turkic swastika." (I offered the chocolate without the swastika.) The site of a few weddings and jaw harp competitions, their experimental temple and religious movement is thus far better known by rumor than experience.

In all these centers of contested cultural revitalization, and in a few others like them throughout the republic in villages and towns, Sakha are trying to reconstruct ancient calendrical rituals, with the blessing-prayers that their ancestors considered crucial to their relations with each other and with spirits. In July 2007, I attended, with a few members of *Aiyy Diété* including Téris, their monthly prayer ritual. Honoring Baianai, the Hunting God, and, in their adaptation, god of wealth, we chanted and rolled in the tall grasses of the sacred green Lena marsh. At *Archy Diété*, monthly rituals follow the lunar calendar. For March, named to honor the Sky God protector of horses, *D'øhøgøi*, a pregnant mare has been hitched to the ceremonial horse post just outside the temple (and near its parking lot). Significantly, *Archy Diété* trains and supplies prayer specialists (*Algyschittar*), or White Shamans (*Aiyy-oiuunnar*), to lead the major June summer solstice *yhyakh* ceremonies of annual renewal.

Except for the annual *yhyakh* ceremonies, held at village, township, and republic levels throughout the republic, most of the revived rituals are poorly attended and critiqued as "artificial." As with other cultural revival efforts in indigenous communities, debates about authenticity and national identity are rife. Sakha complain that many rituals lack the elaborate beauty and efficacy that enable participants to connect with the spirits of Nature. Some wonder whether Buriats or Tuvans have been more effective, and thus I was not surprised to learn that in 2010, Andrei Krivoshapkin had traveled to Buriatia to meet with spiritual leaders there.

Buriatia: Shamanic Rock of Ages?

Buriatia has had a booming revival of local and urban shamans, alongside its more Mongolian-oriented Buddhist heritage.[19] In the post-Soviet years, shamanic revival has not only focused on individual curing, but also on major group shamanic ceremonies. As elsewhere, these have sometimes been associated with mixed academic-practitioner international conferences on shamanism, in the Buriatia case led by activists Irina Urbanaeva (2000), Taras Mikhailov (2004) and others. I attended such a conference in the Tunka Valley in 2010, during which we were able to participate in an already planned major sacrifice ceremony (*tailgan*) honoring a Mountain God revered throughout the republic, organized by the Buriat shamans' association *Tengri*.

Several Sakha colleagues interested in comparing Sakha and Buriat organized religious-shamanic movements attended the conference. Buriat revival has also encompassed such urban extravaganzas as the shaman-led spring and fall sacrifice ceremonies held on the outskirts of the republic's capital, Ulan-Ude, at the Ethnographic Museum, at the hippodrome, and elsewhere, with participants numbering in the hundreds (Metzo 2008: 217; Quijada 2008: 1–22).

In less publicized cases, revival has meant the rekindling of relatively closed kin group ceremonies with newly energized shamans. Some have reconnected with their extended families by sponsoring sheep sacrifices at original familial sacred sites, where all that remain are graves and sacred horse posts (interestingly called *sérgé*). One secret family ritual involved a group who hired a well-known shaman to help a son escape serving in Chechnya. He later successfully failed his army medical exam. An unusual Buriat group of combined shamans and lamas were credited in 2006 with having prevented an oil pipeline from coming too near Lake Baikal.[20]

A particularly high profile ritual brought male healers from all over the world to the justifiably famed and magnificent "shamanic rock" sacred site, variously called "Shamanka," "Böö"[shaman in Buriat] or Burkhan [spirit] Rock, of Olkhon Island, in Lake Baikal. I heard the ritual described somewhat sarcastically on Russian radio in 2003. The fascinating Buriat historian-turned-shaman Valentin Valerievich Khagdaev, keeper of the Olkhon region, hosted this unconventional *tailgan*, incorporating a sheep sacrifice, prayer, and purification ceremony.

I landed on Olkhon Island in 2005, not for a shamanic ceremony inside the rock's cave (where women are not allowed in any case) but for more private respect nearby. Early on, I learned that totemic legends animate this sacred island, in numerous versions and with multivocal significance. One is that Swan-girls came from the sky and landed on the island. A young man spied on them, and stole the plumage of one, preventing her from returning to the heavens. She was forced by her circumstances to become the wife of this man, this mere earthling, and eventually bore him a son. That son became the ancestor/forefather of the Khorin Buriats, who proudly recount this tale to their children, not just visiting foreigners. Local residents explained that the swans themselves have diminished in numbers, whether due to climate change, human "evil," celestial punishment against humans, or a combination of reasons. They worry about losses of a whole range of animals, and have recently renewed their offerings to lessen ancestral offense. They also continue to prohibit hunting nearby in an area now designated as a national park, and hope that shamanic rituals may lessen the extensive poaching that has plagued this area. Retelling the legends reinforces the perceived need for the rituals.[21]

Various zones constitute different degrees of sacredness on Olkhon—the most sacred is the hard to reach cave that opens onto the water around the rock from its main beach. The beach and beribboned trees near it constitute the second zone. And the third is the upper-level cliff overlook. With an Olkhon woman, I passed several ribbon-laden trees, and emerged onto the pebble beach. A Tibetan prayer flag flew between two of the trees. Lamas have claimed the spot as theirs, and have sometimes removed shamanic attributes. A St. Nicholas icon was once placed in the nearby cave—but that was later removed by Valentin's shamanic followers. As in Sakha, religious competition is constantly played out.

Valentin's often stated narrative concerning his shamanic legacy begins with the concept of heredity in an illustrious Olkhon line. He terms himself a "hereditary shaman of the ninth generation, of the Buian clan, Khagdai subclan."[22] His grandfather was a shaman, but, he adds with irony, his father was a communist. Significantly, before going to Soviet schools, Valentin was raised with nomadic traditions by his grandparents, who noticed that he had inherited shamanic capabilities, *utkha*. Since his clan was divided by the late 1980s into family groups of Olkhon, Ulan-Ude and far off Magadan, the shamanic heritage was split and nearly lost. As his friend, the filmmaker-anthropologist Anya Bernstein puts it, "Valentin often refers to Soviet-time shamans not as shamans but as shamanizing elders." At the end of the Soviet period, when hidden shamanic practice came to be valorized, these elders "decided it was necessary to unite two parts of the clan by initiating Valentin to be the main shaman of the clan. He underwent his first initiation in 1990, when he was 30 years old...due to the urgency of the situation." This initial private ritual anointed Valentin the keeper of the shamanic traditions of the reunited clan, and transferred their blacksmith tools and other shamanic objects to him, revealing his ancestors to have been shaman-blacksmiths (*darkhat*), renowned in the literature on Mongolic and Turkic shamanism (compare Alekseev 1984, 1997). Valentin has explained: "To be a shaman is not a profession but an obligation" (Krupnov 2005).

Valentin was chosen by the elders as well as "by the spirits" because of a very special sign on his body. He was born with a sixth finger on one hand. Far from letting Soviet doctors remove it to make him normal (as some family members suggested), elders urged that this special mark be revered. A further source of his knowledge has been diligent fieldwork, talking to elders throughout his region, gathering their accounts and memories. Anya Bernstein sees his impressive understanding of sacred geography to be "key to his 'cultural capital,'" as he is the only one who can identify ancestral spots for different (often long-scattered) local clans." Further, as a literate and exceptionally bright Soviet and post-Soviet student of history, Mongolic folklore and Buriat cosmology, Valentin uses and gives credit to the books of scholars like Natalia Zhukovskaia and Vladimir Basilov.[23]

I am not in a position to judge Valentin's discourse or his vagueness about the purposes, contexts and number of his initiations.[24] After his first initiation, relieved shamanizing elders (one in his eighties, the other 93) of his scattered family in Ulan-Ude and Olkhon stopped their practices. Valentin's social networks connect him to reopened Buriat channels of shamanic initiations with revitalization-minded spiritual seekers apprenticed to Mongolian shamans (compare Fridman 2004). His career incorporates personal curing with more broadly significant repatriation of living and dead Olkhon Island families back to their ancestral sites for heartfelt ceremonies of spiritual reunion. To earn money for his local historical museum and for his own family, he also provides more superficial séance-like performances for rich foreign and Russian tourists at local resorts. Commercial activities, the chaotic rock-star adapted *tailgan* ceremonies for international healers, and offers of personal fate predictions to foreigners have lessened his reputation with local Olkhon Island families.

Valentin has positioned himself as one of the stars of the Buriat shamanic revival, a religious philosophy he considers fully comparable in complexity and tolerance to Buddhism. He deems Russian Orthodoxy, at least as represented by local Russian priests, less encompassing and less tolerant. His strategic location presiding over one of the most sacred sites of the Buriat people, purposefully located by Soviet gerrymandering legacy in Irkutsk Oblast not the republic, makes his social-moral leadership significant. Locals hope he will not undermine his personal and social healing talents to chase foreign money.

When my Sakha friend Uliana Vinokurova interviewed Valentin on Olkhon Island in 2010, she found a Buriat patriot who was offering: "traditional ceremonies and rituals; lectures and discussions on history and Buriat-Mongol culture; healing through folk medicine;

excursions to shamanic sites; predictions according to the Mongol astrology book Éurkhai." As a prophet, his cleverly syncretic "codex," begins with the principle: "Every people is original and unrepeatable," and ends with the epigraph about the right to justice that began this chapter. Most significant, he includes a variation on the Judeo-Christian "golden rule" exhorting everyone to "live in harmony with oneself, with all beings surrounding one, with Nature, so that one does not do to others what one would not wish done to oneself."[25]

Other major male shamans have also gained national Buriat and international reputations, such as the elder Bair Tsybiekovich Rinchinov, an early member of the shamanic organization *Khese Khengereg* (glossed as rambling drum) that later merged into *Böö Mürgel* (Association of all-Buriat Shamans). He has also led the shamanist group *Altan Gadahan* (Polar Star) that has been superceded by an Aga Buriat group called *Khukhé Munkhé Tengeri* (Eternal Blue Sky). Rinchinov is based in the satellite region Aga that merged in 2007 with Chita Oblast, much to many Buriats' distress. Trained first by a local Aga female elder, he went on to an apprenticeship with a Mongolian shaman. As he explained to a group of healers and scholars (including me) in Moscow in 1995: "My teachers were very kind and strict, constantly testing. I know my own and the Russian language, but also have been able to speak other languages.... My ancestors, now spirits, knew such languages as Évenki, and Altai languages. I speak them fluently during ceremony. I somehow understand them." In the mid-1990s, Rinchinov was concerned with *Khese Khengereg's* gatekeeping against charlatans: "I passed my education trials. I can hold hot water, and do other things that seem hard.... We have to check on those pretenders who haven't really endured the shamanic illness. Who is acting? Who really is able to walk on water and hold hot things?"[26] In 2010, he sent a representative to the Tunka Valley conference on shamanism with a message of thanks for foreign support from the California-based Foundation for Shamanic Studies.

The respected, educated, and articulate former Russian teacher Nadezhda Stepanova, based in Ulan-Ude, founded the Society for the Revival of Buriat Religious Traditions in 1993 that later merged into the Association of all-Buriat Shamans (*Böö Mürgel*). In 2000, she lamented the distortions of shamanic practice that had been necessary in the Soviet period: "Fear controlled the world (our world, of course) and therefore many people had to turn away from their traditional responsibilities, for them traditional culture and traditional worldview in relation to the land... to Mother Earth" (Metzo 2008: 223–4). Overt respect for the earth and for ancestors faded, but could be recovered because the values were still passed on. Nadia conducts rituals in her tiny apartment, as well as in mass ceremonies, opening the window for offerings to the sky, feeding the gas stove for offerings to the fire spirit (as in Sakha Republic) (Humphrey 1999: 3–10). She also travels widely, helping people repair the damage of ancestral spirit neglect. Active in the Women's Crisis Center of Irkutsk, and an advisor on religious issues for the past president of the republic (Leonid Potapov), she helped push Khural legislation in the republic to ensure that shamanism would be recognized as an official religion alongside Orthodoxy and Buddhism. Nadia has also helped coach younger would-be shamans who are worried about their calling and their rituals. Her own shamanic illness included visions and a burst eardrum before she accepted her "call." She explains: "God's gift is given so that one can help people and not to make them lower [*nizhe*], so that the[y] fall still deeper on their knees."[27]

The Association of All-Buriat Shamans *Böö Mürgel*, whose members are scattered in areas throughout the republic and beyond, numbers close to 100, while that of the more recently founded and somewhat competitive *Tengeri* (*Tengri*) number about half that, with 15 claiming to be full-time practicing shamans.[28] *Tengeri* was founded by Bair Zhambalovich Tsirendorziev in 2003, with some of its members formerly in *Böö Mürgel*. It has sponsored *tailgan* ceremonies in the hippodrome on the outskirts of Ulan-Ude, and its leaders hope to create a shamanic ceremonial center on nearby land. But the territory is in dispute, with squatters and local Buddhist leaders against *Tengeri* aspirations. To broaden their base, their shamans suggest that *tailgan* participants need not know their clan roots, and can receive blessings from spirits of the whole Ulan-Ude region (Quijada 2008: 13–14).

In 2010, Bair Tsirendorziev similarly affirmed that the daylong *tailgan* ceremony we witnessed in the Tunka Valley was primarily to honor the Mountain God Bøhø Noyon, a god for everyone. However, he stressed that: "We had our own ancestors arrive [into us] first, before Bøhø Noyon, and we asked for them to ask for Bøhø Noyon to come." The God eventually came, in a culminating moment of the innovative ceremony led by Bair that involved the sacrifice of two sheep and a goat, a festooned birch tree cluster that was later burned in a huge bonfire, as well as the simultaneous drumming of an unprecedented 27 extravagantly dressed and masked shamans going into trance. At least one, a woman, was a Buriat from Mongolia, revealing ongoing cross-border ties of the spiritual communities.[29]

Several of my Buriat interlocutors sensed that shamanic ancestors who were repressed and frustrated in the Soviet period have finally been able to recoup spiritual losses in the nick of time by arranging a bumper crop of genuinely talented younger shamanic leaders. Many look to their Mongolian roots with nostalgia, bridging the divide that Soviet authorities tried to instill, as is evidenced by the poetry of Bayir Dugarov (1996), then president of the Geser Society:

> ...And the tips of my family tree extend into the mute depths of the Mongolian steppe.
> I could have listened to them day and night. I remember all that they have told me.
> And I am proud that the youth of my village consider me an elder.[30]

In sum, it takes more than conditions of political and social crises to reactivate shamanic communities, especially in places like Buriatia, where alternative religious traditions, whether Buddhism, Orthodoxy, or newer brands of Christianity, are easily available. Buriat shamans, crediting ancestral inspiration, have proved themselves to be more than a passing post-Soviet fad. However competitive, they have created active associations, have appealed to many urban and dislocated Buriats to reconnect with their homelands, and regularly sponsor and perform major, adaptive *tailgan* ceremonies. They are a conduit through which an impressive range of Buriat-Mongolic ancestor-oriented values and rituals have been rekindled in new ways for new times. Buriat (not Tuvan or Sakha or Altaian) shamans make up the overwhelming majority of an incomplete and controversial list of shamans of Russia that appeared on the internet in 2009.[31] However, like spiritual leaders elsewhere, the degree of their personal charisma and social effectiveness is varied, as is the longevity of their popularity. International recognition may hurt, not help, their credibility. Their activities, mostly with personal clients, small kin groups, or within competing organizations, are far too eclectic and their traditions far too ruptured (as yet?) to coalesce into a religious movement under a single shamanic leader. Only a few *böö* like Valentin would aspire to such a movement in any case.

Republic of Tuva: Dizzy with Success?

Perhaps the most famous, or at least cacophonous, shamanic revitalization is centered in the Republic of Tuva (Tyva), where both spiritual continuity and change across generations has been great and well-documented.[32] An argument could be made that "vitalization," as a more continuous flow of spiritual power into cultural practices, was relatively more possible in Tuva, given the impressive demographic majority of Tuvans in their own republic throughout the Soviet period. Tuvans' nomadic herder ties to their environment remained strong, and their urbanization processes relatively more recent (Anaiban 1999). And yet, as in the Sakha Republic, the locus of conscious cultural revitalization has been strongest in an urban context, with some of the main protagonists well-educated intellectuals (compare Humphrey 1999; Hoppál and Kosa 2003). Few represent this process more overtly than the renowned and widely respected scholar of Tuvan shamanism, Mongush Kenin–Lopsan, himself from a family of shamans. His personal saga of travel from novelist and folklore-collector of shamanic poetry to healer with clients waiting for audiences, blessings, and cures is quite dramatic. (See also Hoppál 2000: 48–52.) More politically complex and perhaps spiritually fraught have been his efforts to ensure his own stamp on the next generation of practicing shamans, the *kham* (from which *kamlanie* "séance" comes) of Tuva/ Tyva.

Mongush Kenin-Lopsan has his receiving room, with spacious porch for waiting supplicants, in the courtyard of the local history museum in the capital of Tuva, Kyzyl. The courtyard, filled with symbolic resonance with the past, is dotted with Altai mountain *stelae*, stone sculpture-figures (*kizhi-khøzh*) used as monuments to the dead in pre–Chingis Khan times when the early Turkic-based Orkhon script was prevalent. During a long wait in this courtyard in 2005, I had flashbacks of my first meeting with Kenin-Lopsan, who is one of my journal's authors, in the mountains of Garmish, Germany, during the 2000 conference "Wanderers Between Worlds: Functions and Forms of Contemporary Shamanism." He had performed in a neat German park in full brocaded regalia, with a group of much younger elegantly robed Tuvans. Their exuberant ritual included dancing, drumming, throat-singing, and jaw harp (also called *khomus*) playing around a large stately tree that was then adorned with prayer ribbons (*chalama*), rendering it incongruously a sacred "shaman's tree" (*kham-dit*), at least for a day.

When the aging elder finally appeared, being led by a young assistant since he is nearly blind, he appropriately took two men who had been waiting even longer than I into his inner sanctum. They were a Russian and a Tuvan, a welcome sign that Kenin-Lopsan, like most shamans in Sakha, is perfectly willing to help needy petitioners of any nationality, not solely Tuvan or indigenous Siberian.

Eventually, after mutual present giving, Kenin-Lopsan answered my urgent question concerning the state of shamanism in the republic: "The importance of keeping our religion and the traditions of our people cannot be underestimated. I was just at a Turkic people's congress in Kazan. I said there and I say to you that I am happy that in our land of Tuva, we have been able to keep the traditions of our people pure, have preserved shamanism despite repression. We have kept the original shamanism. Shamanstvo is not only a dead, folklore religion, it is a living breathing practiced religion of today."[33]

Kenin-Lopsan's extensive publications (1987, 1995a,b, 1997, 2006) include a collection of prayers (*algysh*) that he feels represent the essence of shamanic continuity with the past. He explained: "Tuvans have saved for the world their religion, the archaic religion of shamanism." His claims for shamanic (re)vitalization are thus bigger than merely salvation of Tuvan cultural traditions. Rather, they extend into the ideology that has also resonated with Michael Harner's (1990) concepts of "core shamanism," including the messianic potential of shamans of this generation to recover lost ecological and spiritual knowledge crucial to the 21st century world. Kenin-Lopsan proudly displays his designation as a Foundation for Shamanic Studies "Living Treasure of Shamanism." His main hope for a personal legacy has been recovery of Tuvan shamanic healing traditions, first through the association of healers he founded called *Düngür* [Drum] and then, when that split due to political dissension, through sponsorship of the group called *Tos Déér*, Nine Heavens.

Kenin-Lopsan went to considerable trouble to dispel some of the more negative stereotypes of Siberian shamans, insisting on the diversity of shamanic practitioners in both the past and present, and the wide range of their functions and intents. In this context, he proclaimed: "We do not have a sharp distinction between good and bad shamans." He elaborated: "We have some who are hereditary shamans, deriving their power from their ancestors, who they know. Others get their gifts from the spirits of the earth. And some from spirits of water, and some from masters of the underground.... We have many experts in healing. We also have some shamans who are experts in changing people's luck. We have some shamans who are able to perform surgery without knives, without cutting..." But the highest category of shamans, he stressed, were those "who derive their spiritual energies from the Sky." His current protégé, Ai-Churek Shiizhekovna Oiun, known widely as Aichurek (Benevolent Spirit Heart), is one of these. He called her to arrange a meeting, saying with a fond smile, "she is very special."

I had learned that Aichurek has a reputation for terrorizing people, including her co-workers and clients, but she is also said to be one of the best healers in the republic. Her healing center, with sacred sculptures, a large central eagle image, yurts, a shamanic world tree (*kham-yiash*), and colorful streamers in its front yard, is on the banks of the stunning Yenesei, near the monument proclaiming Tuva the "heart of Asia." I arrived with my Tuvan friend Aldynai Seden-Kurak, professor at Kyzyl State Teacher's Training Institute, whose useful *Tuvan-English Phrasebook* (2003: 99–107) equates Shamanism and Buddhism as local religions, glossing the Tuvan word *chüdülge* for religion. A guard ushered us to couches where he showed us Aichurek's publicity packet, stressing her reputation in Europe and America as well as Tuva. Her usual charges were on another page: 300 r for a consultation or healing session, 1,000 r for a ritual of purification, 3,000 r for a full ceremony. A nearby room was filled with shamanic instruments, tables laden with animal parts and shamanic cloaks. The walls were also decorated with animal heads, drums, and Buddhist hangings. The whole place was permeated with the scent of herbs, incense, and smoke.

Aichurek ushered us into her back room, down a long corridor in a building that used to be a school. She was wearing a long dress, had long loose hair, and ash on her forehead. We sat on stools in a room filled with incense and decorations on the walls, including feathers and a framed portrait of an Apache leader with ribbons adorning it. Her shamanic cloak, with its numerous ribbons in patterned splendor, was hung with a headdress nearby. Her face softened with our enthusiasm for her center, and she flowed easily into her fascinating life history:

> I started to shamanize when I was in seventh grade, around 1977. Even before that I'd had some people tell me I had talent, and I'd been able to see things others didn't. But one teacher's husband had disappeared and she feared he'd been lost, on a hunting trip.... I felt what had happened through her intuition, her fear. I conjured, saw a vision of a man with his face down in the water, at the edge of a riverlet. He'd been killed... I described where they might find the body, and it was right.

After a long silence, this former teacher influenced Aichurek's future: "In 1993, she refound me and thanked me, and told me to come with her to talk to Kenin-Lopsan." He passionately urged Aichurek to help her own people: "You need your people, to save your people... [to] practice and help people in the new group, *Düngür* (Drum)." Aichurek attributed her success with Kenin-Lopsan to her hard work, her openness to new experience, and her own family history. "He was worried about me, and told me to take a role in the [first Tuvan Republic] symposium on shamanism. I began to help people, to drum, and so became one of several children in my family who took up shamanizing as they had in the past." Her confidence increased after the visit of the Foundation for Shamanic Studies group: "Even Americans were using the drum. I was one of the shamans who was with the Americans when they came in the early 1990s" (compare Peters 1993; Brunton 1994).

Aichurek's view of shamanic revitalization was through the prism of her own experience: "Shamans are the people who can see the spirits, and are being respected for this again. Before, people had kept their shamanic heritage hidden. But secretly, people came to me to be cured. It has been hard to accept this ancestry." She pursued her awakening by returning to her natal village: "I went back to my region, my homeland, and found out that people had always thought me odd..." When asked how Tuvans had managed to keep their traditions alive, Aichurek smiled conspiratorially: "People said and did ritual prayers, *algysh*, even in the 1930s, and 1940s, when it was strictly forbidden. The *algysh* I sing today come from absorbing the chants of my childhood, and from nature. Those called by the spirits can become suicidal if they don't listen to the call, to begin to help people themselves." Renewed enthusiasm for healers has come at the price of some false claims of shamanic talent, but, Aichurek warned, "If pretenders don't have the spirit calling, then people can tell, and they won't come to them for cures." When it became possible, in the early post-Soviet period, healers began to recognize each other's talents: "We started gathering healers in a group... so people would not be called charlatans. It began with *Düngür*.

Sadly, some of the main healers began to call each other charlatans. To avoid getting sidetracked into personal recrimination, I gently jumped to asking about Düngür's competition, the center we sat in: "We started *Tos Déér* because he [Mongush Kenin-Lopsan] thought of it. People come here as a last resort. They come when doctors call them crazy. We had five last spring like that. They were psychic, they were talking to themselves, or to spirits, to devils. We help them and try to return them to their families as they were, but if it turns out that they need to start curing others, then that is what we help them do. It depends on the person."

Aichurek's own "spirit torture" was considerable. She explained that she had "three years without sleeping at night, as if a spirit was nearby and strangling me." She also reminded, after we discussed Joan Koss-Chioino's theories of "radical empathy" (1992) that not all come out of spirit torment as healers: "Some just get stronger, so they can help their children, for example. Or become better leaders." On the more negative use of special spirit powers, she warned: "People know that bad can come back on themselves. They know this all too well."[34]

In sum, Mongush Kenin-Lopsan and Aichurek represent one strand of Tuvan cultural revitalization, with claims of shamanic purity and antiquity, despite considerable adaptation of their practices in the current political environment. A Tuvan-Russian healer of more openly mixed ethnic background and ideology is Nadia, whose lovely drumming and singing séance overlooking an *arzhaan* (healing spring) in 2005 brought a falcon circling close over the heads of my impressed Tuvan and non-Tuvan friends. Tuvan shamans' reputations have shifted enough in the post-Soviet period to create several bases, not all in Kyzyl. Sailyk-ool (L. D. Mongush), who took over the group *Düngür*, is said by many to be past president Oorzhak Sherig-ool's favorite. In one account, the president himself requested a group shamanic ritual for rain to be performed in the mountains (and filmed); it successfully dispelled a drought. Indeed, authorities officially have supported *Düngür* and *Tos Déér* to some extent, but many say that officials support the local Buddhist community more.[35]

The healing centers of *Düngür* and *Tos Déér* function in tandem and competition with each other and, to some extent, also in competition with the thriving, revitalized Buddhist temples of Tuva. While for individual Tuvans these modes of spirituality are rarely mutually exclusive, for their major representatives they are increasingly distinct. Cultural leaders may use syncretic discourse without explicitly valuing syncretic thinking. Shamanic activism has not coalesced into a sustained movement that, despite its archaic roots, could be called a new contemporary religion. Routinization, in Weber's sense, is elusive, problematic and conflicted (Weber 1947; compare Crumbly 2008: 108; Kendall 2009). Nonetheless, competition with the prestige of Buddhism has caused Tuvan leaders like Kenin-Lopsan to frame shamanic practice and ideology in relatively institutionalized religious terms, including the partial written codification of oral *algysh* traditions.

Millennial Faith Healing for All?

In the interrelated realms of politics, development, ecology, conscious cultural changes, and human psychological potential, shamans and shamanic rituals can mediate interconnectivity, encourage social morality, radiate love, and promote interethnic tolerance. To do this effectively, shamans must speak in a language followers can understand, in times and contexts that resonate. As masters at trickster-like creativity, shamans also push the limits of all culturally available metaphors, especially symbols of spiritual power (Hyde 1998). In this fluid system, Jesus Christ can become Aiyy Urung or a shamanic helper spirit, as can and has Chingis Khan. But the system is undermined without faith, without confidence in the mediator, and, especially, when a mediator-shaman loses confidence in him/herself after being called psychotic or given inappropriate drugs by "modern" medical doctors.

The terrifying Soviet propaganda and punishment apparatus was one of the worst confidence destroyers of indigenous belief systems ever known. Yet some shamanic healers and visionaries have emerged to piece together faith in spirit powers, human-animal rapport, and a cosmology beyond the arrogance of Soviet-style "scientific materialism." Siberians, hungry for such faith, nonetheless eat tentatively at the tables of newly-forged-for-the-times shamanic mediators-between-worlds. "Are they real?" "Did they go through a genuine shamanic initiation, being torn apart by spirits and reconstituted?" "Do they use drumming séances?" Siberians themselves ask, not just outsider ethnographers. Unlike some Native Americans, who have explained to me that they experience and shape ongoing cultural processes of "vitalization," Native Siberians consider cultural revitalization all too necessary. As stressed throughout this book, their disruptions were too great and their underground too deep to see the post-Soviet emergence of shamans as a steady or normal process.

Sakha, Buriats, and Tuvans all have leaders in spiritual revitalization who are literate and articulate historians, or sometimes linguists. They are precisely the kind of needed interpretive philosophers whose deep cultural knowledge is combined with conscious yearning to transcend the banality and economic dislocations of everyday post-Soviet, Russified, and Westernized urban life. Their spiritually oriented and ecologically oriented activities are often impressive, using personal shamanic experiences to galvanize others into creating more institutionalized centers of healing and more general ritual observance. A few are charismatic, with loyal spiritual followers in villages and towns. But no one figure has yet emerged in these communities who qualifies as the messiah of a sustained new religious movement, such as Chot Chelpan in early twentieth century Altai or Handsome Lake for the Iroquois (Wallace 1972; Balzer 2003; Funk 2006; Halemba 2006). New generations of shamanic practitioners are often conscious of the messy incompleteness of their cultural reconstruction efforts. In Siberia, revitalization can be viewed as a regionally and temporally variable continuum. It is as often dependant on grants from newly cooperative Ministries of Culture (if not Health) as on visions. It is more institutionally supported in the republics. However, some major Buriat leaders have developed followings in areas rimming the Buriat republic, as if they sense a desperate need for a nick-of-time renaissance.

Have the leaders profiled here successfully begun revitalizing movements, or merely seized millennial moments to piece together in new ways older Siberian traditions? Several are living icons of their time, very much in current self-renewing spiritual agony, so it is premature to artificially slap labels of "new religion," "cult," "fraud," or "aborted reform movement" on them. Causes of shamanic movement mobilization go well beyond the need for professionalization through associations, the impact of literacy and educated shamans, new concerns about licensing of folk healers, fury over neocolonial Russian exploitation of nonrenewable resources, or the stimulus of competition from other more established religions. Yet these causes play into the psychology of leaders and followers to various degrees, with different synergistic mixes.

In each Siberian context, these social-spiritual movements represent conscious attempts at personal and community rejuvenation in crisis times by troubled charismatic leaders. Particularly striking is the diversity and sincerity of their followers, although they may be a relatively small proportion of the total population in various republics. Whether an urban folklorist experiencing conversion from Soviet atheism, a former Communist leader-turned-politician, or a rural cleaning lady once cured by a shaman in childhood, each supplicant and some cynics have found resonance in messages of ecological renewal, national identity, community solidarity (*communitas*) and return to traditional family values.[36] While the processes of cultural revitalization are uneven, messy and at times disillusioning, the urge toward spirituality using shamanic idioms continues to inflame and enrich indigenous and scholarly perceptions. In the global history of revitalization movements, few have reached the point of constructing a new religion or a genuine revolution (compare Wallace 1956; Van der Veer 2000; Lester 2002; Daschke and Ashcraft 2005). But many, including those described here, have been catalysts for more modest individual and community spiritual renewal. They thus simultaneously create and represent a kind of social medicine that Siberians call shamanic.

Photo 10 Buriat shaman with supplicant, *tailgan* ceremony Tunka Valley. Photo by Marjorie Mandelstam Balzer, 2010.

Reflections

Spiritual Vacuum?

In the late 1990s, I was at a conference in Alaska on indigenous peoples with my Sakha colleague and co-author Uliana Vinokurova, and decided to ask her an obvious question that anthropologists might pose more often before they write grant applications: "What do *you* think I should study next summer?" She laughed and confessed that she would appreciate my being her eyes and ears on a problem that had come to worry her: "Why do those [American] missionaries think we have a spiritual vacuum in the Sakha Republic?" The following summer, I followed her suggestion, expanding it to understand the multiple sides of religious "conversion" processes, and renewing my sense that the English word "conversion" sounds far more decisive than everyday experience often reveals. In retrospect, it was a peak time of spiritual experimentation.

During the project, a young mixed Russian-Sakha ("Sakhalar") Evangelical deacon named Aleksei Evertsov told me he had never felt comfortable in either the Russian or Sakha ("Yakut") worlds of Yakutsk. "I have only come to feel comfortable with myself through religion, this evangelical religion," he proclaimed. After a technical education at Yakutsk State University, he went to Moscow for missionary training with American Evangelicals. Typical of many children of mixed ethnic marriages in the republic, he had been brought up without religion.[1] "I do not really know the Yakut religion," he said, using their Russian exonym, "nor do my friends." Hinting that the Sakha religious revival has been superficial, he added: "I hear a small group of scientists have gotten together recently to recreate Yakut traditional religion."

An American missionary couple from Alaska named the Henrys stood beaming nearby with their Russian translator, greeting their mostly Russian parishioners in a downtown Yakutsk movie theater, the only venue they had been permitted. Down the road, the refurbished Russian Orthodox cathedral of St. Nikolai, with shining new gold cupolas, was home to a more flourishing congregation, also of mostly Russian believers.[2]

The leaders of these spiritual options, the official Russian Orthodox, the upstart and disadvantaged Evangelicals, and the indigenous Sakha, reveal enormous variations within themselves and considerable ignorance about each other. All are in competition with each other for followers, including indigenous Siberian followers, with the Orthodox and the Protestants most likely to use idioms of exclusivity and conversion. In contrast, some Sakha, such as the shaman and doctor Aleksandra Chirkova, calmly adhere to a long tradition of combining Russian Orthodoxy and indigenous belief. As we have seen in other Siberian republics, similar but not identical processes of religious experimentation, syncretism, and competition are ongoing. Those with Buddhist traditions, especially Tuva (Tyva) and Buriatia, have particularly strong, multicultural claims to rich indigenous spiritual legacies.

I have shown in this book that the complexities and ranges of Siberian beliefs go far deeper than the recent concoction of traditional religion by "a small group of scientists." Yet creation, adaptation, and "construction" are understandable aspects of the process of recent generations' urgent attention to spiritual roots. During Soviet repression of religion, shamanic knowledge was lost and many rituals went underground or were domesticated and feminized. Aleksei Evertsov's marginalization of Sakha religion was biased, and his post-Soviet association of Sakha religion with those old Soviet gods, "Scientists," was ironic. It is his small Evangelical group who are marginalized, especially under the 1997 Russian Federation "Law on Freedom of Conscience and Religious Associations" that in its preamble and in practice has come to privilege the Russian Orthodox.[3] Most poignant, however, was his query to me: "Do you know about this? I would love to know more about Yakut [Sakha] religion."

The scholar best matching Alexei's depiction of a scientist-religious leader is the Sakha linguist-philosopher Lazar Afanasev, a cofounder of the group *Kut-Siur*, proselytizer of the wisdom that one's heart-soul-mind-body can be blended for personal and community health. As we have seen in the previous chapter, Lazar's group has coalesced around their *Aiyy Diété* (Spirit House), a traditional log *balagan* on the outskirts of Yakutsk. They have had some success campaigning for school programs that explain Sakha religion as "benevolent spirit teaching." However, their sponsorship of rituals to honor gods of the Sakha Turkic pantheon has attracted only a small group of loyal followers.

Introspective Sakha reflect on a growing divide within their society, both rural and urban, between those who see the revival of shamanic beliefs as medically oriented and those who see it as part of a larger, indigenous religious movement. It may be more accurate to suggest three main strands of shamanic "useable past" knowledge and inspiration: the medical, the cultural-artistic, and the religious, with each known through their dominant representatives. Yet the most effective of the shamans and spiritual activists featured here combine these strands to varying degrees, and all use several different Sakha words for intuition to explain their practices.

These creative healers and spiritual leaders draw heavily but not rigidly on Siberian traditions and methods. Many use literacy in productive ways, especially the late Vladimir Kondakov (1997), who wrote entertaining historical novels to teach Sakha beliefs. Some use modern European medical vocabularies of psychological well-being, for example Aleksandra Chirkova. The late Klavdia Maksimova, Saiyyna, tapped into human yearning for reincarnation, creatively adapting indigenous beliefs that were predominant in the Far North. The diviner Natalia Ivanova conceives her powers as partially channeled through an energy column that resembles a Sakha horse hitching post.

Contemporary shamanic practitioners are women and men. Without full surveys, I cannot claim to know the proportions but my sense is more women are self-identifying as healers in the Sakha Republic and more men do so in Buriatia. The most successful are sensitive to socially constructed gender differences and (en)gendered power at many levels; their followers may be predominantly one gender or more balanced. They have loyal followers because of proven successes in both personal healing and social "purification." Gender issues may contribute to the way they critique rivals as "charlatans," also common in earlier periods. Their human frailties are magnified by their prominent yet insecure, often weakly institutionalized, social positions.

Pre-Christian shamans, conventionally defined as mediators between cosmic and earthly worlds, were oriented toward problem solving, especially healing the integrated bodies and minds of people in small communities. They did not proselytize, but had a deeply spiritual, mystical world view that opened vistas of thought and philosophy. The crux of the difference between "world religions" and "shamanic belief systems" is not spiritual depth, nor literacy, but rather social organization and missionizing.[4] "Traditional" shamans had no need to ambitiously convert others. But today, post-Soviet shamans do need to rebuild their communities and reharmonize their ill and bewildered followers. Competition with established Russian Orthodoxy and invigorated Western Christian missions is part of the dynamic driving religious revitalization (compare A. Nikolaev 2007). Hope for community renewal also comes from within, from non-chauvinist rediscovery of indigenous shamanic local and homestead-based pasts (Vinokurova 1994; Morokhoeva 1995; Anaiban 1999).

At the (dis)junction between personal healing and community well-being, contemporary spiritual practitioners are and need to be the most creative and adaptive. Shamanic troubleshooting these days extends from healing the ill to finding lost bodies and stolen cars; from facilitating business ventures and marriages to influencing court cases and army drafts. The manipulation (literally and figuratively) of the personal and community interstice is precisely what is most vulnerable to accusations of "artificiality" and "charlatanism" against people striving for cultural revitalization and community solidarity. At stake are trickster-like shifting definitions of cultural legitimacy and subversion (compare Hyde 1998: 252–280).

In the early 1990s, a young Sakha healer decided to call herself "Sakhai." Her effort was perhaps too blatant, or premature, and her practice suffered from undue dramatization. So too, Lazar Afanasev's group has lost followers, partly from uneasiness about his almost missionary style of writing strident Sakha-centric ("nationalistic") newspaper articles. By 2010 in Yakutsk, three buildings were associated with claims to be indigenous-led "temples" of spirituality. Their leaders competed with each other and also with rival Christian churches. This was far from a spiritual vacuum. But precisely the multiplicity of options was bothering those Sakha who wanted their own non-chauvinist yet coherent and organized religion as a symbol of their coming of age as a nation.

"Too Many Coincidences?"

The eclectic and sometimes competitive belief communities described here illustrate that neither current nor historical Siberian "beliefs" are monolithic. As has happened frequently in the history of religion, some charismatic activists have tried to delineate gospel and position themselves in "more fundamental (pure) than thou" polemics. For many followers, however, faith remains eclectic, situational, or elusive, as do the ways people discuss it. Trust can be fragile and rationality itself culturally relative (Handler 2004; Lindquist and Coleman 2008).

People who have bouts of doubts about their faith are not fickle intellectuals, they are human. My analyses, acknowledging local skeptics, has neither presumed the wholeness of Siberian "cultures" nor assumed that "gods and spirits" are indisputably part of the "natural world." Nonetheless, healers and elder-experts composing Sakha prayers and blessings have repeatedly used the expression "there are too many coincidences [to be real coincidences]" to explain to me why they believe in the spirits they address in their magnificent, poetic prayers sampled in Chapter 4. Interlocutors in or from various parts of Siberia in recent conversations enthusiastically stress dramatic successes in shamanic healing or divining by living as well as legendary shamans. As in the past, reputations build: success reinforces successive success.

When Sakha say that words have spirit (*ichchi*), this literally can mean that certain sacred sung phrases may provide entry points into other dimensions of reality. Similar dimensions are also tapped when a craftsman envisions or dreams a designated tree for making sacred healing drums. They are manifest when a hunter refrains from killing an eagle thought to be the reincarnation of an ancestor, but joyfully kills an elk perceived to be offering itself. Some fear that such sensitivities are themselves endangered, but these examples are taken from optimistic conversations about spiritual rebirth that I had in 2010.

In the post-Soviet period, popular discourse in the Sakha Republic has focused on spirits (*aiyy, ichchi*, and *abaaghy*), as well as very specific sky gods, using the term *tangara*, glossed as god but sharing its Turkic root with *tangalai*, sky. Comparable discourse concerning *Tengri* also has taken hold in other Turkic and Mongolic communities of Siberia and Central Asia.[5] Interestingly, those who have come to worship as well as study *Tengri* tend to say "Thank *Tengri*" instead of "Thank God," including when speaking Russian to each other. It has become a kind of Siberian Turkic-Mongolic peoples' solidarity code.

Some Siberians, striving for collective spiritual solidarity and pride at national and supranational levels, have imbued projects like the "Purification House," the "Spirits House," and numerous "folk healing" centers with meaning beyond political symbolism. Whether called shamanism or neo-shamanism, shamanic, or animistic, popular religion or benevolent spirit teaching, nature worship, or ancestor worship, such faith-based striving links indigenous Siberian peoples to spiritual revitalization trends throughout the world.[6] Implicit, and sometimes explicit, is an us/them sentiment that pits indigenous groups against dominant cultural "others," in the Sakha, Buriat, and Tuvan cases, Russians. Dangers of homegrown fundamentalism combined with national chauvinism lurk, but are not dominant (compare Van der Veer 2000; Vitebsky 2005: 191–195). "Strategic essentialism," a concept of literary scholar Gayatry Chakravorty Spivak (2008), may be relevant for more subtle, mutual us/them positioning.

Do stable communities exist where shamanic practice, despite some degree of political repression, has maintained a more isolated and "traditional" basis of credible belief and authority? Many romantics, spiritual seekers, and ethnographers (sometimes overlapping categories) have searched Siberia looking for such places. The mountainous Republic of Tuva (Tyva) in particular has been identified not only with spiritual revival but spiritual continuities of archaic beliefs, rituals, and throat singing harmonized to running rivers (Kenin-Lopsan 1997; Van Deusen 2004; Levin, Suzukei 2006; Lindquist and Coleman 2008). However, the more one learns of the politics of spirituality and of permeating outside influences, the less consistent over the generations a particular "people's" shamanic practice appears. Like a disturbed archeological dig, interpenetrating layers of beliefs, be they Buddhist, Christian, or Islamic, distort our ability to discern what is a revitalization process and what is a more "natural," flowing vitalization. Perhaps the line should be declared too fuzzy for us to fuss over, although vitalization may reduce dangers of fundamentalism.

As we have seen, much of the traditional power of synergistic, intense group belief was squashed by Soviet political repression in most of Siberia. Group practices representing or encouraging shamanic faith and ritual have had to be recreated in ways that may look artificial, although their vocabulary may be "ancient," derived from epics. Some Siberian practitioners in Sakha, Tuva, and Buriatia say that the spirits themselves, some of whom are ancestors, are helping them to reconnect with their past. They learn what they need as they go, usually with some degree of altered consciousness to assist entry into non-ordinary realities.[7] To pervert the famous Levi Strauss "bricolage" metaphor (1966: 16–22), the cultural crafting materials exist, but are put together in reconstructive, imaginative and intuitive ways, with enormous gaps (compare Fortun et al. 2010). Tuvan and Buriat intellectuals have indicated to me that such gaps worry practitioners there as well as in the Sakha Republic. In these areas, the shamanic revival is strong yet eclectic, controversial and subject to changing public opinion.

When recalling any and all Siberian rituals remotely shamanic that I have observed or participated in, I must differentiate those oriented to public "white shamanic" practice (such as those occurring in *Archy Diété* in Sakha Republic, at *tailgan* in Buriatia, or at national festivals and blessing ceremonies throughout Turkic and Mongolic Siberia) and those explicitly for healing that are much more personal, intimate, and private.[8] These are in turn separate from the rituals of Russian or Russian-influenced Siberian practitioners called "extrasense," who sometimes conduct mass meetings and workshops they call "séances."

More intriguing and problematic to categorize are the group sessions of several powerful Sakha women shamans, Aleksandra Chirkova, Saiyyna, and Ed'ii Dora. Comparable sessions are led by Aichurek and others in Tuva; Nadezhda Stepanova and Svetlana Daribazarova (Arsiia) with Buriats. While drawing on elements of pre-Soviet séances, each has brilliantly reconfigured the "traditional" yet maintained the essence of shamanic practice: evoking and communicating with spirits for a purpose.[9] Svetlana's articulate insights into the process may be more generally relevant. She explains that she helps women exorcize their personal and community concerns, using the power of "scent, drum, dance, and songs" to produce "a positively charged memory" that will help not only a single ill patient, but also a whole network of that person's kin, friends, and associates. She uses the Buriat *ongon*, an image or stone to attract a spirit for a purpose, similar to an *émégét* in Sakha shamanic tradition. She recommends larger kin group sacrifices (*tailgan*) only when necessary, and she becomes a medium through whom pathologies, both individual and community, can be healed "by changing clients' consciousness."

Fragile beliefs are today socially and politically activated in a skeptical, worldly milieu. Messages concerning an urgent need for ecological and social healing as well as personal healing resonate strongly but unevenly. In 2009, a well-traveled young Sakha doctor from Yakutsk told me that she prefers telemedicine to shamans. But she affirmed that when she travels in northern villages, she sees that many families have photos of Ed'ii Dora on their walls—"Just like the Tibetans have the Dalai Lama." I saw this too in 2010, but I also saw that eclectic global media and violent internet games have reached Siberian villages, piercing any romantic illusions that isolated, bravura, tradition-permeated séances are dominant sources of group solidarity.

Finding Fault Lines?

Interpretive studies of shamans and their practices and worldviews are bound to reveal variations in approaches, writing styles, and the virulence of their culturally saturated debates. Acknowledging the extraordinarily subjective nature of this and any study of shamans, I nonetheless see patterns in the sharpest fault finding and claims. Differences in approaches are worth making explicit, in an effort to bridge some of these comparative and applied divides. Several interrelated issues deserve review: definitions, especially attempts to differentiate "shamanism" and religion; origins, pitting theories focused on bioneurology against social context; psychology, characterizing indigenous mental health and naiveté; and authenticity, claiming dichotomies between "indigenous" and "new age" shamanic practices and beliefs. Readers need not be specialists to jump into the fray by thinking about these hot issues that can reflect refracted light on wider societal and global concerns.

Many of the narratives featured in this book reveal that contemporary shamanic perception and activities often incorporate more than Mircea Eliade's definition of shamanism as an "archaic technique of ecstasy." No one definition of shamanism, whether as "controlled trance," "local religion," "an ancient belief system," "spirituality," or "gnosis" (direct experience of the Divine), suffices for all contexts. I share Jacques Derrida's concern about the Westernized over-abstraction of "Religion? In the Singular?" and am partial to Jane Atkinson's plea for contextual study of shamanship and shamanism*s*, while acknowledging Åke Hultkranz's eloquent rebuttal.[10] As open-mind-bodied searchers in a globalizing world, we can respect increasing communications among creolized shamanic practitioners and their insistent messages of human-animal communication and mutual influence. No pure version of shamanic practice, devoid of layers of cultural contexts, exists. Searches for a "First Shaman" (an ur-shaman birthplace), including in Siberia, are equally unproductive.[11]

As boundaries of world religions and local religions become increasingly blurred, it is harder to maintain concepts of the purity of Culture (for anthropologists) and Gospel (for missionaries). The complementarity as well as clashing of shamanic world views with conventionally defined "world religions" (Christianity, Buddhism, Islam, and Judaism) make a mockery of attempts to isolate or purify our study of shamanism into a single coherent complex (compare M. Bloch 2008). Much of my research on Siberian groups has emphasized empirical variations and debates within specific shamanic cultural contexts (Ob Ugrian, Turkic, Mongolic), rather than trying to derive general patterns of shamanic behavior, belief, and cosmology. Yet comparisons provide striking parallels. In addition to exploring common cultural roots, a way to summarize these parallels is to contrast the goals of shamanic practitioners with those of other religious authorities:

1) Shamans have rarely been missionaries, although competition with missionaries, whether Christian, Buddhist, or Islamic, has sometimes led to greater institutionalization of shamanic movements. This has happened in Native North America and is happening in Siberia today, particularly in the republics of Sakha, Buriatia, Tuva, and Altai.
2) Shamans usually have local, not universal, canons. Yet their focus on both individual and community curing leaves open widening, situational, and multileveled definitions of "community." Shamans in Siberia are interested in meeting other indigenous healers and have begun to do so, especially in the context of ecological and climate change concerns.
3) Shamans have not needed literacy, but some make excellent contemporary use of it, whether in court cases, life histories, or presentations of philosophy. Indigenous healers have become articulate authors in Eurasia and North America, and this need not delegitimize them. "World religion" distinctions designating "peoples of the book" (the Bible, the Koran) dissolve with the potential for new sacred texts and syncretic versions of older moral codes. "Live and direct" communication with other worlds need not be hindered (compare Engelke 2007).
4) Contemporary shamans come from social-political groups often identified as "minority," "indigenous," "Native," "countercultural," or "non-hegemonic." As subjects, not perpetrators of colonialism, theirs has been a special form of identity-building resistance, sometimes secretive and recently more open (compare Ortner 1995; Fortun et al. 2010). Whether open or closed (a matter of degree), the very localization of shamanic communities often has been their strength. But this may be changing and the definition of "colonial" may also be a matter of degree.

It is unwise to try to fit shamans into a box, conceptually with our definitions, psychologically by pegging them as abnormal, or politically, by giving authorities intellectual ammunition to repress them. Shamans have survived into the twenty-first century because their own communities recognize them as addressing ongoing needs for interrelated individual, community, and ecological health. Their outstanding, sustainable use of local herbs and pharmacopeia is the most basic of their skills (Plotkin 1993, 2000). Their often-virtuoso coalescence of culturally salient symbols, myths, and rituals provides further aesthetic, heuristic, and emotional value. Their experiential knowledge paths derive from lifetimes of attunement to "imagination, intuition, visions, dreams, the senses, and the body" (Krippner 2000: 115).

For those focused on origins, such as archeologist David Whitley (2009), this attunement derives from a dramatic shift in human neurobiology around the time of the magnificent Lascaux cave paintings (35,000–10,000 years ago) that enabled great capacity for art, the emotional ranges of manic-depressives, charisma, and much else associated with shamans. Unfortunately, he links this provocative theory to early ethnographic reports of shamans as deranged. But early writers, whether missionaries, explorers, or traders, perceived shamans as deranged and vindictive because they arrived with the baggage of extreme prejudice against shamans, whether in Europe, Siberia, or the Americas.[12] Shamans, representing the epitome of the Christians' pagan devil, often perceived themselves to be at war with many of the newcomers.

How do we reconcile the biases of early accounts, that made most shamans psychotic, with those of later accounts, that stress shamanic healing? Certainly it is clever but too over-generalized to claim, as George Devereaux did (1956), that shamans are cured psychotics, harnessing their emotional energies into troubleshooting for the benefit of their communities. Equally problematic are explanations portraying shamans of yore as wild (savage, pure, and brilliant) but ones today as kind and tame. How do we explain contemporary threats (including against me) and the continuity into the twenty-first century of the fear of shamanic curses in indigenous Siberian communities? When did I realize, during the ostensibly basic "purification and blessing" séance described in Chapter 1, that V.'s "smallest helper-spirit" was "a real predator," who "could have eaten [my] heart?" How can we understand a Siberian family, today living far from their original homeland, who do not want their children to return even for a visit because they believe in the curses extending through the generations of shamans who hated their famous Soviet Commissar great grandfather?

My approach has been to learn from the diverse social-cultural contexts that could result in individual and community fear of shamans as well as healing by them. I do not dare generalize about the psychological state of all shamans, especially as it changed over individual lifetimes. However, I admire their huge and widely recognized capacities for altered consciousness (Furst 1972, 2004; Kremer 1999, 2000, Krippner and Elis 2009). If we stress the social constraints on shamans' potential to use their powers to do evil, however derived, then we find a salient and probably quite archaic belief, since it is widespread in Siberia and elsewhere: that shamanic revenge or abuse of power can come back to haunt either the shaman or close family members. This spirit-attributed social enforcement mechanism constrains misuse of shamanic power enormously effectively, although not in all cases. It may well have enabled shamans to maintain their dignity, leadership, spiritual authority, and healing powers in earlier times as well. Shamanic psychological qualities within their social and political milieus are too mixed and complex to be rendered into a linear evolutionary story line (compare Wilber 1981; Winkelman 2000). That shamans did not need to be loved, and sometimes enjoyed being feared, is well documented. The revered and gentle Sakha shaman Niikon occasionally lost his temper and used shamanic powers in competitive ways that we might condemn.

Neurobiologically driven mood swings may help us partially understand shamanic brilliance, greatness, and extravagant personalities. Manic flair perhaps sheds some light on shamanic flexibility, the ability to change with the times, trickster-like. But such reductionist or "leading cause" medical explanations downplay the very wisdom that the whole Sakha *kut-siur* philosophy is built on: the integration of heart-soul-mind-body. I argue, at least for Sakha shamans, if not other Siberian shamans, that they were and often are better at this integration in themselves, before stimulating it in others, than most of their contemporaries in each generation. This is no "new-age" fad or Orientalist romanticism. It derives from my Siberian interlocutors. And far too often, certainly historically, discussion of shamanic vengefulness, spiritual mysteries, altered consciousness exploits, and shamanic initiation through "illness," curdles into the pathologizing of shamans and their practices through time (compare Silverman 1967; Narby and Huxley 2001). The historical literature, and the multitude of experiences it imperfectly reflects, should not be used as an excuse to demonize shamans of yore, any more than the current literature, and the multitude of experiences it perhaps more accurately reflects, should be used to make them all into angels.

Curing hurt people battered by social and political circumstances is a widespread survival value shared in pre-colonial, colonial, and post- or neocolonial times. While classics of anthropology are filled with shamanic exploits recovering "lost souls" (Boas 1909, 1930; Levi-Strauss 1963), today we usually think of this in metaphorical terms. Michael Jackson (2009: xiii) eloquently states: "Lost souls variously hit the bottle, do drugs, distract themselves in work, appeal to God, or seek out some wilderness, real or symbolic where they take refuge and regroup. I refuse to pathologize any of these transmutations, or to interpret connectedness with nature, the cosmos, the divine or an imagined community as escapes from reality, mere opiates, illusions, or defenses."

What if we accepted, as smaller scale shamanic societies probably did, a greater range of what is "normal" and what is needed to attain "normalcy"? In a lecture to the Quest Society, the Russian ethnographer of the shaman-led "Tungus" (Évenki) Sergei Shirokogoroff (1924: 370) long ago contrasted European and Tungus psychological approaches, using the vocabulary of his day: "I have already noted that some kinds of psychic and nervous maladies in the conditions of European life are never cured at all and the persons who are *de facto* ill live without medical survey. Among the Tungus all these persons would be cured by the Shaman's hypnotic influence and would return to their normal activity. This explains why the Tungus, in spite of their very unstable psychology, have usually such a normal and healthy method of acting and thinking, and at the same time *assimilate new knowledge very easily*" (my emphasis).

This passage, from an ethnographer steeped in many languages and perceptions, points to the nexus of learning, intelligence, and health. It contrasts emblematically with Patriarch of the Russian Orthodox church Kirill's embarrassing 2010 pronouncement on indigenous peoples' psychology at the opening of a new cathedral complex in Yakutsk: "Meeting with local people, looking at them in the eye, I suddenly saw their childishness...a preserved childishness in their hearts...a purity of the heart." His deputy, answering a direct question about shamans, warned: "...evil spirits always spoil human life, and if you begin to communicate with them, they will make you their hostage."[13]

Backsliding into recurring clichés about Siberians as crazy, dangerous, naïve, or childish is hardly an effective bridge for communication or learning from indigenous experience. How then are we to better understand one of the hallmarks of shamanic intelligence through the generations, the shamanic illness? Sakha, Tuvan, and Buriat shamans have resonated with my descriptions of Joan Koss-Chioino's theories concerning the "radical empathy" of traditional healers. They explain that their tormenting by spirits was not only purposeful, in that it forged them as shamans, but also that it was targeted to help them cure specific illnesses. One (Sakha) shaman revealed that he expected, by the end of his healing career, to be able to cure exactly 41 illnesses, as that would fulfill his fate. Alcoholism was definitely included. Another (Tuvan) shaman felt that it was crucial for her to live through how a sufferer feels, in order to be able to cure ailments of that particular sufferer. If shamanic empathy was not experienced either during the cure or during an initiatory shamanic illness, then that supplicant would need to seek help elsewhere. This is one of the reasons that shamans continually mention (in the field, in the literature) that they have repeated bouts of "spirit torture," including dismemberment and reconstitution, to bring them to increasingly higher levels of ability. This resembles graduating levels of psychiatric training rather than some naive "devil's deal" or the pathological need of a doctor to "cure thyself." Knowing that spirits have chosen the shamans, and that shamans have suffered through illness, helps make them credible to supplicants.

Credibility, gatekeeping, and issues of "authenticity" plague indigenous shamans and healers in their local communities. Such issues also vex indigenous and other scholars intent on preserving shamans' reputations and cultural or perceived national purity. "Western" shamanic practitioners (misnamed "new age") can and have become their targets or allies, depending on the context. In practice these seemingly distinct categories of people cannot be easily valorized or demonized as two specific groups.[14]

Criticizing false dichotomies need not mean analytically merging European shamanic and indigenous spiritual practices. But the strident sharpening of their borders needs softening. They have in common a deeply democratic access to spiritual worlds beyond everyday realities, through trance and intense purpose. Few claim that drum circles spawned from the "core shamanism" workshops of Michael Harner's Foundation for Shamanic Studies are the same as a Lakota sweat lodge or a Sakha shamanic séance. All are venues I have experienced with Siberian friends and all have their own charms, music, cultural contexts, and altruism. Each is worth studying and taking seriously for what it may offer an unselfish spiritual seeker. Premature judgements concerning who is "real" in their human-animal encounters and mystical experiences may cut off our ability to understand "natural" worlds. In a multileveled, multicultural world of expanding connections, spirited kindred humans are finding each other for diverse reasons.[15]

One of the most significant connections is that of indigenous or so-called "fourth world" peoples talking to each other. When they do, in environments they consider safe from mockery of their faiths, they find not only rapport as activists but considerable commonality in spiritual orientations. I saw this in the rapport of Sakha, Buriat, and Khanty colleagues in 2010. My Native American friends who host sweat lodges and are also professional psychologists say that this is because "the spirit worlds are the same." Their generalization helps them relate to the multicultural people who feel grounded in their lodge. Siberians who experience their own and other forms of séances nonetheless are animated by particular spirit animals or special ancestors or warrior-leaders or epic heroes. At a different level of communication, possibly telepathy, is the Canadian First Nations leader who told me his drum circle had sent their souls to the Amazon to check on a friend who was an ecology activist living with death threats. When they returned from their "trip," several of them had seen the same scene: their friend safely but sadly walking along a newly cut road in the forest.

Who Cares?

Cultural leaders, political activists, anthropologists, and spiritual seekers have helped to raise the credibility of shamans and shamanic thinking, with varied success, personal passion, and "pluriversal" orientation. Increased international interest in "traditional" spirituality may propel those who mediate among the most worlds into becoming media savvy twenty-first century shamans. But the perils of going beyond community healing and spirituality into shamanic rock-star status are also great. How well does shamanic thinking travel beyond indigenous communities? Is respect for ancient wisdom increasing and coming into our global cultural mainstream in the nick of time or just too late?

I have outlined shifting ways that healers and healing communities are creating effective yet altered ritual environments in western and eastern Siberia, transcending harsh legacies of Soviet and missionary repression. At times such processes work in synergistic ways, reinforcing indigenous community confidence, Northern ecological activism, and inter-indigenous contacts and communication. This positive synergism is the context of the Sakha cultural revitalization movement that was supported by republic authorities during the peak of 1990s sovereignty. It also helped propel other spiritual revitalization urges in republics where indigenous leaders could align cultural and political policy to recognize Native potential. Buriat and Tuvan shamans undoubtedly are more numerous than Sakha ones. But numbers do not always add up to community or republic level success, and should not mask the cold reality that many of the 1990s cultural revitalization movements seem to have stalled.

Looking at broader Russian Federation trends, the fledgling and fragile positive synergism of local cultural renewals has more recently been pulled apart and twisted by counter-trends of political recentralization, unemployment, increased alcohol and drug abuse, burst Siberian dams and pipelines, and finally acknowledged dangers of human-induced climate change. Disturbing causes and effects are hard to separate, because they interact with each other in a negative spiral. In unpublished statistics that were later suppressed in 2008, the Sakha republic was revealed to have some of the highest youth suicide rates in the Russian Federation. Siberian indigenous groups have long had some of the lowest life expectancies in the county.[16]

With such colossal interrelated problems, we must ask whether shamanic and other kinds of cultural and spiritual renewal could possibly be effective in any but the most superficial "morale-building" terms. Russian nationalists, Russian Orthodox authorities, and some lingering "scientific atheists" regularly disparage the "shamanist" republics and peoples. They have used a propagandized regression into "primitive faiths" as an excuse to recover resources feared lost in sovereignty drives. Presidents of the Republics of Sakha and Tuva have felt impelled to make public statements distancing themselves from shamanism, for whatever reason. The prestige of folk healing throughout Russia, having hit a possible peak in the 1990s, has itself been declining.

In this context, international attention to the significance of folk wisdom, to the dignity of indigenous rights, and to the preservation of Northern ecological systems recognized to play a magnified role in global health may help pull Native communities back onto the synergistic track they had begun to find in the 1990s. Indigenous Siberian leaders, having tasted degrees of sovereign control over their resources, are alarmed that they have been forced yet again into dependency positions. This is a recipe for radicalization that is dangerous, and Siberians themselves need to counteract it. The moderates among them, reaching out to learn more of international experience, find encouragement in fora such as the Northern Forum, the Arctic Council, the United Nations Non-Governmental Organizations, and Many Strong Voices (a coalition of island and northern indigenous peoples).[17]

A better, more informed awareness of shamanic communities, sacred sites, and indigenous ecological values must go beyond clichés or paternalism, all too common in the past. Spiritual allies (kindred spirits) are finding each other as some land management and climate change negotiators incorporate indigenous perspectives and indigenous leadership, especially in Alaska and Canada (Nadasdy 2007). Indigenous Siberians recently have been collaborating with the ecology organizations Sacred Earth, Foundation for Sustainable Development of Altai, Pacific Environment, Cultural Survival, and others. This is important, because the history of indigenous rights leaders' and ecology activists' communication has been filled with tensions and incongruent agendas.[18]

Further indicators of respect for indigenous spirituality may be relatively more symbolic, focused on ceremony or public lectures. In Greenland in 2009, the Évenk shaman Sobei with his assistant Oktiabrina helped open a conference on problems of climate change attended by scientists and shamans from Asia, Africa, America, and Australia. At the United Nations in New York, performances by Siberian shamans were held in 2007 and 2009. Was this more than entertainment, more than the catering to curiosity for the exotic akin to the sensation of indigenous performances at historical World Fairs? Perhaps slightly, since one of the U.N. performances was held in conjunction with highlighting the Year of Polar Awareness.[19]

We need more than one year of Polar Awareness to make up for the devastation done to Native communities throughout the North and likely to increase with the opening of the Northern Sea Route. This book is meant as a small contribution to raising the credibility of Siberian shamans and their struggling communities, without trying to whitewash frightening aspects of shamanic traditions, including curses and internal competitions. The best of the talented twenty-first century shamans and shamanic trickster-artists combine social leadership, charisma, creative talent, ecological sensitivity, and healing gifts in their activist lives. Their gifts may perpetuate family histories of X-ray vision, synesthesia, telepathy, clairvoyance, empathy, endorphin stimulation, manic depression, and more that we have not yet defined in scientific terms. Shamanic functions are impossible to separate, since shamans of the past and today are usually the most talented, adaptable, and perceptive individuals of their communities.

Photo 11 Olkhon Island, Lake Baikal, near sacred rock, with sun-kissed offerings tree. Photo by Marjorie Mandelstam Balzer, 2005.

Notes

Introduction: Shamans, Spirituality, and Cultural Revitalization

1. Those effectively stressing healing language include Feld (1990); Riboli (2000); Roseman (1991); Vitebsky (1993). Compare Vitebsky's overview (1995).
2. See Bogoras (1909); Czaplicka (1914); Lot-Falk (1956: 378–83); Shternberg ([1933]1999). For gender-sensitive comparisons across Siberia concerning shamanic practice, "bear ceremonialism," and "menstrual taboos," see Balzer (1981;1996). See also Buckley and Gottlieb (1988); Grambo (1989: 103–113); Hamayon (1990, 2007); Kehoe (1992:344; 2000); LaBarre (1972a:138–40, 156–7, 179–81); Lang (1997); Saladin d'Anglure (1992 b, c; 1993); Oosten (1989: 334); Tengan (2008:152); Williams (1992).
3. See Cruikshank (1998, 2005); Goulet and Miller (2007); Ingold (2000); McClellan (1975); Nadasdy (2007); Nelson (1983). Compare Anderson and Nuttall (2004); Stammler and Takakura (2010); Willerslev (2007). Pedersen (2001: 422) overgeneralizes about "North Asian indigenous ontologies," exposes his own worldview with the word "spooky," while calling Chukchi spirit beliefs "beautifully symmetrical."
4. Compare the angry Sidky (2008) and the "radical" Jackson (1989, 2009).
5. Compare Thomas and Humphrey (1994); Balzer (1999); Ssorin-Chaikov (2003); Cruikshank and Argounova (2000); Bloch (2004); Grant (1995); Vitebsky (1990; 2005); Kharitonova (2006).
6. A large older literature focuses on whether the shaman is "neurotic" or "schizophrenic." Proponents included Czaplicka (1914); Bogoras (1909); Zelenin (1936); Devereaux (1956, 1961); and, with reservations for "shaman-saviors," LaBarre (1972b). Opponents included Ackerknecht (1943); Honigman (1960); Nordland (1967); Opler (1959, 1961); and Murphy (1964). Beck (1967) and Torrey (1974) argued the shaman is more psychiatrist than psychotic, whereas Eliade (2004 [1951]) believed that shamans are cured psychotics. Silverman (1967) stressed that schizophrenic tendencies are put to good supportive-creative use by shamans.

7. Compare Durkheim (1965: 267–272); Chadwick (1942:16–17); V. Turner (1977: 52); Metcalf (1989); Friedrich (1991); Laderman and Roseman (1996); Wautischer (1998); Grenoble and Whaley (2006); M. Bloch (2008); Dulam (2010).
8. A few examples include, but are hardly limited to, Humphrey with Onon (1996); Kendall (1985, 2009); Funk (2005); de Laguna (1972); Mills and Slobodin (1994); Radin (1949); Ridington (1990); V. Turner (1969); E. Turner (1996).
9. "Classical" forms of shamanism are recognized to be rooted in Siberia among Tungus-Manchu peoples (Diószegi 1968; Kasten 2009; Laufer 1917; Nowak and Durrant 1977:38; Siikala 1978: 14–15; Siikala and Hoppál 1992), although the linguistic origins of the Tungus word *šaman* are also sought in more southern, Turkic, traditions, as well as in Sanscrit *sramana*, and Vedic *śram* (Shirokogoroff 1935:270; Demitri Shimkin, personal communication April, 1979).

1 Sacred Trust: Ethnography as Renewed Relationships

1. For sample drops in the ocean of excellent collaborative anthropology, see Michael M. J. Fischer with Mehdi Abedi (1990); Caroline Humprey with Urgunge Onon (1996); Theodore Levin with Suzukei (2006). For sensitive reflection, see Charles Hale (2006); David Gow (2008); Rappaport (2005).
2. A Soviet period example of a scholar who became a shaman's patient is Kulemzin (1984).
3. Compare Kendall (1996, 2010); Vitebsky (1993); King (1999).
4. This séance description is slightly edited from the notes I wrote just after the séance. Later V. put his cloak back on and said: "I do not really feel this is so secret you cannot know about it. Look at my cloak, look at the symbols of the spirits who help me...a whole army." On the cloak, with long fringes at the bottom, fur under, skin outer, were sewn a plethora of metal ornaments. Underneath larger clackers were metal images, mostly on the breast. At the top were an ancestor pair and a lone figure, clan progenitor Tokunai *oiuun*. Below was an *abaaghy* pair, near an "especially predatory" spirit image. A round disk depicted a whirlwind, with a dog-wolf spirit image nearby. A round sun disk was central. To its side was a bear image, V.'s mother-beast-spirit, *iié kyl*. Nine white Northern owls lined the edge, above the fringe.
5. I reveal this story with trepidation, knowing that the anthropology memoir literature is littered with tell-too-much tales of lovers. Perhaps more salient ethnographically is V.'s creative use of shamanic spirit intimidation threats, something he had honed to an effective art in his practice with alcoholics.
6. On European "new age" shamans and their popularity, see Lindquist (1997); Jakobsen (1999).
7. For a sample of the Khatylaev's exquisite music, see www.sakhaopenworld.org.

8. The phrase "willing suspension of disbelief" comes from literature studies, most often applied to the theater. On shamanism and the arts, see Hyde (1998).
9. These range from historical ones such as Ksenofontov (1992[1928]); Oiyunsky (1975); and Popov (1947, 1949, 2006) to senior scholars such as N. Alekseev (1984); E. Alekseev (1976, 2008); and Gogolev (1983, 2002); to newer path-breakers such as Bravina (2005); Kolodesnikov (2000); Romanova (1994, 1997, 2008); Sleptsov (1989, 1993); and Yakovlev (1992, 2000). They include folklore projects (Emelianov and Mukhopleva 1993) and histories of shamanism (Boeskorov 2001; Il'iakhov 1995, 1997; Vasil'eva 2000). See also Afanas'ev [Téris] (1993, 2002); Egoreva (2010); Kondakov (1992, 1999, 2005).
10. "Controlled equivocation" and "perspectivalism" derive from F. Nietzsche and E. Viveiros de Castro; see Fortun et al. (2010). While "emic" and "etic" come from linguistic theory, anthropologists have adapted them to show gradations of insider knowledge. An outstanding syncretism of insider and outsider approaches in ethnomusicology is Levin with Suzukei (2004). See also E. Alekseev (2008), Fernandez (1991).
11. See Utkin [Nuhulgen] (1990, 2000) on Zakharov's life and Boeskorov (2001) on Niikon's.
12. In 2005, I was a study leader for the American Museum of Natural History of New York in Tuva and at Lake Baikal (Irkutsk Oblast and Buriatia). I returned to Buriatia in 2010. On the anthropology of pilgrimage, tourism, and its moral dilemmas, see especially Badone and Roseman (2004).
13. See Funk (1993, 1995); Kharitonova (2000, 2006); Hoppál and Kosa (2003).
14. For example, Utkin (1996); Koledesnikov (2000); Vinokurova and Dambaeva (2008).

2 Spirits Under Siege: Shamanic Communities of the North

1. The larger Siberian groups, the Sakha, Buriats, Tuvans (Tyvans), Altais and Khakas were not included in the official 'small nationalities' grouping, and some of the Amur River groups were missed. In the post-Soviet period, the indigenous activist group RAIPON (Russian Association of Indigenous Peoples of the North) includes over 39 in its membership. See their website www.raipon.org (accessed November 4, 2008). For perspective, see Fondahl (1993: 477–510).
2. My approach combines field and archival research with a review of Soviet literature from the period, especially that of cultural activists writing for the journal *Sovetskii Sever* (1930–32). Western summaries include, in order of usefulness, Chichlo (1981a); Slezkine (1994); Kuoljok (1985); Forsyth (1992). See also Humphrey and Thomas (1994); Ramet (1993).
3. Marfa Mikhailovna Zamorshikova, Tiuktiur village, Megino-Kangalas Region, Sakha Republic, 1995 told this story, recorded in the Sakha language.

4. The legend may have some historical basis, since Khanty ancestors did move north from more southern steppes. See Gerhard Friederich Miller (1787: 126–127); and Grigory Novitskii ([1715] 1884: 24). Novitskii was a missionary assistant to Metropolitan Filofei Leshinksii (Feodor) under Peter the Great. See also Balzer (1999: 54–74).
5. Startsev (1928: 92). For a dangerously negative review of Startsev, who was faulted in the 1930s for defending shamans and rich Khanty and Samoyed "kulaks," see G. Prokof'ev (1931).
6. This was reported by the later-repressed Sakha ethnographer A. E. Kulakovskii (1979: 284).
7. Compare B. Laufer (1917: 261–9); R. Austerlitz (1986: 143–4). On shamanism as "black faith," see V. F. Troshchanskii (1903).
8. See Waldemar (V. L.) Jochelson (1933: 183–5); V. L. Prikolonskii (1896: 188–189); E. S. Shishigin (1991).
9. Alykhardaakh's life spanned Tsarist and Soviet periods, according to her kinsman, Vladimir Kondakov. See Kondakov (1992: 42–4). On priests appealing to shamans for help, see V. G. Korolenko ([1880] 1965: 751, and 797 on Orthodox influences).
10. W. Sieroshewskii (V. L. Seroshevsky) (1901: 102).
11. Stories of the exile I.A. Khudiakov's dangerous friendships with Verkhoyansk shamans were recalled when I traveled there in 2010.
12. See Slezkine (1994: 228–9); compare Forsyth (1992: 289). From 1928–30, about 250 churches and parishes were closed in Siberia, according to Chichlo (1981a: 290). See also Shil'diashov (1982).
13. See the major authority on Tungus (Évenk) shamanism S. Shirokogoroff (1935). See also A. Siikala and M. Hoppál (1992); and M. M. Balzer (1997).
14. Examples are from fieldwork and the archive of *Leningradskoe Otdelenie Akademiia Nauk*, fond 14, opis 3, delo 13, list 3, A. A. Popov. See also Popov (1947; 1949: 255–323; 2006) and Jochelson (1933: 103–123). Compare N. A. Alekseev (1975; 1984: 188; 2008).
15. I. M. Suslov (1931: 129–32; I. Skachkov (1934: 50–4); V. G. Bogaras (1932: 142–157).
16. Its formal name was "Committee for the Assistance to Populations of the Far North." It was disbanded when economic interests caused its jurisdiction to be transferred and gutted. See M. A. Sergeev (1955); I. S. Gurvich (1971: 9–49); V. A. Zibarev (1972); P. E. Terletskii (1930, 1935).
17. On Alykhardaakh, see M. M. Balzer (1997: xiii); E. N. Romanova (2008: 311–2). Other examples are from Y. Slezkine (1994: 227); N. I. Leonov (1930: 86–91).
18. One Khanty president of a native council (*tuzsovet*) continued covert shamanizing, according to S. Golubev (1931: 111). See also I. S. Gurvich (1971); I. Skachkov (1933: 50–4).
19. This was told to the schoolteacher I. Panov (1937: 98).
20. The late Alexander Pika generously shared his notes from a closed archive. See E. Aipin (2010); T. Moldanova (1990: 24–28); I. Panov

(1937: 97–119); D. I. Kopylov, V. F. Retunskii (1965: 168–9); M. E. Budarin (1968: 214–27). See also Art Leete (2007). Other "rebellions" in the 1930s in the Soviet Union are more famed and valorized. See Viola (2002).
21. Oiunskii became famous for collecting and singing the major Sakha epic (*olonkho*) Niurgun Bootur and he founded what is currently the Institute of Humanities Research (IGI). He died in jail in 1939, at the peak of Stalinist repression in the Far East, but was rehabilitated under Krushchev. See P. A. Oiyunsky [Oiunskii] (1962, 1975); V.A. Semenov (1980: 21).
22. The phrase "kulak-shamans" was used in party documents through the North. Anti-Soviet Sakha "rebellions" of the 1920s, especially one centered in Omiakon, where Soviet rule was not established until 1927, were not predominantly led by shamans. Compare S.A. Tokarev (1940: 230–3); I. Nikolaev, I. Ushnitskii (1990: 15–16); N. Vasil'eva (2000).
23. Chichlo (1981a: 300). A range of donations and barter arrangements were common, and did not make shamans any less "professional."
24. "O merakh borby s shamanismom" *Sbornik postanovlenii i rasporazhenii IaASSR 1922–26* Yakutsk, Kanseliariia ATSIk i SNK, November 3, 1924, adapted that year to make it illegal to practice any kind of medicine without a special medical education and degree.
25. See Kuoljok (1985: 226); Slezkine (1994); and Kline (1968: 146–71) for perspective on the insidious way that formal legality masked rampant repression of religion.
26. Igor Semenovich Laptev, Srednaia Kolyma region, Sakha Republic, 1994.
27. The shaman's daughter was Anna Spiridonovna Semenova. Data on Kachagatsa come from work there in 1986 and 1993.
28. This typical story about Niikon was shared by the ethnographer Semen Ivanovich Nikolaev (pen name Somogotto), near Yakutsk, July 1991. See also Boeskorov (2001). Some exploits fit older patterns. Compare G. V. Ksenofontov (1929; 1992 [1928–9]); A. E. Kulakovskii (1979: 88–101).
29. For insights into Niikon's skill and personality, see the magnificent film "Time of Dreams" (*Vremia Snovedenie* 1984) directed by Eduard E. Alekseev and Elena Novik, with the great cinematographer, the late Andres Slapinch.
30. Conversations with William Fedotovich Yakovlev in 1986, 1995, and 2010.
31. Insights into the psychology of youths in boarding schools come from collecting life histories. Anecdotal evidence of high suicide and accident rates beginning in the 1930s and increasing through the Soviet period is buttressed by statistics in A. I. Pika and B. B. Prokorov (1994: 162–75). The school discipline story is from Slezkine (1994: 228). See also the excellent monograph of Alexia Bloch (2004), who prefers the term "residential schools."
32. On the abuse of psychiatry, see Sergei Grigoryants (1989: 34–47). Compare George Devereaux (1956); Julian Silverman (1967: 21–31).

33. Galina A. Obatyna, Kazym, 1991; Maina A. Lapina, Tatiana V. Voldina, Maria K. Vagatova at the 2010 conference "Shamanism and Art" in the Buriat Republic.
34. Major sources are Gondatti (1887a, b); Boris Chichlo (1981b); A. Irving Hallowell (1926); and Eva Schmidt (1989). For comparative analysis, see Babcock (1978) on rituals of reversal; and Bakhtin (1965) and his 1920s contemporary Freidenburg (1973: 490–512) on "carnival."
35. A controversial law "On traditional folk medicine" drafted by the Sakha parliament attempted to limit and license healers, and was superseded by Russian Federation law in the first Putin administration.
36. Early Soviet accounts are from points of view of culture base workers exulting in small everyday victories over "defeated" shamans who turned in their drums, or from Marxists who saw isolated bits of pre-Christian beliefs as insignificant "survivals" (*perezhitki*). Activists such as Gurvich (1971); Leonov (1930); Prokof'ev (1931); Sergeev (1955); Sergeeva, Ankudinov, and Dobriev (1939); Skachko (1931); Skachkov (1934); Suslov (1931); and Zibarev (1972) were under considerable pressure to report successes.
37. Uliana Alekseevna Vinokurova, New York City, Spring 1994, while analyzing a diorama of a "Yakut shaman" in the American Museum of Natural History.

3 Doctors or Deceivers?

1. Pioneer examples include Gillin (1948); V. Turner (1964); Romanucci-Ross (1977: 481–87); Ohnuki-Tierney (1976, 1980); Kleinman (1979).
2. See Shirokogoroff [(1935: 270); Diószegi (1978: 135–62); Siikala (1978: 14–15); Siikala and Hoppál (1992).
3. Fieldwork was in the Northern Khanty village of Tegy, a fishing collective (summer 1976), and Kazym, a reindeer-breeding center (1976, 1991), supplemented by meetings with Khanty friends in diverse venues, including at conferences and in my home. Compare Jordan (2003).
4. Karjalainen (1921: 21) and Raun (1955: 50–71) discussed dual souls, Chernetsov (1963: 5) and Sokolova (1976:57) saw them as multiple. Russian Orthodox Northernist Lydia Black insisted multiple soul manifestations were "the relationship of parts to the whole" (personal communication February 16, 1978). Named distinctions are nonetheless made, and when asked about a gender-based discrepancy in souls, an elderly Tegy woman explained: "Males are higher and females are lower. Males are stronger."
5. See especially Moldanova (2007; 2001). See also Kulemzin (1976: 52).
6. Tatiana V. Voldina, in 2010, mentioned Khanty "black" shamans called *chepan* could take away "life spirit" or import illness. See also Karjalainen (1927: 245–95); Startsev (1928: 90–91); Minenko (1975: 204). Mongolic Buriats and Turkic Sakha sometimes divide shamans into "black," dealing with lesser and evil spirits of the lower and eastern world; and "white,"

dealing with major, pure spirits of the upper or western world (Zelenin 1936: 294–98; Krader 1954: 334–37; Krader 1978: 192).
7. I have no evidence of *Amanita muscaria* use today, but did see it growing near Kazym. Khanty consultants loathe all mushrooms, but a few Khanty shamans may secretly maintain the mushroom tradition. Evidence for Ugrian shamanic use of *Amanita muscaria* comes from Munkasci [1907] reprinted in Wasson (1960: 306), Dunin-Gorkavich (1904: 95), and Patkanov (1897: 121). Czigany (1980: 213) confirms the antiquity of mushroom use. As in Central Asia, Khanty shamans probably used hemp seeds thrown on fires to produce intoxication and blue smoke (Balazs 1968: 59–61; Shimkin 1967: 624).
8. Several films feature Ivan Stepanovich Sopochin (1910–1992), including that of Finnish anthropologist Juha Pentikainen, director "Reindeer Sacrifice of a Khanty Shaman" (State Audio-Visual Centre of Finland, University of Helsinki, 1991, 25 min.); and that of the Hungarian anthropologist Márta Csepregi. See Csepregi (2007). See also the work of Natalya Koshkarova (Institute of Philology, Siberian branch RAN) and folklorist Olga Balalaeva.
9. The importance of the number seven and of a multilayered cosmology may reveal Tatar influences on Khanty communities (Karjalainen 1927: 245–331; Siikala 1978: 224). Ob Ugrian myths describe seven layers of the universe: three upper and three lower worlds, with the earth as central (Chernetsov 1935). See also Lapina (2008); and Moldanova (2007; 2010).
10. Iron and other metals may have once been impressive markers of trade wealth. The religious significance of metal in Khanty symbolism has been shown by Sokolova (1978), and is studied by Ugrian specialist Ildiko Lehtinen (curator, Helsinki's National Museum of Finland). Shamanic materials in the National Museum of Finland are from Potanin, Alquist, and Karjalainen (e.g., numbers 4866:6; 1870:22; 4934:216). Metal images of spirit helpers, associated with shaman equipment and ancestor images, include a bear, lizards, and birds.
11. Complex issues of "faith healing," "beliefs," and how to convey them, are reviewed in a special issue of the journal *Social Analysis*, edited by Galina Lindquist and Simon Coleman (2008). See also Joan D. Koss-Chioino (2006); Joa'o Biehl, Bryan Good and Arthur Kleinman (2007); Charles (1953: 95–122); Revunenkova (1974: 110); Hultkranz (1978); and Peters and Price-Williams (1980).
12. The moment of reindeer killing in an annual sacred grove ritual honoring Khanty ancestors was considered too sacred to film, but some of the ritual is captured.
13. Neher (1962) posited important trance-inducing effects of near-alpha brain wave frequencies in shamanic drumming, but the French ethnomusicologist Rouget (1980) forcefully refuted Neher's "reductionist" claims. A compromise position is that drumming may help create conditions for trance that susceptible individuals, in conducive cultural contexts, can then utilize.

14. Shatilov (1931: 125–129) carefully recorded the full séance chant that his main Khanty source, Andrei Grigorivich Prasin, gave to him during the séance. My translation is as close to Shatilov's as possible, including switches in tense and in person.
15. My most striking experience in 1976 of *Numi-Torum*'s reality for some Khanty came literally with a thunder clap. Just prior to a storm, the elderly woman I was visiting jumped up with alarm, and ran outside. There she stood, with arms outstretched, appealing to the Sky-God to spare her house and children. She had earlier explained: "I am still afraid of thunder. Last year a house near here burned from thunder."
16. V. Turner (1964: 237) concluded that Ndembu doctors "are well aware of the benefits of their procedures for group relationships, and they go to endless trouble to make sure that they have brought into the open the main sources of latent hostility in group life." See also Edith Turner (2006); Arthur Kleinman (1979: 363–65); and Kleinman, Veena Das, and Margaret Lock (1997).
17. Candace Pert, a discoverer of endorphins (nicknamed natural morphines) with Sol Snyder at the National Institute of Health, in 1982 provided me with leads to biochemical responses of patients during shamanic séances. See Snyder (1977); Foster and Anderson (1978: 99–100); Dow (1986). In 1980, McGill University sponsored a pioneering conference in Montreal entitled "Shamans and Endorphins," exploring linkages of endorphins with pain control, memory, acupuncture, and shamanic trance. The connection has widened and deepened, including study of the endorphin subgroup, enkephalins. See also Amy Hardie's 2010 masterpiece "Edge of Dreaming" (Lorber films).
18. Compare for approaches and data the classic Reo Fortune (1932: 144–7) on Melanesia; Jane Atkinson (1992: 307–30), whose fieldwork was based in Southeast Asia; and Homayun Sidky (2008), based in Nepal. See also Linda Connor and Geoffry Samuel (2001).
19. The issue of increase in "witch-fear" during periods of intense cultural change has been described elsewhere, for example Inuit (Eskimo) by Edmund Carpenter (1961: 508–15); and South Africa, by John and Jean Comaroff (2004: 188–204). Compare Comaroff (1985).
20. A public-private distinction between effective hope-producing atmosphere in ritual curing was also made by Frank (1961:6 2). Theories of Freud (1949) and Sargant (1964) fit less well. Cathartic acting out of suppressed desires by a Khanty sufferer is rare. While therapies may be similar, cultural contexts alter the healing process (Crapanzano 1973: 212–29; Csordas 2002; Moyers and Flowers 1993; E. Turner 2006).
21. For statistics on Soviet period medical improvements, see Diachkov (1979: 20–4). Some clinics supported into the 1990s had to close by the end of the decade, although the Khanty-Mansiski *Okrug* was better off economically than many regions of the North (Heleniak 2009).
22. Lola Romanucci-Ross (1977) explains that Manus frequently choose Native medicine, basing decisions on a moral component of illness, whereas choices of European medicine are often last resorts (compare

Landy 1977; Nichter 1978). Studies of "resort" must cope with haphazard elements of choice, and with sampling accurately enough to reflect cultural trends and change.
23. Compare Greenfield and Droogers (2001); Kitiarsa (2005: 461–487); Leopold and Jensen (2004); Matory (2005).

4 Poetics of Sacred Language Through Time and Space

1. For more on Fedot, see ahead. My approaches to the embeddedness of poetry in ritual draw on E. Bruner (1984); J. Fernandez (1986; 1991); P. Friedrich (1991); C. Laderman and M. Roseman (1996); P. Metcalf (1989); and V. Turner (1977: 52). On the significance of language for cultural recovery, see Grenoble and Whaley (2006).
2. For a musical taste of the richness, see ethnomusicologist Eduard Alekseev's website at Sakha Open World, for example "Sledy zabytoi pesni" on singer and shaman's assistant Sergei Zverev http://sakhaopenworld.org/alekseyev/work8.html. An excerpt of a séance was also famously recorded by Sergei Zverev, taped by Eduard Alekseev in 1978 on Melodiya records (no. 33 D 030639-40). The epic Niurgun Bootur was recorded in a multiset album, also on Melodya. See also Aleksei Romanov's film "Orto Doidu"(The Middle World), 1993.
3. Konstantin Chirkov had a mother who was Yukaghir. See also Il'iakhov (1995, 1997).
4. My collection (Balzer 1997) is dedicated to Matriona Petrovna Kurbel'tinova and includes Nadezhda Bulatova's description of Matriona's *algys* blessing ritual. Several excellent films have been made of her, for example by Viacheslav Semenov (with A. Myreeva) "Chokhotui's Prediction" Sakhafilm 1996. For more on Sobei, see Anatoly Alekseev (1994: 1,3); Piers Vitebsky (2005). Sobei, his assistant, and Éven scholar Anatoly A. Alekseev have traveled to England, New York, and Greenland presenting Éven shamanism. See http://www.annews.ru/news/detail.php?ID=188579. (accessed July 17, 2009). An unlikely circus venue was the site of a ticket-taking séance featuring Sobei (needing an eye operation) in 2009.
5. Arsan Laptev (personal communication July 1994). Accounts could be compared for shamans Ard'amaan-D'ard'amaan, Keken, Cheriktė, Matriona Kurbel'tinova, Kiktei, Chuonakh, Tius'piut, Konstantin, and Niikon as told by representatives of various ethnic groups.
6. Aleksandra K. Chirkova (personal communication July 1993).
7. Mikhail Bogorov of Borogonsk ulus, 1924, recorded by Ksenofontov ([1928-9]1992: 229–230). For the rich metaphorical language of Évenk references to animals, especially predators, see Myreeva (1988: 9–30). For context, see Togolukov et al. (1997).
8. Galina Keptuké's shamanic memoir is significantly called "Having its own name."

NOTES

9. Their shamanic background is also revealed in the description of their extended family's "izgorod'-marylia [a sacred fence of young larches], [ritually] placed by shamans of the Keptuké clan" (Keptuké 1989: 3).
10. On the controversial black/white distinction, see N. Alekseev (1975, 1984, 1997); Basilov (1992, 1997); Novik (1997: 214); Popov (1947, 1949, 2006); Shirokogoroff (1935); and Troshchanskii (1903).
11. Words for shamanizing in Tungusic dialects are similar, eg. *jaja*, *iaia*, *iaia(n)*, revealing their antiquity and Éven-Évenk common ancestry. Compare A. Petrov (1988: 69). See also linguist G. M. Vasil'ievich's chart comparing key words in Évenk and Yakut (Sakha) (1948: 253–4).
12. Kyys Djebelije is enacted at www.youtube.com/watch?v=GT1YXRiEw6w (accessed Sept. 15, 2010). Sakha folklorist N. Emelianov (Burnashev et al. 1993: 307) saw Khoro as "a tribe met in folklore not speaking in the Yakut language. According to historical legends, their ancestor Uluu Khoro (Great Khoro) with his many-in-number people came from the east on a bison-*skakune*." See also Emelianov (1996); F. Zykov (1992: 102); Ksenofontov (1992: 214–7) linking Adzharai and Khoro.
13. Later sacred expressions also reveal complex mutual influences. Over time, Sakha, Éven, Évenk and Yukaghir groups intermarried and visited each other's summer festivals. Compare Khudiakov (1969: 101).
14. On epic poetry and shamans, see Hatto (1970). My reading and excerpted notes of the Mas Batyia Bukhatyyr *olonkho* come from the Oiusardakh village museum archive of Sredne Kolymsk ulus. This version was sung by Profirii Nikolaevich Nazarov of Sien-Kiuol, recorded in 1945 in the Sakha language by folklore enthusiast Dmitri Gavrilovich Zhirkov.
15. Aleksandra K. Chirkova about a friend of her father (personal communication 1993).
16. See Nadasdy (2007) for insights into "human-animal sociality," reciprocity and personhood from hunting-dependent First Nations of the Yukon that resonate well with Sakha views.
17. The root of the Sakha word for "purify," a complex concept much analyzed (eg. Douglas 1975, 1996), is *sul*, meaning clear, cleanse, strip bare. My version in the Sakha language comes from the archive of Aleksei Mikhailov. A version was also printed in Ksenofontov (1935).
18. This fragment from Ksenofontov (1929:135) is analyzed in N. Alekseev (1984: 183), and translated and reprinted in Balzer (1997: 54). Sexuality and sexual symbolism are under-acknowledged but common in Siberian shamanic practice. See also Shternberg (1904); Kenin-Lopsan (1987; 1995 a,b); and Austerlitz (1984).
19. Spiridon's poetry is in a life history given to me by Nikolai Ignat'ev (1990 ms.) of Viliuisk.
20. "Iakovlev-Kruuppa" archive, Institute of Languages, Literature and History, fond 5, op. 3, ed. kh. 537, page 57, Nikita Petrovich Iakovlev's shamanic texts, handwritten in Sakha by Sakha folklorist Kristofor Konstantinov in 1941, my translation.
21. On "world tree" symbolism, compare Eliade ([1951] 2004). Some shamanic trees are less secret than others, with offerings of ribbons, food or coins common, described more ahead.

22. This ceremony was in July 1993, with family members of Evdokiia Semenova, village officials, and a few guests from Yakutsk.
23. This *algys* from the IaLI archive (otd. folklora, opis 2, delo 1, ctr. 59-67) was published by G. V. Ksenofontov (1961: 77-88).
24. Such ambiguous language about "enemies" can be viewed variously by participants. The Romanian poet Andrei Codrescu (1990: 110) explains: "The tonal ambiguities developed by oppressed cultures to communicate different things in the same words to friends and foes become urgently important." In accord with Kondakov's wishes, I have a transcript not a recording.
25. My video and cassette tapes of many hours of *okhuokhai*, deserving separate treatment, capture its spirit far better than the printed text. See also N. Petrov (1990, 1995).
26. This chant is printed in a Sakha pamphlet about Ivan Zakharov (Utkin 1990: 28–9), and I also taped it in June 1991 at his Viliuisk smithy. Zakharov was renowned as a maker of the Sakha national instrument, the shamanic *khomus*, jaw harp.
27. See Sleptsov (1989: 149), or an English transcription and translation in Sleptsov (1993: 8–9).
28. Major *olonkho* collections are Oiyunsky (1975), and Mirbatalaeva with the singer Timofeev-Teploukhov (1985). *Toiuk* sources include E. Alekseev (1976) and the series Ergis et al. (1976, 1977, 1980, 1983).
29. Examples of some of the first recent poets using shamanic themes and symbolism are Ivan Gogolev (1987, 1989), and Sargilaana Gol'derova (1987). The group of poets called "White Horse" (1991), includes Aisen Doidu (whose pen name means homeland), Anatolii Shvetsov, Oleg Chermyshentsev, Vladimir Orosutsev, and Kirill Alekseev. The poet Omsuura, whose pen name is from the Sakha root for questing, is especially popular for her sexual symbolism.
30. An early example is Aleksei Romanov's 1989 film called Maappa (the name of a beautiful suicide ghost), shown on Sakha television. "Shamanic rock" groups (in constant flux) include Choron [Chalice], Cholbon [Star], Aiarkhaan [Cry Out], D'aangy Saryala [Mountain Lights]. Sergei Rastorguev has turned an "original stage-circus synthetic theater" called "Oyuun" into the republic's well-traveled "Sakhacircus."
31. Afanasy Fedorov helped found the Sakha College of Culture, and the urban *Archy Diété*, "Purification House," in Yakutsk. When he constructed a basic text for enacting his séance simulation in 1991, he was careful not to use the opening calling chants of any one particular shaman, but rather syncretized an archival sampling, so as not to offend any deceased shamans, nor mis-signal helping spirits.

5 Flights of the Sacred: Birds, Trees, and Open-Body-Mindedness

1. Tokoyeu, who died in 1959, was so strong by reputation that the novel *Khanido I Khalerkha* by Yukaghir writer Sémën Kurilov, widely read in

the republic, dramatizes his usually benevolent deeds. An acclaimed version was directed by Andrei Borisov for the Yakut National Theater in 1986. Tokoyeu was nearly dragged into court in 1947 when the sister of a local Komsomol leader died after a séance.
2. See also Balzer (1997); Balzer and Vinokurova (1996); Ramet (1993); and Grigoryants (1989).
3. These are only a sample of the range of terms. Compare Eliade (2004); Gogolev et al. (1992); Siikala and Hoppál (1992).
4. A valuable séance (re)creation by former shaman assistant Sergei Zverev, taped by ethnomusicologist Eduard E. Alekseev in 1978, is on Melodiya records (no. 33 D 030639-40).
5. Every Sakha shaman cloak I have seen, whether on grimacing museum mannequins or in private possession for use, features bird symbolism. Examples are in Yakutsk (Museum of Music and Folklore and the Republic Yaroslavsky Museum), and in St. Petersburg (State Museum of the Peoples of Russia and the Kunst Kamera Peter the Great Museum).
6. Arsan Laptev, grandson of Kursan (Ébé oiuun), August 1994 in Khatingnaakh Village, Sredn'iaia Kolyma.
7. Arsan Laptev (August 1994), who knew both Parilop and Kharkha.
8. Sakha folklore enthusiast Dmitry G. Zhirkov (August 1994) coaxed Tokoyeu into talking on World War II Victory Day, when everyone was in an unusually open mood. Zhirkov took notes and later sent them to the Institute of Languages Literature and History (IIaLI) in Yakutsk. He related the interview from memory, since he considered it one of his most important deeds.
9. Troshchanskii (1903) exemplifies a Christian-biased ethnography. A special *ichchi* exhibit was mounted in the Republic Yaroslavskii Museum in 1992, with numerous examples of *émégét*. Some Sakha visitors, commenting the images had not lost their spirit power, gave coin offerings at a display honoring the sky goddess Aiyyhyt.
10. See Afanas'ev (1993); Afanas'ev et al. (1990); and Utkin (1994).
11. Innokenty F. Volkhov, of Oiusardaakh Village, Sredn'aia Kolyma, August 1994. During some fertility rituals, various "sins" and relationships are revealed. In older versions, the focal woman was surrounded by eight virgins and nine pure youths (Kulakovskii 1979: 93–100). Aiyyhyt is similar to other fertility goddesses of Turkic and Mongolic peoples (Sleptsov 1989: 85–118).
12. To return to earth, daughters of dark sky clouds (rain and fertility bringing) wrap the *salgyn-kut* in a swan skin, or, by some accounts, if the shaman is to have dealings especially with the lower world, a raven skin. Compare Ksenofontov (1992); Kulakovskii (1979: 59–61); and Popov (1947: 283).
13. The site is near Belaia Gora; the story again reveals complexities of defining "white shaman" (*aiyy-oiuun*) implying "ours" versus "black" (*khara* or *semiekh*) meaning "theirs," enemy shaman. *Semiekh-oiuun* glosses as "eating-shaman," one who can cause predator spirits to eat your soul, as I nearly discovered first hand.

14. Compare Alekseev (1984: 80); Ksenofontov (1992: 50, 69–71); Kulakovskii (1979: 92); and Seroshevsky (1896: 626).
15. The quote is from Kulakovskii (1979: 92); I have heard similar eagle epithets.
16. Compare Alekseev (1984: 81); Anisimov (1958: 136–8); and Ksenofontov (1992: 52).
17. Ksenofontov (1992: 58, 54). Sakha ethnographers decided to reprint Ksenofontov's work in time for an international conference on shamanism in 1992. See also Balzer (1993a).
18. Aida was forthcoming with me and active as a local healer until family responsibilities later impinged. Aleksandra subsequently moved to Yakutsk. See also Balzer (2000).
19. Vladimir Kondakov is featured ahead. The passage is from a pamphlet (Kondakov 1993: 38).
20. Compare Basilov (1997); Bogoras (1930); and Lake-Thom [Medicine Grizzly Bear Lake] (1991). See also David Gellner (1994) on Nepal.
21. See the UNESCO sponsored Sakha site www.kuyaar.ru.
22. From the Ionov archive in the St. Petersburg branch of the Institute Vostokovedenie. A version was published in N. F. Katonov (1996: 166–8).
23. Compare Chowning (1962); Dzeniskevich (1976); Furst (1977, 2004); Jochelson (1904); Meletinsky (1980); and Seamans and Day (1994) for raven and eagle beliefs and distribution. Swiss ethnographer A. Métraux ([1944] 2001: 99–100) discusses the kite-like *kumalak* bird and other birds as key to Akawaio shamans' abilities to fly with the tobacco spirit. See also A. Irving Hallowell's (1926) masterful survey of bear ceremonialism. See Fitzhugh and Crowell (1988).
24. Compare Furst (1977: 95–117); Hall (1919); and Siikala and Hoppál (1992: 65, 134–7) for discussions of shamanic bird symbolism in diverse geographical regions and time periods. On the healthiness of cognitive classification, see Yoon (2009).
25. At other sessions, Klavdia Maksimova used a drum to induce trance in the patients, though not herself. Klavdia later transformed herself into Saiyyna (Summer), founding a special healing center at the edge of Yakutsk, described ahead, and dying in 2009. See Saiyyna (2000).
26. The wise white-clad elder shaman turning into an eagle was part of a video song contest: http://www.nvksakha.info/tv/projects/clip2008 /03_19/ clip 19 (accessed April 12, 2009).
27. A depiction of this is in Aleksei Romanov's film "Orto Doidu"(The Middle World), made in 1993. Klavdia Maksimova (as Saiyyna) developed laughter therapy further at her healing center. Parallels include Native American clowning, trickster and coyote traditions, teachings of the Hindu mystic Osho, and the Dutch Center in Favor of Laughing.
28. Examples are Friedson (1996); Geertz (1973); Jackson (2009); Lutz and Abu-Lughod (1990); Roseman (1991); Stoller (1994, 2009); Taussig (1993, 2009), and Vitebsky (2005).

6 Urban Shamans? Unmasking Leadership and Creativity

1. Through Soviet history, policies and theories about nationalism fluctuated (Tillett 1969, Krupnik 1990, Tishkov 1992, Balzer 1999). But emphasis was on expunging all traces of nationalism for the glory of Soviet "internationalism." See also Vitebsky (1990). For a fuller version of my conversations with Andrei Borisov see Balzer (1993b).
2. Speculation abounds on the origins of the term "Yakut" and whether it is derogatory. It is probably a Russian corruption of an Évenk word (Kulakovskii 1979: 414).
3. Dmitri K. Sivstev, the author of the play and a venerable though controversial Sakha elder, viewed the role of the Russians in Sakha history as predominantly benevolent into the 1990s (interview, July 1991).
4. See Oiyunsky (1975), Pukhov (1975), and Chapter 4.
5. On the1920s, see the contemporary journal *Sakha Keskile*, and Sakha Omuk's journal, *Ilin*. Andrei's rivals in the 1990s included the linguist Lazar Afanasev, who criticized him for not being Sakha enough (interviews with Lazar Afanasev, June-July, 1991). Lazar later founded *Aiyy Diété* [Spirit House] outside Yakutsk, discussed ahead.
6. Similar ideas of the group *Kut-Siur*, only partially absorbed by *Sakha Omuk*, are in L. Afanasev, A. Romanov, R. Petrov, and V. Illarionov (1990). Andrei's mixed ethnic background is exemplified in the saying "ikki atakhmaakh kihi aimakh" (person from clan with two legs).
7. A version of Kyys Djebelije is at www.youtube.com/watch?v =GT1YXRiEw6w (accessed Sept. 15, 2010).
8. The true hosts were Vladimir and Zina Ivanov, and additional guests were ethnomusicologist Aiza Reshetnikova and the actress Stepanida Borisova.
9. In 2010, I learned that a Russian friend feels Vladimir caused her lingering back pain in 1992, after she defended a theory concerning genetic roots of the illness "Viliuisk encephalitis" that Vladimir took as personal insult. In August 1991, I checked with a friend who is a Cherokee healer, C. W. Duncan Sings Alone, on whether shamanic amnesia was a common occurrence, and he confirmed that he does not always remember his séance spirit journeys but messages are spoken in sweat lodges so that others remember. This is similar to Buriat trance messages.
10. A "bioenergy" wave swept Russia in the 1990s, with many curers, some from Yakutia, training with the Russian spiritualist Juna in Moscow. I have been the subject of this technique, based on auras and energy fields, and have gained temporary headache relief.
11. Aiza, whose own superb music training in Moscow led her to be receptive to "Russian medicine," was bitterly torn after this encounter. Compare Feshbach and Friendly (1992) on the traumas of Soviet medicine and general medical ignorance about cancer.
12. Nadezhda Senkina (1991: 5) was a reporter whose father, Vasilii Lukich Senkin, had a wide reputation as a folk curer. Nadia, a friend since 1986, also explored her own curing skills.

13. This comment was a pun on the Greek *Iliad* epic and a reputed ancestor, Ellei, who is the hero of some Sakha epics, and the founder of the annual *yhyakh* festival. See Ksenofontov's (1977) *Elleiada*.
14. See Efimova (2009); and the Association's website www.aaraiyyitegele.ru /index_rus.php?id=1&i=56 (accessed 7/20/09). See also the obituary in the Sakha parliament's online journal "Vladimir Kondakov Aiyy Shaman has Left Life" at www.v-yakutia.ru/?id=11984 (accessed 7/20/09); and Kim (1992).
15. Saiyyna added "the woman who had ridden with Napoleon loved marches, she loved parade music, and from childhood always loved the assemblies, the formal parades in pioneer camps. And she loved the sound of the drum." For other reincarnation accounts focused on indigenous peoples of the North, see Mills and Slobodin (1994); Jochelson ([1910] 1975).
16. Compare Durkheim ([1915] 1965); Descola (1994); Yamada and Irimoto (1997); Conklin (2001); Willerslev (2007).

7 Sustainable Faith? Multiple Generations of Healing and Spirituality

1. Fieldwork in Belaia Gora (1992), the Viliuisk region (1991, 2002), Tatta (1986, 2003), Yakutsk (2007), and Verkhoyansk (2010) is particularly relevant.
2. For historical background, see N.A. Alekseev (1984); Il'iakov (1995, 1997); Znamenski (1999).
3. On curing, see Crandon (1987); Csordas (2002, 2009); Koss-Chioino and Hefner (2006).
4. On group séance dynamics, see Ksenofontov (1992); Csordas (1994); Jakobsen (1999); Kendall (2001). Compare Chapter 3.
5. See Basilov (1997). Compare Brown and Cousins (2001); Hultkranz (1992); Mehl-Madrona (1997). On the significance of women shamans through history, see Tedlock (2005). See also Perrone et al. (1989); Koss-Chioino (1992); Kendall (2009).
6. Maria, another of Konstantin's children with healing talent, practices in her home region near Belaia Gora. When Aleksandra moved to Yakutsk, she briefly worked in Yuri Prokopiev's healing center, without using the cloak or drum. Compare Chapter 1.
7. This approach is also practiced by the healer-shaman V. featured in Chapter 1. It brings out negative, fear-inducing aspects of dealing with spirits, who can be vengeful if not appeased and respected. Compare Brown (1989); Whitehead and Wright (2004).
8. On *menerik*, see the Russian doctor S. I. Mitskevich (1929); and ethnomusicologist E. E. Alekseev (2008). For a social interpretation of similar phenomena, see I. M. Lewis (1971).
9. The body-purifying liver is as or more important than the heart in Sakha conceptions. On the three souls and health, see Grigor'eva (1996); Kulakovskii (1979); Kolodesnikov (2000); Kondakov (1992; 1999).

10. Mikhail called the tree a "sacrifice tree," *kérék mas*. Sacred trees for more general offerings are usually termed *aal luuk mas*, also associated with shamans, and are often oaks. On the distinction, see also Cruikshank and Argounova (2000: 104–105). On the shamanic world tree, compare Eliade (2004: 269–74); Ksenofontov (1992); Novik (1997: 228).
11. This account is from the ethnographer S. I. Nikolaev (Somogotto), told to me in July, 1991.
12. This appeared in a collection honoring Niikon (Boeskorov 2001).
13. The late Nobel prize winner Carleton Gaidushek with former Soviet doctor Lev Goldfarb created an NIH team to solve the mystery of Viliuisk encephalitis, theorizing that it involves a combination of genetic, social, and environmental factors. After I heard the blood transfusion story, I contacted Lev Goldfarb to explain that doctors and villagers in Viliuisk were wondering whether the case should be treated as more than an anomaly. With kind skepticism, Lev answered that they have detailed records for everyone with the illness, that many of the cases are not really encephalomyelitis but another long-term debilitating disease (spinocerebellar ataxia type 1) and that I would need to learn the patient's name. See Goldfarb et al. (2009).
14. I have collected accounts of Fedot for years and plan further contact.
15. See also Kondakov (1999) and Chapter 6. The stunning 1984 documentary film *Time of Dreams*, directed by E. Alekseev and E. Novik and shot by A. Slapinch, includes Niikon.
16. Was it really cancer? This sensational summer 2010 account is from a satisfied patient, Svetlana Nikolaevna Alexandrova, who had her wrist successfully reset by Anna.
17. See also Csordas (2000, 2009) and Davies (2004) on Navaho healing in new culturally mixed contexts.

8   Social Medicine? Religious Movements in the Siberian Far East

1. One of the best documented is the "White Faith" movement of the Altai peoples, also called "Burkhanism," that was partially shamanic. For a range of perspectives, see the two issues of my journal *Anthropology and Archeology of Eurasia* on Burkhanism (Balzer 2006) and Filatov (2001). The indigenous ethnographer Liudmilla I. Sherstova (2010) correlated Burkhanism and national identity in her sensational Kandidat dissertation (1985). For revival-related Burkhanism compendiums, see Danilin (1993) and Maidurova and Tadina (1994). See also the flawed (commandments were missed) but fascinating debut of the topic in Western anthropology by Lawrence Krader (1956: 282–92), strategically placed in the *American Anthropologist* just after Wallace's famous article on revitalization (1956: 264–81).
2. Compare Wallace (1956, 1972); Kopytoff (1964); LaBarre (1972b); De Vos (1976); Trompf (1990); Trott (1997); Nagel (1996); Balzer (1999: 75–98); Daschke and Ashcroft (2005); Smith (2008: 215–239). Wallace

(1956: 265) defined a revitalization movement as "a deliberate, organized, conscious effort by members of a society to construct a more satisfying culture."
3. For historical background, see N. Alekseev (1984); Gogolev (1992, 1993); Il'iakov (1995); Znamenski (1999). For context, see the stunning 1984 documentary "Time of Dreams" of E. Alekseev and E. Novik with cameraman A. Slapinch; and 1994 "Shamanism: Past and Present," of M. Hoppál, with B. Kovacs.
4. Compare Hamayon (1990); Atkinson (1992); Siikala and Hoppál (1992); Hultkranz (1993); Humphrey with Onon (1996); Balzer (1997); Pentikainen (1997); Humphrey (1999); Schenk and Ratsch (1999); Znamenski (1999); Narby and Huxley (2001); Eliade (2004).
5. The term "dvoieverie" has a long and complicated history in Russian studies. Compare Billington (1970: 18); Balzer (1999: 54–74).
6. Some Sakha say palms should wave the rays of the sun gracefully inward, towards the chest. Sun-greeting ceremonies have become a feature of the Sakha *yhyakh*, with some of the first led by the actor-turned-spiritual leader Afanasy Fedorov, in the capital, Yakutsk. Afanasy is adamant that those who place palms outward are shunning, not receiving the rays. The debate symbolizes passion over reconstructed rituals; my 1997 notes mention "people are seriously agitated about this difference." Ethnographer Anatoly Gogolev doubts that sun-greeting was part of earlier Sakha *yhyakh*, but the ceremony has become popular.
7. Kyta Baaly's huge drum, made by one of the only drum masters left in the republic, Afanasy Brodnikov, is nine-pointed and sided, with three old bells hanging from a steel frame in back. Most Sakha and Tungus drums have numerous bells and sacred figures on their inner frames. Many Sakha consider that a nine-point drum, with metal symbols, should be spiritually earned
8. Sakha such as Kyta Baaly have made the linguistic distinction between *aiyy* and *abaaghy* shamans a way to celebrate their tradition of an indigenous priesthood. For a Russian Orthodox view, see Troshchanskii (1903). For Sakha perspectives, see Gogolev (1983); N.A. Alekseev (1984); Gogolev et al. (1992); Afanas'ev (1993); Utkin and Fedorov (1993); Utkin (1996).
9. Polygamy advocacy and Sakha nationalism are closely linked, since an important goal is to demographically increase the proportion of Sakha in the republic as fast as possible. An advocate of this is the Sakha university professor N. K. Antonov. See Tumusov, Popov et al. (2001) on the traditional Sakha polygamous family.
10. For perspective on Sakha cosmology, see Popov (1947); Ksenofontov (1992); Kolodesnikov (2000); Vasil'ev (2000); Vinokurova et al. (2002); Bravina (2005); Vinokurova and Artamonov (2009); Egorova (2010).
11. This revisits the theme of shifting authenticity and morality through time. See also Approsimova (1992); Afanas'ev (1993); Koriakin (2007); Popov (1947); Vasil'ev (2010).
12. Nina I. Protopopova, an elderly Sakha journalist, makes clear her great respect for Dora. Her interviews spanned numerous sessions and were published in several forms.

13. Note the similarity of "sucking cure" traditions to those of Native Americans, for example as featured in the California Indian films "Sucking Doctor," and "Pomo Shaman," produced by William Hieck, 1964, available through University of California Extension Center for Media and Independent Learning, catalogue numbers 37454 (original), 37439 (edited).
14. Especially relevant is the Native American (Handsome Lake) spiritual revitalization that Anthony Wallace (1956, 1972) long ago called "goal culture." Compare E. Turner (2006).
15. Protopopova (1999: 185). The earth and rivers are personified as grandmothers (*ébé*), while the protector-guide of taiga, tundra and forest hunters, is the male Baianai. Dora mourns recent massive destruction of Baianai's animals, as well as increasing forest fires, attributing them to the pollution of Nature and violation of customs. "The land weakens, suffers and needs purification...this can be done with incantations...Nature and Earth itself has told me how to help. I've put out many fires." (Protopopova 2006: 38).
16. Compare Protopopova (1999: 177-8) and the Russian translation of Protopopova (2006: 59-60). See also Emelianov and Mukhopleva (1993); Funk (2005); and Funk and Alekseev (2008).
17. The passage acknowledges that each community may celebrate *yhyakh* in its own way (Protopopova 1999: 186-7). This alleviates pressures that some indigenous ethnographers have put on communities planning the celebrations to follow specific ritual details. Ethnographers leading the *yhyakh* revival include Anatoly Gogolev, Ekaterina Romanova, and Villiam Yakovlev; plus Andrei S. Borisov (Minister of Culture); Afanasy S. Fedorov (College of Sakha Culture); Nadezhda S. Tolbonova (head, *Archy Diété*); Uhhan (journalist); Uliana A. Vinokurova (sociologist), and many others in rural and urban venues.
18. Ekaterina Romanova (2008: 317, 325). See also Balzer (1997: xiii, xiv). Dora has also claimed that she is the tenth person in a line shamanic defenders of nature through incantations.
19. See Hamayon (1990, 2007); Morokhoeva (1995); Humphrey and Urgunge (1996); Humphrey (1999); Bazarov (2000); Zhukovskaia (2000, 2001, 2002, 2008); Fridman (2004).
20. These two unusual cases are from Natalia Zhukovskaia (personal communication, June 2007; presentation Tunka Valley conference August, 2010). See also Metzo (2005).
21. The tale correlates well with an explanation the female shaman Maria Tsibenova of Olkhon Island told Mihály Hoppál (2000: 60) in 1996 about *tailgan* origins from the swan. On Buriat origins and shamanic flexibility compare Klementz (1924); Krader (1954, 1978).
22. Anya Bernstein personal communication May 4, 2007. See the excellent film of Anya Bernstein featuring Valentin Khagdaev 2006 "In Pursuit of the Siberian Shaman" Cinetrance. Compare Hoppál (2000: 79-84).
23. Valentin cites Basilov (1997: 8) as confirming that "shamans must have an extra bone," using academic as well as spiritual authenticity. Elders throughout Siberia also looked for signs of a child drawn early to the drum or other shamanic accouterments. See also Hoppál (2000: 79).

24. He provided Mihály Hoppál (2000: 83) with a colorful out-of-body soul flight description provoked by a roofing accident. He told a smoother version to the journalist Dmitri Krupnov (2005): "Have I died or something, I thought? I rose in a soap bubble, ever higher. I was amazed at the colors in unfathomable variety. I heard all the sounds of the world in one gamma. Then I landed on something like moss and the bubble shattered. I was asked a thousand questions ..."
25. The quotes are from Valentin's 2010 business card. Uliana knew I was distressed in 2005 that Valentin had stood up my American Museum of Natural History group. The focus of her interview was on Valentin's cultural revitalization efforts through his history museum.
26. I remember Rinchinov with mixed feelings, for when he conducted a dramatic, fully robed and masked purification and prognosis seance on a tennis court outside Moscow, with two assistants to guide him when he whirled into trance, he predicted the imminent death of my elderly mother-in-law. She died many years later. See also Tkacz et al (2002).
27. Metzo (2008: 231). I knew Nadia as an historian, before she became a shaman. Another impressive Buriat shaman is Svetlana Daribazarova, who I was able to meet in 2009 in Alaska, discussed ahead.
28. The estimates are from Katherine Metzo (2008: 231–5), and Justine Buck Quijada (personal correspondence September 24, 2009). See also C. Allione "Nadia Stepanova, Buryatian Shaman" *Mystic Fire Video*, 1995; and the video "Siberian Dream", http://www.gardnerdocgroup.com/siberian/characters.html.
29. Describing this "communitas" inducing ceremony is beyond my scope. But local specialists confirmed its innovation, since having as many as 27 shamans drumming and trancing at once was highly unusual, even for the sacred setting we were in. See especially the work of Olga A. Shoglanova, a graduate student of Natalia Zhukovskaia.
30. The translation is mine from Russian. The Geser (Gesar) Society, celebrating the famed Mongolian epic, is another example of cultural revitalization that explicitly valorizes Mongolian roots. The positive spin on ancestral shamanic legacies interestingly contrasts with that described by Manduhai Buyandelgeriyn (2007: 135), who mentions repressed shamans in Mongolia as avenging ghosts, or *uheer*, literally raised corpses. The name and concept is similar to the Sakha *iuor*. See also the work of the Mongolian Cambridge-educated anthropologist Bumochir Dulam (2010) and Natalia Zhukovskaia (2002).
31. A list of shaman candidates for the "Chief Shaman of Rossiia," at www.shamanstvo.ru , was compiled in 2009 without consulting with all the candidates, some of whom were already deceased. The list included many folk curers, and some musicians, artists and actors; it is not clear how it was compiled. The self-appointed head of the commission for determining the "chief shaman" was Shonshalai Khovemei. Valentina Kharitonova (personal communication May 2009) explained that the Moscow-based Altaians who organized the competition were hoping to gain recognition for shamanic representatives on par with those of the other "traditional

religions of Russia" named in the preamble to the 1997 Law on Freedom of Conscience and Religious Associations of Rossiia.
32. See Vainshtein and Moskalenko (1995); Kharitonova (2000, 2006); Johansen (2001); Lindquist (2005, 2008); Levin and Suzukei (2006).
33. Note that Mongush Kenin-Lopsan used both the terms "shamanism" in Russian, and "shamanstvo," stressing practice over ideology. For context, see Anaiban (1999) and Moskalenko (2004).
34. A film was made by the Foundation for Shamanic Studies "Tuvan Shamanic Healing" featuring "Ai-Churek." See www.shamanism.org . See also their 1993 film: "Tuva: Shamans and Spirits" on the famous trip led by Bill Brunton (1994) to the republic. Compare Peters (1993).
35 . The rain séance was filmed by Valentina Kharitonova, who confirmed in 2010 that it had brought rain after a long and serious regional drought. Zoia Anaiban (personal communication April 2007) discussed tensions between shamanists and Buddhists. Official support, requiring registration, includes leasing of valuable Yenesei front property to *Tos Déér* and potential tax breaks. A list of prominent shamans and their organizations in the republic, provided by Zoia Anaiban (May 2007) includes L. D. Mongush (Sailyk-ool) of *Düngür*; Aichurek Sh Oiun of *Tos Déér*; A.D. Choodu of *Ovaa*; K.T. Dopchun of *Adyg Eeren*; Kanchir-ool of *Zolotaia Orba*; D. S. Saryglar of *Solangy Eeren*; B.T. Anykai of *Ush-Mooruk*. Such groups are under renewed siege as Russian Federation law requiring medical licences is enforced.
36. These examples of followers are all taken from people I have interviewed.

Reflections

1. As the Soviet period ended, the Sakha Republic had among the highest rates of interethnic marriage, but these declined in the 1990s (Bragina 1996). The pattern of the children of mixed ethnic marriages turning to Protestantism holds for other congregations I have visited.
2. I periodically attend Russian Orthodox services in Yakutsk, and have watched their congregations grow since 1986. By 2000, about ten percent was indigenous Siberian. This held steady or perhaps declined by 2010. See also Balzer (2005).
3. On the 1997 Law and its human rights ramifications, see Balzer (2011).
4. See also the fine-grained ethnographies of V. Turner (1969; 1977), M. Taussig (1987), R. Ridington (1990), A. Fienup-Riordan (1994), E. Turner (1996), C. Humphrey (1998).
5. On *Tengri* concepts and cultural renewal in Central Asia and Turkic Siberia, see Sarygulov (2002). For relevant Mongolic and Turkic connections, see Bezertinov (2000); Zhukovskaia (2008). Conferences in Siberia have enabled scholars to reinforce commonalities in the past decade, for example a conference on Turkic peoples and folklore in Yakutsk in 2007.

6. Compare Atkinson (1992); Vitebsky (1995); Balzer (1996, 1997); Lindquist (1997); Pentikainen (1997); Humphrey (1999); Kendall (1996, 2000, 2010); Niezen (2000); Csordas (2002);.
7. The widely used phrase "non-ordinary reality" is part of the terminology of Michael Harner's "core shamanism" workshops. See Harner (1990); compare Lindquist (1997); Jacobsen (1999); Kharitonova (2000, 2006). Altered consciousness is a matter of degree, not a yes/no state of "ecstasy" subdivided into "controlled" (shamanic) and "out of control" (possession) states. Compare Eliade (2004); Lewis (1971).
8. This contrasts with the familiar and misleading white "benevolent" and black "ill-willed" shaman distinction. Compare Troshchanskii (1903); Kulakovskii (1979). On variations concerning the mixed powers of healing and sorcery, see Radin (1949) for North America; Reid (1983) for Australia; J. Smith (2008) for Africa; Whitehead and Wright (2004) for Amazonia.
9. See Shirokogoroff (1935); Ksenofontov (1992); Diószegi and Hoppál (1978); Hoppál and Kosa (2003); D. Funk (1995); Basilov (1997); Narby and Huxley (2001).
10. Compare Eliade (2004); Derrida and Vattimo (1998); M. Bloch (2008); Atkinson (1992); Hultkranz (1993). See also Toby Lester's "Oh, Gods!" (2002).
11. On Tungusic and other origins and definitions, see Balzer (1997); Kehoe (2000). On romanticism of Siberia, see Hutton (2001); Znamenski (2007).
12. Contrast the typical Troshchanskii (1903) with the sensitive Shirokogoroff (1935). On changing views of shamans, see Flaherty (1992); Narby and Huxley (2001); Hutton (2001). Others linking art, archeology, religion, and folklore include Wallis and Lymer (2001). Compare Francfort et al. (2001: 31–294); Hick (2007); Seaman and Day (1994).
13. See http://rusk.ru/newsdata.php?idar=44024 (accessed 9/25/10) for the statement by the priest Vsevolod Chaplin, at the university in Yakutsk during celebrations opening the new cathedral and seminary. See http://www.blagovest-info.ru/index.php?ss=2&s=3&id=36815 (dated 9/24/10, accessed 9/24/10) for the Patriarch's comment.
14. Improving communication between indigenous and non-indigenous healers and academics is a goal of part-Ojibwa (Anishinaabe) scholar Barbara Tedlock (2008) in founding the journal *Shamanic Practice*. See also Brunton (1994); M. Kenin-Lopsan (1994); and L. Peters (1993) on the 1993 Foundation for Shamanic Studies trip to Tuva.
15. Some Native spiritual leaders have welcomed sincere seekers ready to endure vision quests and other spirit testing or spiritual initiations, although this continues to be controversial in indigenous communities. These networks extend beyond sometimes sensational publicity. Compare the "memoirs" of Carlos Castaneda (1968; 1972), Lynn Andrews (1981); and the "metis" Hyemeyohsts Storm (1972; 1997). See Boyd (1974); John Fire (Lame Deer) with Richard Erdoes (1972); Bobby Lake-Thom, also called Medicine Grizzly Bear (1991); Neihardt (1993).

Analysis includes Fikes (1993); Jakobsen (1999); Kehoe (2000); Wallis (2003); Znamenski (2007).
16. Information on record breaking high Sakha youth suicides appeared at Ivan Nikolaev's (Uhhan) site: www.uhhan.ru/news/2008-06-20-189 (accessed 8/5/08) but later disappeared. Siberian life expectancy averaged around fifty three in recent years, in a country where life expectancy statistics are in general alarming. See Heleniak (2009) and Orlov (2008).
17. See Osherenko and Young (2005); Yalowitz et al (2008); and www.arctic-council.org/article/about (accessed 6/28/09). See also Paul Goble (2006); www.arcticpeoples.org/2008/04/23 (accessed 6/28/09); and www.manystrongvoices.org (accessed 3/28/09).
18. On ecology activist group projects, see www.pacificenvironment.org . For indigenous perspective, see Sergei Khariuchi (2008), head of the Russian Association of Indigenous Peoples of the North (RAIPON) and of the Yamal duma. RAIPON is a member of the Arctic Council: www.raipon.info.
19. Other hopeful signs include beloved primatologist Jane Goodall, now a U. N. "peace representative" reinforcing the need to "return to indigenous wisdom." The National Geographic Society was launching an "Ancient Wisdom" project, including filming of shamanic communities but funding was curtailed in 2010.

References

Ackerknecht, Erwin H. 1943. "Psychopathology," *Bulletin of the History of Medicine* 14: 30–67.
Afanas'ev, Lazar A. (Téris). 1993. *Aiyy yoreghé [Teachings of the spirit]*. Yakutsk: Ministry of Culture. [In Sakha.]
———. 2002. *Aiyy suola [The road of the spirit]*. Yakutsk: Bichik. [In Sakha.]
Afanas'ev, Lazar A., A. Romanov, R. Petrov, N. Petrov, and V. Illarionov. 1990. *Aiyy yoreghé [Teachings of the spirit]*. Yakutsk: Sakha Keskile, Kut-Siur. [In Sakha.]
Aipin, Eremei. 1990. "Vdenie: O gnezdyshke odinokom" *Literaturnaia Arktika* (4): 24.
———. 2010. *Bozh'ia Mater' v Krovavykh Snegakh*. St. Petersburg: Amfora.
Alekseev, Anatoly Afanasevich. 1994. "Healing Techniques Among Éven Shamans," *The Journey Journal: A Publication of the Shamanic Film/Video Archive* 2(2): 1, 3.
Alekseev, Eduard E. 1976. *Problemy formirovaniia lada (na materiale Iakutskoi narodnoi pesni)*. Moscow: Muzyka.
———. 2008. "Penie pri kul'turno-spetsifichnyikh psikhicheskikh rasstroistvakh u narodov Sibirskogo Severa" *Mif, Simbol, Ritual. Narody Sibiri.* S. Iu. Nekliudov, ed., 153–173. Moscow: Gumanitarnyi U.
Alekseev, Nikolai A. 1975. *Traditsionnye religioznye verovaniia Iakutov v xiv-nachale xx v.* Novosibirsk: Nauka.
———. 1984. *Shamanizm tiurkoiazychnykh narodov Sibiri*. Novosibirsk: Nauka.
———. 1997. "Shamanism Among the Turkic Peoples," *Shamanic Worlds: Rituals and Lore of Siberia and Central Asia*, M. M. Balzer, ed., 49–109. Armonk, NY, London: M.E. Sharpe.
———. 2008. *Etnografiia i Fol'klor Narodov Sibiri*. Novosibirsk: Nauka.
Anaiban, Zoia V. 1999. "The Republic of Tyva (Tuva): From Romanticism to Realism," *Anthropology and Archeology of Eurasia* 31(3).
Andrews, Lynn. 1981. *Medicine Woman*. San Francisco: Harper and Row.
Anisimov, Arkady F. 1958. *Religiia Evenkov*. Moscow: Akademiia Nauk.
———. 1963. "The Shaman's Tent of the Évenks and the Origin of the Shamanistic Rite," *Studies in Siberian Shamanism*, H. Michael, ed., 84–123. Toronto: U. of Toronto Press, Anthropology of the North, 4.
Anderson, David and Mark Nuttall, eds. 2004. *Cultivating Arctic Landscapes: Knowing and Managing Animal Populations and the Environment in the Circumpolar North*. Oxford: Berghahn.

Appadurai, Arjun. 1996. *Modernity at Large: Cultural Dynamics of Globalization.* Minneapolis: U. of Minnesota Press.

Approsimova, Liudmilla. 1992. *Aiahym ortoturgar syld'abyn* [I'm in the Middle of the Path]. *Sakha Siré* 8 Aug. 92, 5. [In Sakha.]

Asad, Talal. 2002. "From the History of Colonial Anthropology to the Anthropology of Western Hegemony," *The Anthropology of Politics: A Reader in Ethnography, Theory and Critique,* Joan Vincent, ed., 133–142. Malden, Massachusetts: Blackwell.

Atkinson, Jane Monnig. 1989. *The Art and Politics of Wana Shamanship.* Berkeley: U. of California Press.

———. 1992. "Shamanism Today," *Annual Review of Anthropology* 21: 307–30.

Austerlitz, Robert. 1984–85. "Ten Nivkh (Gilyak) Erotic Poems," *Acta Ethnografica Acad. Sci. Hung.* 33: 33–44.

———. 1986. "Shaman," *Ural-Altaic Yearbook* 58: 143–4.

Babcock, Barbara. 1978. *The Reversible World: Symbolic Inversion in Art and Society.* Ithaca: Cornell U. Press.

Badone, Ellen, Sharon R. Roseman, ed. 2004. *Intersecting Journeys: the Anthropology of Pilgrimage and Tourism.* Urbana: U. of Illinois Press.

Bakhtin, Mikhail M. 1965. *Rabelais and His World,* Helen Iswolsky, trans. Cambridge: MIT Press.

Balazs, J. 1968. "The Hungarian Shaman's Technique of Trance Induction," *Popular Beliefs and Folklore Tradition in Siberia,* V. Diószegi, ed., S. Dunn, trans., 53–57. Bloomington: Indiana U. Press, Uralic and Altaic Studies, 57.

Balzer, Marjorie Mandelstam. 1980. "The Route To Eternity: Cultural Persistence and Change in Siberian Khanty Burial Ritual," *Arctic Anthropology* 17:77–90.

———. 1981. "Rituals of Gender Identity: Markers of Siberian Khanty Ethnicity, Status and Belief," *American Anthropologist* 83 (4): 850–67.

———. 1993a. "Shamanism and the Politics of Culture: An Anthropological View of the 1992 International Conference on Shamanism, Yakutsk, the Sakha Republic," *Shaman* 1(2):71–96.

———. 1993b. "Two Urban Shamans: Unmasking Leadership in Fin-de-Soviet Siberia," *Perilous States: Conversations amid Uncertain Transitions to the Next Century.* George Marcus, ed., 131–164. Chicago: U. of Chicago Press.

———. 1996. "Sacred Genders in Siberia: Shamans, Bear Festivals and Androgyny," *Gender Reversals and Gender Cultures: Anthropological and Historical Perspectives,* S. P. Ramet, ed. London: Routledge, 164–182.

———. 1999. *The Tenacity of Ethnicity: A Siberian Saga in Global Perspective.* Princeton: Princeton University Press.

———. 2003. "Dynamic Ethnics: Socio-Religious Movements in Siberia," *Extending the Borders of Russian History: Essays in honor of Alfred J. Rieber.* M. Seifert, ed., 481–495. Budapest: Central European U. Press.

———. 2005. "Whose Steeple is Higher? Religious Competition in Siberia," *Religion, State and Society* 33(1): 57–69.

———. 2011. "Religious Communities and Rights in the Russian Federation," *Religion and the Global Politics of Human Rights,* Thomas Banchoff and Robert Wuthnow, eds. New York: Oxford U. Press.

Balzer, Marjorie Mandelstam, ed. 1995. *Culture Incarnate: Native Anthropology from Russia.* Armonk, New York: M. E. Sharpe.
———1997 [1990]. *Shamanic Worlds: Rituals and Lore of Siberia and Central Asia.* Armonk, NY, London: M.E. Sharpe. [2nd revised edition.]
———. 2006. "Buddhism in Russia: Burkhanism" Parts 1, 2. *Anthropology and Archeology of Eurasia.* 45 (2, 3).
Balzer, Marjorie Mandelstam and Uliana A. Vinokurova. 1996. "Nationalism, Interethnic Relations and Federalism: The Case of the Sakha Republic (Yakutia)," *Europe-Asia Studies* 48 (1): 101–20.
Bannerman, R. H. 1977. "W.H.O.'s Programme," *World Health* Nov.: 16–17.
Bartenev, Victor. 1896. *Na Krainem Severo-Zapade Sibirii.* St. Petersburg: M. F. Paukin.
Basilov, Vladimir. 1992. *Shamanstvo u narodov Srednei Azii i Kazakstana,* Moscow: Nauka.
———. 1997 [1984]. "Chosen by the Spirits," *Shamanic Worlds: Rituals and Lore of Siberia and Central Asia,* Marjorie Mandelstam Balzer, ed., 3-48. Armonk, NY, London: M.E. Sharpe.
Basso, Keith. 1996. *Wisdom Sits in Places: Landscape and Language Among the Western Apache.* Albuquerque: U. of New Mexico Press.
Bazarov, Boris. 2000. *Tainstva i praktika shamanizma.* Ulan-Ude: Buri'ia'ad unèn.
Beck, Robert J. 1967. "Some Proto-Psychotherapeutic Elements in the Practice of the Shaman," *History of Religions* 6(4): 303–27.
Bezertinov, Rafael Nurudinovich. 2000. *Tengrianstvo—religii'a tiurkov i mongolov.* Chelny: Ai'a'z.
Biehl, Joa'o; Byron Good, Arthur Kleinman, eds. 2007. *Subjectivity: Ethnographic Investigations.* Berkeley: U. of California Press.
Billington, James. 1970 [1966]. *The Icon and the Axe: An Interpretive History of Russian Culture.* New York: Random House.
Bloch, Alexia. 2004. *Red ties and residential schools: indigenous Siberians in a Post-Soviet state.* Philadelphia, Pennsylvania: U. of Pennsylvania Press.
Bloch, Maurice E. 2008. "Why Religion Is Nothing Special But is Central," *Philosophical Transactions of the Royal Society* 363 (1499): 2055–61.
Boas, Franz. 1909. *The Kwakiutl of Vancouver Island.* Leiden: E. J. Brill; New York: G. E. Stechert.
———. 1930. "The Religion of the Kwakiutl," *Columbia University Contributions to Anthropology* 10(2).
Boeskorov, Stepan T. 2001. *N'iikon.* Yakutsk: Bichik.
Bogoras, Vladimir G. [Waldemar Bogoras-tan]. 1909. *The Chukchee.* Memoirs of the American Museum of Natural History, no. 11. New York: Stechert. [original: Jesup North Pacific Expedition 1904]
———. 1930. "The Shamanistic Call and the Period of Initiation in Northern Asia and Northern America," *Proceedings of the 23rd International Congress of Americanists, New York,* 441-4. Lancaster, Pennsylvania: Science Press Printing Company.
Bohannon, Laura. 1960. "The Frightened Witch," *In the Company of Man.* Joseph B. Casagrande, ed. New York: Harper.

Boyd, Douglas. 1974. *Rolling Thunder; a Personal Exploration Into the Secret Healing Powers of an American Indian Medicine Man*. New York: Random House.
Bragina, Daria. 1996. *Sovremennye Etnokul'turnye Protsessy u Narodov Sakha*. Yakutsk: YaGU.
Bravina, Rosa I. 2005. *Kontseptsiia zhizni i smerti v kul'ture Etnosa: Na Materiale Traditsii Sakha*. Yakutsk: YaGU.
Brem, Alexander. 1897. "Ostiaki-Idolpolkoniki,"*Ezhemesiachniia Literaturniia Prelozheniia k Nive*, 2: 347–83.
Brown, Michael F. 1989. "Dark Side of the Shaman" *Natural History* no. 11: 8–10.
———. 2003. *Who Owns Native Culture?* Cambridge: Harvard U. Press.
Brown, Joseph Epes with Emily Cousins. 2001. *Teaching Spirits: Understanding Native American Religious Tradition*. New York: Oxford.
Bruner, Edward M. 1984. *Text, Play and Sorcery: The Construction and Reconstruction of Self and Society*. Washington, DC: American Ethical Society.
Brunton, Bill with Michael Harner (introduction). 1994. "Tuva, Land of Eagles— The Foundation's 1993 Expedition to Tuva" *Shamanism*, Spring 7 (1).
Buckley, Thomas and Alma Gottlieb, eds. 1988. *Blood Magic: The Anthropology of Menstruation*. Berkeley: U. of California Press.
Budarin, M. E. 1968. *Byli o Sibirskikh Chekistakh*. Omsk: Zapadnoie-Sibirskoe izdat.
Bugaev, N. (Bugay). 1992. "Oborvannaia tsepochka," *Molodezh Yakutii*, August 6: 8.
Burnashev, N. P. with S. K. Diakonov et. al. 1993. *Yakutskii geroicheskii epos 'Kyys Debeliie.'* Novosibirsk: Nauka, series *Pamiatniki folk'lora narodov Sibiri i Dal'nego Vostoka*.
Businskii, P. O. 1893. *Kreshchenie Ostiakov i Vogulov Pre Petre I*. Kharkhov: Gub. Pravleniia.
Buyandelgeriyn, Manduhai. 2007. "Dealing with Uncertainty: Shamans, Marginal Capitalism, and the Remaking of History in Postsocialist Mongolia," *American Ethnologist* 34(1): 126–147.
Carpenter, Edmund S. 1961. "Witch-Fear Among the Aivilik Eskimos," *Social Structure and Personality*, Yehudi A. Cohen, ed., 508–15. New York: Holt, Rhinehart and Winston.
Carter, Lewis F. 1996. *The Issue of Authenticity in the Study of Religions*. London: JAI.
Castaneda, Carlos. 1968. *The Teachings of Don Juan; a Yaqui Way of Knowledge*. Berkeley, U. of California Press.
———. 1972. *Journey to Ixtlan: the Lessons of Don Juan*. New York: Simon and Schuster.
Chadwick, Nora Kershaw. 1942. *Poetry and Prophesy*. Cambridge: Cambridge University Press.
Charles, Lucile Hoerr. 1953. "Drama in Shaman Exorcism," *Journal of American Folklore* 66: 95–122.
Chatterjee, Partha. 1993. *The Nation and its Fragments: Colonial and Post-Colonial Histories*. Princeton: Princeton University Press.

Chernetsov, Valerii N. 1935. *Vogulskie Skazki*. Leningrad: Soslitizdat.
———. 1963. "Ideas of the Soul Among Ob-Ugrians," *Studies in Siberian Shamanism: Anthropology of the North*, vol. 4. Henry Michael, ed. Ethel Dunn and Stephen Dunn, trans., 3–45. Toronto: U. of Toronto Press.
Chirkova, Aleksandra Konstantinovna. 2002. *Shaman: Zhizn' i Bessmertie*. Yakutsk: Sakhapoligrafizdat.
———. 2009. *Shaman: Life and Immortality*. Vladimir Riazanski, ed. and trans. Charleston, SC: BookSurge Publishers.
Chichlo, Boris. 1981a. "La Collectivisation en Sibire: un problem de nationalites," *L'Experience Sovietique et le probleme National dans le Mond (1920-1939)*. Paris: Centre National de la Recherche Scientifique, t.1.
———. 1981b. "L'Ours Shamane," *Études Mongoles*, vol. 12, 1981, pp. 35–112.
Chowning, Ann. 1962. "Raven Myths in Northwestern North America and Northeastern Asia," *Arctic Anthropology* 1:1–5.
Codrescu, Andrei. 1990. *The Disappearance of the Outside: A Manifesto for Escape*. Reading, Massachusetts: Addison-Wesley.
Comaroff, Jean. 1985. *Body of Power, Spirit of Resistance: The Culture and History of a South African People*. Chicago: U. of Chicago Press.
Comaroff, John, Jean Comaroff. 2004. "Criminal Justice, Cultural Justice: The Limits of Liberalism and the Pragmatics of Difference in the New South Africa," *American Ethnologist* 31(2): 188–204.
Conklin, Beth A. 2001. *Consuming Grief: Compassionate Cannibalism in an Amazonian Society*. Austin: U. of Texas Press.
Conner, Linda and Geoffrey Samuel, ed. 2001. *Healing Powers and Modernity: Traditional Medicine, Shamanism, and Science in Asian Societies*. Westport, Connecticut: Bergin & Garvey.
Crandon, Libbet, ed. 1987. "Beyond the Cure: Anthropological Inquiries in Medical Theories and Epistemologies," *Social Science and Medicine* 24 (12): 1011–1118.
Crapanzano, Vincent. 1973. *The Hamadsha: A Study in Moroccan Ethnopsychiatry*. Berkeley: U. of California Press.
———. 1991. "The Postmodern Crisis: Discourse, Parody, Memory," *Cultural Anthropology* 6 (4): 431–46.
Cruikshank, Julie. 1998. *The Social Life of Stories: Narrative and Knowledge in the Yukon Territory*. Lincoln: U. of Nebraska Press.
———. 2005. *Do Glaciers Listen. Local Knowledge, Colonial Encounter and Social Imagination*. Vancouver: U. of British Columbia Press.
Cruikshank, Julie and Tatiana Argounova. 2000. "Reinscribing Meaning: Memory and Indigenous Identity in Sakha Republic (Yakutia)," *Arctic Anthropology* 37(1): 96–119.
Crumbly, Deidre Helen. 2008. *Spirit, Structure, and Flesh: Gendered Experiences in African Instituted Churches among the Yoruba of Nigeria*. Madison: U. Wisconsin Press.
Csepregi, Márta. 2007. "An Eastern Khanty Shaman Song," *Shaman* 15 (1 & 2).
Csordas, Thomas J. 1994. *The Sacred Self: A Cultural Phenomenology of Charismatic Healing*. Berkeley: U. of California Press.
———. 2002. *Body/Meaning/Healing*. New York: Palgrave Macmillan.

Csordas, Thomas J., ed. 2000. "The Navaho Healing Project," *Medical Anthropology Quarterly* 14 (4).
———. 2009. *Transnational Transcendence: Essays on Religion and Globalization*. Berkeley: U. of California Press.
Czaplicka, Maria. 1914. *Aboriginal Siberia: A Study in Social Anthropology*. Oxford: Clarendon.
Czigany, L. G. 1980. "The Use of Hallucinogens and the Shamanistic Tradition of the Finno-Ugrian People," *Slavonic and East European Review* 58: 212–217.
Danilin, A. G. 1993. *Burkhanizm: iz istorii natsional'no-osvoboditel'nogo dvizheniia v Gornom Altae*. Gorno-Altaisk: Ak-Chechek.
Daschke, Dereck and W. Michael Ashcraft, eds. 2005. *New Religious Movements: A Documentary Reader*. New York: New York U. Press.
Davies, Wade. 2004. "Western Medicine and Navaho Healing," *The Politics of Healing: Histories of Alternative Medicine in Twentieth-Century North America*, R. D. Johnson, ed., 83–94. New York: Routledge.
de Laguna, Frederica. 1972. *Under Mt. St. Elias: The History and Culture of the Yakutat Tlingit*. Washington, DC: Smithsonian Contributions to Anthropology, 7.
De Vos, George, ed. 1976. *Responses to Change: Society, Culture, and Personality*. New York: Van Nostrand.
Derrida, Jacques and Gianni Vattimo, eds. 1998. *Religion*. Stanford, CA: Stanford University Press.
Descola, Phillippe. 1994. *In the Society of Nature: A Native Ecology in Amazonia*. Cambridge: Cambridge U. Press.
Devereaux, George. 1956. "Normal and Abnormal: The Key Problem of Psychiatric Anthropology," *Some Uses of Anthropology: Theoretical and Applied*, 23–48. Washington, DC: Anthropological Society of Washington.
———. 1961. "Shamans as Neurotics," *American Anthropologist*. 63: 1088–90.
Diachkov, V. I. 1979. "Sostoianie i Perspektivy Razvitiia Zdravookhraneniia v Iamalo-Nenetskom i Khanty-Mansiiskom Avtonomnykh Okrugakh Tiumenskoi Oblasti," *Zdravookhranenie Rossiiskoi Federatsii* 4: 20–24.
Diószegi, Vilmos. 1968. *Tracing Shamans Through Siberia*. Antia Rajkay Babo, trans. Oosterhout, the Netherlands: Anthropological Publications.
———. 1978. "Pre-Islamic Shamanism of the Baraba Turks and Some Ethnogenetic Conclusions," *Shamanism in Siberia*. V. Diószegi, M. Hoppál, eds., S. Simon, Trans., 83–167. Budapest: Akadémiai Kiadó.
Diószegi, Vilmos and Mihály Hoppál, eds. 1978. *Shamanism in Siberia*. Budapest: Akadémiai Kiadó.
Douglas, Mary. 1970. *Natural Symbols: Explorations in Cosmology*. New York: Vintage.
———. 1975. *Implicit Meanings*. London: Routledge.
———. 1996. *Purity and Danger: an Analysis of Concepts of Pollution and Taboo*. New York: Praeger.
Dow, James. 1986. *The Shaman's Touch: Otomi Indian Symbolic Healing*. Salt Lake City: U. of Utah Press.

Dugarov, Bair. 1996. *Sagan-Dali, Flower of My Mountain Land.* Elizabethtown, NY: Ecologically Sustainable Development Project.

Durkheim, Emile. 1965 [1915]. *The Elementary Forms of the Religious Life.* J.W. Swain, trans. New York: Free Press.

Dulam, Bumochir. 2010. "Degrees of Ritualization: Language Use in Mongolian Shamanic Ritual," *Shaman* 18(1&2): 11–42.

Dunin-Gorkavich, A. A. 1904, 1910, 1911. *Tobol'skii Sever,* vols. 1–3. Tobolsk: Gub. Tip.

Durrant, Stephan. 1979. "The Nišan Shaman Complex in Cultural Contradiction," *Signs* 5(2): 338–47.

Dzeniskevich, Galina I. 1976. "Skazaniia o Vorone u Atapaskov Alaski," *Sovetskaia Etnografiia* 1:73–83.

Efimova, Irina. 2009. "Belyi Shaman Vladimir Kondakov," www.dvmusic.ru/index/articles/one/full/1517 (accessed 7/20/09).

Egorova, Liudmila I. 2010. "Kul't Neba" ms. [presentation to Tunka Valley conference "Shamanism and Art."]

Emelianov, Nikolai V. 1996. "The Orphan Husband: The Epic Forefather of the Uraangkhai Sakha Tribe," *Anthropology and Archeology of Eurasia* 35(2): 57–94.

Emelianov, Nikolai V. and Svetlana D. Mukhopleva, eds. 1993. *Oiuun [Shaman].* Yakutsk: Russian Academy of Sciences. 3 vols. [in Sakha.]

Engelke, Mathew. 2007. *A Problem of Presence: Beyond Scripture in an African Church.* U. California Press.

Eliade, Mircea. 2004 [1974, 1951]. *Shamanism: Archaic Techniques of Ecstasy.* Princeton: Princeton U. Press.

Ergis, G. U., et al. eds. 1976, 77, 80, 83. *Iakutskie Narodnye Pesni. Sakha Narodnai Yryalara* [Sakha Folk Songs]. Yakutsk: Yakutsk Kn. Izd. [Series in Russian and Sakha.]

Feld, Steven. 1990. [1982]. *Sound and Sentiment: Birds, Weeping, Poetics and Song in Kaluli Expression.* Philadelphia: U. Pennsylvania Press.

Fernandez, James. 1986. *Persuasions and Performances.* Bloomington: Indiana U. Press.

Fernandez, James, ed. 1991. *Beyond Metaphor: The Theory of Tropes in Anthropology.* Stanford: Stanford U. Press.

Feshbach, Murray and Alfred Friendly Jr. 1992. *Ecocide in the USSR: Health and Nature under Siege.* New York: Basic Books.

Fikes, Jay C. 1993. *Carlos Castaneda, Academic Opportunism and the Psychedelic Sixties.* Victoria, BC: Millenia.

Filatov, Sergei. 2001. "Altai Burkhanism: Faith or a Dream of Faith?" *Anthropology and Archeology of Eurasia* 39(4): 76–91.

Fienup-Riordan, Ann. 1994. *Boundaries and Passages: Rule and Ritual in Yup'ik Eskimo Oral Tradition.* Norman: University of Oklahoma Press.

Fire, John (Lame Deer) with Richard Erdoes. 1972. *Lame Deer, Seeker of Visions.* New York: Simon and Schuster.

Fischer, Michael M. J. with Mehdi Abedi. 1990. *Debating Muslims: Cultural Dialogues in Postmodernity and Tradition.* Madison: U. of Wisconsin Press.

Fitzhugh, William and Aron Crowell, ed. 1988. *Crossroads of Continents: Cultures of Siberia and Alaska.* Washington, D.C.: Smithsonian.

Flaherty, Gloria. 1992. *Shamanism and the Eighteenth Century*. Princeton: Princeton U. Press.

Fondahl, Gail. 1993. "Siberia: Native Peoples and Newcomers in Collision," *Nations and Politics in the Soviet Successor States*, I. Bremmer and R. Taras, eds. 47–510. Cambridge: Cambridge U. Press.

Forsyth, James. 1992. *A History of the Peoples of Siberia: Russia's North Asian Colony 1581–1990*. Cambridge: Cambridge U. Press.

Fortun, Kim, Mike Fortun, Steven Rubenstein, eds. 2010. "Essay Cluster: Emergent Indigeneities," *Cultural Anthropology* 25(2): 222–370.

Fortune, Reo. 1932. *Sorcerers of Dobu*. New York: Dutton.

Foster, George M. and Barbara Gallatin Anderson. 1978. *Medical Anthropology*. New York: John Wiley & Sons.

Fox, Richard. 1995. "The Breakdown of Culture," *Current Anthropology* 36(1): 1–13.

Francfort, Henri-Paul, Roberte Hamayon with Paul G. Bahn, eds. 2001. *The Concept of Shamanism: Uses and Abuses*. Budapest: Akadémiai Kiadó.

Frank, Jerome. 1961. *Persuasion and Healing*. Baltimore: Johns Hopkins U. Press.

Freud, Sigmund. 1949 [1940]. *An Outline of Psychoanalysis*. J. Strachey, trans. New York: Norton.

Freidenburg, Olga M. 1973. "Proiskhozhdenie parcdii," *Trudy po znakovym sistemam*, 6, vyp. 308. Tartu: Tartu State U.

Fridman, Eva Jane Neuman. 2004. *Sacred Geography: Shamanism Among the Buddhist Peoples of Russia*. Budapest: Akadémiai Kiadó, International Society for Shamanistic Research.

Friedrich, Paul. 1991. "Polytrophy," *Beyond Metaphor: The Theory of Tropes in Anthropology*. J. W. Fernandez, ed. Palo Alto: Stanford U. Press.

Friedson, Steven M. 1996. *Dancing Prophets: Musical Experience in Tumbuka Healing*. Chicago, Illinois: U. of Chicago.

Funk, Dmitri A. 1993. *Bachatskie Teleuty*. Moscow: Russian Academy of Sciences.

———. 2005. *Miry Shamanov i Skazitelei*. Moscow: Nauka.

———. 2006. "In Lieu of an Introduction," *Anthropology and Archeology of Eurasia* 45(2): 9–13.

Funk, Dmitri A., ed. 1995. *Shamanizm i rannie religioznye predstavleniia*. Moscow: Russian Academy of Sciences.

Furst, Peter T. 1977. *Stones, Bones and Skin: Ritual and Shamanic Art*. Toronto: Artscanada.

———. 2004. "Visionary Plants and Ecstatic Shamanism," *Expedition: Magazine of the University of Pennsylvania Museum of Archeology and Anthropology* 46(1): 26–29.

Furst, Peter T., ed. 1972. *Flesh of the Gods: The Ritual Use of Hallucinogens*. New York: Praeger.

Geertz, Clifford. 1973. *The Interpretation of Cultures*. New York: Basic Books.

Gell, Alfred. 1998 *Art and Agency: an Anthropological Theory*. Oxford; New York: Clarendon Press.

REFERENCES

Gellner, David N. 1994. "Priests, Healers, Mediums and Witches: The Context of Possession in the Katmandu Valley, Nepal," *Man* 29:27-48.
Gillin, John. 1948. "Magical Fright," *Psychiatry* 11: 387-400.
Goble, Paul. 2006. "Window on Eurasia: Russia's Northern Peoples Again Look Abroad for Policy Ideas," www.windowoneurasia.blogspot.com (9/27/06 accessed 10/3/06).
Gogolev, Anatoly I. 1983. *Istoricheskaia etnografiia Yakutov: Narodnye znanie i obychnoe pravo*. Yakutsk: Yakutskaia Gosudarstvennaia Universiteta.
———. 1986. *Istoricheskaia etnografiia Yakutov: Problemy etnogeneza i formirovaniia kul'tury*. Yakutsk: YaGU.
———. 1992. "Cultural History of the Yakut (Sakha) People," *Anthropology and Archeology of Eurasia*. 31(2): 1-84.
———. 1993a. *Yakuty: Problemy etnogenez i formirovaniia kul'tury*. Yakutsk: Ministry of Culture, YaGU.
———. 1993b. "Aan tyl [Gateway Language]," *Sakha Oiuunnara* [Sakha shamans]. Yakutsk: Sakha Ministry of Culture, 3-4. [In Sakha.]
———. 2000. "Predislovie," *Sviashennye i pamiatnye mesta Khangalas*. Yakutsk: Akademiia Nauk.
———. 2002. *Istoki mifologii i traditsionnyi kalendar' Yakutov*. Yakutsk: Min. Obrazovanie.
Gogolev, A.I., A.P. Reshetnikova, E.N. Romanova, P.A. Sleptsov, eds. 1992. *Shamanizm Kak Religiia: Genesis, rekonstruktsiia, traditsii*. Yakutsk: YaGU.
Gogolev, Ivan. 1987. *Khara kytalyk* [The black crane]. Yakutsk: Sakha Press.
———. 1989. *Aian Aaryktara* [Poetry]. Yakutsk: Sakha Sirinéékhi. [In Sakha.]
Gol'derova, Sargilaana. 1987. *Khatyng Uuta* [Birch Sap]. Yakutsk: Sakha Sirinéékhi. [In Sakha.]
Goldfarb, Lev, Vsevolod A Vladimirtsev, Fyodor A Platonov, Hee-Suk Lee, Catriona A McLean, Colin L Masters. 2009. "Viliuisk encephalomyelitis in Eastern Siberia—analysis of 390 cases," *Folia Neuropathologica* 47 (2): 171-181.
Golovnev, Andrei V. 1995. *Govoriashchie kul'tury: traditsii Samodiitsev i Ugrov*. Ekaterinburg: Akademiia Nauk.
Golubov, S. 1931. "Pervyi otriad severnykh national'nykh rabotnikov," *Sovetskii Sever* (6): 111.
Gondatti, Nikolai L. 1887a. "Sledy Iazycheskikh Verovanii u Mansov," *Trudy Obshchestva Estestvenii Antropologii i Etnografii* 8: 49-93.
———. 1887b. "Kul't medvedia u Zapadnoi-Sibirskoi inorodtsev," *Trudy obshchestva estestveni nauk antropologii i etnografii*, 8.
Goodenough, Ward. 1963. *Cooperation in Change*. New York: Russell Sage Foundation.
Goodman, Felicitas. 1990. *Where the Spirits Ride the Wind: Trance Journeys and Other Ecstatic Experiences*. Bloomington: Indiana U. Press.
Goulet, Jean-Guy J., and Bruce Granville Miller, eds, Johannes Fabian, preface. 2007. *Extraordinary Anthropology: transformations in the field*. Lincoln: U. of Nebraska Press.
Gow, David D. 2008. *Countering Development: Indigenous Modernity and the Moral Imagination*. Durham: Duke U. Press.

Grambo, Ronald. 1989. "Unmanliness and Seidr: Problems Concerning the Change of Sex," *Shamanism Past and Present*, Mihály Hoppál and Otto von Sadovszky, eds. 103–13. Budapest: Akadémiai Kiadó.

Grant, Bruce. 1995. *In the Soviet House of Culture: A Century of Perestroikas.* Princeton: Princeton U. Press.

Greenfield, Sidney M., A. F. Droogers. 2001. *Reinventing Religions: Syncretism and Transformation in Africa and the Americas.* Lanham, MD: Roman and Littlefield.

Grenoble, Lenore, Lindsay J. Whaley. 2006. *Saving Languages: an Introduction to Language Revitalization.* Cambridge, UK, New York: Cambridge U. Press.

Grigoryants, Sergei. 1989. "Camps with White Gowns," *Glasnost* January 1989 (16–18): 34–47.

Grim, John. 1983. *The Shaman: Patterns of Siberian and Ojibway healing.* Norman: U. of Oklahoma Press.

Grigor'eva, Aleksandra M. 1996. *Narodnoe Vrachevanie v Yakutii (XVII-XXv).* Moscow: Akademiia Nauk.

Gurvich, Il'ia Samoilevich, ed. 1971. *Osushchestvlenie Leninskoi National'noi politiki u Narodov Krainego Severa.* Moscow: Nauka.

Gushin, N. Ia., ed. 1980. *Kul'turnoe razvitie sovetskoi sibiri.* Novosibirsk: Nauka.

Hale, Charles. 2006. "Activist Research v. Cultural Critique: Indigenous Land Rights and the Contradictions of Politically Engaged Anthropology," *Cultural Anthropology* 21(1): 96–120.

Halemba, Agnieszka. 2006. *The Telengits of Southern Siberia: Landscape, Religion and Knowledge in Motion.* London, New York: Routledge.

Hall, H. U. 1919. "Shamanist Bird Figures of the Yenisei Ostyak," *University of Pennsylvania Museum Journal* 10: 210–212.

Hajdu, Peter. 1968. "The Classification of Samoyed Shamans," *Popular Beliefs and Folklore Tradition in Siberia.* V. Diószegi, ed. Stephen Dunn, trans. 147–73. Bloomington: Indiana U. Press Uralic and Altaic Series, 57.

Hallowell, A. Irving. 1926. "Bear Ceremonialism in the Northern Hemisphere," *American Anthropologist* 28(1): 1–175.

Hamayon, Roberte. 1990. *La Chasse à l'âme: Esquisse d'une théorie du chamanisme sibérien.* Nanterre: Société d'etnologie.

———. 2007. "A quel esprit se vouer? Vicissitudes de la notion d'esprit chamanique en Sibérie postsoviétique," *La nature des esprits dans les cosmologies autochtones/Nature of Spirits in Aboriginal Cosmologies*, Frédéric Laugrand, Jarich G. Oosten, eds. 403–425. Quebec: Université Leval.

Handler, Richard. 2004. "Afterword: Mysteries of Culture," *American Anthropologist* 106(3): 488–494.

Harner, Michael J. 1990 [1980]. *The Way of the Shaman: A Guide to Power and Healing.* New York: HarperCollins.

Harner, Michael, ed. 1973. *Hallucinogens and Shamanism.* London: Oxford U. Press.

Hatto, Arthur Thomas. 1970. *Shamanism and Epic Poetry in Northern Asia.* London: U. of London.

Heleniak, Timothy. 2009. "Growth Poles and Ghost Towns in the Russian Far North," *Russia and the North*, Elana Wilson Rowe, Helge Blakkisrud, eds. Oslo: Norwegian Institute for International Affairs.

———. 2009. *Russia and the North*. Ottowa: University of Ottowa Press.

Hick, John. 2007. *The New Frontier of Religion and Science: Religious Experience, Neuroscience and the Transcendent*. New York: Palgrave Macmillan.

Honigman, John J. 1960. "Review of *Culture and Mental Health*, ed. Marvin Opler," *American Anthropologist* 62: 920–23.

Hoppál, Mihály. 1992. "Urban Shamans, A Cultural Revival in a Postmodern World," *Studies on Shamanism*, 197–209. Helsinki: Finnish Anthropological Society; Budapest: Akadémiai Kiadó, *Etnologica Uralica* 2.

———. 2000. *Shaman Traditions in Transition*. Budapest: Akadémiai Kiadó.

Hoppál, Mihály and Gabor Kosa, eds. 2003. *Rediscovery of Shamanic Heritage*. Budapest: Akadémiai Kiadó.

Hultkranz, Åke. 1978 "Ecological and Phenomenological Aspects of Shamanism," *Shamanism in Siberia*. V. Diószegi, M. Hoppál, eds., S. Simon, Trans., 27–58. Budapest: Akadémiai Kiadó.

———.1992. *Shamanic Healing and Ritual Drama*. New York: Crossroad.

———. 1993. "Introductory Remarks on the Study of Shamanism," *Shamanism* 1(1): 3–14.

Humphrey, Caroline. 1998. *Marx Went Away—But Karl Stayed Behind*. Ann Arbor: U. of Michigan Press.

———. 1999. "Shamans in the City," *Anthropology Today* 15(3): 3–10.

Humphrey, Caroline with Urgunge Onon 1996 *Shamans and Elders: Experience, Knowledge and Power among the Daur Mongols*. Oxford: Clarendon Press.

Humphrey, Caroline and Thomas, Nicholas, eds. 1994. *Shamanism, History, and the State*. Ann Arbor: U. of Michigan Press.

Hutton, Ronald. 2001. *Shamans: Siberian Spirituality and the Western Imagination*. London: Hambledon and London.

Hyde, Lewis. 1998. *Trickster Makes this World: Mischief, Myth, and Art*. New York: Farrar, Straus, and Giroux.

Ignat'ev, Nikolai. 1990. "Onokhu Spiridon Chakhchu oiuun saarbata été" [Essay on the Good Works of the Shaman Spiridon]. Ms. [In Sakha.]

Ingold, Tim. 2000. *The Perception of the Environment: Essays in Livelihood, Dwelling and Skill*. New York: Routledge.

Il'iakhov, Petr N. 1995. *Bor'ba s shamanizmom v Yakutii (1920-30)*. Yakutsk: Dom Narodnogo Tvorchestva.

———. 1997. *Shamanstvo na Severe Yakutii (1920-30)*. Yakutsk: Poligrafist.

Ivanova-Unarova, Zinaida. 2000. *Liki Shamana*. Yakutsk: Bichik.

Jackson, Michael. 1989. *Paths Toward a Clearing: Radical Empiricism and Ethnographic Inquiry*. Bloomington: Indiana U.

———. 2009. *The Palm at the End of the Mind: Relatedness, Religiosity and the Real*. Durham: Duke.

Jakobsen, Merete Demant. 1999. *Shamanism: Traditional and Contemporary Approaches to the Mastery of Spirits and Healing*. New York, London: Berghahn Books.

Johansen, Ulla. 2001. "Shamanism and Neoshamanism: What is the Difference?," *The Concept of Shamanism: Uses and Abuses*, H-P. Francfort and R. Hamayon, eds., 297–303. Budapest: Akadémiai Kiadó.

Johnston, Robert D., ed. 2004. *The Politics of Healing: Histories of Alternative Medicine in Twentieth-Century North America*. New York: Routledge.

Jochelson, Waldemar [Vladimir]. 1904. "The Mythology of the Koryak," *American Anthropologist* 6: 413–25.

———. 1933. *The Yakut*. New York: American Museum of Natural History Anthropological Papers, 33.

———. 1975 [1926, 1910]. *The Yukaghir and the Yukaghirized Tungus*. New York: AMS Press. [Jesup reprint; original Memoirs of the American Museum of Natural History, vol. 12.]

Jokić, Želko 2006 "Cosmo-genesis or Transformation of the Human Body Into a Cosmic Body in Yanomami Shamanistic Initiation" *Shaman* 14(1&2): 19–39.

Jordan, Peter. 2003. *Material Culture and Sacred Landscape: the Anthropology of the Siberian Khanty*. Oxford: AltaMira Press.

Jung, Carl G. 1928. *Two Essays in Analytic Psychology*. New York: Dodd and Mead.

———. 1965. *Memories, Dreams, Reflections*. New York: Vintage.

Kara, David Somfai, Mihály Hoppál, János Sipos 2007 "The Sacred Valley of Jay Ata and a Kirghiz Shaman from Xinjiang, China" *Shaman* 15 (1&2): 47–68.

Karjalainen, Kustaa F. 1921, 1922, 1927. *Die Religion der Jugra-Volker* 3 vols. Porvoo: Finnish Academy of Sciences, Folklore Communications 41, 44, 63.

Kartsov, V. G. 1937. *Ocherk Istorii Narodov Severo-Zapadnoi Siberi*. Moscow-Leningrad: Gos. Sots. Ekon Izdat.

Kasten, Erich, ed. 2004. *Properties of Culture- Culture as Property*. Berlin: D.Reimer.

———, ed. 2009. *Schamenen Sibiriens: Magier, Mittler, Heileri*. Stuttgart: Linden-Museum Stuttgart, Dietrich Reimer Verlag.

Katonov, N. F. 1996. *Shamanskie Pesnopeniia Sibirskikh Tiurkov*. Moscow: Lit-Ekspress.

Kehoe, Alice Beck. 1992. *North American Indians: A Comprehensive Account*, Englewood Cliffs, NJ: Prentice-Hall.

———. 2000. *Shamans and Religion: an Anthropological Exploration in Critical Thinking*. Prospect Heights, Ill.: Waveland Press.

Kendall, Laurel. 1985. *Shamans, Housewives and Other Restless Spirits: Women in Korean Ritual Life*. Honolulu: University of Hawaii Press.

———. 1996. "Korean Shamans and the Spirits of Capitalism," *American Anthropologist* 98(3): 512–527.

———. 2001. "Encounters with Korean Ancestors," *Ancestors in Post-Contact Religion: Roots, Ruptures, and Modernity's Memory*, S. Friesen, ed., 13–56. Cambridge: Harvard U. Press.

———. 2009. *Shamans, Nostalgias, and the IMF: South Korean Popular Religion in Motion*. Honolulu: U. of Hawaii Press.

Kennedy, Walter P. 1961. "The Nocebo Reaction," *Medical World*, 95 (September 1961): pp. 203–205.
Kenin-Lopsan, Marina. 1994. "Vtrecha Tuvinskikh i Amerikanskikh Shamanov," *Shamanism v Tuve* Tamara Budegechi, ed., 3–4. Kyzyl: Gos. Komitet po delam Nauki i uchebnykh zavedenii r. Tyva.
Kenin-Lopsan, Mongush B. 1987. *Obriadovaia praktika i fol'klor Tuvinskogo Shamanstva*. Novosibirsk: Nauka.
———. 1995a. "Tuvan Shamanic Folklore," *Culture Incarnate: Native Anthropology from Russia*. Balzer, Marjorie Mandelstam, ed. Armonk, NY, London: M.E. Sharpe.
———. 1995b. *Algyshi Tuvinskikh Shamanov: Tyva Khamnarnyn'g algyshtar* [Tuvan Shamans' Prayers]. Kyzyl: Kraeved. Muzeia. [In Russian and Tuvan.]
———. 1997. *Shamanic Songs and Myths of Tuva*. Hoppál, M., Buckbee, C. eds., Seden-Khurak, A. trans. Budapest: Akadémiai Kiadó..
———. 2006. *Traditsionnaia Kul'tura Tuvintsev*. Dugerzhaa, A. A., Dembirel', A.S., trans. Kyzyl: Tuvinskoe Knizhnoe Izdat.
Keptuké, Galina [Varlaamova]. 1989. *Imeiushchaia svoe imia, Dzheltula-reka*. Yakutsk: Yakutskoe Kn. Izdat.
Khariuchi, Sergei. 2008. "Arktika dolzhna iskat' zashchitu ot ugrozy ekolologicheskikh katastrof" www.indigenousportal.com/index2.php?option=com October 15, 2008 (accessed 12/9/08).
Kharitonova, Valentina I., ed. 2000. *Shamanskii dar*. Moscow: Nauka.
Kharitonova, Valentina I. 2006. *Feniks iz pepla? Sibirskiy shamanizm na rubezhe tysyacheletiy*. Moskva: Nauka.
Khudiakov, Ivan A. 1969. *Kratkoe opisanie Verkhoianskogo Okruga*. Leningrad: Nauka [from 1866–9 ms.].
Kim, Natalia. 1992. "Ia chuvstvyiu vlianie belykh sil," *Yakutia* 15 Aug. 1992: 1–2.
King, Alexander. 1999. "Soul Suckers: Vampiric Shamans in N. Kamchatka," *Anthropology of Consciousness* 10(4): 57–69.
Kiselev, L. E. 1974. *Ot patriarkhal'shchiny k sotsializmu*. Sverdlovsk: Sredne-Ural'skoe Kn. Izdat.
Kitiarsa, Patana. 2005. "Beyond Syncretism: Hybridization of Popular Religion in Contemporary Thailand," *Journal of Southeast Asian Studies* 36 (3): 461–487.
Kleinman, Arthur. 1979. *Patients and Healers in the Context of Culture*. Berkeley: U. of California Press.
Kleinman, Arthur, Veena Das, and Margaret Lock, eds. 1997. *Social Suffering*. Berkeley: University of California Press.
Klementz, Dmitri. 1924. "Buriats," *Encyclopedia of Religion and Ethics* 3: 1–17.
Kline, George. 1968. *Religious and Anti-Religious Thought in Russia*. Chicago: University of Chicago Press.
Kolodesnikov, Sergei K. 2000. "The Person in the Traditional Yakut (Sakha) Worldview," *Anthropology and Archeology of Eurasia* 39 (1): 42–79.
Kondakov, Vladimir A. 1992. *Émtéëhin kistéléngnérittén* [About a few secrets of folk curing]. Yakutsk: Sakha Republic Association of Folk Medicine. [In Sakha.]

Kondakov, Vladimir A. 1993. *Dobyn khallaan byyhyn* [Sky's power brings health]. Yakutsk: Association of Folk Medicine. [In Sakha.]
———. 1997. *Aiyy oiuuna* [White Shaman]. Yakutsk: Soruk [In Sakha.]
———. 1999. *Tainy sfery shamanizma.* Yakutsk: AiyyArchyta.
———. 2005. *Algystar: Én Komuskélléring* [Prayer-Blessings: To Protect You]. Yakutsk: Scientific Center for Sakha Republic Association of Folk Medicine. [In Sakha.]
Kopylov, D. I.; V. F. Retunskii. 1965. "Bor'ba partiinkhy organizatsii krai za kollektivizatsiiu sel'skogo khozaistva i nastuplenie sotsializma po vsemu frontu" *Ocherki istorii partiinoi organizatsii Tiumenskoi oblast,* D. A. Smorodinskokov, ed., 141–76. Sverdlovsk: Sredne-Ural'skoe Knizhnoe Izdat.
Kopytoff, Igor. 1964. "Classification of New Religious Movements: Analytic and Synthetic," *Symposium on New Approaches to the Study of Religion, Proceedings of the American Ethnological Society,* June Helm, ed., 77–90. Seattle: U. of Washington Press.
Koriakin, Petr I. 2007. "Nabliudaiushchee uchastie v izuchenie Ucheniia Aiyy" Ms.
Korolenko, V. G. 1965 [1880]. *Istoriia moego sovremennika.* Moscow: Khudozhestvennaia literatura.
Koss-Chioino, Joan D. 1992. *Women as Healers, Women as Patients: mental health care and traditional healing in Puerto Rico.* Boulder: Westview.
———. 2006. "Spiritual Transformation and Radical Empathy in Ritual Healing and Therapeutic Relationships," *Spiritual transformation and healing: anthropological, theological, neuroscientific, and clinical perspectives,* Koss-Chioino, Joan D. and Philip Hefner, eds., 45–61. Lanham, MD : AltaMira Press,
Koss-Chioino, Joan and Philip Hefner, eds. 2006. *Spiritual Transformation and Healing: Anthropological, Theological, Medical and Biological Perspectives.* Lanham, MD: AltaMira Press.
Krader, Lawrence. 1954. "Buryat Religion and Society," *Southwestern Journal of Anthropology* 10: 322–51.
———. 1956. "A Nativistic Movement in Western Siberia," *American Anthropologist* 58 (2): 282–92.
———. 1978. "Shamanism: Theory and History in Buryat Society," *Shamanism in Siberia,* V. Diószegi, M. Hoppál, eds., S. Simon, Trans., 181–233. Budapest: Akadémiai Kiadó.
Kremer, Jurgen Werner. 1999. "Shamanic Inquiry as Recovery of Indigenous Mind," *What Is a Shaman?* Schenk & Ch. Rätsch, eds., 125–40. Berlin: Verlag für Wissenschaft und Bildung.
———. 2000. "Shamanic Initiations and their loss—decolonization as initiation and healing," *Etnopsychologische Mitteiluneen* 9 (1–2): 109–148.
Krippner, Stanley. 2000. "The Epistemology and Technologies of Shamanic States of Consciousness," *Journal of Consciousness Studies* 7 (11/12): 93–118.
Krippner, Stanley and Debbie Joffe Ellis. 2009. *Perchance to Dream: The Frontiers of Dream Psychology.* Hauppauge NY: Nova Science Publishers.
Krupnik, Igor. 1990. "Natsional'nyi vopros v SSSR: poiski ob'iasnenii" *Sovetskaia Etnografiia* 4: 3–15.

Krupnov, Dmitri. 2005. "Interv'iu so znamenitym Buriatskim shamanom Valentinom Khagdaevym" www.portal-credo.ru August 17, 2005.
Ksenofontov, Gavril V. 1929. *Krestes, shamanizm i khristianstvo*. Irkutsk: Russkoe Geograficheskoe Obshchestvo.
———. 1935. "Sochetaniie shamana s priezhaiushchimi" *Buriatievedenie* 1.
———. 1961. "Prazdnichnyi algys na ysyakhe," *Sbornik statei i materialov po etnografii narodov Iakutii*. S. I. Nikolaev, ed., 77–82. Yakutsk: Yaktuskoe kn. izd. [In Russian and Sakha]
———. 1977. *Elleiada: Materialy po mifologii i legendarnoi istorii Iakutov*. Moscow: Nauka.
———. 1992 [1928–9]. *Shamanizm: Izbrannye trudy*. A.N. Diachkova, ed. Yakutsk: Sever-Iug. for Museum of Music and Folklore.
Kulakovskii, Alexei E. 1979. *Nauchnyie Trudy*. Yakutsk: AN. Yakutskoe Knizhnoe Izdatel'stvo.
Kulemzin, Vladislav M. 1976 "Shamanstvo Vasiugansko-Vakhovskikh Khantov, konets XIX–nachala XX vv," *Iz istorii shamanstva*. N. V. Lukina, ed., 3–154. Tomsk: Tomsk Universitet.
———. 1984. *Chelovek i priroda v verovaniiakh Khantov*. Tomsk: Tomsk U.
Kuoljok, Kirstin Eidlitz. 1985. *The Revolution in the North: Soviet Ethnography and Nationality Policy*. Uppsala: Acta Universitatis Upsalensis.
LaBarre, Weston. 1972a. *The Ghost Dance: Origins of Religion*. London, New York: Dell.
———. 1972b. "Hallucinogens and the Shamanic Origins of Religion," *Flesh and the Gods: Ritual Use of Hallucinogens*. Peter Furst, ed., 261–78. New York: Praeger.
Laderman, Carol, Marina Roseman, eds. 1996. *The Performance of Healing*. New York: Routledge.
Lake-Thom, Bobby (Medicine Grizzly Bear). 1991. *Native healer: initiation into an ancient art*. Wheaton, IL: Quest Books [also 1991 *Native Healer: Path to an Ancient Healing Art*. New York: HarperCollins.]
Landy, David. 1977. "Role Adaptation: Traditional Curers Under the Impact of Western Medicine," *Culture, Disease, and Curing*, D. Landy, ed. New York: Macmillan.
Lang, Sabine. 1997. *Two-Spirit People: Native American Gender Identity, Sexuality and Spirituality*. Urbana: U. of Illinois Press.
Langford, Jean. 2003. "Traces of Folk Medicine in Jaunpur" *Cultural Anthropology* 18 (3): 217–303.
Lapina, Maina A. 2008. *Etika i Etiket Khantov*. Tomsk: Basko.
Laufer, Berthold. 1917. "Origin of the Word Shaman," *American Anthropologist* 19: 261–78.
Leete, Art. 2007. *La guerre du Kazym*. Paris: L'Harmattan.
Leonov, N. I. 1930. "Kul'tbaza v taige," *Prosveshchenie natsional'nostei* (9–10): 86–91.
Leopold, Anita Maria, Jeppe Sinding Jensen, eds. 2004. *Syncretism in Religion*. New York: Routledge.
Lester, Toby. 2002. "Oh Gods!" *The Atlantic Monthly* Feb. www.theatlantic.com/issues/2002/02/lester.htm.

Levi-Strauss, Claude. 1963 [1958]. *Structural Anthropology*. C. Jacobsen, B. Grundfest Schoept, trans. New York: Basic.

———. 1966. *The Savage Mind*. Chicago: U. of Chicago Press.

Levin, Theodore with Valentina Suzukei. 2006. *Where the Rivers and Mountains Sing: Sound, Music and Nomadism in Tuva*. Bloomington: Indiana U. Press.

Lewis, I. M. 1971. *Ecstatic Religion: An Anthropological Study of Spirit Possession and Shamanism*. New York: Penguin.

Lindquist, Galina. 1997. *Shamanic Performances on the Urban Scene: Neo-Shamanism in Contemporary Sweden*. Stockholm: Stockholm Studies in Social Anthropology.

———. 2005. "Healers, Leaders and Entrepreneurs," *Culture and Religion* 6(2): 263–285.

———. 2006. *Conjuring Hope: Magic and Healing in Contemporary Russia*. New York, London: Berghahn.

———. 2008. "Loyalty and Command: Shamans, Lamas, and Spirits in a Siberian Ritual," *Social Analysis* 52(1): 111–126.

Lindquist, Galina and Simon Coleman. 2008. "Introduction: Against Belief?" *Social Analysis* 52(1): 1–18.

Lot-Falk, Eveline. 1956. "Eroticism and Shamanism," *Sexology*, 22 (1, January): 378–83.

Lutz, Catherine A. and Lila Abu- Lughod, eds. 1990. *Language and the Politics of Emotion*. Cambridge: Cambridge U. Press.

MacCormack, Carol and Marilyn Strathern, eds. 1980. *Nature, Culture and Gender*, Cambridge: Cambridge University Press.

Maidurova, N. A. and N. A. Tadina, eds. 1994. *Burkhanizm: dokumenty i materialy* .2 vols. Gorno-Altaisk: Gorno-Altaisk Gos. U.

Malinowski, Bronislaw. 1945. *The Dynamics of Culture Change*. New Haven: Yale U. Press.

Marcus, George and Fischer, Michael M. J. 1986. *Anthropology as Cultural Critique*. Chicago: U. of Chicago Press.

Matory, J. Lorand. 2005. *Black Atlantic Religion*. Princeton U. Press.

McClellan, Catharine. 1975. *My Old People Say: An Ethnographic Survey of Southern Yukon Territory*. 2 vols. Ottawa: National Museum of Man.

Mehl-Madrona, Lewis. 1997. *Coyote Medicine*. New York: Scribner.

Meletinsky, Eliazar M. 1980. "The Epic of the Raven among the Paleoasiatics. Relations between Northern Asia and Northwest America in Folklore," *Diogenes* 110: 98–133.

Metcalf, Peter. 1989. *Where are YOU/SPIRITS: Style and Theme in Berawan Prayer*. Washington D.C. and London: Smithsonian Institution Press.

Métraux, Alfred. 2001 [1944]. "Climbing the Twisted Ladder to Initiation," *Shamans Through Time: 500 Years on the Path to Knowledge*, J. Narby and F. Huxley, eds., 97–102. New York: Tarcher/ Putnam.

Metzo, Katherine. 2005. "Articulating a Baikal Environmental Ethic," *Anthropology and Humanism* 31(1): 39–54.

———. 2008. "Shamanic Transformations: Buriat Shamans as Mediators of Multiple Worlds," *Reclaiming the Sacred: Morality, Community and Religion after Communism*, Mark Steinberg and Cathy Wanner, eds., 215–246. Washington DC: Woodrow Wilson Center Press.

Mikhailov, Taras M. 2004. "Shamanskaia Praktika," *Buriaty*, Abaeva, L., Zhukovaia, N., eds. 371–380 Moscow: Nauka,.

Miller [Müller], Gerhard Friedrich. 1787. *Opisanie Sibirskogo Tsarstva*. St. Petersburg: Izdat. Imperskogo Akademii Nauk.

Mills, Antonia and Richard Slobodin, eds. 1994. *Amerindian Rebirth: Reincarnation Belief among North American Indians and Inuit*. Toronto: U. of Toronto Press.

Mirbadaleva, A. S. with I. G. Timofeev-Teploukhov, V. N. Vasil'ev. 1985. *Kuruubai khaannakh Kulun Kullustuur: Yakutskoe olonkho*. Moscow: Nauka for Glav. red. vostochnoi literatury. [In Sakha and Russian.]

Mitskevich, S. I. 1929. *Menerik i emiriachen'e*. Leningrad: Akademiia Nauk.

Moldanova, Tatiana. 1990. "O gnezdyshke odinokom," *Literaturnaia Arktika* (4): 24–28.

———. 2001. *Arkhetipi v mire snovidenii Khantov*. Tomsk: Tomsk Press.

———. 2007. "Dreams in Khanty Culture," *Anthropology and Archeology of Eurasia* 45(2): 55–72.

———. 2010. *Pel'ymskii Torum - ustroitel' medvezh'ikh igrish*. Khanty-Mansiisk: Politgrafist.

Morokhoeva, Zoia P. 1995. "Cultural Norms in the Baikal Region," *Culture Incarnate: Native Anthropology From Russia*, M. Mandelstam Balzer, ed., 123–139. Armonk NY: M.E. Sharpe.

Moskalenko, Nelli P. 2004. *Etnopoliticheskaia istoriia Tuvy v XX Veke*. Moscow: Nauka.

Moyers, Bill, Betty Sue Flowers. 1993. *Healing and the Mind*. New York: Doubleday.

Murphy, Jane. 1954. "Psychotherapeutic Aspects of Shamanism on St. Lawrence Island, Alaska," *Magic, Faith and Healing*, Ari Kiev, ed., 53–83. New York: Free Press.

Myreeva, Anna N. 1988. "Leksika vostochnogo narechiia Evenkiiskogo iazyka (zhivotnyi mir)," *Iazyki narodnostei severa: Leksika, toponimika*. 9–30. N. E. Petrov, ed. Yakutsk: Institut Iazyki, Literatury, i Istorii.

Nachtigall, Horst. 1976. "The Cultural-Historical Origins of Shamanism," *The Realm of the Extra-Human: Agents and Audiences*. A. Bharati, ed., 315–22. The Hague: Mouton.

Nadasdy, Paul. 2007. "The Gift in the Animal: The Ontology of Hunting and Human-Animal Sociality," *American Ethnologist* 34(1): 25–43.

Nagel, Joane. 1996. *American Indian Ethnic Renewal: Red Power and the Resurgence of Identity and Culture*. Oxford: Oxford U. Press.

Narby, Jonathan and Francis Huxley, ed. 2001. *Shamans Through Time: 500 Years on the Path to Knowledge*. New York: Putnam.

Neihardt, John (Flaming Rainbow), Black Elk. 1993. *Black Elk Speaks: Being the Life Story of a Holy Man of the Oglala Sioux*. Alexandria, Virginia: Time-Life Books.

Neher, Andrew. 1962. "A Physiological Explanation of Unusual Behavior in Ceremonies Involving Drums," *Human Biology* 34: 151–160.

Nelson, Richard K. 1983. *Make Prayers to the Raven: A Koyukon View of the Northern Forest*. Chicago: U. of Chicago Press.
Neu, Jerome. 1975. "Levi-Strauss on Shamanism," *Man* 10(2): 285–92.
Nichter, Mark. 1978. "Patterns of Resort in the Use of Therapy Systems and their Significance for Health Planning in South Asia," *Medical Anthropology* 2(2): 29–56.
Niezen, Ronald. 2000. *Spirit Wars: Native North American Religions in the Age of Nation Building*. Berkeley: U. of California Press.
Nikolaev, Afanasy. 2007. "Sovremennaia religioznaia situatsiia v Respublike Sakha: Problemy i perspektivy," July 19 http://religare.ru/analytics43720.htm (accessed 7/25/2007).
Nikolaev, I., Ushnitskii, I., eds. 1990. *Tsentral'noe Delo: Khronika Stalinskikh Repressii v Yakutii*. Yakutsk: Yakutskoe Kn. Izdat.
Nikolaev, Ivan N.[Ukhkhan, Uhhan]. 2008. "Yakutia: Pervoe mesto v mire po urovniu detskoi suistida" www.uhhan.ru (accessed 7/20/2008).
Nikolaev, Semen I. [Somogotto]. 1992. "Otkuda vyi rodom, personazhi olonkho?" *Molodezh Yakutii*. 32 July: 5.
Nordland, Odd. 1967. "Shamanism as an Experiencing of the 'Unreal'," *Studies in Shamanism*. C. Edsman, ed., 166–85. Stockholm: Almquist and Wiksell.
Nosilov, K. D. 1904. *U Vogulov*. St. Petersburg: Suvorin.
Novik, Elena S. 1997 [1984]. "Ritual and Folklore in Siberian Shamanism," *Shamanic Worlds*, M. M. Balzer, ed., 185–234. Armonk, NY: M. E. Sharpe.
Novikova, Natalia. 2004. *Olen' vsegda prav: issledovanie po iuridicheskoi antropologii*. Moscow: Nauka.
Novitskii, Gregory. 1884 [1715]. *Kratkoe opisanie o narode Ostiakom*. St. Petersburg: Maikov.
Nowak, Margaret and Stephen Durrant. 1977. *The Tale of the Nišan Shamaness: A Manchu Folk Epic*. Seattle: U. of Washington Press.
Ohnuki-Tierney, Emiko. 1976. "Shamanism and World View: The Case of the Ainu of the Northwest Coast of Southern Sakhalin," *The Realm of the Extra-Human: Ideas and Actions*. A. Bharati, ed., 175–200. The Hague: Mouton.
———. 1980. "Ainu Illness and Healing: A Symbolic Interpretation," *American Ethnologist* 7: 132–51.
Oiyunsky, P. [Sleptsov, P. A.]. 1962. *Auymn'ylar*. Yakutsk: Sakha sirineekhi knizhnoe izdat., t. 7. [In Sakha.]
———. 1975. *Niurgun Bootur Stremitel'nyi*. trans. V. Derzhavin.Yakutsk: Yakutskoe kn. Izdat. [In Sakha and Russian.]
Okladnikov, Aleksei Pavlovich. 1970. *Yakutia Before Its Incorporation into the Russian State*. trans. Stephen P. Dunn and Ethel Dunn. Henry Michael, ed. Montreal: McGill-Queen's University Press.
Omar, Dilmurat. 2003. "Modern Kazakh shamanism," *Rediscovery of Shamanic Heritage*. M. Hoppál and G. Kosa, eds., 227–240. Budapest: Akadémiai Kiadó.
Oosten, Jarik. 1989. "Theoretical Problems in the study of Inuit Shamanism," *Shamanism Past and Present*, M. Hoppál and O. von Sadovszky, eds. Budapest: Akadémiai Kiadó.

Opler, Marvin. 1959. *Culture and Mental Health: Cross Cultural Studies.* New York: Macmillan.
———. 1961. "On Deveraux's Discussion of Ute Shamanism," *American Anthropologist.* 63: 1091–92.
Orlov, Mikhail. 2008. "Prodol'zhaem vymirat,'" *Trud* 201, Oct. 24, 2008, 8.
Ortner, Sherry. 1995. "Resistence and the Problem of Ethnographic Refusal," *Comparative Studies in Society and History* 26(1): 173–93.
Osherenko, Gail and Oran R. Young. 2005. *The Age of the Arctic: Hot Conflicts and Cold Realities.* Cambridge: Cambridge U.
Panov, I. 1937. "Gorod v lesu," *Narody Severnogo Urala,* V. A. Popov, ed., 97–119. Sverdlovsk: Sredne-Ural'skoe izdat.
Patkanov, S. K. 1897 *Die Irtysch Ostyaken und ihre Volkspoesie.* St. Petersburg: Suvorin.
Pedersen, Morten A. 2001. "Totemism, Animism and North Asian Indigenous Ontologies," *Journal of the Royal Anthropological Institute.* 7(3): 411–427.
Pentikainen, Juha. 1997. *Shamanism and Culture.* Helsinki: Etnika.
Perrone, Bobette, H. H. Stockel, V. Krueger. 1989. *Medicine Women, Curanderas, and Women Doctors.* Norman: U. of Oklahoma Press.
Peters, Larry G. 1993. "In the Land of Eagles. Experiences on the Shamanic Path in Tuva," *Shaman's Drum* (Fall–Winter): 42–49.
Peters, Larry G. and Douglas Price-Williams. 1980. "Towards an Experiential Analysis of Shamanism," *American Ethnologist* 7: 397–418.
Petrov, A. A. 1988. "Leksika, otrazhaiushchaia narodnoe pesenno-tantseval'noe isskusstvo Evenov," *Iazyki narodnostei severa: Leksika, toponimika.* N. E. Petrov, ed. Yakutsk: Institut Iazyki, Literatury, i Istorii.
Petrov, Nikolai E. 1990. "Khorovodnyi pesni okhuokhai kak zhanr Iakutskogo Fol'klora," *Sovetskaia Tiurkologiia.* 1990, 3.
———. 1995. *Alguoy, blagopozhelaniia, toiuki* [Prayers, Blessings, Songs] Yakutsk: Sakha Ministry of Culture. [In Russian and Sakha.]
Pika, Alexander I.; Boris B. Prokorov, 1994. *Neotraditsional'izm na Rossiiskom Severe.* Moscow: Nauka.
Plotkin, Mark J. 1993. *Tales of a Shaman's Apprentice: an Ethnobotanist Searches for New Medicines in the Amazon Rain Forest.* New York : Penguin Books.
———. 2000. *Medicine Quest: In Search of Nature's Healing Secrets.* New York: Viking.
Popov, Alexander A. 1947. "Poluchenie 'Shamanskogo Dara' u Viliuiskikh Yakutov," *Trudy Instituta Etnografii* II: 282–93.
———. 1949. "Materialy po istorii religii Yakutov Viliuiskogo okruga," *Sbornik muzeia antropologii i etnografii* T. 11: 255–323.
———. 2006. *Kamlanie Shamanov.* Novosibirsk: Nauka [from ms. 1922–25 texts, ed. by R. I. Bravina.]
Powers, William. 1992. *Yuwipi, vision and experience in Oglala ritual.* Lincoln: U. of Nebraska Press.
Pukhov, I. V. 1975. "Olonkho- Drevnii epos Iakutov," *Niurgun Bootur Stremitel'nyi.* V. Derzhavin, trans., 411–30. Yakutsk: Yakutsk Press.
Priklonskii, V. L. 1896. *Letopis' Yakutskogo Krai.* Krasnoyarsk: Eniseiskaia Gubernskaia Tipografiia.

Prokof'ev, G. 1931. "Vulkany v Tundre," *Sovetskii Sever* 1931 (5): 141–144.
Prokof'eva, E. D. 1971. "Shamanskie kostiumy narodov Sibiri," *Religioznye predstavleniia i obriady narodov Sibiri v XIX-nachale XX v. Sbornik muzeia antropologii i etnografii*, 27. Leningrad: Nauka.
Protopopova, Nina I. 1999. "Ed'ii Dora," *Aiyy Dalbar Khotuna* [Women Masters of Pure Spirits]. Yakutsk: Republic Press. [In Sakha.]
———. 2006 [2003]. *Ed'ii Dora*. Yakutsk: Bichik.
Quijada, Justine Buck. 2008. "What if We Don't Know Our Clan? The City Tailgan as New Ritual Form in Buriatia," *Sibirica* 7(1): 1–22.
Radin, Paul. 1949. *The Culture of the Winnebago: As Described by Themselves*. Baltimore: Waverly.
Ramet, Sabrina P., ed. 1993. *Religious Policy in the Soviet Union*. Cambridge: Cambridge U. Press.
Rappaport, Joanne 2005 *Intercultural Utopias: Public Intellectuals, Cultural Experimentation, and Ethnic Pluralism in Colombia*. Durham: Duke U. Press.
Reid, Janice. 1983. *Sorcerers and Healing spirits*. Canberra: Australian National U. Press.
Revunenkova, E. V. 1974. "O Lichnosti Shamana," *Sovetskaia Etnografiia* 3: 104–11.
Riboli, Diana. 2000. *Tunsuriban: Shamanism in the Chepang of Southern and Central Nepal*. Kathmandu: Mandala.
Ridington, Robin. 1990. *Little Bit Know Something: Stories in a Language of Anthropology*. Vancouver: Douglas and McIntyre.
Ridington, Robin and Antonia Ridington. 1975 [1970]. "The Inner Eye of Shamanism and Totemism," *Teachings from the American Earth: Indian Religion and Philosophy*. Denis Tedlock and Barbara Tedlock, eds. 190–204. New York: Liveright.
Roheim, Geza. 1954. *Hungarian and Vogul Mythology*. New York: Augustin, Monographs of the American Ethnological Society, 23.
Romanova, Ekaterina N. 1994. *Yakutskii prazdnik ysyakh: istoki i predstavlenia*. Novosibirsk: Nauka.
———. 1997. 'Liudi Sol'nechnykh luchei s povod'iami za spinoi'/(Sud'ba v kontekste miforitual'noi traditsii Yakutov). Moscow: Russian Academy of Sciences.
———. 2008. "Mifologiia sovremennogo shamanstva. K interpretatsii fenomena 'pomniashaia kul'tura'," *Mif, Simbol, Ritual. Narody Sibiri*. S. Iu. Nekliudov, ed., 309–326. Moscow: Gumanitarnyie U.
Romanucci-Ross, Lola. 1977. "The Hierarchy of Resort in Curative Practices: The Admiralty Islands," *Culture, Disease and Curing*, David Landy, ed., 481–87. New York: Macmillan.
Roscoe, Will. 1998. *Changing Ones: Third and Fourth Genders in Native North America*. New York: St. Martin's Press.
Roseman, Marina. 1991. *Healing Sounds from the Malaysian Rainforest: Temiar Music and Medicine*. Berkeley: U. of California Press.
Rouget, Gilbert. 1980. *La Musique et la Trance*. Paris: Galimard.
Rouget, Gilbert. 1992b. "Rethinking Inuit Shamanism through the concept of the 'Third Gender,'" *Northern Religions and Shamanism*, M. Hoppál, J.

Pentikainen, eds. Budapest: Akadémiai Kiadó; Helsinki: Finnish Literature Society.

———. 1993. "Sila, the Ordering Principle of the Inuit Cosmology," *Shamans and Cultures,* M. Hoppál, K. Howard, eds.,160-8. Budapest: Akadémiai Kiadó.

Saiyyna [Maksimova, Klavdia I.] 2000. *Min kuiaar oghoto…* [I am a child of wide-open spaces]. Yakutsk: Sakha Keskile [In Sakha.]

Saladin d'Anglure, Bernard. 1992a. "Le 'Troisieme' Sexe," *Etnologiei* 23: 836-844.

Sargant, William. 1964. *Battle for the Mind.* London: Pan.

Sarygulov, Dastan Islamovich. 2002. *Tengrianstvo i global'nye problemy sovremennosti.* Bishkek: Fond "Tengir Ordo."

Schenk, Amelie and Christian Ratsch, eds. 1999 *What is a Shaman? Shamans, Healers and Medicine Men From a Western Point of View.* Berlin: Verlag fur Wissenschaft und Bildung.

Schmidt, Eva. 1989. "Bear Cult and Mythology of the Northern Ob-Ugrians," *Uralic Mythology and Folklore,* Mihály Hoppál and Juha Pentikainen, eds.,187-232. Budapest: Akadémiai Kiadó; Helsinki: Finnish Literature Society.

Scott, James C. 1985. *Weapons of the Weak: Everyday Forms of Peasant Resistance.* New Haven: Yale U. Press.

Seaman, Gary, and Jane Day, eds. 1994. *Ancient Traditions: Culture and Shamanism in Central Asia and the Americas.* Denver: U. of Colorado, Denver Museum of Natural History.

Seden-Khuurak, Aldanai. 2003. *Tuvan-English Phrase book.* Kyzyl: Tyvanyng nom undurer cheri.

Semenov, V. A. 1980. *Tvorchestvo P. A. Oiunskogo.* Novosibirsk: Nauka.

Senkevich, V. 1935. "Skazka i Pesni Khantov," *Sovetskii Sever* 6 (3-4): 151-159.

Senkina, Nadezhda. 1991. "V. A. Kondakov: Tselitel'- lish' posrednik mezhdu vyschimi silami i liud'mi," *Molodezh Iakutii* March 14, 5.

Sergeev, M. A. 1955. *Nekapitalisticheskii put' razvitiia malykh narodov Severa.* Moscow: Akademiia Nauk.

Sergeeva, K.S., N. Ankudinov, A. Dobriev. 1939. *Shamany Obmanshchiki.* Leningrad: Glavsemorput.

Seroshevsky, Vladimir L. [Sieroshewskii, W.] [Sierozhevskii, Waslav]. 1896. *Yakuty.* St. Petersburg: Izdat. Imperatorskogo Russkogo Geograficheskogo Obshchestva. [reprint edition 1993 Moscow: Rossiiskaia Politicheskaia Entsykopediia.]

———. 1901. "The Yakuts," W. G. Sumner, trans. *Journal of the Royal Anthropological Institute* 31.

———. 1902. "Du chamanisme d'aprés les coryances des Yakoutes," *Revue de L'Histoire des Religions* 46: 204-33, 299-338.

Shashkov, S. 1864. *Shamanstvo v Sibiri.* St. Petersburg: Morichegovskogo.

Shatilov, M. B. 1931. *Vakhovskie Ostiaki.* Tomsk: Trudy Kraevogo Muzeia, 4.

Sherstova, Liudmilla I. 2010. [1985] *Burkhanism: istoki etnosa i religii.* Tomsk: Tomsk Gos. Izdat.

Shil'diashov, I. M. 1982. *Religiia v Sibiri i ateisticheskoe vospitanie.* Novosibirsk: Nauka.

Shimkin, Demitri. 1967. "Pre-Islamic Central Asia," *Canadian Slavic Studies*. 1(4): 618-39.
Shirokogoroff, Sergei. 1924. "What is Shamanism?" *The China Journal of Science & Arts* 2 (4): 275-279, 368-371.
———. 1935. *The Psychomental Complex of the Tungus*. London: Kegan, Paul, Trench, Trubner.
Shishigin, Egor S. 1991 *Rasprostranenie Khrestianstva v Yakutii* Yakutsk: Yakutskii Nauchnyi Tsentr.
Shternberg [Sternberg], Lev Iakovlevich [Leo]. 1904. "Gilyaki," *Etnograficheskoe Obozrenie*, No. 1: 1-42; No.2: 9-55; No. 4: 66-119.
———. 1999. *The Social Organization of the Gilyak*, B. Grant, ed. Seattle: U. of Washington Press for American Museum of Natural History, 82.
Sidky, Homayun. 2008. *Haunted by the Archaic Shaman: Himalayan Jhākris and the Discourse on Shamanism*. Lanham MD: Rowman and Littlefield.
Siikala, Anna-Leena. 1978. *The Rite Technique of the Siberian Shaman*. Helsinki: Finnish Academy of Science, Folklore Communications, 22.
Siikala, Anna-Leena and Mihály Hoppál, 1992. *Studies on Shamanism*. Helsinki: Finnish Anthropological Society; Budapest: Akadémiai Kiadó.
Silverman, Julian. 1967. "Shamans and Acute Schizophrenia," *American Anthropologist*. 69: 21-31.
Skachko, A. 1931. "Ocherednye zadachi sovetskoi raboty sredi malykh narodov Severa" *Sovetskii Sever* (2): 5-28.
Skachkov, I. 1934. "Ob Anti-religioznoi rabote na Severe," *Revoliutsiia i National'nosti* 7(53): 50-54.
Sleptsov, Platon A. 1989. *Traditsionnaia sem'ia i obriadnost' u Yakutov*. Yakutsk: Academy of Sciences.
———. 1993. "Blessing (*Algys*) of a Bride's Father Before Leaving Her Home," *Anthropology and Archeology of Eurasia* 31(3): 8-9.
Slezkine, Yuri. 1994. *Arctic Mirrors: Russia and the Small Peoples of the North*. Ithaca: Cornell U. Press.
Smith, James Howard. 2008. *Bewitching Development: Witchcraft and the Reinvention of Development in Neoliberal Kenya*. Chicago: U. of Chicago Press.
Snyder, Solomon H. 1977. "Opiate Receptors and Internal Opiates," *Scientific American* 236(3): 44-57.
Sokolova, Zoia P. 1971. "Perezhitki Religioznikh Verovanii u Obskikh Ugrov," *Sbornik Muzeia Antropologii i Etnografii* 27: 211-39.
———. 1976. *Strana Ugrov*. Moscow: Mysl'.
———. 1978. "The Representation of a Female Spirit from the Kazym River," *Shamanism in Siberia*, V. Diószegi, M. Hoppál, eds. S. Simon, trans., 491-501. Budapest: Akadémiai Kiadó.
Spivak, Gayatri Chakravorty. 2008. *Other Asias*. Malden, MA : Blackwell.
Ssorin-Chaikov, Nikolai V. 2003. *The Social Life of the State in Subarctic Siberia*. Stanford: Stanford U. Press.
Stammler, Florian and Hiroki Takakura, eds. 2010. *Good to Eat, Good to Live With: Nomads and Animals in Northern Eurasia and Africa*. Sendai: Tohoku U. Press. Northeastern Asia Study Series, 11.

Startsev, Georgi. 1928. *Ostiaki: Sotsial'no-etnograficheskii ocherk*. Leningrad: Priboi.
Stoller, Paul. 1994. "Embodying Colonial Memories," *American Anthropologist* 96: 634–648.
———. 2009. *The Power of the Between: An Anthropological Odyssey*. Chicago: U. of Chicago Press.
Storm, Hyemeyohsts. 1972. *Seven Arrows*. New York: Harper and Row.
———. 1997. *Lightningbolt*. New York: Ballantine Books.
Suslov, I. M. 1931. "Shamanstvo i bor'ba s nim," *Sovetskii Sever* (3-4): 129–132.
Tamir, Yael. 1993. *Liberal Nationalism*. Princeton, N.J.: Princeton U. Press.
Taussig, Michael. 1987. *Shamanism, Colonialism and the Wild Man: A Study in Terror and Healing*. Chicago: U. Press.
———. 1993. *Mimesis and Alterity: A Particular History of the Senses*. New York: Routledge.
———. 2009. *What Color is the Sacred?* Chicago: U. Press.
Tedlock, Barbara. 2005. *The Woman in the Shaman's Body: Reclaiming The Feminine in Religion and Medicine*. New York: Bantam Dell.
———. 2008. "Shamanism and Shamanic Practice Today and Into the Future," *Journal of Shamanic Practice* 1(1): 7–11.
Tengan, Ty P. Káwika. 2008. *Native Men Remade: Gender and Nation in Contemporary Hawai'i*. Durham: Duke U. Press.
Tkacz, Virlana, Sayan Zhambalov, and Wanda Phipps. 2002. *Shanar: Dedication Ritual of a Buryat Shaman in Siberia as conducted by Bayir Rinchinov*. New York: Parabola.
Tillett, Lionel. 1969. *The Great Friendship: Soviet Historians on the Non-Russian Nationalities*. Chapel Hill: U. of North Carolina Press.
Tishkov, Valery Aleksandrovich. 1992. "Sovetskaia Etnografiia: Preodelenie krizisa," *Etnograficheskoe Obozrenie*. (1): 5–20.
Togolukov, V. A. et al. 1997. *Istoria i kul'tura Évenov*. St. Petersburg: Nauka.
Tokarev, S. A. 1940. *Ocherk istorii Yakutskogo Naroda*. Moscow: Gos. Sotsial'no-ekonomicheskoe izdat.
Torrey, E. Fuller, MD. 1974. "Spiritualists and Shamans as Psychotherapists: An Account of Original Anthropological Sin," *Religious Movements in Contemporary America*. Irving I. Zaretsky and Mark P. Leone, eds. 330–37. Princeton: Princeton U. Press.
Trompf, G. W., ed. 1990. *Cargo Cults and Millenarian Movements: Transoceanic Comparisons of New Religious Movements*. Berlin: Mouton de Gruyter.
Troshchanskii, V. F. 1903. *Evoliutsiia chernoi very (shamanstvo) u Yakutov*. Kazan: Uchenyi zapiski Kazanskogo U.
Trott, Christopher G. 1997. "The Rapture and the Rupture: Religious Change Among the Inuit of North Baffin Island," *Études Inuit* 21(1-2): 209–28.
Tsing, Anna Lowenhaupt. 2005. *Friction: An Ethnography of Global Connection*. Princeton: Princeton U. Press.
Tumusov, F. C., B. N. Popov et al, eds. 2001. *Yal Bii Biliité* [World of the Family Encyclopedia]. Yakutsk: Kuduk. [In Sakha.]
Turner, Edith L. B. 1993. "The Reality of Spirits: A Tabooed or Permitted Field of Study?," *The Anthropology of Consciousness* 4(1): 9–12.

Turner, Edith L. B. 1996. *The Hands Feel It: Healing and Spirit Presence among a Northern Alaskan People*. De Kalb: U. of Northern Ill Press.

———. 1999. "Experiential Shamanism and Its Implications for the World of Knowledge," *Etnologicheskie issledovanie Shamanizma*...D. Funk and V. Kharitonova, eds., v. 5, 205-22. Moscow: RAN.

———. 2006. *Among the Healers: Stories of Spiritual and Ritual Healing Around the World*. Westport, CN: Praeger Publishers.

Turner, Victor. 1964. "An Ndembu Doctor in Practice," *Magic, Faith and Healing*. A. Kiev, ed., 230-63. New York: Free Press.

———. 1969. *The Ritual Process: Structure and Anti-Structure*. Ithaca: Cornell.

———. 1977. "Process, System and Symbol: A New Anthropological Synthesis" *Daedalus* 106(3): 61-80.

Turner, Victor, ed. 1982. *Celebration: Studies in festivity and ritual*. Washington, DC: Smithsonian Institution Press.

Urbanaeva, Irina S. 2000. *Shamanskaia filosofiia Buriat-Mongolov : tsentral'no-aziatskoe tengrianstvo v svete dukhovnykh uchenii*. Ulan-Ude:Izdat. Buriatskogo nauchogo tsentra.

Utkin, Ksenofont D. [Nuhulgen]. 1990. *Khomuhunnaakh uus I. F. Zakharov* [Jaw Harp Master I. F. Zakharov]. Yakutsk: Sakha Ministry of Culture. [In Sakha.]

———. 1996. "The Kut-Sür Philosophy," *Anthropology and Archeology of Eurasia*. 35(2): 33-56.

———. 2000. *Kylyad'y uus* [The sharpest blacksmith]. Viliuisk: Ulus press. [In Sakha.]

Utkin, Ksenofont and P. N. Fedorov, eds. 1993. *Sakha oiuunnara* [Sakha shamans]. Yakutsk: Sakha Ministry of Culture. [In Sakha.]

Vagatova, Maria Kuz'minichna. 2007. *Materinskoe serdze - Aāki sam* [The Maternal Heart]. Ekaterinburg: Sredne Ural Izdat. [In Russian and Khanty.]

Vainshtein, S. I., and N. P. Moskalenko, N. P. 1995. "Problemy Tuvinskogo shamanstva: generis, izbrannichestvo, effektivnost' lechebnykh kamlanii, sovremmennyi renessanc," *Shamanizm i Ranne religioznye predstavleniia* D.Funk, ed., 62-75. Moscow: Nauka.

Van Deusen, Kira. 2004. *Singing Story, Healing Drum: Shamans and Storytellers of Turkic Siberia*. Montreal: McGill-Queen's U. Press.

Van der Veer, Peter. 2000. "Religious Nationalism in India and Global Fundamentalisms," *Globalization of Social Movements*. J. Guidry, M. Kennedy, M. Zald, eds, 315-339. Ann Arbor: U. of Michigan.

Vasil'ev, Valery E. 2000. *Drevnie istoki kul'ta Bozhestva Aiyy*. Ulan-Ude: Institut Mongolovendeniia, Kanditatskaia dissertatsiia.

———. 2010. "Razkazy o "belykh" shamanakh v srednei kolyme," *Psykhofiziologiia i Sotsial'naia adaptatsiia (Neo)Shamanov v Proshlom i Nastoiashchem V. I. Kharitonova, ed., 147-60. Moscow: Nauka.

Vasil'ev, F. F. 1995. *Voennoe delo Iakutov*. Yakutsk: Bichik.

Vasil'ievich, G. M. 1948. *Ocherki dialektov Evenkiiskogo (Tungusskogo) Iazyka*. Leningrad: Ministerstvo prosviashcheniia.

Vasil'eva, Nina D. 2000. *Yakutskoe shamanstvo (1920-1930s)*. Yakutsk: IGI.

REFERENCES

Vértes, E. 1968. "On the Trail of Ostyak (Khanty) Mythical Songs," *Popular Beliefs and Folklore Traditions in Siberia.* V. Dioszegi, ed., 113-122. Bloomington: Indiana U. Press, Uralic and Altaic Series, 56.

Vinokurova, Uliana A. 1994. *Skaz o Narode Sakha.* Yakutsk: Bichik.

———. 1997. *Sanaabyn sanaanan samnardym* [Thinking, searching, asking] Ms. [In Sakha.]

Vinokurova, Uliana A., Roza I. Bravina et al. 2002. *Kiun D'øhøgei Aiyy* [Sun Horse-Protector God]. Yakutsk: Bichik. [In Sakha.]

Vinokurova, Uliana A. and Liliia P. Dambaeva. 2008. "Sacred Sites of the Sakha People-Custom and Law," *Anthropology and Archeology of Eurasia* 47(3): 38-52.

Vinokurova, Uliana A. and Arkhan Artamonov. 2009. *Kul't Sterkha v Kul'ture Naroda Sakha.* Yakutsk: Bichik.

Viola, Lynne, ed. 2002. *Contending With Stalinism: Soviet Power and Popular Resistance in the 1930s.* Ithaca: Cornell U. Press.

Vitebsky, Piers. 1990. "Yakut," *The Nationalities Question in the Soviet Union.* G. Smith, ed., 304-19. London: Longman Press.

———. 1993. *Dialogues with the Dead: The Discussion of Mortality Among the Sora of Eastern India.* Cambridge: Cambridge U. Press.

———. 1995. *The Shaman: Voyages of the Soul, Trance, Ecstasy and Healing From Siberia to the Amazon.* London: Duncan Baird.

———. 2005. *The Reindeer People: Living with Animals and Spirits in Siberia.* Boston: Houghton Mifflin.

Wallace, Anthony F. C. 1956. "Acculturation: Revitalization Movements," *American Anthropologist* 58 (2): 264-281.

———. 1972. *Death and Rebirth of the Seneca.* New York: Vintage.

Wallis, Robert J. 2003. *Shamans/neo-Shamans: Ecstasy, Alternative Archaeologies, and Contemporary Pagans.* London; New York: Routledge.

Wallis, Robert J. and Kenneth Lymer, eds. 2001. *A Permeability of Boundaries?: New Approaches to the Archaeology of Art, Religion, and Folklore.* Oxford, England: British Archaeological Reports.

Walter, Mariko Namba and Eva Jane Neumann Fridman, eds. 2004. *Shamanism: An Encyclopedia of World Beliefs, Practices, and Culture.* Santa Barbara: ABC-CLIO.

Wautischer, Helmut, ed. 1998. *Tribal Epistemologies: Essays in the Philosophy of Anthropology.* Aldershot: Ashgate.

Wasson, Robert Gordon. 1960. *Soma: The Divine Mushroom of Immortality.* New York: Harcourt, Brace, Jovanovich.

Weber, Max 1947. *Theory of Social and Economic Organization.* A. M. Henderson and Talcott Parsons, trans. Oxford: Oxford University Press.

———. 1963 [1922]. *The Sociology of Religion.* Boston: Beacon.

Whitehead, Neil and Robin Wright. 2004. *In Darkness and Secrecy: The Anthropology of Assault Sorcery and Witchcraft in Amazonia.* Durham, NC: Duke.

White Horse. 1991. "Belaia loshad' literaturnaia studiia" *Ilin* 1:42-43; 2:42-54; 3:40-45. [In Russian and Sakha.]

Whitley, David. 2009. *Cave Paintings and the Human Spirit: The Origin of Creativity and Belief.* Amherst, New York : Prometheus Books.

Wilber, K. 1981. *Up From Eden: A Transpersonal View of Human Evolution.* Garden City, N.Y.: Doubleday.
Williams, Walter L. 1992. *The Spirit and The Flesh: Sexual Diversity in American Indian Culture.* Boston: Beacon Press.
Willerslev, Rane. 2007. *Soul Hunters: Hunting, Animism, and Personhood Among the Siberian Yukaghir.* Berkeley: U. of California Press.
Winkelman, Michael. 2000. *Shamanism: The Neural Ecology of Consciousness and Healing.* Westport, CT: Bergin and Garvey.
Yakovlev, Viliam I. 1992 *Sergé (Konoviaz')* Yakutsk: Min. Kul'tury. [In Sakha.]
———. 2000. "Erkeeni khohotyn ytyk sirdere [Sacred Places in the Erkeeni Valley]," *Khangalas,* Shadrina, G., ed., 14–19. Yakutsk: IGI. [In Sakha.]
Yalowitz, Kenneth and James F. Collins, Ross A. Virginia. 2008. *The Arctic Climate Change and Security Policy Conference.* Washington: Carnegie Endowment; Hanover: University of the Arctic, Dartmouth College.
Yamada, Takako and Takashi Irimoto. 1997. *Circumpolar Animism and Shamanism.* Sapporo: Hokkaido U. Press. (Part III. "Northern Eurasia" 183–283).
Yoon, Carol Kaesuk. 2009. *Naming Nature: The Clash Between Instinct and Science.* New York: W.W. Norton.
Zelenin, D. K. 1936. *Kul't Ongonov v Sibiri.* Moscow-Leningrad: Akademii Nauk.
Zhukovskaia, Natalia. 2000. "Neo-Shamanism in the Context of the Contemporary Ethno-cultural Situation in the Republic of Buryatia," *Inner Asia* 2: 25–36.
———. 2001. "The Revival of Buddhism in Buryatia," *Anthropology and Archeology of Eurasia* 39(4): 23–47.
———. 2002. *Kochevniki Mongolii.* Moscow: Vostochnai'a Literatura RAN.
Zhukovskaia, Natalia, ed. 2008. *Religii'a v istorii i kul'ture mongolo-iazychnykh narodov Rossii.* Moscow : Vostochnai'a literatura RAN.
Zibarev, V. A. 1972. *Bol'shaia Sudba malykh narodov.* Novosibirsk: Zapadnoe Sibirskoe Knizhnoe izdat.
Znamenski, Andrei. 1999. *Shamanism and Christianity: Native Encounters with Russian Orthodox Missionaries in Siberia and Alaska, 1820-1917.* Westport, CT: Greenwood Press.
———. 2003. *Shamanism in Siberia: Russian records of indigenous spirituality.* Dordrecht; Boston, Massachussetts: Kluwer Academic Publishers.
———. 2007. *The beauty of the primitive: shamanism and the Western imagination.* Oxford; New York: Oxford U. Press.
Zykov, Fedor M. 1992. "O poniatiiakh 'adzharai' i 'abacy'," *Shamanizm Kak Religiia: Generis, rekonstruktsiia, traditsii.* A. I. Gogolev et al, eds., 102. Yakutsk: Yakutsk Gos. Universitet.

Index

Aar-Toyon (sky god), 99, 149, 187;
  see also God, gods/goddesses
abaaghy (evil spirit), *see* spirit(s), evil
acetylcholine, 69
acupuncture, 6, 53, 149
Afanasev, Lazar (Téris), 212, 214
ahaghas éttéékh kihi (open-bodied
  person), *see* shaman(s),
  powers of
ahynyy (empathy), *see* empathy
Aichurek (Tuvan shaman), 184,
  204–7, 217
Aida (Abyi region healer), 107, 116
Aipin, Eremei, 41–2
aiyy (good or benevolent spirit), *see*
  spirit(s), good
Aiyyhyt (sky goddess), 113, 126
  see also God, gods/goddesses
aiyylgha (nature), 4, 172
Aiyy Urung (sky god), 187, 188, 208
  see also God, gods/goddesses
aiyy yoreghé (teaching spirit), *see*
  spirit(s), teaching
alcoholism, alcoholic, 5, 17, 88,
  119, 169, 170, 172, 180,
  188, 193, 223, 225
Alekseev, Eduard E. (Alekseyev),
  185, 237n, 244n
Alekseev, Egor, 137
Alekseev, Ivan E., 176
Alekseev, Nikolai A., 28, 102, 112,
  122, 143, 198
Alekseeva, Tatiana I., 44
algys (prayer), *see* prayer

Altai, Altais, 102, 184, 200, 202,
  203, 208, 219
Alykhardaakh (Anna Pavlova),
  16–17, 38, 40, 194
Amanita muscaria (mukhomor),
  61, 65
Anaiban, Zoia, 30
animism, 35, 215
  see also human-animal
  communication
Antonov, Nikolai K. (Professor),
  188
aptaktaakh (séance, all that occurs
  in a séance), 109
  see also séance, description of
Archy Diété (Purification House),
  in Yakutsk, 32, 118, 194–6,
  217
  see also Sakha, spiritual
  revitalization
Arctic hysteria (*menerik*), 164, 171–2
Argounova, Tatiana, 128
art(s), 12, 16, 35, 34, 48, 64, 80,
  81, 87–8, 99, 102, 104, 126,
  134, 141, 195, 220
Åry Darkhan (sky god), 114
  see also God, gods/goddesses
Association of All-Buriat Shamans
  (*Böö Mürgel*), 200–1
Association of Folk Medicine (Sakha,
  founded by Kondakov), 11,
  27, 53, 106, 116, 132, 139,
  140–2, 145, 149
Atkinson, Jane, 3, 127, 218

Atlasov, Vasily N., 195
Baaly, Kyta (Anatoly Yurevich Mikhailov), 185–190
Bahylai, (Sakha shaman), 111
Baianai (god of hunting), 196
  see also God, gods/goddesses
Baikal, Lake, 30, 86, 122, 184, 197, 228
balagan (winter house), 18, 44, 137, 138, 141, 141, 195, 212
Balalaeva, Olga, 235
baqshi (Kyrgyz shaman), 5
Basilov, Vladimir, 3, 10, 102, 199
bear(s), 3, 18, 21, 48, 49, 52, 57, 62, 65–6, 70, 76, 77, 83, 112, 114, 116, 124, 157, 168, 177
  see also spirit(s), guides/helpers
bioenergy, 77, 144–5
birds (e.g. raven, eagle, owl), 11, 19, 61, 66, 76, 77, 109–17, 122–5, 127, 155–6, 165–6, 190–1
  see also spirit(s), guides/helpers
blacksmiths, 80, 99–100, 198
blindness, 76
boksuruiuu (sucking), see shaman(s), powers of
Böö Mürgel (Association of All-Buriat Shamans), 200–1
Borisov, Andrei Savich (Minister of Culture, Sakha Republic), 130, 132, 133–40, 160, 193
Borisov, Egor Afanas'evich (President, Sakha Republic), 158, 160
Borisova, Stepanida, 139
Buddhism, Buddhist, 5, 30, 31, 155, 196, 199, 201, 202, 205, 207, 212, 216, 218, 219
Bugaev, N., 107, 128
buor-kut (earth-clay soul), 113
  see also soul(s), reincarnation
Buriats, Buriatia (Buryatia), Republic of, 30, 31–2, 184, 196–202, 208–10, 212, 213, 216–17, 219, 223, 224, 225
Burkhanism, 183, 244n
Burkhan, 197
Burnashev, Anatoly, 84, 156

cancer, 1–2, 7, 123, 145, 163, 169, 177, 178
Castaneda, Carlos, 9, 16
Center for Prophylactic and Sports Medicine, see Center for Traditional Healing
Center for Traditional Healing (Sakha, founded by Prokopiev), 53, 179, 180, 189
Center of Folk Medicine (Sakha, founded by Kondakov), 6, 179
Chaashka, see Chashkin, Foma Petrovich
chants, chanting, 79–80, 81, 84–7, 89, 91–101, 103, 104, 120–1, 139, 185, 215
Chashkin, Foma Petrovich (Chaashka *oiuun*), 29, 155–6, 163, 165, 169–73, 174, 179, 180, 181
Chashkin, Mikhail Fomich, 29, 170–3, 180
Chechnya, war in, 31, 197
Cheriktê (Evenki shaman), 83
Chernetsov, Valerii N., 58
Chingis Khan, 132, 203, 208
Chirkov, Konstantin Ivanovich, see Konstantin (*oiuun*)
Chirkova, Aleksandra Konstantinovna, 3, 21–2, 25, 46, 81, 116, 160, 162, 163, 165–9, 179, 181, 212, 213, 217
Chirkova, Matriona Konstantinovna, 81
Chot Chelpan, 208
Christianity, Christian, 5, 31, 35, 36, 37–8, 39, 40, 55, 74, 77, 83, 113, 127, 143, 149, 188, 189, 194, 195, 200, 202,

INDEX

211–12, 213, 214, 216, 218, 219, 220
  see also Evangelism (Protestant); Russian Orthodoxy
Chuonakh (Sakha shaman), 84
Chukchi, 122
chuval (hearth), see hearth
cloak(s), see shaman(s), attributes of
colonialism, 10, 134, 219
community solidarity (*communitas*), 96, 209, 214
cosmology (shamanic), legends, 52, 53, 62, 71, 74, 99, 103, 104–5, 126, 142, 187, 189, 197
Cruikshank, Julie, 128
Csordas, Thomas, 8, 75, 181, 185
cult(s), 12, 22, 38, 43, 143, 209
cultural relativism (also perspectivalism), 27, 160, 215
culture brokers, 75
Cuna (Kuna) Indians, 69–71
curing, curing rituals, 6, 7, 8, 17–20, 53–54, 58, 60–71, 89, 104, 123, 125, 141–2, 147, 148–9, 151–2, 155, 165–6, 168, 170, 172, 174–6, 180
  fertility, 113–14, 192
  hierarchies of resort, 74–77, 180
  see also medicine, modern; healing, spiritual healing

Dalai Lama, 31, 217
d'albyii (escorting or removing spirits), see spirit(s), powers of
dance, dancing, shamanic (also *okhuokhai*, or line dance with chanting), 19, 40, 44, 62, 64, 66, 78, 80, 88, 90, 95, 97–100, 103–4, 116, 125, 138–9, 166, 171, 185, 195, 203, 217
Daribazarova, Svetlana (Arsiia, Buriat shaman), 217
death, 26, 36, 41, 44, 50, 61, 66, 73, 77, 82, 84, 86, 91, 109, 113, 117, 120, 122, 127, 137, 143, 148, 150, 167, 170, 173, 176, 177, 179, 180, 195, 224
Derrida, Jacques, 218
divination, 52, 72
Dora, Éd'ii (Dora Innokentievna Kobiakova, Elder Sister), 26–7, 190–4, 217
Dostoevskii, Fyodor, 42
Douglas, Mary, 123
dreams, dream interpretation, dreams of shamans, 23–4, 47, 60, 69, 76–7, 126, 175, 190
drum, drumming, see shaman(s), attributes of, drums, drumming
Dulam, Bumochir, 7, 89
düngür (drum), see shaman(s), attributes of, drum, drumming
Düngür (shamanic healing center in Tuva), 30–1, 204, 205, 206, 207
Duranova, Zoia (Sakha shaman), 88, 143, 148
dvoeverie (Russian: double faith), 185
d'ylgha (fate), 36, 94, 114

ecology, 8, 12, 26, 53, 128, 181, 184, 193, 194, 195, 207, 224, 226
Eliade, Mircea, 61, 115, 117, 218
émchité (curer), see curing, curing rituals
émégét, see spirit(s), protector, holder
emotion, anthropology of, 126
empathy (*ahynyy*), 4, 6–7, 61, 69, 164, 167, 174, 179, 206, 223, 227
endorphins (enkephalins), 4, 69, 70, 166, 227
epics (*olonkho*), 80, 81–7, 103, 115, 135, 138–9

ethics, *see* morality
ethnicity, ethnic consciousness, 7, 11, 29, 32, 37, 46–7, 49, 54, 74, 76, 80, 81, 82, 83, 84, 85, 89, 102, 114, 126, 128, 132, 133, 159, 186, 193, 194, 207, 208, 211
éttéénei (spirit torture or torment), *see* spirit(s), torment, torture
éttéétén (spirit illness from spirit torture), *see* spirit(s), torment, torture
Evangelism (Protestant), Evangelists, missionaries (Protestant), 19, 31, 189, 211–12, 214
Éven, Évenk (also Tungus, Tungusic), 11, 12, 39, 52, 81–7, 89, 102, 110, 115, 122, 222
Evertsov, Aleksei, 211, 212
Evseev, Mikhail Mikhailevich, 99

family (also family values), 85, 149, 209, 211, 214, 248
divorce, 188
polygamy, 43, 188
fate (*d'ylgha*), 36, 94, 114
Fedorov, Afanasy, 104
Fedorov, Klim, 156
Fedot, *see* Ivanov, Fedot
Feld, Steven, 123
fire spirit (*iot ichchi*), 18, 19, 92, 94, 95, 99–101, 137, 142, 176
Foundation for Shamanic Studies (Michael Harner), 200, 204, 206, 223
functionalism, 2, 122, 184
fundamentalism (also essentialism), 214, 216

gender, 7, 21, 45, 49–50, 62, 134, 142, 152, 156, 158, 191, 213
gender ambiguity, 45, 134; *see also*, shamanism, gender issues

Gerasimov, Igor, 146–7
Germany, German, 5, 22–3, 203
God, gods/goddesses (e.g. God of the Dead, Sky-God, Sky-Goddess), 42, 101, 113, 114, 115, 120–1, 126, 143–4, 155, 187, 188, 195, 201, 212–13, 215
Gogolev, Anatoly I., 28, 29, 54, 84, 102, 111, 118, 119, 122, 134
Goodale, Jane, 24
groves, trees (sacred), 11, 29, 117–21, 123, 137, 173, 215

Hale, Charles, 33
Harner, Michael, 6, 125, 204, 223
healing, spiritual healing, 7, 8, 10, 29, 53–4, 116–17, 123, 126, 128, 148–9, 154–6, 164, 177, 181, 185
among the Khanty, 57–8, 62–8
of individuals 10, 69–70, 123, 144–5, 177, 180, 191
mind-body, 20, 69–70, 76, 164
kut-siur ("heart-soul-mind-body"), 53, 104, 105, 129, 138, 139, 164, 212, 221
open-body (soul) mindedness, 7, 107, 128–9, 218
see also curing, curing rituals
hearth (*chuval*), 18, 19, 47, 94, 95, 100, 101, 135, 138, 141, 144, 151, 166, 176, 192
historical diffusionism, 122
homeland, 31, 84, 86, 93–4, 97, 105, 136, 150, 158, 160, 191, 192, 202, 206, 220
Hoppál, Mihály, 4, 5, 11, 12, 123, 203
horse(s), 3, 19, 26, 31, 43, 62, 65, 66, 73, 76, 88, 90, 91, 93, 95, 97, 101, 103, 108, 112, 113, 124, 135, 137, 158, 171, 176, 186, 192, 193, 196
see also spirit(s), guides/helpers

Hultkranz, Åke, 3, 218
human-animal rapport,
   communication, 208, 218, 224
Humphrey, Caroline, 201, 203
Hyde, Lewis, 8, 208, 214
hysteria (Arctic hysteria, *menerik*),
   164, 171-2

ilbiihut (curer, massage ritualist), *see*
   curing, curing rituals
Iéiékhsit (sky-goddess), 121
   see also God, gods/goddesses
iie-kut (Sakha mother soul), *see*
   soul(s), reincarnation
iié-kyyl (mother-beast-spirit), 112,
   114
   see also spirit(s), guides/helpers
integrated medicine, 3, 76, 164, 213
   see also healing, mind-body
intuition, 7, 99, 138-9, 150, 155,
   164, 172, 205, 213, 220
Ionov, V. M., 120-1
iot ichchi (fire spirit), *see* spirit(s), fire
Islam, 5, 216, 218, 219
isyl'ta-ku (Khanty: soul-crying man
   or woman), *see* shaman(s),
   Khanty
Ivanov, Fedot Petrovich (Sakha
   shaman), 1-2, 79, 108, 123,
   145, 148, 163, 165, 175-9
Ivanov-Unarov, Vladimir, 25, 126
Ivanova, Natalia Dmitrievna,
   153-9, 160, 213
Ivanova-Unarova, Zinaida, 25
Izbekov, Iakim, cover, 120

Jackson, Michael, 102, 222, 229n
Jesus Christ, 185, 188, 208
Jochelson, Waldemar (Vladimir), 110
Jorgen (Khanty shaman), 62
Jung, Carl, 126, 192

Karjalainen, Kustaa F., 59, 62, 65-6
Kazym Resistance (of Khanty,
   Nentsy, 1931-33), 41-2, 45,
   47-8, 51, 183

Kékén, Semen Popov, 83
Kendall, Laurel, 9
Kenin-Lopsan, Mongush (Tuvan
   scholar and shaman), 183,
   203-7
Keptuké, Galina Varlaamova, 83
kérék mas (sacred tree), 29
   see also trees, groves (sacred)
Khagdaev, Valentin Valerievich
   (Buriat shaman), 31, 183,
   197-200
Khakas, Khakassia, 184
Khanty, Khanty-Mansi
   Autonomous Okrug (also
   Ob Ugrians), 35-6, 37,
   41-2, 47, 48, 50, 51-2, 54,
   56, 59-69, 71-3, 224
Khanty healing practices, *see*
   healing, among the
   Khanty
Khanty Rebellion, *see* Kazym
   Resistance 1931-33
Khatylaev, German, 14, 23, 139,
   153, 156
Khatylaev, Klavdia, 14, 23-4, 32,
   139 153, 156
khomus (jaw harp), 6, 53, 125-6,
   130, 176-7, 185, 192
khomusun (séance, obs.), 109
   see also séance
Khotoi-aiyy (sky god), 115
   see also God, gods/goddesses
Khudiakov, Ivan A., 39, 84, 110
kiusym karaha ("hidden eye"),
   139
   see also shaman(s), powers of
Kobiakova, Dora Innokentievna, *see*
   Dora, Éd'ii (Elder Sister)
køkhauger khararkhiakh ("eyes on
   the spine," perceptiveness), 7
   see also curing, curing rituals
Kondakov, Vladimir Alekseevich
   (Sakha shaman), 6-7, 27,
   53, 97-8, 106, 116-17, 131,
   132-3, 140-50, 154, 157,
   160, 213

Konstantin *oiuun* (Sakha shaman), 3, 21, 22, 47, 48, 81, 89, 116, 124, 162, 164–9, 178, 179
kørbøchur (telepathy, lit. "clear seeing"), 53, 70, 128, 154, 171, 176, 177, 224, 226
Korea, Korean, 4, 9, 140
Koss-Chioino, Joan (radical empathy), 4, 71, 206, 223
Krivoshapkin, Andrei, 195, 196
Ksenofontov, Gavril, 92–3, 112, 113, 115, 125
Kul'betinova, Matriona Petrovna (also Maria Kurbeltinova), 4–5, 81
Kulemzin, Vladislav, 59, 60, 63, 66
kul'tbaz (Russian: Soviet culture base), *see* shamanism, Soviet persecution of
Kumin, Aleksei (Khanty shaman), 62
kumiss (fermented mare's milk), 95, 96, 97, 98, 100, 104, 114, 186
Kunin, Aleksei, 62–3
Kurilov (Yukaghir shaman), 46
kut-siur ("heart-soul-mind-body"), *see* shaman(s), powers of, *kut-siur*
kuturar (séance, emphasizing chanting and songs), 109
see also séance; séance, description of; chants, chanting
Kyrgyz, 5
kyryylar (séances, lit. "over the edge"), *see* séance

de Laguna, Frederica, 25
lama(s), 31, 197, 198, 217
laughter therapy, 6, 11, 91, 126, 130, 131
leadership, 43, 52, 73, 131, 135, 136, 158, 159–60, 184, 199, 221, 226
charisma, 21, 23, 60, 150, 184, 185, 202, 208, 209, 220, 226
legends, *see* cosmology (shamanic); epics
Lena River, 82, 86, 95, 119, 134, 136, 139, 153, 185, 192, 194, 196
Leshinskii, Filofei, 37
Levin, Theodore (Ted), 30, 216
Levi-Strauss, Claude, 10, 30, 69, 70, 75, 123, 216, 222
l'iaksas (Khanty: soul), *see* soul(s), reincarnation)
Likhanova, Evdokiia Semenova (Sakha curer), 79, 95–6
liminality, 4, 124, 192

Maksimova, Klavdia (Saiyyna), 125, 131, 150–3, 160, 175, 213, 217
Malinowski, Bronislaw, 122
Manchari, Sakha historical folk hero, 136–7
Manchikai (Sakha shaman), 84
Mansi, *see* Khanty-Mansi Autonomous Okrug, Ob-Ugrians
Marquez, Gabriel Garcia, 138
Matrena (Sakha curer), 36, 49
medicine
mind-body (healing), *see* healing, mind-body
modern (Western, European, Soviet), 40, 57–8, 73–7, 145
shamanic, *see* curing; healing
see also hierarchies of resort
Mehl-Madrona, Lewis, 7, 125
Mékhélé, Tumus (Mikhail Pavlov), 149
menerik (hysteria, Arctic hysteria), 164, 171–2
metaphor, 9, 11, 67, 69, 90, 93, 95, 103, 104, 117, 119, 124, 133, 139, 208, 216, 222
Mikhailov, Anatoly Yurevich, *see* Baaly, Kyta

INDEX 283

mind-body medicine/healing, see healing, mind-body
"heart-soul-mind-body" (*kutsiur*), see shaman(s), powers of, *kut-siur*
Moldanova, Tatiana, 42, 60
Mongolia, Mongolian, 22, 89, 153, 196, 199, 200, 201, 202
morality, 18, 53, 58, 65, 189, 195, 208
music, musicians, 2, 6, 7, 14, 23–4, 30, 103, 104, 105, 125, 133, 137, 139, 144, 150, 157, 177, 223
see also chants, chanting

Nadia (Tuvan shaman), 4, 207
Natasha (Tuvan-Russian shaman), 182
nationalism, 6, 11, 29, 105, 128, 132, 185
Sakha nationalism, see Sakha, nationalism, national identity of
Native Americans, 7, 20, 25, 117, 124, 127, 176, 205, 208, 219, 223, 224
Apache, 205
Cuna, 69–71
Iroquois, 208
Navaho, 181, 244n
Tlingit, 25
Yurok, 124
nature (*aiyylgha*), 4, 172
Ndembu, Ndembu séance, 68–9
Nentsy, 47
neo-shamanism, 12, 215
new age, 6, 125, 126, 223
new religious movements, 12, 184, 189, 192, 208
Niikon (Nikon Alekseevich Vasilev, of Viliuisk), 1, 6–7, 28, 48, 49, 100, 106, 114, 127, 153, 165, 173–8, 179, 181, 221
Nikolaev, Ivan (Uhhan), 195, 250n

Nikolaev, Mikhail Efimich (first Sakha Republic President), 136, 190
nocebo, 74
see also placebo
Novik, Elena, 123

Ob Ugrians, see Khanty
oiuun (male shaman), see shaman(s), male
Oiyunsky (also Oiunskii; Platon Sleptsov), 42, 87, 135, 139
okhuokhai (line dance with improvisational chant), see dancing
Olkhon Island (Buriatia), 31, 197–200
olonkho (epic), see epics
Omar, Dilmurat, 5
Ommolon, Suoron (Dmitri Konovich Sivtsev), 133
omuk (people, collective identity), see Sakha, history of; national identity of
ongon (Buriat: spirit holder), see spirit(s), protector, holder; see also Buriats, Buriatia
Osipova, Maria (Sakha musician), 14
Ostiak, see Khanty
otohut (bone setter), 142, 180
see also curing; healing

Parilop (Sakha shaman), 83, 111, 114
Pavlova, Ekaterina, 27
Pavlov, Mikhail (Tumus Mékhélé), 149
Pavlov, Platon, 116
Pentikainen, Juha, 12, 64
Perspectivism, 27, 231
Petrova, Evresenia Dmitr'evna, 175
placebo, 2, 70, 74
poetry (in shaman rituals), 80–7, 89, 91–105, 120–1, 185, 186
polygamy, 43, 188
Posokov, Z. N., 41

Potapov, Leonid, 201
power, spiritual, 62, 81, 179, 203, 208
Prasin, Andrei, 67
prayer, shamanic (*algys*), 79–105, 149–50, 158, 172, 206
priest(s), 37, 38, 39, 41, 42, 189, 199
Prokopiev, Yuri Sidorevich, 53, 179, 180
Protopopova, Nina, 27, 190, 191
psychological trauma (including fear of), 51, 108, 168
psychiatry (including abuse of), 51, 57, 71, 108, 168, 223
psychotherapy, 71, 165
Putin, Vladimir Vladimirovich, 29, 53, 158, 160

Rebrova, Maria Ivanovna, 90
reincarnation, 17, 32, 52, 58, 66, 76, 137, 152, 164, 194, 213, 215
see also souls, reincarnation
Reshetnikova, Aiza (Director, Museum of Music and Folklore), 144–5
revolution, revolutionary, 35, 39, 42, 43, 66, 120, 133, 135, 136, 139, 184, 193, 209
Rinchinov, Bair Tsybiekovich (Buriat shaman), 200
rituals, 5–6, 25, 35, 39, 52–3, 77, 89, 100, 113, 125–6, 143, 159, 176, 183–4, 190, 192, 195–9, 201–2, 208, 212–13
of reversals, 234n
routinization of, 207
typology, 219
Romanova, Ekaterina, 190, 192
Russian Orthodoxy, Russian Orthodox Church, 9, 35, 37–8, 39, 48, 77, 107, 149, 155, 164, 195, 199, 212, 214, 222, 225

Safroneeva, Ann Vasil'evna, 180
Saiyyna, *see* Maksimova, Klavdia

Sakha
history of, 36, 38–9, 42–6, 81–5, 134, 136, 142, 143
nationalism, national identity of, 29, 97, 105, 128, 131–2, 135, 136, 138, 181, 184, 188, 194–6, 209, 214
Republic of, 29, 32, 52, 54, 103, 117, 131–2, 225
Sakha-ness, 135, 138
spiritual revitalization of, 11, 52–3, 125, 128, 141–2, 159, 164, 185–96, 208–9, 212–16, 219, 225
Purification House (*Archy Diété*) in Yakutsk, 32, 118, 194–6, 217
Sakha Omuk ("Sakha People," political cultural movement in the 1990s), 84, 132, 136–8, 140, 160–1
salgyn-kut (air-breath soul), 113, 173
see also soul(s)/reincarnation
šaman (Tungusic), *see* shaman(s)
Savvinov, A. A., 100
science, 49, 175, 180
Scott, James, 47
séance(s) (spirit calling ritual; *kuturar, kyryylar*), 4, 5, 20, 44, 48, 51, 63–71, 74, 77, 81, 88, 90, 102–4, 109, 110, 123–6, 152, 165–6, 169, 217
description of (*aptaktaakh*),16–20, 22, 40, 65, 90–6, 110–11, 124, 151
diagnostic, 16–17, 36, 64
Seden-Khuurak, Aldynai, 30
Sémënchik (Sakha shaman), 115
Senkevich, V., 65, 73
sergé (ceremonial horse hitching post), 115, 153, 154, 185, 186, 197, 213
Seroshevsky, V. L. (also W. Sieroshewskii), 7, 39, 89–90, 91, 112, 124

INDEX

sexuality, see shamanism, gender issues
shaman(s), 6, 12, 16–17, 19, 47, 59–69, 60–1, 89–96, 102–5, 107–12, 114, 115, 117, 122, 124, 127–8, 140–53, 179, 204, 212, 218–22
  accouterments
    cloaks, 19, 22, 61, 62, 63, 110, 123, 124, 147, 162, 167–8, 175; drums (*düngür*), drumming, 4, 19, 37, 44–5, 49, 62, 63, 123, 124, 147, 185, 187, 191, 205–6, 223; jaw harp (*khomus*), 6, 53, 125–6, 130, 176–7, 185, 192
  black/white, 8, 19, 54, 60, 83, 114, 123, 143–4, 159, 187
  community leaders/protectors, 47, 60, 94, 127, 140–53, 159–60, 178
  descriptions of, 16–17, 21, 40, 89–90, 91–6, 140–53, 167–79, 186–94, 198–201, 205
  female (*udagan*), 23, 24, 26, 36, 82–3, 86–8, 142, 143, 180
    see also individual names
  gender issues, 7, 45, 49–50, 93, 103, 113, 142, 143
  graves of, 26, 33, 84, 107–8, 127, 171, 173, 176
  Khanty (*isyl'ta-ku*), 59–69, 71–3
  male (*oiuun*), 17, 42, 20, 80, 82, 94, 96, 105, 141–3, 145, 171, 187–8
    see also individual names
  power(s) of, 3, 4, 7, 59, 60, 80, 128, 176, 191
    kut-siur ("heart-mind-soul-body"), 53, 104, 105, 113, 129, 138, 139, 164, 212, 221
  response to repression, 46–50
  Soviet persecution of, 5, 21, 26, 32, 35–7, 39–46, 50–1, 64, 71–4, 77, 83, 108, 111, 112, 123, 127, 169, 189, 208
  training of, 60–1, 63, 115
  shamanic illness, see spirit(s), torment/torture
shamanism, 2, 12, 22, 28–9, 38, 43–4, 46, 54–5, 68, 73, 117, 122–6, 128, 142–3, 148, 185, 189, 204, 218–20
  Christian (Russian Orthodox) repression, disparagement of, 5, 35, 37–9, 74, 77, 127, 164, 189, 222, 225
  credibility of, 10, 12, 54, 127, 180, 214, 223
  history of, 12, 38–9, 46, 73, 81–4, 134, 220
  neo-shamanism, 12, 215
  new age, 6, 125, 126, 223
  recovery (revival) of (post-Soviet), 51–5, 159, 164, 184, 196–7, 199–201, 202–4, 206–9, 212–17
Shashkov, S., 59, 64
Shatilov, M. B., 67, 68
Shirokogoroff, Sergei, 68–9, 81, 122, 222
Shishigin, Egor Spiridonovich, 45
Shishigin, Spiridon, 125
shock therapy, 69
Shtyrov, Viacheslav Anatol'evich, 158, 160
Siberiak(i), 37, 38
Siikala, Anna-Leena, 4, 61, 66, 123
Sivtsev, Dmitri Konovich (Suoron Ommolon), 133
Sleptsov, Piotr, 125
Sleptsov, Platon (ethnographer), 118
Sleptsov, Platon A. (Oiyunsky), 42, 87, 135, 139
Sobei (Evenk shaman), 81, 178–9, 226
Solovyev, Vera, 27
Solovyev, Zhargal, 27

286 INDEX

solstice, summer, festival (*yhyakh*), 78, 84, 87, 88, 96–9, 103, 114, 118, 138, 141, 143, 153, 185–7, 189, 192–3
songs, singing, *see* chants, chanting
Sopochin, Ivan (Khanty shaman), 62
soul(s), reincarnation (Khanty [soul]: *l'iaksas*), 52, 58, 76, 113, 114, 115–17, 152, 164, 172–3
sovereignty, 29, 136, 138, 192, 225
Spiridon (of Viliusk), 47, 93–4
spirit(s) (*ichchi(ler)*; *aiyy*), 3–4, 18–19, 49, 59, 61–5, 76, 80, 89, 90, 94–5, 98–101, 104, 109–12, 115–17, 118, 126, 142, 167–9, 176, 187–90, 195, 215, 221
ancestral, 8, 59, 80, 201
calls, calling, communication with, 19, 49, 50, 120–1, 126, 176
evil (*abaaghy*), 15, 19, 20, 83, 95, 112, 122, 142, 144, 148, 176, 187–8, 215
fire (*iot ichchi*), 18, 19, 92, 94, 95, 99–101, 137, 142, 176
good spirits, intercessors, (*aiyy*), 94, 112, 143, 187–8
guides/helpers, 3–4, 5, 7, 19, 21, 61–5, 76–7, 88, 103, 108,109–17, 120, 122, 123–4, 142–3, 156, 168, 176, 187–8, 190
protector, holder (*émégét*), 89, 113, 120, 123, 135, 217
teaching(s) (*aiyy yoreghé*), 53, 195
torment/torture (*éttéénei*), also spirit illness (*éttéétén yald'ar*), 4, 6, 17, 61, 108, 112, 115–16, 153, 159, 167–9, 171, 175, 201, 206–7, 221, 223
Spivak, Gayatry Chakravorty, 216
Startsev, Georgi, 37, 59, 64, 66, 73

Stepanova, Nadezhda, 200, 217
structuralism, 9, 70, 123
sullérdééhii (a kind of telepathy), 176
  see also telepathy
sunrise ceremony, 138, 186, 192
Suzukei, Valentina, 30, 216
symbolism (multivocal), 8, 37, 39, 68, 69, 70, 81, 88, 93, 95, 104, 117, 123, 134, 135, 185, 197, 215
synecdoche, 55, 135, 160
synesthesia, 7, 70, 226

tailgan (Buriat sacrifice ritual), 32, 196, 197, 199, 201, 202, 210, 217; *see also* Buriats, Buriatia
Taussig, Michael, 10, 35, 82, 124
telepathy (*kørbøchur*, lit. "clear seeing"; also *sullérdééhii*), 53, 70, 128, 154, 171, 176, 177, 224, 226
temple(s), 31, 32, 118, 184, 194, 195–6, 207, 214
Tengri (Turkic: God), 215
  see also God, gods/goddesses
theater, 2, 3, 11, 16, 90, 104, 132, 133–4, 135, 136, 139, 193, 221
therapy (laughter, psychological, shock), 6, 11, 69, 71, 91, 126, 130, 131, 165
Tiumaada Valley, 193
Tius'piut (Sakha shaman), 89, 91
toiuk (Sakha song), 103
  see also poetry; chants, chanting
Tokoyeu (Sakha shaman), 46, 107, 111, 123
Tolbanova, Nadezhda S., 194
Tolstoy, Leo, 42
Tomskaia, Maria, 87
Tos Déér ("Nine Heavens," shamanic healing center in Tuva), 30–1, 204, 206, 207
totemism, totemic legends, 38, 61, 156, 197

INDEX 287

trance (*turuk*), see séance
trees, groves (sacred), 11, 29,
   117–21, 123, 137, 173, 215
Tretiakov, Iuban Gavrilovich, 44
Tretiakov, Philip (Sakha elder), 79,
   82–4
Tsirendorziev, Bair Zhamalovich, 201
Tuberculosis (also TB), 54, 71, 147
Tungusic (Amur River) people, see
   Even, Evenk
Tunka Valley (Buriatia), 32, 196,
   200, 201, 210
Turner, Edith, 10, 71, 192
Turner, Victor, 68, 76, 123, 135,
   192
turuk (trance or visualization), see
   séance
Tuvans, Tuva (Tyva), Republic of,
   30–1, 184, 202–7, 208, 212,
   216–17, 219, 223, 225

udagan (female shaman), see
   shaman(s), female
Uighur, 1, 5
Uiuskhaana, Irina, 195
Uhhan, 195
   see also Nikolaev, Ivan
ulus (a local district in the Sakha
   Republic, mini-homeland),
   29, 45, 82, 119, 157, 160,
   180, 185, 188, 189, 192
Uluu Aiyy Toyon (sky god), 143–4;
   see also God, gods/goddesses
Urangkhai Sakha (early ethnonym),
   see Sakha, history of
urasa (Sakha conical, tee-pee–like
   summer house), 21, 38, 137
Urung Aar Toyon (sky god), 187;
   see also God, gods/goddesses

Vagatova, Maria (also Voldina), 41,
   56, 77
Varlaamova, Anatassiia, 137, 177
Vasilev, Nikon Alekseevich, see
   Niikon (of Viliuisk)
venereal disease, 147

Veniaminov, Innokentii, 38
Vinokurova, Uliana A., 15, 28–9,
   32, 55, 173, 194, 199, 211
vision quests (North America), 117
visualization, 151–2, 154
Vitebsky, Piers, 10, 126, 216
Voldina, Tatiana, 57
Volkhov, Innokenti, 35, 44

Whitley, David, 12, 220
world religions (Buddhism,
   Christianity, Islam, Judaism),
   213, 218, 219
   see also under individual religions
world tree(s), 11, 68, 115, 117, 185,
   205
   see also trees, groves (sacred)
World War II, 45, 72, 75, 94, 96

Xinjiang, 1, 5
x-ray vision, 17, 128, 226

Yakovlev, William, 119
Yakut, Yakutia, see Sakha
Yakutsk (capital of Sakha), 1, 5, 11,
   21, 24, 28, 32, 38, 39, 42,
   53, 84, 87, 99, 104, 113,
   118, 119, 125, 128, 131,
   132, 133, 136, 141, 148,
   153, 154, 158, 168, 175,
   178, 179, 185, 191, 194,
   195, 211, 214, 222
Yarkin (of Narikarsky), 73
Yeltsin, Boris, 103
Yenesei River, 205
yhyakh (summer solstice festival), see
   solstice
Yukaghir, indigenous Northern
   (Siberian) people, 50, 52, 81,
   102, 110, 122, 152

Zakharov, Ivan, 28, 99–100, 114,
   127
Zverev, Asen, 87, 139
Zverev, Sergei, 87, 90, 101, 150
Zvereva, Anya, 101

CPSIA information can be obtained at www.ICGtesting.com
Printed in the USA
BVOW011718110512

290018BV00004B/2/P